'THE GLEAM OF SOCIALISM'

Britain's Communist Party *1920-2020*

ROBERT GRIFFITHS

PRAXIS PRESS 2024

'THE GLEAM OF SOCIALISM'

Britain's Communist Party *1920-2020*

ROBERT GRIFFITHS

PRINT EDITION ISBN: 978-1-899155-27-9
DIGITAL EDITION ISBN: 978-1-899155-28-6

Published by Praxis Press 2024
Email: praxispress@me.com
Website: www.redletterspp.com

PRAXIS Press
C/O 26 Alder Road
GLASGOW, G43 2UU
Scotland, Great Britain

Contents

ABBREVIATIONS v

FOREWORD vii

1 100 years of struggle for the working class and humanity 1

2 Thora Silverthorne and the 'new Nightingales' 67

3 Party crises, recovery and re-establishment, 1928-1988 74

4 'Red Robbo': A giant of the labour movement 127

5 Not our history: *Endgames and New Times:*
The Final Years of British Communism 1964-1991 130

6 Gordon McLennan: 'A heavy responsibility' 133

7 John Haylett: A great editor and comrade 137

8 In defence of Palme Dutt: *Cold War, Crisis and Conflict:*
The CPGB 1951-68 143

9 'Botched Autopsy': *Cold War, Crisis and Conflict:*
The CPGB 1951-68 147

10 'Worth a warrant': Dora Cox 151

PHOTOGRAPHS and illustrations between pages 154 and 155

11 'The new imperialist offensive' and CP international policy
1977-88   155

12 'Ideological Grave-robbing': *Arthur Horner:*
A Political Biography vols I & II   163

13 Man of anthracite: Dai Dan Evans   167

14 The Communist Party and the national question   173

15 The worlds of TE Nicholas   197

16 Annie Powell and 'Red Rhondda'   211

17 The Communist Party 1920-2020: A thematic summary   217

18 Our history: A Centenary for Socialism   239

   FURTHER READING   242

   NAME INDEX   245

   SUBJECT INDEX   253

Abbreviations

AES	Alternative Economic Strategy
AEU	Amalgamated Engineering Union
AFL-CIO	American Federation of Labor and Congress of Industrial Organizations (USA)
ANC	African National Congress
AON	Association of Nurses
ASLEF	Associated Society of Locomotive Engineers and Firemen
AUEW-TASS	Amalgamated Union of Engineering Workers – Technical, Administrative and Supervisory Section
BNP	British National Party
BRS	British/Britain's Road to Socialism
CC	Central Committee
CCG	Communist Campaign Group
CIA	Central Intelligence Agency
CND	Campaign for Nuclear Disarmament
CP	Communist Party
CPB	Communist Party of Britain
CPGB	Communist Party of Great Britain
CPSU	Communist Party of the Soviet Union
CPUSA	Communist Party of the USA
EC	Executive Committee
EU	European Union
ILP	Independent Labour Party
IRA	Irish Republican Army
KGB	Committee for State Security
LCDTU	Liaison Committee for the Defence of Trade Unions
MI5	Military Intelligence 5 (the Security Service)
MML	Marx Memorial Library
NALGO	National and Local Government Officers Association
NATO	North Atlantic Treaty Organisation
NCP	New Communist Party
NMM	National Minority Movement
NUM	National Union of Mineworkers
NUPE	National Union of Public Employees
NUR	National Union of Railwaymen
NUT	National Union of Teachers
NUWM	National Unemployed Workers Movement
OMS	Organisation for the Maintenance of Supplies
PB	Political Bureau
PC	Political Committee

PCS	Public and Commercial Services union
PLO	Palestine Liberation Organisation
PPPS	Peoples Press Printing Society
PR	Proportional Representation
RILU	Red International of Labour Unions
RMT	Rail, Maritime and Transport workers union
SACP	South African Communist Party
SAS	Special Air Service
SDP	Social Democratic Party
SLP	Socialist Labour Party
SMA	Socialist Medical Association
SNP	Scottish National Party
SRN	State Registered Nurse
STUC	Scottish Trades Union Congress
SWLF	South Wales Labour Federation
SWMF	South Wales Miners Federation
SWMIU	South Wales Miners Industrial Union
SWP	Socialist Workers Party
TGWU	Transport & General Workers Union
TSSA	Transport Salaried Staffs Association
TUC	Trades Union Congress
UCS	Upper Clyde Shipbuilders
UKIP	United Kingdom Independence Party
UN(O)	United Nations (Organisation)
USSR	Union of Soviet Socialist Republics
WFDY	World Federation of Democratic Youth
WNP	Welsh National Party
YCL	Young Communist League

Foreword

This book is a collection of previously published pamphlets, chapters and articles on the history of the Communist Party in Britain since its formation.

Some of the texts have been restored to their original length. Others have been extended. In some cases, titles have been changed from those decided by sub-editors. Minor factual inaccuracies have been corrected and small improvements made in terms of style and translation. However, none of my judgments or predictions have been altered; they remain as originally published, regardless of their fate at the hands of subsequent events.

Readers will notice a disproportionate representation of Welsh Communists among the biographies featured in this volume. This reflects my work done on particular projects over the years. No disrespect is meant for the tremendous contributions made by English and Scottish Communists to the CP and the labour and progressive movements in the course of the 20th century. Many of their stories can be found in Meddick, Katz and Payne eds., *Red Lives – Communists and the Struggle for Socialism* (2020).

The absence of reference notes is intentional. This book is for a readership beyond academia. The sources for many facts and contentions can be found in the books suggested for further reading, or are easily available online. Queries may also be addressed to me via Praxis Press.

Many authors and researchers have contributed to the commonwealth of knowledge about Britain's Communist Party in the 20th century. Special thanks must go to those who have been of particular assistance in the production of this book and its contents, namely: Irene Green, Michael Walker, Roger Jones, Martin Levy, Sian Cartwright, Jimmy Macintyre and Kenny Coyle.

Harry Pollitt, probably the most popular and widely known of Communist Party general secretaries, often spoke of 'the gleam of socialism'. We don't know whether this gleam derived from the poetry of Wordsworth, who longingly recalled the gleam of childhood and would have added his own gleam to a painting of Peele Castle and thus transformed the world. More aptly, it reflects Alfred Tennyson's poem 'Merlin and the Gleam', which ends by beseeching the young Mariner:

Down to the haven,
Call your companions,
Launch your vessel,
And crowd your canvas,
And, ere it vanishes
Over the margin,
After it, follow it,
Follow The Gleam.

Finally, I'd like to dedicate this book to the memory of two great friends and comrades.

Er cof cymrodyr annwyl
GARETH MILES, JOHN HAYLETT

Robert Griffiths,
Caerllion, November 2023

1

100 years of struggle for the working class and humanity

This chapter is based on a text first published in 2000 as a pamphlet to mark the 80th anniversary of the Communist Party in Britain, updated and extended in 2010 (with Ben Stevenson) and then again in 2023.

Introduction

The formation of the Communist Party in July 1920 was considered significant not only by revolutionaries in Britain and internationally. The editorial in the *Daily Herald* – soon to be taken over by the Trades Union Congress – declared:

> The founding of such a party we can count emphatically a gain to the movement in the country. It is not a new split. It is indeed a fusion. But it is more than that. It is the creation of an organisation for the expression in action of a definite and existent body of revolutionary thought ... They are preparing to face the problem which too many of us are inclined temperamentally to evade – the problem of the 'how' and 'now' of the British revolution ... The strong point of the Communist Party is its steady realism.

The question of the how and now of the British revolution may seem like a more distant prospect today than it did in 1920, yet the experiences of politics in the first decade of this new century demonstrates that it is certainly no less necessary.

Throughout its history the Communist Party has sought to fulfil its role as the vanguard party of the broader working class movement, and in doing so has at various points had the entire capitalist state apparatus brought down upon it. Yet throughout its history, it has combined a propensity for building unified working class militancy in Britain with a steely commitment to internationalism.

This pamphlet is not intended as a complete official history of the Communist Party in Britain. There are already four substantial volumes on the Party's history from 1920 until 1951, written by James Klugmann and Noreen Branson. A new volume covering the next 13 years is currently being prepared by the re-established Communist Party History Group. Nor does this pamphlet shirk its responsibility to point out the Party's weaknesses and failures during the past 90 years, as well as highlighting some of the successes. The lessons to be learnt from our rich history can be used to help shape the tactics and strategies of revolutionaries in the labour and progressive movements today.

Since the attempts to destroy the Communist Party in the 1980s and early 1990s, and against the background of counter-revolution in the Soviet Union and eastern Europe, a cottage industry of historians has developed in Britain. They proclaim themselves experts in Communist Party history. But their aim is to misrepresent the record of the Party, especially since the 1950s, as having been one of almost unmitigated wrong-headedness and failure. The crucial flaw in these bourgeois, liquidationist and anti-Communist accounts – apart from them not being written from a Marxist dialectical and historical materialist perspective – has been their fundamental misunderstanding of the role and record of Communists, collectively and individually.

It is not surprising, then, that the narrative they strive to present is one of a party which is the cat's paw of the Kremlin, incapable of asserting independent political thought or activity. While they have to concede that many Party members are dedicated, talented and even courageous, ultimately they are portrayed also as naive and misguided. This pamphlet is a refutation of that analysis and an assertion of the Communist Party's invaluable role as an independent but integral part of the British labour movement. It seeks to prove that, despite difficulties, Communists in Britain have always striven to uphold the highest principles of revolutionaries.

In our view, the experiences, successes and achievements of the Marxist party of the labour movement continue to be a source of inspiration and an example to workers, socialists and revolutionaries. After the deepest capitalist crisis for 60 years, as the ruling class offensive against workers and their families intensifies, and after thirty years of almost unbroken neo-liberal policies carried out by Tory and New Labour governments, the need to build united working class resistance in Britain is greater than ever. A new generation of militant activists can draw upon the battles of the 20th century in order to win the struggle for socialism in the 21st.

1920 The party of a new type

The call from Lenin to the 'international Communists' to break from the 'social traitors' and form Communist parties found an echo across the world, including in Britain. While thousands of people were inspired by the example of the first workers' state established by the 1917 Bolshevik revolution, the left in Britain was even more divided than it sometimes appears to be today.

Since the highpoint of militant political struggle around the Chartists in the 1830s and '40s, revolutionaries had failed to connect in any significant away to the new working class created by intense industrialisation and the supremacy of British capital. From the late 1880s and early '90s, an upsurge of militancy among the unskilled and semi-skilled workers of the 'New Unionism' had swollen the ranks of the Marxist-oriented Social Democratic Federation. The SDF carried this revolutionary tradition into the British Socialist Party in 1911. Many workers, especially women, joined trade unions during the huge strike wave of 1910-13, although more working class men continued to vote Liberal rather than for the fledgling Labour Party and its more left-wing affiliate, Keir Hardie's Independent Labour Party.

But old loyalties began to shift profoundly during and immediately after the 1914-18 Great War between the main imperialist powers. Millions of workers had slaughtered each other in the name of 'patriotism', empire, the rights of small nations and even 'a war to end all wars'. In reality, they had died needlessly in a predatory struggle between the capitalist ruling classes of each country. It was a case of thieves and exploiters falling out with each other, each group seeking to redivide the world's colonial territories to their own advantage. During the war, more and more sections of industrial workers – Yorkshire and Lancashire engineers, Clydeside munitions workers, south Wales coal miners – organised and took action to defend their rights and living standards. Most trade union and Labour Party leaders chose instead to support the war effort. In Britain as elsewhere, the majority of 'socialist' and social-democratic party leaders lined up behind their 'own' ruling class, betraying pre-war pledges by the Socialist International to oppose the warmongering governments.

But the Russian Bolsheviks showed how imperialist war and carnage could be turned into civil war and revolutionary victory. After the Great October Socialist Revolution of 1917, Soviet Russia withdrew from the bloodbath, only to face White counter-revolutionary terror and, soon afterwards, the intervention of 14 foreign armies including forces from Britain, the USA, Poland and Japan.

Many workers were profoundly inspired by the example of the Bolsheviks. Harry Pollitt, then a boilermaker in the London docks and later Communist Party general secretary, said that his first thoughts were: 'The workers have done it at last ... lads like me had whacked the bosses and the landlords, had taken their factories, their lands and their banks'. In this spirit, socialists formed the great 'Hands Off Russia!' movement which spread through Britain to stop the imperialist military intervention against the world's first socialist state. Led by a younger generation of militant workers such as Pollitt, together with older stalwarts like Tom Mann, the campaign received a massive boost on May 10, 1920, when London dockers refused to coal the 'Jolly George', a ship loaded with arms to be used against the Soviet Republic.

Therefore, the call for the formation of Communist parties across the globe was seized upon by militant workers, socialists and working-class organisations in Britain. After months of difficult negotiations, the first Communist Unity Convention was held in London on July 31 and August 1, 1920, attended by delegates from the British Socialist Party, the Communist Unity Group (expelled members of the Socialist Labour Party), the South Wales Communist Council and other socialist and shop stewards' organisations. The delegates were united by deep revolutionary feelings, a profound hatred of capitalism and utter disgust at the repeated betrayal of workers' interests by corrupt reformist leaders. Yet they also had different approaches to solving the problems of the working class, reflecting their different backgrounds, experiences and group loyalties.

There was complete agreement on the basic aim of establishing working class political power through Workers' Councils, with the dictatorship of the proletariat as 'the necessary means for combating the counter-revolution during the transition period between capitalism and Communism'.

But there was vigorous debate and disagreement on whether the infant Communist Party of Great Britain (CPGB) should participate in bourgeois elections, and on what its attitude should be to the Labour Party and the official trade union movement. The British Socialist Party had been affiliated to the Labour Party, which then more clearly fulfilled its role – proclaimed upon the party's foundation in 1906 – as the parliamentary expression of the whole labour movement. Consequently, many Communist Unity Convention delegates favoured affiliation to the Labour Party as a way forward for the new Communist Party. Other delegates expressed the contrary view, born of their own experiences, that parliamentary politics were a diversion and that the CPGB should concentrate on industrial struggle.

The majority of delegates supported the views of Lenin expressed at the Communist International (founded in 1919) and in his letter of greetings to the Unity Convention, where he advocated 'participation in Parliament, and affiliation to the Labour Party on condition of free and independent Communist activity'. In speeches at the Comintern congress and in talks with leading Communists such as Willie Gallacher, Sylvia Pankhurst and William Paul, Lenin rejected fears that Britain's Communists might become infected with careerist and conformist parliamentarianism, arguing that the Party had to develop a new type of flexible yet incorruptible approach to parliamentary work.

It was decided by the founding convention of the CPGB to take part in electoral work and to affiliate to the Communist International. But delegates had not been anywhere near unanimous in their decision to seek Labour Party affiliation, which was only carried by 100 votes to 85 votes. The nature of the Communist Party's relationship with Labour would continue to be a major issue of debate throughout the Party's history.

In January 1921, at a conference in Leeds, Communist unity took a second major step forward when the CPGB merged with the Sylvia Pankhurst's Communist Party (formerly the Women's then the Workers' Socialist Federation) and the Communist Labour Party (recently established in Scotland by sections of the shop stewards movement). The unified CP set itself the formidable task of offering leadership to the working class in what was then still the world's biggest imperialist power, presided over by the most experienced – and ruthless – ruling class. Moreover, in the world's oldest and most industrialised economy, this was a working class whose labour movement was dominated by the ideology of class collaboration.

Britain's Communists immediately went into action to mobilise workers against another, much bigger military invasion of Soviet Russia, proclaiming the slogan 'Not a Man, Not a Gun, Not a Penny'. In response to the Communist Party's manifesto and a call from the Labour Party – both carried in the *Daily Herald* – protest meetings were held across England, Scotland and Wales and 350 Councils of Action were set up. The campaign forced Lloyd George's Tory-Liberal coalition government to retreat on the pretext that war had never been intended. It was a momentous victory, showing what could be achieved by united working class action.

Getting that lesson understood, organising militant struggle and turning the labour movement away from right-wing influence were the vital tasks taken on by the newly-established Communist Party. The growth of unemployment in the economic crisis of the early 1920s encouraged the bosses in their offensive for wage cuts. The disastrous class-collaboration policy that dominated the leadership of the trade unions led to the defeat of the miners in 1921, the engineers' lockout in 1922 and in the dockers' six-week strike in 1923.

In response to the return of mass unemployment, Communists took the lead in forming the National Unemployed Workers' Movement, led by Wal Hannington. It was the also the Communists who raised the slogan 'Stop the Retreat'. The Labour Party leadership's inability or unwillingness to challenge the capitalists consistently in the class struggle – politically and ideologically – lay behind its rejection of Communist Party affiliation 1920, 1922 and 1924.

Despite these rejections, individual Communists were still able to function as members of the Labour Party, often in their capacity as trade union delegates. Hundreds played an active part in their local constituency Labour parties and some Communist candidates stood with official Labour support. Thus Shapurji Saklatvala became the MP for Battersea North at the 1922 General Election, while J. Walton Newbold won in Motherwell.

The British ruling class and the Labour Party leaders feared the growth of Communist influence, particularly when Ramsay MacDonald headed Britain's first-ever minority Labour government from January 1924. In office but not in power, it quickly collapsed in a frenzy of ruling class anti-Communism. The government's attempt to prosecute JR Campbell, editor of the Communist Party's paper the *Workers' Weekly*, ended in a fiasco. MacDonald resigned and the election in October was dominated by another 'Red scare'. The *Daily Mail* and other right-wing newspapers 'leaked' a letter allegedly written by the head of the Communist International, Grigory Zinoviev, to the CP in Britain containing instructions for a military seizure of power. Today, it is beyond dispute that the letter was a forgery, and that the whole affair was concocted and orchestrated by British and French intelligence circles, in league with Russian emigres. But at the time, it signalled the beginning of an intense, unending campaign by agencies of the British state to disrupt the Communist Party through an extensive programme of infiltration, bugging, burglary and harassment.

Within the Labour Party, too, left unity on the ground came under heavy fire from the Labour right wing and over the next few years Communists were gradually driven out of the Labour Party, despite fierce resistance. Nonetheless, as Communist influence grew in the trade union movement and among shop stewards, Party militants and their allies initiated the National Minority Movement in 1924 to co-ordinate left-wing sections in the unions.

From the outset, Britain's Communists acted in solidarity with the oppressed and super-exploited peoples of the British Empire. As the first Labour government was suppressing the Iraqi Arabs with mustard gas, the 6th CP congress was insisting that 'the continued enslavement of the colonial peoples makes our own freedom in this country absolutely impossible', sending its comradely greetings to Communists and workers in British imperialism's prisons from Egypt to India. From the beginning, too, the Party did not waver in its support for the principle of an independent united Ireland, free from British rule.

As the British section of the Communist International, the CP was subject to its principles and direction. This also necessitated the construction of a centralised apparatus to lead the Party, staffed by full-time revolutionaries. 'Bolshevisation' also entailed the formation of factory cells. Like many other Communist organisations in other countries, the CP in Britain began to receive substantial financial assistance from the Comintern – as did the Labour Research Department (LRD) and, briefly, the then left-wing *Daily Herald*.

The Communist Party's own paper, the *Workers' Weekly*, sought to unite the streams of left opinion, reaching some 40,000 readers (well beyond the Party's membership of a little over 2,000). In 1925, with the backing of Comintern funds, the *Sunday Worker* was launched which, with its broad left outlook and content, reached a high-point in circulation of around 100,000. By this time, and distrustful of the National Council of Labour Colleges, the CP had set up its own 90 Marxist study centres around Britain.

Unlike other Communist parties in Europe, the CP in Britain was slow to react to the call of the Young Communist International to establish a dedicated youth section. This was primarily because there was little or no history on the British left of separating 'youth' from 'adult' organisations. The few progressive youth organisations that existed in Britain were new, raw, lacked coordination and were primarily concerned with socialist political education. Additionally, many of the leading cadres in the Party were young and there was no appetite to segregate them in a separate organisation. Even so, the Young Communist League held its founding congress in 1922, although the new organisation exercised little influence in its early years, with only a small number of functioning branches in London, Glasgow, Manchester and Yorkshire. Yet it was unique in publicising the anti-colonialist, anti-imperialist struggle among young people in Britain through its propaganda and educational schools.

The Communist Party's strength – its base in the industrial unions – also pointed to a major weakness: its failure to recruit and promote more women. Nevertheless, female emancipation featured in the Party's publications from the beginning. The first national conference for Communist women, in 1924, established a CP central women's department headed by organiser Beth Turner.

Throughout 1925, preparations mounted for the coming class battle with Britain's miners, who were determined to resist the coalowners' attack on their wages and conditions. Demands throughout the labour movement for solidarity resulted in a special TUC conference on July 24 and a renewal of the Triple Alliance between the mining, railway and transport unions. In response, on July 30, Tory prime minister Stanley Baldwin issued a declaration of war on behalf of the capitalist class: 'All the workers of this country have got to take reductions in wages to help put industry on its feet'. The next day, 'Red Friday', his government had to retreat before the unity and determination of the mass movement by giving a subsidy to the coal industry to prevent wage cuts.

This victory would not have been won without the tremendous organisational drive of the Communists and their left allies to put trade union leaders under mass pressure. In the words of the resolution moved by miners' leader Arthur Horner at the Party's 7th congress:

> Only through working-class loyalty and working-class
> solidarity can the workers hope to improve their conditions,
> and make a successful fight against the attacks of the
> employers.

1926 Nine Days in May

In October 1925, the Labour Party conference once again rejected the Communist Party's application for affiliation. It also banned Communists from representing unions and other affiliated organisations inside the Labour Party. Communists were now to be excluded from the Labour Party altogether, even those who had become Labour councillors and parliamentary candidates.

This sent a clear signal to the Tory government. A few days later, twelve leading Communists were arrested on charges of 'seditious conspiracy'. These included Tom Bell (editor of the *Communist Review*), Willie Gallacher, Albert Inkpin (the Party's general secretary), Harry Pollitt (at that time secretary of the National Minority Movement) and YCL general secretary Bill Rust. The Old Bailey judge described them as members of 'an illegal party carrying on illegal work in this country'. Five were sentenced to a year in prison and the others to six months, keeping them out of the battle to come. The intention was to paralyse the political and organisational leadership of the Party and intimidate the whole left into compliance. However, far from being cowed into submission, Communists intensified their activities. Party publications grew in circulation and new members were made. Above all, Britain's Communists tried to prepare the labour movement for the next round of struggle, warning again and again that the government was determined on a showdown with the miners when the 'Red Friday' subsidy expired in May 1926.

The government was well-prepared for the conflict, having conspired with employers and ex-army officers to set up the strike-breaking Organisation for the Maintenance of Supplies. The TUC general council had made no contingency plans of its own. Rank and file pressure forced the decision for a general strike from midnight on May 3, in support of the miners locked out again for refusing a wage cut.

The nine days of the General Strike saw more than three million workers uniting in tremendous class solidarity and initiative. Although too few in number, Communists played an outstanding role in many localities. The TUC cautiously called out only about half of Britain's trade unionists, but more demanded the right to participate as the days went by. Despite the efforts of the OMS, Britain was at a standstill.

Well in advance, the Communist Party had initiated the call for Councils of Action. They were set up in many areas, representing the whole local working class movement, organising pickets, coordinating activities, issuing publicity materials and in some cases controlling transport and the local distribution of food. Throughout the strike, the Party issued a daily news sheet – the *Workers' Bulletin* – reaching a circulation of 200,000 at times. Many local Party groups issued their own bulletins repeating its reports. Nearly half of the 2,500 people arrested by police during the General Strike were Communists.

The YCL also threw itself into the battle, with its newspaper the *Young Worker* doubling its circulation and coming out weekly. By its fourth congress at the end of 1926, the League had more than trebled its membership to nearly 2,000. Its work in the Councils of Action meant that young miners now comprised more than three-quarters of the YCL membership, giving it a real working class base for the first time.

Likewise, the Communist Party doubled its membership in just four months to more than 10,000. But despite these advances, the Party's influence in the trade unions was not sufficient to prevent the betrayal of the strike by the right-wing leadership of the labour movement.

The TUC called off the strike when it was strongest and closest to victory. Indeed, most workers thought that a victory had been won. The reality was that the General Council had accepted a 'peace' formula which implied wage cuts and longer hours for the miners. When other strikers returned to work, they faced oppressive new terms of employment, no-strike rules and widespread victimisation. The miners were left to battle on alone for seven more months, until hunger brought defeat. Communists continued to fight for solidarity with the miners, campaigning for a levy on wages to give them financial support and for an embargo on the transport of coal. It was a tragic end to a titanic struggle, yet it stimulated the demand for nationalisation of the mines, which finally became irresistible. Arthur Horner wrote later: 'If there had been no '26, there would not have been such a tremendous feeling for the nationalisation of coal after the Second World War'.

For the Communist Party, the General Strike confirmed the need to strengthen the militancy of the trade unions, step up the fight against class collaboration, work for a new leadership of the labour movement and to build and strengthen the Party itself as an integral part of such developments.

For the right wing of the labour movement, the lesson in the words of one union leader was: 'Never Again!'. They had not wanted the strike, were pushed into it and called it off as soon as possible. For them, the Communists and the left were 'troublemakers' who had to be removed. The leadership of the labour movement set about a purge of the left, excluding Communists and Minority Movement supporters from union office and redoubling efforts to drive them out of the Labour Party. This would clear the way to diluting Labour's programme and establishing the machinery of class collaboration with the big employers, who were seeking to 'rationalise' industry and eliminate industrial action. The aim was a corporate state, in which employers, the government and 'responsible' trade union leaders would rule together as 'partners' – the economic model, minus any democratic rights, preferred by fascism.

Two views emerged within the Communist Party's central committee about how to respond. The majority favoured continuing the resistance inside the Labour Party, keeping up the demand for CP affiliation, working with Labour allies in the National Left Wing Movement and calling for the return of a Labour government. The minority argued for abandoning or severely modifying this perspective and concentrating on the Communist Party's independent and separate role in the working class movement.

With the Communist International executive committee putting its enormous prestige behind the second view, the majority gave way in February 1928. Then the Comintern went further at its 6th world congress, attacking social democrats across Europe for propping up a capitalist system which could follow Italy and turn fascist. With capitalism hurtling towards a new and unprecedented crisis, there could be no middle way between siding with the interests of the working class – which in every country meant supporting the Communist Party – or siding with those of the capitalist class, as the social democrats were doing. The left wing were denounced as the 'most dangerous faction' in the social democratic parties, 'essential for the subtle deception of the workers'. There were, the Comintern warned, 'social fascist tendencies' in social democracy.

This new 'Third Period' line has since been presented by historians as one simply imposed by the Communist International without regard for local conditions or views. Certainly, the Comintern regarded the Party in Britain as one which lacked rigour and ruthlessness in dealing with ideological and political deviations; while its sense of solidarity was admirable, Presidium member Manuilsky told the British delegates in Berlin, it was too much like a 'society of great friends'. But another part of the truth is that, in Britain, many rank and file Communists adopted the 'New Line' with enthusiasm. One of its leading advocates, Harry Pollitt, backed by the Comintern, was elected CP general secretary in 1929 to carry it through. It appeared to provide a political rationale for uncompromising retaliation against the campaign of bans, expulsions and organisational manipulation already underway in the Labour Party and the unions.

Reinforced by Comintern policy, the Communist Party allowed its responses to take on a sectarian character. The Labour left, notably the ILP, was singled out for especially sharp attack, and Communists raised the need to form revolutionary new unions. In Scotland – under the greatest provocation – Party members and sympathisers actually established a breakaway, militant miners' union. A separate, Communist-led union for clothing workers arose from a strike in north London.

In some cases the Comintern acted as a restraining force, opposing moves to fight for trade union disaffiliations from the Labour Party and to drop the demand for CP affiliation to it. At the same time, the new turn provided a further pretext for Labour's national executive committee to expel scores of constituency organisations for refusing to implement anti-Communist bans. For years, this resulted in the existence of two Trades and Labour Councils in some towns and cities – one affiliated, the other not.

At the 1929 General Election, the Communist Party's manifesto *Class Against Class* had called for a 'Revolutionary Workers' Government' rather than a general vote for Labour. The second right-wing, minority Labour government led by Ramsay MacDonald confirmed Communist fears. Clinging to orthodox Treasury policies, it neither anticipated the great financial crash which broke out on Wall Street, nor had any idea how to counteract the economic slump that followed. Instead, at the command of US and British bankers, plans were drawn up to slash public spending including unemployment benefits and public sector wages.

1930 The 'Daily Miracle'

The experience of the General Strike and the political degeneration of the *Daily Herald* had convinced the Communist Party of the need for a daily working class paper, one which would challenge the monopoly of the press barons. On New Year's Day, 1930, the *Daily Worker* appeared for the first time, under the clandestine editorship of Bill Rust. A reporter from the *Daily Herald* telephoned to ask if a second issue would be coming out tomorrow. Within months, the TUC had sold a majority shareholding in its own paper to a capitalist publishing company.

The *Daily Worker* was immediately boycotted by advertisers, wholesalers and distributors. The Communist Party had to establish its own distribution apparatus, with daily rotas of volunteers collecting parcels at their local railway stations for delivery to newsagents and other sellers. This remarkable saga of dedication to the paper continued for the next eleven years. By 1932, the paper's circulation reached 20,000 daily, with 30,000 on Fridays and 46,000 on Saturdays. By 1935, it would sell 30,000 daily and 100,000 on the weekend. This was no mean feat and showed what could be achieved by even a small number of devoted supporters working in a collective manner. Without massive financial resources, and in complete opposition to the capitalist state and big business, workers in struggle now had a daily voice – soon dubbed the 'Daily Miracle'.

Day in, day out, the paper railed against mass unemployment, wage cuts, the profligacy of the idle rich and the rise of fascism. The state hit back with police raids, censorship, prosecutions, fines and the gaoling of managers Kay Beauchamp, Frank Priestley, Bessie White and numerous other staff members. Party cells in industry produced their own papers as well, such as the *Salford Docker* and, for railway workers in west London, the *Old Oak Star*. Party organiser Idris Cox wrote:

> The foundation of the Communist Party must be in the factories. This is where the class struggle is seen most clearly in actual practice. It is therefore in the factories that the workers can best protect their everyday interests, deal the most serious blows against the boss and organise the struggle for the overthrow of Capitalism. Factory cells, therefore, are the basis of Communist organisation.

In fact, the first issue of the *Daily Worker* had highlighted a dispute in the Yorkshire woollen industry, where the Communists were seeking to exercise 'independent leadership' outside official union structures as part of the 'Third Period' line. In the Lancashire cotton industry, the millowners were trying to replace women weavers with men working more looms each. Communists Lily Webb, Margaret McCarthy, Rose Smith and Bessie Dickenson led the resistance in a series of strikes and lockouts, eventually producing their own paper, the *Cotton Strike Leader*.

But attempts to provide 'independent leadership' to that of the South Wales Miners Federation proved a fiasco, prompting Arthur Horner to challenge the whole 'Third Period' line in industry. The Party's central committee charged him with 'Hornerism', but the Comintern declined to take serious disciplinary action.

In 1931, in the ultimate betrayal, Ramsay MacDonald entered secret talks with the Tories and Liberals to emerge at the head of a 'National Government'. In the General Election that followed, the Labour Party was reduced to a rump in Parliament. Twenty-six CP candidates – five of them in prison – won 75,000 votes between them. In West Fife, Willie Gallacher polled 22 per cent of the vote. Militant activity trebled Party membership to 9,000 by January 1932, and Communist candidates scored impressive votes in local elections that year, especially in the Welsh and Scottish industrial belts. In March 1933, Arthur Horner won 11,228 votes (38 per cent of the total) in the Rhondda East parliamentary by-election, less than three thousand votes behind the victorious Labour candidate. But many of the new recruits did not stay in the Party for long, having joined in a flush of militant enthusiasm. Differences within the CP leadership over 'independent leadership' and unofficial strike committees eased, as 'life itself' demonstrated that Communists should fight for influence within the unions rather than apart from them.

When the National Government announced fresh cuts in the pay of Royal Navy ratings, a thousand sailors mutinied in Cromarty Firth, even raising the red flag above their vessels. The action prompted panic on the London Stock Exchange. Bankers and speculators deserted sterling, forcing the pound off the Gold Standard. Communists were widely blamed for the 'Invergordon mutiny', although it was at root a spontaneous outbreak of discontent. One of its leaders, Len Wincott, joined the CP and later accepted an invitation to live in the Soviet Union, while another, Fred Copeman, went on to command the British Battalion of the International Brigades in Spain.

On dry land, meanwhile, the National Unemployed Workers Movement led by Wal Hannington was galvanising mass resistance to the hated Means Test, house evictions and a new round of proposed benefit cuts. Despite official hostility from the TUC and Labour Party, it built up a dues-paying membership of 50,000 unemployed workers, organised into more than 300 branches. The NUWM agitated outside the Labour Exchanges, fought welfare cases on behalf of the jobless and marshalled the South Wales miners march of 1927, a Scottish unemployed march in 1928 and the all-Britain Hunger Marches of 1929, 1930, 1932 and 1936. Police violence against NUWM demonstrators prompted left-wing lawyers such as Harry Thompson to establish the National Council for Civil Liberties (known today as Liberty). The London Metropolitan Police planted weapons in a van to secure the imprisonment of Communist organiser Will Paynter, later leader of Britain's miners. YCLer and future Party general secretary John Gollan received a six-month sentence for inciting soldiers to 'disaffection' with His Majesty.

In solidarity with national liberation movements in the British Empire, Communists and socialists had formed the League Against Imperialism in 1927. As the British section of the Comintern, the Party assisted workers and revolutionaries in the colonies. Members Ben Bradley and Philip Spratt were among those gaoled in the Meerut Conspiracy Trial in 1933, accused of undermining British rule by organising trade unions, strikes and the Communist movement in India.

In January 1933, as the monopoly capitalists helped Hitler and the Nazis into power in Germany, the Communist International dropped the 'Class against Class' line in favour of working class and left unity to counter the fascist menace. In Britain, the TUC response was to issue the first of a new series of 'Black Circulars', once more urging unions to ban Communists from all official positions in the movement including local trades councils.

On a more positive note, Communists and socialists marked the 50th anniversary of the death of Karl Marx by opening the Marx Memorial Library & Workers School. Whereas the Nazis were burning books – as the prelude to burning people – the library would collect them for workers to study.

By the end of 1934, the CP in Britain was urging votes for Labour candidates who supported left unity. In January 1935, a huge wave of protests called by the NUWM across Britain forced the government to abandon its vicious new unemployment benefit and Means Test regulations. There were other, more unorthodox victories too. In 1932, Manchester Communist Benny Rothman had led a mass trespass to the Kinder Scout in the Peak District, defying the closure of large tracts of the countryside by big landowners. They were members of the British Workers Sports Federation, in which many Communists and socialists participated as an alternative to sports clubs organised by Christian, 'patriotic' and militaristic bodies. Although a jury of the landed establishment jailed Rothman and four other young people, controversy around the case led to the first legal rights for ramblers everywhere. Communists launched the *Country Standard* newspaper in 1935 to highlight the battles of farm labourers for decent wages, safety at work, secure housing and trade union rights. Among its earliest contributors was the novelist Sylvia Townsend Walker.

The Party's 13th congress in February 1935 called for united action to remove the National Government. It also produced a new programme, *For Soviet Britain*, which advocated the forceful overthrow of capitalism because 'the capitalist class will never allow itself to be gradually expropriated by successive Acts of Parliament'. Parliamentary rule should be replaced by 'Workers' Councils, made up of workers elected democratically from every factory, workshop and mine, and from every other grouping of men and women of this country who have to work for their living'. The new programme also set out the policies that would emancipate women in a socialist society: equal opportunities in the labour market and at work; equal pay; time off with full pay and free medical care during pregnancy; creches, clinics and school meals for the children of working mothers; and labour-saving appliances in all new houses. While films and books encouraged young women to marry their boss for the ideal happy ending, Britain's Communists urged them to fight for equality and join the Women's Cooperative Guild instead.

At the General Election that November, in the only two Communist contests, Willie Gallacher won West Fife and Harry Pollitt gained 13,655 votes in Rhondda East. The Party now began to reorganise itself with factory, ward and street groups to be coordinated by local branches and a branch committee. Party fractions in the trade unions were growing rapidly through their work in rank and file and shop stewards' movements among engineers, coal miners and London bus crews, publishing influential papers such as the *New Propeller*, the *South Wales Miner* and the *Busman's Punch*. General secretary Pollitt described this as 'a revolution within the Party'.

1936 '¡No Pasaran!'

In the 1930s, Communists across Europe rose to the challenge of fascism: 'the open terrorist dictatorship of the most reactionary, most chauvinistic and most imperialist elements of finance capital', as Comintern secretary Georgi Dimitrov defined it. The leading role of Britain's Communist Party in the fight against fascism was only made possible by its expanding base in the working class, both in workplaces and in local communities. So strong had the Party become in small towns and villages such as the Vale of Leven, Chopwell, Maerdy and Nelson in Lancashire that each had earned the nickname 'Little Moscow'. Leiston in Suffolk became the countryside equivalent.

The British Union of Fascists had emerged in 1933 under the leadership of former Labour Party junior minister Sir Oswald Mosley. Among its most enthusiastic backers was Lord Rothermere, proprietor of the *Daily Mail*. The real character of Mosley's thugs was shown at his 1934 rally in Olympia, when black-shirted storm troopers savagely beat anti-fascist protestors. Later that year, a BUF rally in Hyde Park was 'drowned in a sea of working class activity' by a counter-demonstration of 150,000 people.

Many socialists and progressives fought alongside the CP in the struggle against the Blackshirts. On many occasions, the BUF were drowned out or routed: from Manchester, Leeds and Hull up to Newcastle, Stockton and Sunderland; from Glasgow down to Worthing; and from Pontypridd across to Oxford. Following the 'Battle of De Winton Field' in June 1936, some 37 anti-fascists from a crowd of 6,000 faced criminal charges; upon their release from prison, four miners set off for Spain with the International Brigades.

Mosley's biggest, symbolic defeat came on Sunday October 4, 1936. His announcement of a march through a heavily Jewish-populated district of East London provoked a wave of resistance. The Communist Party decided – after heated internal debate – to cancel a proposed youth rally in Trafalgar Square in solidarity with the Spanish Republic against General Franco's fascist-backed rebellion. Stepney anti-fascists proclaimed the Spanish slogan against Franco's forces: 'No Pasaran!' (They Shall Not Pass). On the Friday before Mosley's march, the *Daily Worker* urged a giant turnout to bar the Blackshirts. On Saturday, a supplement in the paper declared: 'Save the East

End of London from Fascism … No Liberty for the Assassins of Liberty'.

Communist organiser Phil Piratin's house in New Road became a major centre of operations even before Sunday broke. On the day, messengers by foot, bicycle and motorbike connected him and his team with large groups of protestors. Piratin, later the area's MP, correctly predicted that the Blackshirts would choose Cable Street as their main route into the heart of the East End.

Although the Jewish Board of Deputies had urged people to stay at home, more than 200,000 demonstrators thronged the surrounding thoroughfares. They included the local Irish community and industrial workers from as far away as Glasgow, together with members of trades unions, left-wing parties and the Jewish Ex-Servicemen's Association. Drivers abandoned a string of tramcars to block the road as fierce clashes broke out between the police and protestors at Gardiner's Corner. Groups of tooled-up Blackshirts were pounced upon as they tried to make their way to Royal Mint Street, where thousands of besieged fascists assembled under police protection.

Meanwhile, Dr Hugh Faulkner had infiltrated Mosley's medical team. He was shown a map of the Blackshirts' intended route and slipped away twice to phone through the changing details to the New Street HQ. The barricades were reinforced in Cable Street, one with a lorry donated 'for overturning purposes' (as Piratin put it). The fascists began to march along Royal Mint Street, chanting: 'The Yids, the Yids, we're gonna get rid of the Yids'. But it proved impossible for the police to fight their way through, bombarded as they were by tons of rubbish from the tenement windows above. Thousands of anti-fascists blocked the way. The Blackshirts and their guardians in blue had to beat a humiliating retreat westwards. Then the evening celebrations began. The slogan sprang to everyone's lips, now louder than before: 'THEY SHALL NOT PASS – THEY DID NOT PASS!'

One particularly important factor in the Party's ability to mobilise large numbers of people in major towns and cities was its growing work among tenants. In particular, women such as Jessie Eden and Ella Donovan played a prominent part alongside Bob Graves and 'Tubby' Rosen in ferocious battles against 'decontrolled' tenancies, rack-renting, unsanitary conditions, evictions and the other features of slum landlordism. Stepney Communist councillor Phil Piratin later explained how this campaigning undermined the fascists in his classic book, *Our Flag Stays Red (1948)*. The right wing of the labour movement advocated ignoring the fascists and abstaining from anti-fascist activity. The Communist response – that retreat before fascist aggression merely increased its appetite – proved correct time and again throughout the decade.

In mid-1935, the 7th world congress of the Communist International had elaborated its call for a united working class front of Communists and social democrats at the core of a broad people's front, to rebuff the fascist tide. That fascism led directly to war had already been shown in 1931, when

Japan attacked China, and in 1935 when Italy invaded Abyssinia (Ethiopia).

In 1936, German and Italian military forces intervened to assist General Franco's revolt against the democratically elected socialist and republican government of Spain. This struggle became the focal point of a worldwide campaign against fascism. Millions of people in Britain rallied in solidarity with the Spanish Republic, while Tory and right-wing Labour leaders adopted a shameful policy of 'non-intervention'. For Britain's Communists, the Spanish cause spawned tenacity and sacrifice on the scale of the General Strike. By the end of December 1936, the Young Communist League had filled the first of 29 food ships. Communist women's leader Isabel Brown was one of many outstanding campaigners, stirring the hearts of open-air crowds with her appeals on behalf of Medical Aid for Spain.

The spirit of Spain also helped produce the biggest vote so far, at the 1936 Labour Party conference, to accept Communist affiliation. More than one-quarter of the votes were cast in favour, including those of the miners, engineers, train drivers and furniture makers. This, in turn, inspired a Unity Campaign from January 1937, launched after talks between the Communist Party, the Socialist League (in which Labour MPs Stafford Cripps and Aneurin Bevan were prominent) and the Independent Labour Party (headed by Fenner Brockway and James Maxton). Large and enthusiastic meetings took place throughout Britain. The campaign drew in the Left Book Club, established in 1936 and soon boasting a network of 1,500 local discussion groups. Its growth reflected the renewed interest in the international situation and in Marxist ideas.

In promoting a 'Popular Front' of anti-fascist forces in Britain, Harry Pollitt pointed out that – unlike in France – it would be overwhelmingly working class in composition:

> Here the decisive majority of the population are industrial
> workers, the most class conscious are already organised
> industrially and politically. Our first job is to bring about
> unity within our Labour Movement.

It is a self-serving myth peddled by ultra-left anti-Communists that the CP in Britain, or in France for that matter, abandoned principled positions in order to chase after middle-class allies for the People's Front.

But Communists were keen to demonstrate that socialist and Communist ideas stood in the progressive traditions of their own country. AL Morton broke new ground with *A People's History of England* (1938) and the first Communist Party history group was founded. Led by Communists, the Unity Theatre movement and the Workers' Music Association expressed the class struggle in cultural forms. Eminent scientists such as JD Bernal and JBS Haldane applied Marxism in their specialist fields, popularising science in the process. Thousands of people flocked to Communist-initiated pageants in London, Glasgow, Manchester, Liverpool and – sponsored by the South Wales Miners Federation and the LRD – across south Wales which celebrated working class and progressive history, linking it to the 'Popular Front' and the struggle in Spain. A theatrical spectacle with 3,000 performers, commissioned by the Cooperative movement and devised by Communists composer Alan Bush, film-maker Montagu Slater and director Andre van Gyseghem, filled Wembley Stadium with 78,000 spectators.

The most heroic aspect of the Spanish crusade was the formation of International Brigades to go and fight fascism. Felicia Brown had been the first Communist from Britain to join a militia in defence of the Spanish Republic. She died on the Aragon front in August 1936. London clothing workers Nat Cohen and Sam Masters set up the Tom Mann Centuria. Beginning with only a dozen British volunteers, it grew rapidly with the direct assistance of Harry Pollitt. In October, Spanish prime minister Francisco Caballero agreed that the Communist International could raise International Brigades to come and defend democracy. A recruiting centre was set up in Paris and a training base at Albacete in Spain.

Around 2,200 volunteers went from England, Scotland and Wales to fight Franco and the fascists. There can be no exact figure because the Tory government threatened to use the 1875 Foreign Enlistment Act against 'illegal' volunteers. Keeping records and lists of names was difficult and dangerous. However, no-passport weekend trips to Paris provided a way around the authorities for those whose ultimate destination was Spain. In France, active support from Communists, workers and peasants opened the paths over the Pyrenees. Volunteers for the British Battalion came from all walks of life, although the great majority were from the industrial areas. They were accustomed to the discipline of work in the factories and pits. From their unions they had learnt the value of organisation, democracy and solidarity. The commissar for English-speaking volunteers in the battalion, Communist Peter Kerrigan, set out the standards expected of volunteers:

> All recruits must understand they are expected to serve.
> Tell them: this is a war and many will be killed. This should
> be put brutally, with a close examination of their hatred of
> fascism.

Many volunteers already knew how to exercise leadership and take action in working class organisations. They understood the importance of setting an example and leading from the front when necessary. They were united in their aims and prepared to fight for them. The International Brigades provided a shock force while the Republican government recruited and trained its own armed forces. The Spanish people knew they were not fighting alone.

In Britain, Communists accounted for about half of the Brigade volunteers and of the 533 killed in action. Party members who served in Spain included Bert Ramelson, Christopher Caudwell, Len Crome, Lou Kenton, Bill Alexander, David Marshall, Ralph Fox and John Cornford. Among the many women in medical units were Communists Thora Silverthorne, Sylvia Townsend Warner, Margaret Powell and Mary Valentine Ackland. Soon after her return, Silverthorne became the founding general secretary of Britain's first independent trade union for nurses.

In September 1938, Juan Negrin, head of the Republican government, announced that the International Brigades would be unilaterally withdrawn from Spain for diplomatic reasons. However, General Franco failed to reciprocate and German and Italian forces remained, continuing their brutal suppression of those standing by the legitimate, elected government of Spain. Before leaving for home, Sam Wild, commander of the British Battalion, declared:

> The British Battalion is prepared to carry on the work begun here to see to it that our 500 comrades who sleep for ever beneath Spanish soil shall serve as an example to the entire British people in the struggle against fascism.

In October, the International Brigades began to depart, the words of Dolores Ibarruri ('La Pasionaria') ringing in their ears: 'You can go proudly. You are history. You are legend'. The Republican government fell to Franco the following year, although Spain's Communists fought to the bitter end.

As fascist aggression was advancing in China, Austria and Spain, Britain's Communists and their allies worked strenuously to build a 'people's front' powerful enough to force the Chamberlain Tory government to adopt a policy of collective security in defence of peace. But the ruling-class traitors would not budge from their determination to appease Hitler, hoping that Nazi Germany would turn its fire eastwards towards the Soviet Union – and away from the British Empire. The *Daily Worker* and Claud Cockburn's journal *The Week* exposed the nest of Nazi sympathisers – leading financiers, industrialists, government ministers, military chiefs and newspaper editors – who plotted at the Cliveden mansion of Lord and Lady Astor.

The Party's 15th congress took place in September 1938, as Prime Minister Chamberlain was scuttling back and forth to settle the fate of Czechoslovakia with Hitler. Palme Dutt and Communist MP Willie Gallacher warned the congress that Chamberlain was preparing to betray Czechoslovakia and therefore to betray peace, rather than form an anti-fascist alliance with the Soviet Union. They were proved right within a fortnight. That same congress also acknowledged that the Communist Party had underestimated the democratic and progressive content of the national question in Scotland and Wales. This rectification opened the way to full support for the establishment of Welsh and Scottish parliaments.

Britain's labour movement leaders refused to rouse the people into mass action against fascist aggression. Cripps and Bevan were expelled from the Labour Party for joining the Popular Front campaign. Communists continued to be ejected from leading elected positions in the Amalgamated Engineering Union and others, while the TUC General Council voted to prevent Arthur Horner taking a seat on behalf of the Miners Federation of Great Britain. Undaunted, Communist policy and leadership continued to attract many people who feared that appeasement was making war inevitable. By 1939, *Daily Worker* circulation had grown to more than 40,000, with a weekend average of nearly 80,000. Communist Party membership reached 15,750 by late 1938 and 17,750 by July 1939. The Young Communist League was also winning young workers through a series of strikes for the 'Apprentices Charter'. It demanded higher pay, day-release training and trade union representation. Clydeside, Tyneside and Manchester were major centres of militancy.

The show trials of former Soviet and Comintern leaders such as Kamenev, Zinoviev and Bukharin did little to check the growing popularity of the Communist Party and Marxist ideas in Britain. For much of the 1930s, the Soviet Union had appeared a bastion of peace and stability amid a world of mass unemployment, fascist aggression and colonial exploitation. Communists everywhere helped publicise its enormous economic, scientific, social and cultural achievements. At the same time, the hostility of the imperialist powers towards the Soviet Union was well understood in working-class and progressive circles. Within the labour movement, the followers of Trotsky – who had been expelled from Russia – were regarded by many who came across them as anti-Communist, anti-Soviet oppositionists, disrupters and defeatists.

When respected lawyers, politicians and diplomats from the US, Britain and elsewhere attended the Moscow show trials and confirmed that the defendants had indeed confessed to being members of a 'Trotsky-fascist' campaign of espionage and subversion, Britain's Communists were not alone in believing that such plots had indeed existed. Reports of mass-scale repression, labour camps and executions in the Soviet Union could all too easily be dismissed as another round of capitalist propaganda against socialism. There is no serious evidence that the British CP leadership knew the full extent of the purges, or the degree to which the incarceration of several million Soviet citizens – many of them loyal Communists – lacked any justification. When they learnt about the arrest and disappearance of British Communist Rose Cohen – who had gone to live in Russia with a Comintern official – Pollitt, Dutt and Gallacher angrily demanded to know the truth from the authorities. But they did not make their protestations public.

1939 A people's peace, the people's war

As late as July 1939, Britain and France had failed to agree to the Soviet Union's requests for an alliance against Germany. On the contrary, the Chamberlain government had pursued a policy of appeasing Hitler and the Nazis, allowing them to annexe Austria and then – in accordance with the Munich Agreement – seize Czechoslovakia. The right-wing Polish government had long rejected Soviet offers of assistance. Nonetheless, the conclusion of a non-aggression pact between the Soviet Union and Germany in August, which included a secret protocol to divide Poland, came as a shock to anti-fascists, Communists and anti-Communists alike. Nonetheless, for the Soviet Union to keep out of the war seemed to many Communists a necessary if temporary tactic. It avoided embroilment in imperialist intrigues while allowing the Soviets time to prepare economically and militarily for the inevitable war with Nazi Germany.

When Britain declared war on Hitler's Germany in September 1939, following the *blitzkrieg* on Poland, the CP at first supported the war while demanding that Chamberlain and the 'men of Munich' be replaced by committed anti-fascists. However, within weeks the Party's central committee reversed this 'fight on two fronts' position, accepting the Comintern's analysis that this was an 'imperialist and unjust war for which the bourgeoisie of all the belligerent states bear equal responsibility. In no country can the working class or the Communist Parties support the war'.

The overwhelming majority of the party leadership backed the change of policy, while the minority – notably Harry Pollitt, JR Campbell and Willie Gallacher – maintained that the earlier position had been correct. In view of their differences, Pollitt was, in effect, replaced by R. Palme Dutt as general secretary and Campbell by Bill Rust as editor of the *Daily Worker*. The majority of Party members also expressed their preference for the anti-war position at a series of well-attended and lively meetings across Britain.

Many had been confirmed in their view by the flow of events. Spain and Albania had succumbed to the fascists. In France, the Popular Front government had fallen and the country's 70 Communist deputies placed under arrest. Nowhere did the capitalist and landowning classes look like mounting a serious challenge to the fascist powers. Nor did the British ruling class appear to be any different. The British Empire belied all the fine phrases about freedom and democracy. The declaration of war on Nazi Germany had fulfilled a diplomatic obligation – but it produced no serious military offensive. The Cabinet refused to bomb German arms factories, because they were 'private property'!

Whereas an ineffective British Expeditionary Force was sent to France to do very little, a 100,000-strong Franco-British army was despatched to assist the right-wing Finnish government in its anti-Soviet endeavours. Meanwhile, in Britain, bunkers were built for the top bureaucrats, business leaders and politicians, while working-class people were left defenceless.

Almost alone, the Communist Party campaigned for proper Air Raid Precautions – especially deep underground shelters – for the general public.

The period of 'phoney war' came to end with the blitz on London and other cities from September 1940. As dockside communities and those closest to the munitions factories sustained devastating damage, Communist councillors and community leaders such as Phil Piratin and Ted Bramley led mass invasions of the Mayfair and Savoy Hotel shelters. They broke into Liverpool Street, Warren Street, Highgate and Goodge Street underground stations, leading thousands of people to safety, and forcing the government to open them every night.

Above ground, the CP and its allies convened a huge People's Convention in January 1941. More than two thousand labour movement delegates demanded a 'people's government' to secure a 'people's peace', an end to profiteering, nationalisation of key industries, democratic and trade union rights, friendship with the Soviet Union and freedom for Britain's colonies. One week later, the British coalition government headed by Winston Churchill decided not to outlaw the Communist Party. Labour home secretary Herbert Morrison banned the *Daily Worker* and *The Week* instead. Government and employers faced another problem soon after. An unprecedented wave of strikes by engineering apprentices hit Clydeside, Edinburgh, Barrow, Tyneside and east Lancashire. Some Communists and their allies were prosecuted, although a Court of Inquiry subsequently improved wages and conditions for young workers.

But by this time, too, the whole character of the war was changing. With the Nazis occupying much of western and central Europe, Communists emerged at the head of popular resistance movements. Then, in June 1941, the fascist powers attacked the Soviet Union.

Quickly restored to the post of CP general secretary, Harry Pollitt declared that 'this is a People's War. One that only the common people can and will win'. For the Party, only the working class could be the driving force in building the national and international unity needed for victory. It had the most to contribute to the anti-fascist struggle, industrially and politically – and the most to lose from a fascist victory. Britain's Communists threw themselves into the fight for maximum production. While the Party continued to argue for higher pay, its policy was to settle industrial disputes as quickly as possible and establish joint production committees with shopfloor participation. Sometimes, notably in the coal industry, Party members found themselves representing strikers in heated disputes with their comrades in official full-time positions in the union.

The wartime influx of women workers into the factories prompted the CP to step up the fight for trade unionisation and equal pay. The *Daily Worker* pointed out that, in the Soviet Union, women were perfectly capable of doing so-called 'men's work'. Communist women blazed a trail in the wartime shop stewards movement, campaigning for welfare and nursery facilities.

Initiated through the People's Convention, the Women's Parliament in July and October 1941 sparked a powerful movement for equal pay. When the House of Commons granted it to women teachers three years later, Prime Minister Churchill stopped it by threatening to resign.

An enormous campaign was mounted to lift the ban on the *Daily Worker*. Just as the TUC was likely to add its support, the paper was restored to legality in August 1942. A new press was bought with £50,000 collected in donations in just three months. Moreover, the wholesalers lifted their boycott so that the *Daily Worker* could, for the first time, be distributed to retailers alongside the other newspapers. Orders for the first post-ban issue totalled half a million, but only 100,000 could be produced due to wartime rationing of newsprint. A telegram of greetings was published from the gunners on the George Cross island of Malta, embattled beneath Nazi dive bombers. The paper's front page splashed on the titanic battle of Stalingrad, then approaching its crucial turning point. It also bore the slogan: 'Ten readers for every copy'. A survey later estimated that the *Daily Worker* had more than half a million daily readers during the Second World War.

As the Soviet people resisted the Nazi invaders with super-human courage, the Communist Party joined Aneurin Bevan and other Labour left-wingers to demand a 'Second Front'. Britain and the USA should launch an offensive through western Europe as the Soviet Red Army took on four-fifths of the German war machine in the east. Britain's Communists exposed ruling-class motives for delaying the Second Front in the hope that the Soviet Union and Nazi Germany would exhaust each other, thereby enabling the imperialist powers to win the war 'on the cheap' and re-establish their predominance after victory.

In June 1944, Churchill at last redeemed his pledges to Soviet leader Stalin as 'D-Day' arrived. The Communist Party's tireless campaigning in the workplaces, local communities and the labour movement helped convince masses of workers that this war – and thereafter the peace – could be won by the working class. Thrilled by the stunning victories of the Red Army, thousands of people in Britain joined the CP. Membership more than doubled, from 17,756 in September 1939 to 45,435 by March 1945.

At the Labour Party conference in spring 1945, Amalgamated Engineering Union president Jack Tanner proposed a policy of 'progressive political unity' for the working class movement – including Communist affiliation to the Labour Party. The CP could no longer be portrayed as an organisation controlled from Moscow (by agreement of its affiliates, the Communist International had been dissolved in June 1943). Against this background, Herbert Morrison's Labour Party machine only managed rejection of left unity on a card vote of 1,314,000 to 1,219,000. With an eye to industrial demobilisation in peacetime, and to joint work with Labour Party organisations in the localities, the CP had reassigned Party factory branch members to residential branches. It proved a costly mistake, losing workplace influence and activists, although the re-establishment of many of the larger factory branches a few years later recovered some of the lost ground.

On May 12 1945, four days after the defeat of fascism in Europe, 500 delegates representing nearly two million organised workers attended a *Daily Worker* conference on the way forward. Editor Bill Rust spoke of plans to develop 'a front rank national newspaper with a circulation of 500,000 copies daily'. Ownership of the *Daily Worker* would be transferred from the Communist Party to a cooperative society, thereby guaranteeing 'readers' ownership and control, which is the distinguishing feature of our press'.

1945 From victory to Cold War

As the war drew to a close, the Communist Party called for a Labour-led coalition to win the peace, before switching to support an outright Labour victory in the 1945 General Election. The working class, especially in the armed forces, voted for a new society based on public ownership of key industries, economic planning, full employment, progressive taxation and a welfare state 'from cradle to grave' including a National Health Service. The people swept Churchill aside, giving Labour a 147-seat majority in the House of Commons.

Twenty-one Communist candidates won a total of 102,780 votes. Phil Piratin was elected in Mile End, east London, to join Willie Gallacher in the Westminster parliament. Harry Pollitt narrowly missed victory in Rhondda East by fewer than a thousand votes. In local elections soon after, 215 Communist councillors were elected across Britain.

Young people celebrated the new post-war world, too. In November 1945, in London, the Young Communist League and the National Union of Students participated in the founding congress of the World Federation of Democratic Youth. Within a few years, WFDY and its affiliates representing 30 million young people would hold their first spectacular World Festival of Youth and Students in Prague.

But at its 18th congress, also in November 1945, the Communist Party warned that 'unless the labour movement compels the government to change completely its present foreign policy, which is simply the continuation of the imperialist line of the Tory Party and the reactionary monopoly capitalists, there can be no fundamental social progress in Britain, and the whole future of this country is in grave peril'. The progressive alternative was a 'Britain free and independent', freedom for the colonies and drastic cuts in military expenditure.

On the domestic front, the Labour government enacted a substantial programme of reform. Coal, electricity, the railways, road transport and the Bank of England were all taken into public ownership. Communists supported these measures, while pointing out that generous compensation to the previous capitalist owners and the lack of workers' participation in the running of the nationalised industries would store up problems for the future. With its National Insurance system, Labour's welfare state guaranteed state benefits for the sick, the unemployed, parents and widows; a pension for all retired workers; and free health care at the time of need. But means testing remained for some benefits, while the NHS and pensions system failed to make full or equal provision for women.

The Labour government's plans to build millions of new houses ran into difficulty through shortages of building materials, workers and finance. Yet military camps and apartment blocks stood empty, while returning troops and bombed-out families cried out for decent accommodation. In July and August 1946, a wave of occupations hit former Army and RAF bases. From Middlesbrough, Doncaster and Scunthorpe to Birmingham and High Wycombe, local Communists led people to take over the huts and press the authorities to provide water, gas and electricity. Backed by some local Labour MPs and councils, the squatters elected camp committees to allocate resources and carry out repairs.

In London, Communist councillor and district secretary Ted Bramley spearheaded the invasion of vacant luxury flats in Tory-controlled boroughs. Stepney councillor Tubby Rosen shepherded a hundred homeless families into Duchess of Bedford House. Lord Ilchester's mansion was next. Another Communist councillor, Joyce Alergant, guided hundreds of people into a vacant block of flats formerly occupied by US soldiers. Councillor Joan McMichael, a member of the Party's executive committee, helped launch a second wave of occupations the following month. The Labour Cabinet went into action, too, on September 9. It declared that 'this action has been instigated and organised by the Communist Party and must result in hindering rather than helping the arrangements made for the orderly rehousing of those in need of accommodation'. Writs and eviction orders were issued against squatters and their leaders, four CP councillors were charged with conspiracy to incitement and trespass, and orders sent out to cut off supplies of power and water. Rather than place children at risk in violent confrontations with the police, the Party argued for a peaceful withdrawal from some of the main properties. Under pressure from mass demonstrations, many local authorities began to requisition empty premises and find accommodation for the squatters.

Communists, especially young Jewish ex-servicemen, were readier to use physical force against Britain's re-emerging fascist movement. Many took part in the activities of the '43 Group' which fought ferocious battles to deny Ridley Road and other London streets to Mosley's front organisations and, from 1948, his Union Movement.

Instead of making deeper inroads into the wealth and power of the capitalist class, including through far-reaching democratisation of the state apparatus, the Labour government yielded to pressure from the City of

London and US imperialism. They wanted the re-imposition of Treasury orthodoxy in place of loans and taxes to fund the welfare state and rebuild basic industries now in public ownership. Labour renewed war-time credits with the US, but strings were attached. The US monopolists wanted control over the British economy to promote the dollar as an international currency at the expense of the pound and create more profitable conditions for US capital in Britain.

This was, of course, linked to US foreign policy objectives to turn back the tide of socialism and Communism in Europe and launch an ideological, diplomatic and militarist offensive against the Soviet Union. Borrowing a phrase from chief Nazi propagandist Goebbels, Winston Churchill declared in the US that an 'iron curtain' had descended across Europe, dividing the continent and the world between Western 'freedom' and Soviet 'tyranny'.

From 1947, the Labour government tried to enforce austerity measures against the working class, supported by trade union leaders who agreed to police a regime of wage restraint. The Communist Party went into action as troops were used to break transport and power strikes.

Hard on the heels of socialist revolution in Czechoslovakia, national docks strikes in 1948 and 1949 brought anti-Soviet, anti-Communist hysteria to Britain. Hundreds of Communists were purged in the civil service and the power stations. The TUC, the Labour Party and their joint National Council of Labour issued a new series of diktats demanding that CP members be banned from elected positions in unions and trades councils, and denouncing so-called 'Communist-front' organisations such as the Labour Research Department. In the National Union of Teachers, MI5 orchestrated a dirty tricks campaign against union president GCT Giles, who had pioneered the case for comprehensive education. Nonetheless, unions such as the firefighters, boilermakers and furniture makers continued to elect Communist leaders.

The *Daily Worker* also retained broad support on the left of the labour movement. In February 1948, a special issue reprinted the *Manifesto of the Communist Party* by Marx and Engels to mark its centenary and sold 230,000 copies. Even more readers bought the May Day special. In July, a big peace conference called by the paper and sponsored by the British Peace Committee featured Hewlett Johnson – the 'Red Dean' of Canterbury – as a principal speaker.

When the new-look *Daily Worker* came off the Goss press in the new building in Farringdon Road, a torchlight procession of 20,000 supporters carried editor Bill Rust shoulder-high to Clerkenwell Green, where he auctioned the first two copies for £45 each. The next day, he received a telegram from George Loveless, a descendant of one of the Tolpuddle Martyrs of 1834: 'Today is a proud day for us all. This is what our ancestors fought for. Long live the people's paper'.

Rust collapsed and died just three months later, still in his prime. His successor Johnny Campbell called him 'the greatest editor in British working-class history'.

On the other wing of the labour movement, the TUC and Labour Party leaders were taking their anti-Communism into the international arena. The TUC assisted the American AFL-CIO in splitting the international trade union movement along Cold War lines in 1949. A cabal headed by Prime Minister Attlee within the Labour Cabinet authorised the production of British atomic bombs, under US control. British troops waged war to defend British business interests against the Communist-led national liberation movement in Malaya. Foreign earnings and cheap imports were the vital proceeds of imperialist super-exploitation.

When Royal Navy gunboats exchanged fire with Chinese Communist forces fighting the Nationalists across the river Yangtse, in April 1949, the deaths of 42 British military personnel prompted some Tory papers and politicians to incite violence against the Communist Party at home. Public meetings in Dartmouth and Plymouth – both naval towns – were attacked by mobs and Pollitt sustained a severe back injury. As China threw off Nationalist and imperialist rule, the Labour government helped found the North Atlantic Treaty Organisation (NATO) – six years before the Soviet Union and its allies established the Warsaw Pact. Soon after, US military bases spread across Britain, although for many years they were falsely badged as 'Royal Air Force' stations.

A new round of show trials, this time in the 'People's Democracies' of central and eastern Europe, followed a breach between the Soviet Union and Josef Tito's Communist regime in Yugoslavia. Once again, despite private reservations, most Communists in Britain and around the world believed that erstwhile comrades in Bulgaria, Hungary and Czechoslovakia were in fact saboteurs, imperialist spies and 'Trotskyist agents' in league with Tito. The Party in Britain paid a price for such blind loyalty, losing some allies on the left while performing somersaults as Tito fell out of favour and then back in. It later became undeniable – especially once state, party and Comintern archives were opened – that these and previous show trials stemmed from the arbitrary abuse of power, involving severe breaches of socialist legality and gross violations of human rights.

Labour narrowly retained its parliamentary majority in February 1950. Gratitude to Labour for nationalising the coal industry helped defeat Willie Gallacher in the mining constituency of West Fife, while extensive boundary changes hit Phil Piratin's share of the poll even harder. Some of their closest allies in the Commons, members of the Labour Independent Group of so-called 'crypto-Communists' (Lester Hutchinson, John Platts-Mills, DN Pritt and Lesley Solley), all lost their seats to official Labour candidates as well. The Communist vote slumped everywhere, not least as the consequence of unrelenting Cold War propaganda.

But the Party continued to fight Labour's austerity programme, with

Electrical Trades Union general secretary Wally Stephens leading the charge to overturn the TUC general council's wage restraint policy in September 1950. Two months later, Home Secretary Chuter Ede and the intelligence services tried their utmost to sabotage the congress of the World Peace Council in Sheffield. Eminent scientists, artists and philosophers were refused entry visas to Britain, although Pablo Picasso managed to get through the net and go for a much publicised haircut.

The Labour government decided to boost the armaments budget by two-thirds – in return for a further US loan – and send troops to help the US prop up the tottering dictatorship of Syngman Rhee in South Korea. Consequently, when charges were imposed on NHS dentures and spectacles, three ministers resigned including Nye Bevan. An Old Bailey jury refused to convict Communist dockers' leaders, killing off the wartime ban on strikes in essential industries. The Attlee government went down to defeat in the 1951 General Election, although Labour still polled more votes than the Tories.

1951 *The British Road To Socialism*

In January 1951, the Communist Party's executive committee published a new programme for discussion, namely, *The British Road to Socialism* (BRS). Its main propositions had been extensively discussed and agreed with Stalin and the Soviet leadership, although the most significant features had already emerged in previous British congress resolutions and Party publications. Militant trade unionists, socialists and progressives welcomed the programme's sharp condemnation of the Tories and right-wing Labour:

> If the people are to advance, both Tories and their allies in the
> Labour Movement, the right-wing Labour leaders, must be
> fought and defeated. The lesson of the failure of the Labour
> Government is not the failure of socialism. It is the failure
> of Labour reformism and Labour imperialism, which is the
> servant of the big capitalist interests.

At the core of the *BRS* was the need to take state power out of the hands of the capitalist minority and implement a policy of socialist nationalisation:

> The people of Britain can transform capitalist democracy
> into a real People's Democracy, transforming Parliament, the
> product of Britain's historic struggle for democracy, into the
> democratic instrument of the will of the vast majority of the
> people.

With Communist victories in eastern Europe and China tilting the world balance of forces against imperialism, the *BRS* argued that ruling-class resistance could be overcome without civil war:

> A people's Parliament and Government which draws
> its strength from a united movement of the people, with
> the working class as its core, will be able to mobilise the
> overwhelming majority of the people for decisive measures to
> break the economic and political power of the big exploiters.

Warning that the capitalist class will resist 'by all means in their power, including force', the programme insisted that the people and their government 'should be ready decisively to rebuff such attempts'. Britain could break free from US domination, dismantle the British Empire and pursue an independent foreign policy for peace and cooperation. The *BRS* also confirmed the Communist Party's call for British military withdrawal from northern Ireland, for a united Ireland and for full recognition of the national claims of Scotland and Wales.

Within three months, more than 150,000 copies of *The British Road to Socialism* had been distributed. It stimulated a huge debate throughout the labour movement on the nature of the British state and how people's democratic control could be exerted over the mass media, the civil service, the Foreign Office, the armed forces, the police and the judicial system. Despite the intense hostility of the British establishment, the 'secret state' and the mass media, the CP carried out political agitation on an extraordinary scale. With membership down to 35,124, the Party nonetheless held 2,000 indoor and 5,000 outdoor public meetings – many at factory gates – in the course of 1952. Weekend sales of the *Daily Worker* averaged 49,000 copies.

With the Bevanites vacillating, it fell to the Communist Party to galvanise resistance to US and British imperialism abroad and Tory policies at home. On April 28, 1952, the *Daily Worker* carried front-page pictures of British soldiers in Malaya displaying the heads of freedom fighters, cut off by bounty hunters. They made worldwide news. The Tory Cabinet thought about prosecuting the paper for treason, but then had to admit that the photographs were genuine. Only a few courageous Labour MPs such as SO Davies, Emrys Hughes, Sydney Silverman and Harold Davies joined the CP in condemning the mass murder of two million civilians by the US and its Western allies in the Korean War. For sending reports from the wrong side of the Korean divide, *Daily Worker* journalist Alan Winnington was banned from returning home for 14 years. Broader alliances were possible in the battle against plans to rearm West Germany and admit it to the NATO alliance.

Communist women played a major part alongside the Quakers in collecting more than a million signatures for the Stockholm Peace Petition, which urged the major powers to ban all nuclear weapons. They also proposed to the International Women's Day Committee that a National Assembly of Women be convened in March 1952.

Under the Party's international secretary Palme Dutt, assisted by former *Daily Worker* editor Idris Cox, a network of sub-committees produced regular bulletins on developments in different parts of the world. The *Irish Democrat*, published by the Connolly Association and guided by the CP in Britain, sold thousands of copies monthly, notably to Irish building workers, dockers and car workers.

Many thousands of Party members were active trade unionists as required by Party rules, often occupying key positions as shop stewards, convenors, branch and district officers and full-time officials at district and national level. Industrial organiser Peter Kerrigan impressed on them the need to win the respect of workmates by being efficient in their job and conscientious in fulfilling their trade union responsibilities. Such an approach, combined with the re-emergence of economic downturns and oppressive management, helped Communists to combat Cold War prejudices within the trade union movement.

Whole sections of the trade union movement were effectively under Communist influence, despite bans on Communists holding office in the Transport & General Workers Union, the steel union and in local trades councils. Party members were prominent at national level in the National Union of Mineworkers, the Amalgamated Engineering Union, the Fire Brigades Union, the Electrical Trades Union, the Building Workers Union and several smaller ones. The Scottish and Welsh coalfields and the Yorkshire, Lancashire and Clydeside engineering districts were dominated by Communist officials and rank-and-file activists, as were the London docks and many big car factories in the Midlands and south-east England. Union offices staffed by the most experienced and durable Party militants, whether in vehicle plants or coalmining communities, were often referred to by workers, bosses and state bureaucrats alike as 'the Kremlin'.

The Party's cutting edge was felt most keenly in the big factories, mines and mills where it had about five hundred workplace branches. Here were the party's 'shock troops', playing a leading role in strikes such as those at Rolls Royce, Briggs' and Austin Motors, resisting assembly line speed-ups and demanding more rewards for the workers responsible for higher productivity. 'Every factory a fortress' ran the slogan and Napier's (Acton), Metro-Vickers (Trafford Park), Fairey Aviation (Stockport) and Austin Aero (near Longbridge) boasted CP memberships of 200 and more, selling at least as many copies of the *Daily Worker* in every plant every day. Not confining themselves to traditional trade union concerns, they engaged in political education and action including election campaigns.

The Young Communists led a new round of apprentices' strikes in the shipyards and engineering works, attracting the attention of the Economic League with its spying activities on behalf of the Engineering

Employers Federation.

The Communist Party women's department led by Nora Jeffery organised initiatives to defend jobs in the clothing and textile industry and to step up the battle for equal pay, where notable progress was made in the public sector. Many of the Party's two hundred women's sections campaigned against rising prices and for greater nursery, education and housing provision. However, the monthly sales of *Woman Today* were patchy and its finances always precarious.

In many local communities, when the Tories removed rent controls and security of tenure, the Party's area branches organised tenants in mass campaigns. In October 1955, in Crawley new town for instance, thousands of housing corporation tenants refused to pay rent, while factory workers downed tools to join protest marches.

On the ideological and cultural front, the CP waged the battle of ideas with vigour and imagination. A series of national conferences proclaimed the case for indigenous and working-class culture in place of the 'degenerate' products of US monopoly capitalism with their pessimism, cynicism and gratuitous violence. However, a tendency to impose orthodoxy fragmented the Engels Society, where Haldane and other scientists had disputed the theories of Soviet geneticist Lysenko. Professor Bernal, on the other hand, participated prominently in the Science for Peace committee and the World Peace Council before writing his influential work *Science in History* (1956).

In a series of classic books and articles Dona Torr, Christopher Hill, Rodney Hilton, Dorothy and EP Thompson, Margot Heinemann, Eric Hobsbawm and Noreen Branson reclaimed British history for the working class. They launched the prestigious journal *Past and Present* and the CP history group published a ground-breaking bulletin, *Our History*. The Party writers' group helped produce periodicals such as *Our Time* and *Arena*. Literary giants Pablo Neruda and Dylan Thomas were among the contributors.

Celebrated Welsh and Scots poets TE Nicholas and Hugh MacDiarmid were equally well known in their respective countries as members of the Communist Party. The Unity Theatre movement confused the censorship authorities by its use of agitprop and improvisation. It nurtured actors such as Lionel Bart, Alfie Bass, Michael Redgrave, Bill Owen, Herbert Lom, Bob Hoskins and Warren Mitchell, some of whom joined the Party. Producers Ivor Montagu and Stanley Forman made films for the labour movement.

Communists helped launch an international campaign to restore his US passport to black singer and actor Paul Robeson. He enjoyed a special relationship with the Welsh miners led by Party members such as Will Paynter and Dai Dan Evans. Folk and jazz was the music of choice for many comrades, reflecting the mixture of traditionalism and avant guardism that characterised their Party. Communist folk singers Ewan McColl and Hamish Henderson provided the imagination – and organiser Martin Milligan the drive – to establish the Edinburgh People's Festival in 1951, alongside the city's international festival of the arts. Its inaugural week of events featured plays, poetry, lectures, Gaelic songs and an address by Communist miners' leader Abe Moffat. Although administered by a broad labour-movement based committee, the People's Festival was soon proscribed as a 'Communist front' by the Scottish TUC and the Scottish Labour Party. It survived until 1954, later to be reincarnated as the Edinburgh Fringe.

1956 Crisis and recovery

The year that saw the erection of Laurence Bradshaw's powerful monument to Karl Marx in Highgate Cemetery also shook the international Communist movement to its foundations.

In February 1956, at the 20th congress of the Communist Party of the Soviet Union, general secretary Khrushchev exposed some of the crimes and abuses of the Stalin period. Many Communists around the world were shocked to learn that violations of socialist, democratic and human rights had taken place on such a scale. In fact – as CPSU and state archives were to confirm – millions of Soviet citizens had been incarcerated in the late 1930s for sabotage or subversion, hundreds of thousands executed and whole peoples accused of disloyalty and deported from their homelands. Anti-Communist propagandists in academia and the mass media quickly inflated the number of deaths to 20 or 30 million and more, adding the real or imagined casualties of war, famine, disease and anything else that could be blamed – rightly or wrongly – on the Soviet system.

In Britain, the Communist Party held its 24th congress in March in a mood of bewilderment and disbelief. Party leaders reported the undoubted economic, social and cultural advances being made in the Soviet Union, which were shifting the world balance of forces towards socialism and colonial liberation. The positive role and legacy of Stalin was emphasised, while criticisms were made of a 'cult of personality' deemed to be safely in the past. But as details of Khrushchev's revelations gained widespread circulation, a growing number of CP members demanded more information and debate. Those involved in producing the monthly *Jewish Clarion* reacted sharply to reports of anti-Semitic policies in the Soviet Union. Even Palme Dutt was compelled to concede that 'criminal misdeeds' had occurred in the pre-war period. Pollitt fell ill, to be replaced as the Party's general secretary by John Gollan. In July, the CP executive committee appointed a commission to consider how inner-party democracy might be improved, although pressure to drop democratic-centralism for a more social-democratic type of organisation was resisted. A number of academics including EP Thompson and John Saville published a factional journal of dissent.

Mass protests in Poland and then Hungary indicated significant discontent with economic and social conditions in the 'People's

Democracies', which some reactionary elements wanted to transform into a challenge to Communist rule and the socialist system itself. For a short time, the headlines were grabbed by Britain's military escapade – in league with France and Israel – to stop Egyptian president Nasser nationalising the Suez Canal. Communists held hundreds of workplace and public meetings to mobilise mass opposition to the war alongside the Labour left.

Then Soviet armed forces intervened in Hungary to protect the socialist state. Britain's CP and the *Daily Worker* echoed the Soviet leadership's initial justification and then its self-criticism for being too provocative. But the Red Army's withdrawal at the end of October was followed by brutal killings of Hungarian party and state officials. The new government in Budapest announced an end to the one-party system and then Hungary's withdrawal from the Warsaw Pact. When Soviet troops and tanks returned to crush 'counter-revolution' after heavy fighting, their action was supported – with qualifications and criticism – by the Communist Party in Britain after the most intensive and open debates in every party organisation and in the *Daily Worker*. Khrushchev's revelations together with these events in Hungary prompted thousands of members of all kinds to leave the Party, including the *Daily Worker*'s chief correspondent in Budapest, militant trade unionists and prominent intellectuals. Membership fell from 33,095 in February 1956 to 26,742 in 1957, although this drop of 20 per cent was accentuated by stricter enforcement of Party rules relating to activity and dues payment.

Shortly after this crisis in the international Communist movement, the CPSU recommended financial assistance to the CP in Britain. It continued until 1979, when the latter ended the arrangement. The amounts were small in comparison with the funds raised by the Party's own members. That they did not 'buy' the loyalty of the British CP would be demonstrated by later events. Anyway, Communists have always been at least as ready as the capitalists and their states to extend international solidarity.

For many Party members, the class struggle at home provided reason enough to stay put. An economic downturn had begun to bite, prompting the British Motor Corporation to sack 6,000 workers at Longbridge without notice or pay. The shop stewards' committee, led by Communists, responded by calling a six-week strike which secured its objectives. This was an historic victory because, firstly, workers would henceforth expect consultation and notice over dismissal; and secondly, BMC workers from each plant sent their representatives to a combine committee – an invaluable mechanism for coordination and solidarity. The dispute also demonstrated that in the bus industry, the docks and now the Midlands car industry, workers at shop-floor level were prepared to defy the TGWU ban on electing Communists to office. It came as little surprise when Britain's biggest union turned left and elected Frank Cousins as its general secretary in 1956.

Throughout the 1950s, the CP economic committee insisted that post-war 'Keynesian mixed economy' capitalism had not and could not abolish crises. While right-wing Labour intellectuals proclaimed the end of crisis, mass unemployment and of capitalism itself, the Communist Party warned that the ruling class still wanted a 'reserve army' of the unemployed to moderate wage demands and undermine strong trade unionism. Professor Maurice Dobb was in the vanguard of theoretical work in areas of Marxist political economy, including problems of planning and distribution in capitalist, 'market socialist' and the centrally planned Soviet economies. John Eaton and Sam Aaronovitch analysed the role of rival state monopoly-capitalisms in the formation and development of the European Common Market, showing that the capitalist monopolies continued to fight to maximise market share and profit in their home economies as well as in the colonies and semi-colonies.

Almost alone on the left, CP economists highlighted the increasingly predominant role of the City of London in shaping British ruling class economic and political policy, especially as British transnational corporations lost ground to US, French and German competition in the developing world. As British imperialism's command of colonial markets and cheap imports weakened, it fought desperately to ensure that countries only gained their independence on terms favourable to British capital. The Communist Party also helped uncover the ongoing trend to monopoly in the British economy, now being driven by US transnationals – not least in the motor industry. In his political report to the 25th party congress in 1957, John Gollan called for a new, independent foreign policy for Britain: one which 'ends subservience to the United States, insists on the withdrawal of American troops and outlaws nuclear weapons, brings about a European Security system, finishes with the colonial wars, and makes Britain a force for new international understanding'.

Later that year, Aneurin Bevan's rejection of unilateral nuclear disarmament at the Labour Party conference angered many on the left. However, like Bevan and the CPSU, the CP in Britain regarded multilateralism as the key issue because it alone could abolish the world's two biggest stocks of atomic weapons. Nevertheless, the Party quickly came to see the value of British unilateralism as a lever to push the US into an agreement with the Soviet Union. From their beginning at Easter 1958, the Communist Party and the *Daily Worker* backed the annual marches between the Aldermaston Atomic Weapons Research Establishment and London. Party members helped turn the Campaign for Nuclear Disarmament (CND) into a mass movement after its formation in 1958. Cousins helped win the Labour Party conference for its policy of unilateral British nuclear disarmament two years later, although the right-wing leadership under Hugh Gaitskell soon reversed the decision.

The Notting Hill riots of 1958 laid bare the ugly racism instilled by empire. Prejudice was mixed with resentment at government-sponsored mass immigration from the Caribbean, as black workers filled low-paid jobs and sub-standard accommodation. White youths went on the rampage. Back in 1952, the Party's 22nd congress had condemned propaganda about Britain being 'flooded' by foreigners and pointed to the 'flagrant and shameful forms of racial discrimination' suffered by immigrants from the colonies, demanding that 'colour bars' against them in employment, housing, pubs and clubs be made a criminal offence. A couple of years later, the CP published a Charter of Rights and distributed 150,000 leaflets and pamphlets which proclaimed 'No Colour Bar for Britain'.

Now, in 1958, Britain's Communists mobilised to resist racist thuggery and urge working class unity. Trinidad-born Claudia Jones, a member of the Party's international committee and editor of the *West Indian Gazette*, not only played an outstanding role in that struggle. She inspired the local black community to celebrate their heritage and culture the following year. The Notting Hill carnival was born.

The Communist Party's black and ethnic minority members tended to be either seafarers in port cities such as Liverpool and Cardiff, or overseas Communists domiciled in Britain. For decades, its best-known black member was the famous Manchester boxer Len Johnson, banned from fighting for a British title by his colour and a frequent local council candidate in Moss Side.

Towards the end of 1959, the Party responded to an appeal from the African National Congress (ANC) to campaign for the boycott of goods from apartheid South Africa. Anger at the Sharpeville massacre transformed the initiative the following year into the Anti-Apartheid Movement. Its headquarters were located in the second Ruskin House, Croydon. The CP opposed the 1961 Commonwealth Immigration Bill which exempted the white 'Old Commonwealth' from any controls. Working with the Movement for Colonial Freedom, it helped establish the Coordinating Committee against Racial Discrimination, drawing in the Indian Workers Association and similar Pakistani and West Indian bodies.

Attempts by followers of Sir Oswald Mosley and neo-Nazi Colin Jordan to rebuild a fascist movement also met Communist-led opposition. During a confrontation in Manchester in summer 1962, Betty Askins floored Mosley with a handbag full of coins from her market stall. Meanwhile, Communists brought together trades unionists and Jewish community leaders to set up the North and East London Anti-Fascist Coordinating Committee. Maurice Ludmer and Gerry Gable collaborated with left Labour MPs to launch the first run of *Searchlight* magazine.

Britain's Communists celebrated heartily when long-time comrade Cheddi Jagan was re-elected chief minister of British Guyana in 1961. He had previously been removed militarily by the British colonial authorities. Despite winning the largest share of the votes in 1964, he was dismissed from office for a second time. Composer Alan Bush, banned from the BBC during the war, added an opera about the Guyanan freedom struggle ('The

Sugar Reapers') to a repertoire which included 'The Men of Blackmoor' (about the Northumberland and Durham miners) and 'Wat Tyler'. They were performed to great acclaim in the German Democratic Republic and other socialist countries, but largely boycotted by the musical establishment at home.

By the late 1950s and early '60s, British monopoly capitalism was concentrating its interests still further in the City of London, financial and property speculation and the export of capital overseas. British manufacturing industry was feeling the strain of under-investment and increasingly fierce competition from the US, West Germany and France. Thus a new ruling class offensive was launched against CP influence in the unions. The US diplomatic and intelligence services had been particularly concerned about Communist influence in the Electrical Trades Union and its security implications. The union's CP leadership had gained unprecedented terms, conditions and union facilities for electricians and apprentices. Disgruntled ex-Party members backed by employers, TUC general secretary Vic Feather, the BBC, Catholic Action, the Economic League and other shadowy right-wing outfits, charged ETU officials with ballot-rigging. In 1961, a High Court judge found the union's general secretary Frank Haxell and other CP members guilty of using 'fraudulent and unlawful' means to win an election. The Party's executive committee condemned such practices, which were more often used by the right wing against Communists and the left. The new leadership of the ETU went on to ban Communists and their allies from office, crushing all dissent and ruthlessly manipulating organisational and electoral arrangements on a scale undreamt of by Haxell and his comrades.

Despite a new wave of anti-Communist frenzy in the mass media, Party membership continued to revive – not least as a result of militant campaigning against high council rents, slum landlords and 'Rachmanism'. Tenants' leader Don Cook was a major target for eviction following a mass rent strike in the London borough of St. Pancras in 1960, where the leader of the council and six of his colleagues had been expelled from the Labour Party and joined the CP. Police laid violent siege to Cook's flat, workers struck in solidarity and 14,000 people marched on the town hall.

In local elections the following year, 450 Communist candidates achieved 100,000 votes and raised the Party's tally of councillors to 28.

Also in 1961, the Tory government imposed a statutory pay pause. This provoked widespread trade union defiance. Workers in the engineering, shipbuilding and motor industries struck for better wages and conditions. In January 1962, the CP executive committee pointed out:

> The ruling class sharpens its weapons for survival in a new and very important stage in the long-drawn-out crisis of British monopoly capitalism.

During the first-ever national strike in the electricity supply industry, Communist Charlie Doyle at Battersea Power Station was attacked by the *Daily Mirror* as 'the most hated man in Britain'. He was used to the hatred of the ruling class, having been hounded out of the US during the McCarthyism madness. But Communist efforts in train drivers' union ASLEF failed to secure united action with the NUR against the Beeching Plan to slash Britain's railway network.

Party recruitment received a boost from the revival of Soviet prestige, due not least to the Sputnik space programme and cosmonaut Yuri Gagarin's orbit around the Earth. Many Communists were very active in the British-Soviet Friendship Society and similar bodies, building links between workers and their families here and in the socialist countries, organising exchange visits between trade union and cultural bodies, selling *Soviet Weekly* and promoting mutual understanding where the British ruling class promoted fear and antagonism.

The CIA-backed 'Bay of Pigs' invasion of Cuba and then, in 1962, the so-called 'Soviet missile crisis' could be pointed to as further evidence of US aggression and nuclear recklessness. Although the US ended its military blockade of the island, an economic embargo has continued to the present day – testimony to US determination that the peoples of Latin America should not see Cuba as a socialist alternative to imperialist domination, military dictatorship, debilitating poverty and untreated disease.

By 1963, British CP membership had returned to pre-Hungary levels. They were barely affected by the departure of small groups of 'Maoists'. The Chinese Communist Party's new line denounced Soviet 'social imperialism', rehabilitated Stalin, dismissed the possibility of imposing 'peaceful co-existence' on the imperialist powers and identified 'Third World' peasants and 'first world' students as the revolutionary forces to replace the 'bourgeois' industrial working class. Britain's CP disagreed with these propositions, clearly but in terms which looked forward to the restoration of unity in the world Communist movement.

Although Communists fared well in British municipal elections the following year, the Party's 36 General Election candidates were squeezed between a reinvigorated Labour Party and a boycott by the mass media. Towards the end of 1964, YCLers in Manchester and Clydeside sparked an all-out strike for the Apprentice Youth Charter. Condemned by envious Trotskyists, the movement won improvements for young workers in their pay and procedures.

Labour prime minister Harold Wilson survived for two years with the slenderest parliamentary majority. But it was long enough to indicate that behind the rhetoric about peace, higher pay and productivity (harnessing the 'white heat of the technological revolution') lurked the usual social-democratic commitment to NATO, nuclear weapons and pay restraint. In September 1965, the government appointed a royal commission into the role of trade unions and a Prices and Incomes Board to impose wage controls.

At the Communist Party's 29th congress, John Gollan urged members to put aside Cold War isolationism. The CP was ready to 'talk to anyone now, and consider any proposal, to reach the aim of a united left movement'. The immediate task was, he insisted, to 'halt the swing to the right and force the Government to the left'. Within the British labour movement, the scope for unity on the left was expanding rapidly, especially between the Communists and the Labour left. Broad left alliances developed within the trade unions, as Palme Dutt's *Labour Monthly* carved out a distinctive position as a magazine of left unity.

The growing number of white-collar and women workers reflected changing patterns of industry, work and employment. Trade unionism advanced in these sectors as the decline in coal, steel, shipbuilding and other traditional industries began to accelerate. In 1966, the *Daily Worker* changed its name to the *Morning Star* in a bid to broaden its appeal. That year, too, Labour increased its majority at the General Election to 96. Prime Minister Wilson treated this result as the green light for an assault on trade union strength in the workplace. This was judged essential if labour productivity and corporate profits were to turn upwards.

In May that year, Communist seafarers and their allies in the 'Reform Movement' succeeded in pressing their union's notoriously collaborationist leaders into calling a strike. The main aim was to reduce the standard working week in the industry from 56 hours to 40. Utilising reports gained from MI5 bugs at CP headquarters in King Street, London, Wilson accused a 'tightly knit group of politically motivated men' of plotting to bring down his government. He named the Party's new industrial organiser Bert Ramelson and dockers' leader Jack Dash as among the masterminds. The TUC withdrew its support for the dispute two days after Wilson's speech. The strike was settled after six weeks with agreement on a 42-hour week and a substantial wage rise, but not before the government had declared a state of emergency. Almost immediately, a national wage freeze was announced across the whole economy with TUC support. Prices continued to rise despite the pledge to control them as well, as millions of workers experienced a fall in their living standards. Communists responded by setting up the Liaison Committee for the Defence of Trade Unions. Pay controls were later relaxed, but further battles over trade union power and the cost of living became inevitable.

Around the world, imperialism was reacting viciously to the advance of revolutionary and progressive movements. In Indonesia, US-backed General Suharto organised the slaughter of half a million Communists.

Massive American military intervention in Vietnam tried to shore up a succession of military dictatorships in the south against the Communist-led National Liberation Front. Young Communists took to high streets across Britain, collecting for medical aid to Vietnam. The Vietnamese NLF made clear its view that the solidarity movement here should concentrate on breaking the Labour government's political support for US policy, helping to force the imperialists to negotiate for peace and withdrawal. Even so, the far left in Britain preferred to raise the slogan 'Victory to the NLF!' The US and its allies killed more than two million civilians in Vietnam, Cambodia and Laos before peace talks began and the forces of popular sovereignty triumphed.

Britain's Communist Party unreservedly opposed Israel's 'Six-Day War' in 1967 against its Arab neighbours. Backed by US and British imperialism, Israel illegally occupied the Palestinian territories of Gaza, the West Bank and East Jerusalem, together with Egypt's Sinai Peninsula and Syria's Golan Heights. The CP paid a heavy price in terms of lost support among Britain's Jewish communities – but as nothing compared with the cost of the war to the Palestinian people.

1968 Communists to the fore!

For some Communists, the 'Prague Spring' in 1968 appeared to be a replay of the Hungarian crisis of 1956. But this time, the Czech Communist Party had initiated the mass demonstrations in favour of its 'democratisation' of political and economic life.

The Dubcek government clearly enjoyed public and working class support, and carefully avoided any talk of withdrawing from the Warsaw Pact. The *Morning Star* and CP in Britain welcomed 'the positive steps taken to tackle the wrongs of the past and strengthen socialist democracy'. When Soviet and allied forces entered Prague on August 20, they met overwhelming but passive, non-violent resistance. The next day, like other Communists in the developed capitalist countries, the Party in Britain opposed the 'intervention'. While understanding Soviet security concerns, they could not share the Soviet assessment that counter-revolution had been underway in Czechoslovakia. The YCL went further, characterising the intervention as an 'invasion'. Divisions within Young Communist ranks polarised sharply between 'revisionists' and Marxists-Leninists.

Similar differences had also surfaced during debates around the new edition of *The British Road to Socialism* published in 1968. It identified 'state-monopoly capitalism' as the obstacle to progress on every front and to socialism, because 'the capitalist state is intertwined with the great banks and monopolies'. The immediate need, therefore, was to construct a 'broad popular alliance around the leadership of the working class, fighting every aspect of the power of the monopolies'. However, the programme also emphasised the importance of a 'democratic advance to socialism', with a multi-party system including parties hostile to socialism continuing after working class state power had been achieved. Instead of seeking to undermine, weaken or split the Labour Party, the CP wanted to see it reject reformism, fight capitalism and help build a socialist society. Indeed, such points had featured as a central theme of CP contributions to a 'Christian-Marxist dialogue' conducted in large public meetings and the Party press, led by James Klugmann and Canon Paul Oestreicher.

Other Communists saw the programme as diluting the class basis of the Party's strategy to take and maintain state power, placing too much store by electoral work and capitulating to 'bourgeois' concepts of democracy.

Communist involvement in the struggle against South African apartheid was less contentious. London was becoming an important base for South African CP and ANC exiles. Britain's Communist Party had responded to an appeal from the two organisations to supply white volunteers who, having no connection with South Africa, would not be known to the apartheid regime. Mostly recruited from within the YCL, and with financial and other help from the Soviet Union and other socialist countries, they travelled to South Africa and neighbouring countries to carry out clandestine military and propaganda work. The military work, which lasted into the early 1990s, consisted mainly of reconnaissance, transporting weapons and equipment, and helping ANC fighters to enter South Africa. Some comrades received training in the Soviet Union and Cuba. In Liverpool, the CP recruited Communist seafarers for an abortive mission, organised by Joe Slovo, to land ANC fighters on the South African coast in the good ship 'Aventura'.

During every year from 1967 to 1971, YCL and CP members, along with non-communists recruited in Britain, planted specially-designed 'leaflet bombs' and similar devices in South African cities. These distributed thousands of ANC leaflets to startled crowds in up to five cities simultaneously. The volunteers also arranged street broadcasting of amplified recordings of ANC speeches and songs. These activities helped the ANC to re-establish a presence inside South Africa following the Rivonia trial, after which most ANC and SACP members who were not gaoled had been forced into exile. YCL member Sean Hosey was captured and jailed for 5 years. Communist Party member Alex Moumbaris, sentenced to 12 years, escaped from Pretoria Prison in 1979. The others kept their activities secret for four decades.

In Britain, as access to higher and further education grew in the 1960s and early 1970s, the student movement gained in social weight and political significance. The Communist Party's national student committee, working with the Labour left and the Young Liberals in the Radical Students Alliance, played a central role in breaking the grip of the Labour right wing in the National Union of Students (NUS). After CIA links with the International Student Conference (set up to undermine the International Union of Students) were exposed in 1967, the CP had become the leading political force in the Broad Left which also included left-wing Labour students. The election of Communist Digby Jacks as its president in 1971 indicated the extent to which the NUS was turning into a mass campaigning organisation on issues such as student finances, student union resources, racism, South African apartheid and peace – although the Communist and Labour left leadership increasingly came under attack from Trotskyist and other far left elements.

Even more significantly, the Party was strengthening its alliances in the labour movement. A further shift to the left in the biggest trade unions had been signalled by the election in the late 1960s of ex-CP member Hugh Scanlon and ex-International Brigader Jack Jones to lead the AEU and the TGWU, respectively. Dockers, engineers, airplane pilots, bus workers and train drivers were among those taking action during the period.

But the most historic strike was that of women machinists at Ford's in Dagenham and then Halewood in June 1968. Their demand was for regrading to reduce pay inequality with their male colleagues. Employment minister Barbara Castle intervened and the action ended after three weeks with a wage rise short of parity. But the episode paved the way for the first Equal Pay Act in 1970. A number of the shop stewards organising the action were Communist or broad left activists.

The Communist Party used its influence among London's dockers to combat Enoch Powell's racist scaremongering about 'funeral pyres' and rivers 'foaming with much blood'. Communists liaised with their Asian, African and Caribbean comrades in Britain to launch the Campaign Against Racist Laws to oppose further immigration controls against black and Asian Commonwealth citizens. Two of Britain's biggest-ever anti-racist demonstrations followed.

The Labour government's January 1969 White Paper, 'In Place of Strife', set out to shackle shop-floor trade unionism by imposing strike ballots, delaying industrial action and outlawing so-called unofficial 'wildcat' walk-outs. A labour court would preside over the new system. The Liaison Committee for the Defence of Trade Unions called a one-day general strike on May 1. Other strikes in the motor, refuse collection and coal mining industries showed the determination of workers to take official and unofficial action in defence of their living standards. Wilson and Castle dropped their anti-union proposals, and a divided Labour Party lost the 1970 General Election.

The Tory government under Edward Heath tried to pick up where Labour had been compelled to leave off. But fresh attempts to assert state authority over collective bargaining through compulsory ballots and a labour court proved catastrophic. Five states of emergency were declared between 1970 and 1974 (there had been only seven in the preceding 50 years). A work to rule on the railways created chaos – but an enforced 'cooling off' ballot turned into a six-to-one vote of confidence in the unions and their action.

The LCDTU took the lead in putting unions and the TUC under pressure to resist Heath's Industrial Relations Bill. One-day 'Kill the Bill' stoppages called by the Liaison Committee and the Amalgamated Union of Engineering

Workers in December 1970 and then in March 1971 – when three million workers came out – forced the TUC to respond. At a special congress, the trade unions decided not to cooperate with the anti-union legislation.

In June 1971, the Tory government announced its intention to withdraw trade credits from the semi-nationalised Upper Clyde Shipbuilders, immediately jeopardising more than 6,000 jobs. Former YCL general secretary and CP Scottish secretary Jimmy Reid, together with fellow Communist shop stewards Sammy Barr and Jimmy Airlie, led a work-in which occupied all four yards in Glasgow and Clydebank. As Reid put it: 'We are taking over the yards. We refuse to accept that faceless men can take these decisions'. They ran the company for 15 months, assisted by an enormous outpouring of national and international solidarity including two one-day strikes across Scotland, until the government backed down. The yards were saved, although not all the jobs. The UCS work-in inspired other workers to resist closures as 200 occupations broke out across Britain over the following 12 months. Further action by the women machinists at Dagenham led to improvements in the equal pay law.

In the last week of July 1972, mass working class action called by the LCDTU secured the release from Pentonville prison of five dockers' leaders (two of them Communists). They had been imprisoned for organising 'secondary' (ie solidarity) action in the course of a dispute involving the TGWU. With the TUC finally threatening a one-day general strike, the government used an obscure legal functionary to free the five. The Industrial Relations Act was now a dead duck.

Communists working with allies in the broad left played a central role in the 1972 miners' strike against government pay controls. The Security Service (MI5) and senior civil servants informed Prime Minister Heath that eight of the 28-strong NUM executive were CP members – and therefore 'wreckers' who opposed the 'existing political system generally' and whose aim was to bring down the Tory government. Party militants initiated a mass picket of Saltley coke works in Birmingham, winning the support of shop stewards in the city's giant factories. In what became known as the 'Battle of Saltley Gates', tens of thousands of engineers and car workers left work to swamp the depot, closing it at the very moment that the government had decided to surrender to the miners.

The Tories took revenge for some of these defeats with the arrest of dozens of local militants six months after a national building workers' strike. Communist Des Warren and Ricky Tomlinson were gaoled on trumped-up conspiracy charges, the former remaining in prison even after the Tories had been turfed out.

In the north of Ireland, the unionist regime and sectarian local security forces tried to suppress resurgent demands from Catholics for equal rights. The British Army imposed curfews and rampaged through nationalist communities. Thousands of nationalists and republicans were interned without trial under special powers legislation. As a result of Connolly Association lobbying, the British TUC adopted a substantial policy on Ireland in 1971 which included opposition to the unionist veto on progress towards Irish reunification. In January 1972, a huge anti-Internment rally was organised in Derry. The march itself passed off peacefully, but British paratroopers opened fire on protestors and killed 14 unarmed people on what became known as 'Bloody Sunday'. Heath brought the Six Counties under direct London rule.

Throughout this period, working closely with their Irish comrades, Britain's Communists raised these issues inside the labour movement and beyond. This became increasingly difficult as the British government and media concentrated on the threat of Irish Republican Army 'terrorism'. The Communist Party, on the other hand, condemned state terrorism in Ireland while making clear its opposition to all military actions against civilians. It warned that repressive legislation would be extended to Britain and, arguing that there could be no military solution, called for the reunification of Ireland by peaceful means.

As far as the national question within Britain was concerned, and almost alone on the left, Communists had long advocated parliaments for Scotland and Wales. Scottish TUC general secretary Jimmy Milne and NUM vice-president Mick McGahey championed the cause in the labour movement. Arising from the solidarity of the miners' strike and other battles, South Wales NUM secretary Dai Francis together with trades council leader D Ivor Davies and North Wales TGWU secretary Tom Jones (a former International Brigader) played a vital part in establishing the Wales TUC in 1973, against the opposition of some right-wing trade unions leaders. The Party's particular appeal in the Celtic countries was demonstrated in that year's local elections, when 608 candidates polled 165,743 votes to win 13 seats in Scotland, six in Wales and four in England.

At the beginning of 1973, the CP launched a women's journal, *Link*. It marked the culmination of a debate within the Party about its relationship to the women's liberation movement. Communists had played a major part in drafting the demands of the 1970 Women's Liberation Conference in Oxford for abortion and contraception rights, childcare facilities and equal opportunities in employment and education. Florence Keyworth, Gladys Brooks and others had then joined non-Party members Sheila Rowbotham and Audrey Wise to produce a feminist magazine, *Red Rag*.

In September 1973, the Popular Unity government of Salvador Allende was overthrown in a CIA-backed military coup. Communists initiated the Chile Solidarity Campaign, also assisting many Chilean Communists and socialists to find safety in Britain. Refugee members of the Manuel Rodriguez Patriotic Front, the armed wing of the anti-fascist resistance, were secretly transported across Europe and on some occasions rescued from deportation to Chile by trade union action.

At home, a miners' overtime ban prompted the Tory government to impose a three-day week and power cuts. When ministers threatened harsher measures still, Mick McGahey caused a storm by declaring that he would – if necessary – appeal to soldiers to disobey orders and assist the miners. In the face of an all-out strike in February 1974, Heath called a General Election on the question of 'Who Governs Britain?' The electors gave their answer, twice in one year. Wilson returned to office on the basis of a Labour manifesto which promised 'a fundamental and irreversible shift in the balance of power and wealth in favour of working people and their families'.

Jimmy Reid, one of the leaders of the UCS work-in, trebled the CP vote in Dumbarton Central which included 'Red Clydebank' with its Communist councillors and more than one thousand Party members. His high profile campaign won 5,928 votes, 15 per cent of the poll, in the wake of a vicious anti-Communist and clerical crusade against him. In the fifty or so other seats contested by the Party in the two 1974 elections, its candidates were seen by the mass media and many electors as irrelevant as far as the most important outcome was concerned.

That year, too, Communists and allies on London Trades Council proposed a Working Women's Charter which was taken up enthusiastically by trade unions, women's centres and tenants' associations in other towns and cities. Its demands included equal pay and opportunities, a national minimum wage, equal rights in law, free daytime nursery provision, additional maternity rights, free contraception and abortion and a bigger role for women in trade union and political life.

In the 1975 referendum campaign, the CP fought hard as part of the broad alliance for a 'No' vote against Britain's continuing membership of the European Economic Community. The Communist position had been consistent since the 1957 Treaty of Rome: based on the free movement of capital, goods and labour, the Common Market was a 'bosses' club'. Although Wilson succeeded in keeping Britain in the EEC, the Labour government also replaced Tory laws with new rights for workers and trade unions, repealed punitive council rent legislation and nationalised the aircraft and shipbuilding industries.

Also in 1975, former CP assistant general secretary and *Morning Star* editor George Matthews displayed a live MI5 microphone discovered in a wall at the Party's King Street headquarters. For decades, the intelligence services had conducted an enormous campaign of espionage, burglary and communications interception against many Party activists and sympathisers. Matthews also made a decisive intervention at that year's Party congress, tipping the balance in favour of a resolution opposing discrimination against gays and lesbians. When this was followed by further executive committee statements attacking anti-gay prejudice and calling for full and equal rights in law, the *Gay Times* congratulated the CP for having the 'fullest and most far-reaching such policy ever adopted by a non-gay organisation'.

Hoping to avoid the conflict over statutory wage controls that had brought down its Tory predecessor, the Labour government concluded a 'Social Contract' with the TUC leadership, including Jones and Scanlon. It promised higher social expenditure and public investment in return for higher productivity and voluntary pay restraint. The problem was that Labour also hoped to placate the City of London by trying to prop up the value of sterling through high interest rates. This made industrial investment and imports more expensive. Wage rises fell way behind inflation, while company profits and dividends raced ahead. Bert Ramelson renamed Labour's deal 'the Social Con-trick' and the label stuck. Ken Gill, Communist general secretary of technicians' union TASS, led the counter-attack at successive TUC conferences. He proposed the Alternative Economic Strategy devised by CP and Labour left economists and trade unionists. It called for limits on the export of capital, selective import controls, public ownership of strategic industries and enterprises, planning agreements, lower interest rates, higher public investment, price controls, free collective bargaining, higher pensions and benefits, a shorter working week and reductions in overtime. In 1975, Gill's motion at the TUC conference was defeated by 6.4 million to 3 million on a card vote.

In August 1976, low-paid Asian women went on strike at the Grunwick photo processing plant in London. They struggled on heroically for almost two years, sustained by mass solidarity and Brent trades council with its substantial Communist influence. Locked into a balance of payments crisis, with unemployment climbing towards two million, the Labour government accepted a loan from the International Monetary Fund. The strings included public spending cuts and job losses. A series of strikes, notably by public sector workers in the fire service and local government, engulfed Labour's pay policy.

Alongside these events, the CP and its allies built 'broad left' organisations in the trade unions. Their work was guided and informed by a Party advisory committee in each union, whose work was in turn overseen by CP organisers at the centre, from Bert Ramelson to Mick Costello.

The 25th anniversary of Elizabeth Windsor's accession to the throne was intended to reinforce patriotic feelings of national unity among the British people. Communists saw it as celebration of social inequality, class privilege and undemocratic rule. An alternative 'People's Jubilee' in June 1977 attracted 11,000 people to Alexandra Palace, London, in what the CP leadership declared was 'a great expression of the internationalism of our party. It demonstrated our closeness to the struggles of the British people, and showed the relationship of these to the battle for socialism in Britain'. One of the organisers of the People's Jubilee was jazz musician Paul Rutherford, a Communist in the tradition of bandleader Harry Gold and his 'Pieces of Eight', while the Party's presence on the folk and jazz-rock scenes was about to be renewed by the likes of Dick Gaughan and Robert Wyatt.

Despite its influence in the trade unions, the Communist Party was not strong enough to force new prime minister Callaghan to change course. Even so, newspapers reported Bert Ramelson as claiming that the CP could decide a policy in the autumn, get it adopted by most major unions by the spring, see it become TUC policy in September and Labour Party policy in October. But the Labour Party leadership now simply ignored its own conference policies, as did some compliant right-wing trade union leaders. Abandoned even by the TUC at the end, Callaghan and Labour were defeated in the General Election by Margaret Thatcher's Tories.

The Communist Party ended the decade with a membership of 20,599, compared with its high-point of 29,943 in 1973. The decline had accelerated after 1977, when a new draft of the Party's programme *The British Road to Socialism* was debated and adopted. Once more, deepening political and ideological differences had come into the open, prompting a group around Surrey district secretary Sid French to split and form the New Communist Party.

At the other end of the spectrum, a small faction of 'modernisers' questioned the centrality of the working class to the struggle for socialism. They pointed to the diversity of the working class as evidence that it could no longer be seen as a single force with one overriding identity or even one fundamental class interest. 'New social forces' based on gender, ethnicity and sexual orientation, or motivated by concerns for the environment and peace, could play the leadership role which the working class and the labour movement had failed to fulfil. This was their interpretation of the 'broad democratic alliance' which replaced the programme's perspective of a 'broad popular alliance' aimed at the monopolies and their state. Selecting and distorting some concepts developed by the Italian Marxist-Leninist Antonio Gramsci, the latter-day 'Gramscians' labelled Communists who based their political theory and practice on class as 'left sectarians' who were guilty of 'class reductionism'. Echoing the 'Eurocommunist' outlook expressed by Communist Party leaders in Italy, Spain and to a lesser extent France, the faction emphasised the need to 'democratise' both capitalism and socialism. The Soviet Union was a model to be shunned or repudiated rather than critically or uncritically supported.

Subsequently, the Eurocommunists took control of the YCL and then the Party's national student committee. Breaking traditional alliances with the Labour left, they disorientated and then demobilised both bodies. This was made possible by the patronage of a CP leadership seeking 'new' ideas. Like Eric Hobsbawm in his 1978 Marx Memorial Library lecture 'The Forward March of Labour Halted?', the Eurocommunists were raising some interesting questions – but then providing some very wrong answers. Taking control of the Party's theoretical and discussion journal *Marxism Today* enabled them to spread further confusion and division, not least about the character of the Thatcher government.

1979 Reaction on every front

Tory strategy reflected the interests of monopoly finance capital in the City of London: to restore corporate profitability through privatisation, cuts in public services, lower wages, higher labour productivity, curbs on trade union rights and massive tax reductions for the rich and big business. An ideological offensive was launched in favour of 'free markets' and 'free' (ie monopoly) enterprise, accompanied by rearmament and a renewed ideological Cold War against the Soviet Union.

When the Soviet Red Army intervened in Afghanistan to support one faction of the revolutionary government against another, and to help it resist CIA-backed subversion, the British government supplied military and financial assistance to the Islamic fundamentalist 'mujahideen'. The decision of the CP executive committee to oppose the Soviet intervention provoked open defiance in the Party and the pages of the *Morning Star*.

At home, too, the Thatcher regime was quick to declare war on the working class. It brought new management into British Leyland to sack powerful Communist works convenor Derek Robinson at the Longbridge car plant in November 1979. The security service MI5 also had a hand in the affair, as did the new right-wing leadership of the AUEW. In response, Longbridge workers struck to defend Robinson. But whereas the TGWU was set to back the unofficial action, his own AUEW leaders opted for a joint inquiry with BL management instead. Three months later, with the momentum lost, under a deluge of anti-Red propaganda and fearful for their jobs, a majority could no longer be won for action to reinstate him. Robinson's offence, supposedly, was to have published with others an alternative survival plan – including the possibility of mass action – for the publicly owned, mismanaged and under-funded company. His real crime was to be the leader of a huge, well-organised combine of militant shop stewards facing company plans to shed at least 25,000 jobs. The ruling class wanted to send a message to every workers' representative in Britain: 'If we can sack "Red Robbo", we can sack you'.

The government and state then took on the steelworkers, achieving mass redundancies in exchange for a wage rise. The teachers were next, defeated in industrial action over their terms and conditions. The Tories abolished important trade union rights, hacked away at public services, privatised the nationalised industries, extended the powers of the police and the courts, hammered local government and awarded enormous tax cuts to the rich. *Marxism Today* announced the arrival of a new and fearsome phenomenon – 'Thatcherism' – rather than analyse the switch by state-monopoly capitalism to a more aggressive strategy of class confrontation.

As unemployment soared towards three million, the Communist Party drew on its traditional strengths and alliances to initiate two People's Marches for Jobs. The first, from Liverpool to London in 1981, received support from the Scottish, Welsh and regional TUCs – although a Tory minister attacked it for being politically motivated, quoting from an article by the then left-wing Labour MP Neil Kinnock in the *Morning Star*. On May 30, more than 100,000 supporters accompanied the marchers into Trafalgar Square. A few weeks later, angered by mass unemployment, racist policing and fascist attacks, young and unemployed people rioted in dozens of English towns and cities. The British TUC backed the second march, in 1983, from Glasgow to London with five additional feeder marches. It helped make unemployment a major issue at the General Election in June, although the 'Falklands' factor ensured a Thatcher victory.

Despite having sold a battleship and other weapons to the military junta in Buenos Aires, while reducing British citizenship rights of the islanders, the Thatcher government had sent a naval taskforce to retake the Falklands from Argentina. Labour Party leaders sided with British imperialism and its determination to hold onto mineral rights in the South Atlantic, while the CP and the *Morning Star* called for withdrawal of the military 'Task Force' in order to pursue a peaceful settlement. During the subsequent election campaign, the Tories placed full-page adverts in the national press listing key common policies from the Labour and Communist Party manifestos, under the heading 'Like your manifesto, Comrade'.

There was one country where the Tories joined their ally US president Reagan and the Pope in supporting strikes, mass demonstrations and free trade unionism ... Poland. In the face of big and popular mobilisations by the 'Solidarity' trade union movement, General Jaruzelski and the military had taken over the government there at the end of 1981. The CP leadership in Britain opposed martial law, demanding the release of detained trade union leaders and a return to civilian rule. Many other Party members believed that the real aim of Solidarnosc, with its material and financial support from the US National Endowment for Democracy, was to bring down Poland's socialist system.

Nevertheless, the Communist Party was united in its opposition to the reactionary regimes of Saddam Hussein in Baghdad and the Ayatollah Khomeini in Tehran. Both dictatorships imprisoned, tortured and executed Communists and progressives, while US and British imperialism armed Iraq for its brutal invasion of Iran. Communists in Britain played a vital role in sustaining organisations of solidarity with the Iraqi and Iranian people, working in unity with Communists from those countries now domiciled here, winning widespread support within the British labour movement.

By now in the grip of a fresh bout of Cold War fever, the Tories were determined to install Cruise and Trident nuclear missile systems in Britain. Hundreds of thousands of demonstrators took to the streets and surrounded military bases at Greenham Common and elsewhere. While Defence

Secretary Heseltine denounced Communist Party influence in CND, one of its leaders Bruce Kent hailed the CP as 'partners in peace' at the Party's 38th congress in 1983. He also praised the *Morning Star* for its 'steady, honest and generous coverage of the whole nuclear disarmament case'.

By then, Eurocommunists in the Party leadership had launched a furious attack on the class-based, pro-Soviet politics of the *Morning Star* and its editor Tony Chater. In a period when the resurgent Labour left headed by Tony Benn would have benefited from Communist support and advice about the importance of extra-parliamentary alliances and mass struggle, the Eurocommunists instead denounced Labour Party socialists as the 'hard left'.

On March 12 1984, the NUM struck against the National Coal Board's pit closure programme. President Arthur Scargill and the union's executive turned a collection of local strikes into a national one, on the authority of previous conference resolutions. The Tories had spent the second half of the previous decade drawing up plans – contained in the Carrington and Ridley Reports – for such a confrontation, with the intention of breaking the power of the miners and their union. All the powers of the state – the police, the courts, the intelligence services, the BBC, the Central Electricity Generating Board and even the social security system – were deployed against the miners, whom Prime Minister Thatcher branded 'the enemy within'. Communists across the inner-party divide threw themselves into the struggle with energy and imagination, helping to mobilise solidarity through miners' support groups, Women Against Pit Closures and among lesbians and gays and the black and Asian communities. The *Morning Star* reported the strike prolifically, handing over the front page to the NUM to put its case.

After the defeat, NUM vice-president Mick McGahey told the Party's 39th congress that 'the basic weakness of the miners' strike … was that the Communist Party was not strong enough in industry, was not organised in factory branches'. The full truth was more severe: despite the efforts of so many CP members, the Party itself had failed to provide the united direction to the struggle that it had in 1972 and 1974. The revisionist leadership spent much of its time sniping at Scargill and militant picketing rather than meeting the NUM leadership to plan solidarity activities. Centrally, more CP resources went into attacking the *Morning Star* than into putting the case for solidarity action with the miners. *Marxism Today's* contribution to the struggle was negligible.

Long before the miners – at least those not victimised – returned to work on March 5, 1985, Party members and trade union allies had risen in open revolt against the CP leadership and its Eurocommunist faction. At the AGM in 1984 of the People's Press Printing Society, the cooperative which owns the *Morning Star*, they had voted for the paper's management committee against candidates proposed by the Party's executive. That same year, the large North West and London district congresses had also opposed the CP leadership, despite an attempt by general secretary Gordon McLennan to close down the latter. In 1985, leading dissidents including Chater and *Morning Star* deputy editor David Whitfield were expelled from the CP, as the self-styled 'revolutionary democrats' proceeded to carry out one of the biggest purges in the Party's history. Another casualty was PPPS management committee chair Ken Gill, about to become the first-ever Communist president of the TUC.

Thousands of shareholders in the *Morning Star*'s cooperative, including Arthur Scargill, inflicted a heavy defeat on the revisionist leadership at the 1985 AGM, although the Eurocommunists and their allies tightened their grip on the Party's apparatus and congress. By the end of 1985, around 101 Party members had been expelled and another 600 deregistered. Few industrial advisory committees still functioned and the YCL had shrunk to 44 members.

In these desperate conditions, the Communist Campaign Group (CCG) was formed to unite Marxist-Leninists inside and now also outside the Party, to continue Communist political work and defeat revisionism and liquidationism. It also began to produce a theoretical journal, the *Communist Campaign Review*.

A leading CCG member, former London district CP chair Mike Hicks, came to the fore in the year-long dispute at Wapping. Media baron Rupert Murdoch provoked a strike there in January 1986 in order to replace 6,000 print workers with new technology and a small 'scab' workforce – recruited with the help of the electricians' union, later expelled from the TUC. The plot was revealed first in the *Morning Star*, based on leaked News International documents. Hicks, a union lay official, embodied the militant spirit of the printers and their supporters on the picket lines. But during his imprisonment on a trumped-up charge of assaulting a police chief, the union leadership under Brenda (later Baroness) Dean called off the action.

By this time, it was clear that no immediate prospect of returning the CP to its rules, principles and programme existed. The main danger was further fragmentation and the disappearance of the Communist Party. Extraordinary circumstances called forth extraordinary measures.

1988 Re-establishing the Party

In April 1988, a special congress of delegates from CCG and existing Party organisations declared the re-establishment of the Communist Party in Britain on the basis of democratic centralism, Marxism-Leninism and *The British Road to Socialism*. The rules were amended to drop the word 'Great' from the Party's name and restore support for the *Morning Star*, while the programme was updated soon afterwards and renamed *Britain's Road to Socialism*.

In particular, the programme now unambiguously identified the working class, broadly defined, as the leading force for revolutionary change. It proposed a democratic anti-monopoly alliance which could win a 'new type of left government, based on a Labour, socialist and communist majority in the Westminster parliament, one which comes about through the wide-ranging struggles of a mass movement outside parliament, demanding the kind of policies contained in the Alternative Economic and Political Strategy'. This would require a stronger Communist Party, together with a decisive shift to the left in the trade unions and the Labour Party, making possible future forms of Labour-Communist cooperation including through CP affiliation.

The Communist Party of Britain (CPB) executive committee elected Mike Hicks as general secretary and Derek Robinson as chair. The latter position was later filled by leading NALGO lay official Richard Maybin. The CPB recommenced publication of a theoretical journal, the *Communist Review*, and an inner-party paper *Communist News*.

The revisionist rump of the old party lingered until 1991 when, by this time down to 4,742 members, it dissolved itself into the 'Democratic Left', then the 'New Times Network', the 'New Politics Network' and finally, oblivion. The heavily subsidised – and by then misnamed – journal *Marxism Today* was shut down at the end of 1991; its ideological legacy soon resurfaced, albeit in a distorted form, in the anti-working class politics of New Labour.

From the outset, the re-established Communist Party involved itself heavily in the strike against redundancies, pay cuts and longer hours at the P&O ferry company in Dover. Communists were among the rank-and-file leaders of the dispute and Party branches and trade unionists – especially on trades councils – helped set up local support committees. The employers used court injunctions and sequestration orders to block solidarity as the 16-month struggle went down to defeat. Other campaigns included the fight against the Poll Tax – where the Party backed every form of opposition including non-payment – and cuts in Welfare State provision.

Facing a new round of hostile legislation, a number of major trade unions agreed to establish the Institute of Employment Rights in 1989 to undertake research and educational work. Its driving force and first director, Carolyn Jones, later succeeded LCDTU chair Kevin Halpin as CP industrial organiser.

Communists also played an active role in the 'Time To Go' campaign alongside Clare Short MP and the Labour Committee on Ireland, linking British military withdrawal from the Six Counties with the need for a comprehensive political settlement between all the parties involved.

Another priority was the work of the Committee Against War in the Gulf, as Saddam Hussein refused to withdraw his occupation forces from Kuwait. In January 1991, the aerial bombardment of Iraq began as the prelude to direct intervention, adding more civilian deaths to the hundreds of thousands already killed by the United Nations trade embargo. The committee mounted local and national demonstrations, demanding 'No More Bombings! Lift the Sanctions!'.

In the midst of this turmoil, the CP Youth Section re-established the Young Communist League, which later relaunched its journal *Challenge* and became an active affiliate of the World Federation of Democratic Youth. Youth section secretary Kenny Coyle went on to become the Party's international secretary and the founder of the left-wing publishing house Praxis Press.

From the beginning, the re-established Communist Party struggled to secure equal representation of women on its leading committees. Yet there were always those who stood in the finest tradition of fighting, organising and thinking women Communists. One such was Mary Davis, whose ground-breaking work *Women and Class* was first published by the CP in 1990 as a pamphlet. It has been periodically reprinted and extended ever since, including as a book in 2020, and its Marxist-Leninist approach to questions of women's liberation, sex and gender has guided the Party's policies throughout that time.

Initially, the *Morning Star* and the Communist Party of Britain welcomed *glasnost* (openness) and *perestroika* (restructuring) in the Soviet Union under Mikhail Gorbachev in the late 1980s. As these twin processes fell prey to forces favouring marketisation, privatisation, national separatism and the restoration of capitalism, the CPB organised a series of large pro-socialism public meetings in alliance with former London mayor Ken Livingstone, Socialist Action, Labour Party Campaign Group MPs and others on the left. The downfall of the Soviet Union and the socialist states of eastern Europe in the early 1990s compelled Britain's Communists – and serious Marxists everywhere – to analyse the reasons for counter-revolution. The reconvened 41st congress of the CPB in November 1992 made its assessment:

> The root cause of the collapse lay in the particular forms of economic and political structure which developed in the Soviet Union. Specifically, the great mass of working people came to be progressively excluded from any direct control over their economic and social destiny. This erosion of the very essence of socialism increasingly affected all aspects of Soviet society.

The CPB and *Morning Star* had also been involved in the formation of the Anti-Racist Alliance at the end of 1991. Against a background of multiplying racist attacks and police harassment, the ARA united black community leaders, trade unions and sections of the Labour left including the Socialist Action group. A series of conferences, demonstrations and marches on police stations highlighted aspects of institutional racism, including the nature of Britain's immigration, nationality and asylum laws. The election of the first BNP fascist councillor prompted the TUC to organise a massive 'Unite Against Racism' march through east London in 1994, lifting morale and helping *Searchlight* and others to mobilise the fight-back in working class communities. Although the ARA did not succeed in its campaign to make racist violence a specific criminal offence, the law was eventually changed to recognise racism as an aggravating factor that would attract additional punishment. But divisions within the ARA grew over the question of black leadership, not helped by sectarian manoeuvring on the part of some left-wing groups.

However, the Party swam against the tide in the labour movement to oppose notions of 'social partnership' and a 'social Europe'. European Commission president Jacques Delors had wooed the TUC with his progressive-sounding alternative to Tory government policies. Almost alone on the left in Britain, the CPB echoed Lenin in warning against the drive to construct an imperialist 'United States of Europe' aimed at rival imperialisms, the peoples of the developing countries and at the workers of Europe itself. One by one, trade unions began to be won over, beginning with the local government officers in NALGO. The *Morning Star* worked with left Labour MPs to demand a referendum against the 1992 Maastricht Treaty, while Party activists took the campaign into shopping centres and onto motorway bridges.

Strengthened by a communist unity process in 1995, which brought in comrades who had remained in the old party until its dissolution, the CPB began to rebuild its influence in the trade union, peace, pensioners and international solidarity movements, its work guided by a range of advisory committees. International secretaries Kenny Coyle and John Haylett helped re-establish extensive relations with Communist and workers' parties and national liberation movements around the world.

In 1995, as unemployment rose above two million again – almost 10 per cent of the workforce – Communists and their allies were central to the ten-day 'March for Full Employment' from Liverpool to Sheffield. Much of the drive came through the National Combine of Unemployed Workers Centres, which helped ensure official TUC endorsement.

Unlike many on the left and in the labour movement, the CPB insisted throughout the 1990s that Labour could again win a majority at a General Election, and without a coalition with the Liberals. The prospects for doing so improved when new leader John Smith – a social democrat who had replaced ex-left wing failure Neil Kinnock – committed the next Labour government to full employment, public ownership of the railways, reform of the anti-trade union laws and devolution for Scotland and Wales. Even after the 'New Labour' faction led by Tony Blair dropped the socialist Clause Four from the Labour Party constitution, following Smith's untimely death, Britain's Communists continued to argue against defeatism and breakaways.

The CPB therefore welcomed the overwhelming defeat of John Major's Tory government at the 1997 General Election – while warning that New Labour would not execute a qualitative break from big business policies without mass pressure from below.

1997 'New Labour', same old class struggle

By the late 1990s, the CPB had also rebuilt international links and recommenced electoral work. But the feeling was growing that the Party should be more vigorous in asserting its independent identity and role, alongside its work in broader alliances. Differences over the succession to Tony Chater as *Morning Star* editor led to violations of democratic-centralism. Early in 1998, therefore, the new CPB executive committee elected trade union lecturer Robert Griffiths as general secretary in place of Mike Hicks. When *Morning Star* editor John Haylett was dismissed in retaliation, the paper's journalists struck in solidarity to get him reinstated. Once political relations between the Party and paper were restored, following an overwhelming vote at the PPPS AGM, plans could be laid for expanding the influence of both.

On the trade union front, Communists worked closely with ex-CP members of Arthur Scargill's new Socialist Labour Party (SLP) to build the United Campaign to Repeal the Anti-Trade Union Laws. Its aim was to press the New Labour government to go beyond its plans for a modest expansion of trade union and employment rights. All eleven hostile measures enacted by the Thatcher and Major governments should be repealed. To this end, left-wing lawyers John Hendy and Keith Ewing later drafted a Trade Union Freedom Bill that won widespread support in the labour movement although not, of course, in big business, New Labour or Conservative circles.

In discussions with the SLP leadership, however, the CPB rejected Arthur Scargill's proposal to merge the two parties which, in effect, would have meant the liquidation of the Communist Party and its Marxist-Leninist politics. Instead, the CPB offered a formal coordination between the two parties which was, likewise, refused.

In June 1998, the Communist Party played a major role in organising the 'No to a Big Business Europe – Yes to Jobs, Public Services and Democracy' demonstration during the European Union heads of government summit in Cardiff. A meeting of Communist and workers parties in Europe was held there at the same time.

From spring 1999, NATO forces led by the US and Britain waged a brutal bombing campaign against Yugoslavia to break the Milosevic regime and detach the province of Kosovo. Left Labour MPs Alice Mahon, Tony Benn and Diane Abbott, together with playwright Harold Pinter and journalist John Pilger, worked with the CPB and other left groups in the Committee for Peace in the Balkans. A demonstration drew 25,000 people onto the streets of London in May.

On December 30, 2000, the *Morning Star* revealed the widespread dangers of depleted uranium munitions used by US, British and NATO forces in Iraq and Yugoslavia. It quoted ex-soldiers and NATO politicians to illustrate the thousands of deaths of civilian and military personnel from cancer and leukaemia. Despite subsequent attempts to deny and cover up these consequences, a series of medical studies and reports have since confirmed the upsurge of cancers and congenital abnormalities in contaminated areas.

At the General Election in 2001, the CPB contested six seats – an advance on previous occasions, although the votes remained few. Yet the Party's growing involvement in elections at every level – European, Scottish, Welsh, Greater London and local – reflected a more general revival in local campaigning and propaganda activity.

The Party's 46th congress in 2002 launched the Charter for Women, setting out policies for equality in the economy, the labour movement and in society generally. It has since been endorsed by more than a dozen trade unions, laying the basis for broad-based campaigning. The incoming executive committee elected the first woman chair of the CP, Anita Halpin, who later became one of two women Communists on the TUC general council. Further initiatives included re-establishing the Party's annual Highgate oration at the grave of Karl Marx; founding an annual Communist University of Britain together with similar events in the district and nations; establishing an annual trade union and political cadre school; and publishing *Unity!* bulletins at trade union conferences including a daily edition at the Trades Union Congress.

Following discussions between the CPB, Colombian Communists and British trade union representatives, 'Justice for Colombia' was established as an independent campaign for peace and social justice in that country. Its work to publicise the assassination of trade union and peasant leaders in Colombia, and to expose the links between local reaction and the British and US governments, subsequently won widespread support in the Westminster parliament and the trade union movement. Britain's Communists also continued to play a major role in the Cuba Solidarity Campaign, helping to maintain the broad basis of its work in support of Cuba's right to national self-determination, publicising the country's outstanding social achievements, campaigning for the release of the 'Miami Five' and changing the stance of the Trades Union Congress.

The Party's 46th congress characterised New Labour as an 'openly bourgeois, anti-working class trend' which had hijacked the Labour Party in order to make it a 'wholly reliable government instrument for capitalism'. It pointed out that this trend represented the interests of British state-monopoly capitalism in an emerging new phase of imperialism (called 'globalisation' by its supporters), as a junior ally of the US. On the pretext of a 'war on terror', the aim was to expand imperialism's political, military and economic presence in energy-rich Central Asia and the Middle East, in line with US geo-political strategy.

With CND, the Muslim Association of Britain, the Socialist Workers Party (SWP) and Labour MP George Galloway, the Communist Party helped form the Stop the War Coalition out of the campaign against the invasion of Afghanistan. The CP and the *Morning Star* played a crucial role in securing significant trade union support for the coalition, with ASLEF (and later TGWU) official Andrew Murray taking the post of chair. At the Trades Union Congress in September 2002, a proposal from TSSA transport staff delegate Andy Bain to oppose any attack on Iraq, even with a second UN resolution, was only narrowly defeated. This unique alliance of anti-war forces was able to bring one million people onto the streets of London and Glasgow in February 2003. When Blair and US president Bush launched their murderous, illegal assault on Iraq a few weeks later, thousands of students walked out of school to take part in spontaneous protests. Young Communists were particularly prominent in Birmingham and Glasgow. At the TUC in September, possibly for the first time ever, the British trade union movement condemned an imperialist war while British troops were still in action.

The election of Kate Hudson as chair of CND in September prompted anti-Communist outbursts in the *Daily Telegraph* and elsewhere. While Communists have always played a leading and unifying role in the movement for peace and against nuclear weapons, the war-mongers have usually tried to divide the movement with anti-Communism, ultra-leftism or, most recently, hatred of Islam.

Following discussions with George Galloway (recently expelled from the Labour Party) and the SWP, and an open debate in the *Morning Star*, the Communist Party held a special congress in January 2004 to decide whether to join them in an electoral alliance. By a narrow majority, delegates decided against. The Respect coalition was launched the following weekend.

According to the 48th CP congress in 2004, New Labour represented a 'qualitative break' with classic social democracy. Whereas the Labour Party had traditionally sought to advance working class interests – however partially and inadequately – while also upholding the capitalist system, New Labour brazenly promoted privatisation, monopoly profit and imperialist war. Britain's Communists proposed a Left-Wing Programme of policies to unite and mobilise socialists, social democrats and the labour movement around an alternative to New Labour neoliberalism. The Party and the *Morning Star* began to raise the need for the labour movement to fight to reclaim the Labour Party from the Blair-Brown clique. These perspectives gained currency in some affiliated trade unions. Communists participated in conferences to establish the Labour Representation Committee, which put forward similar positions.

At the same time, while continuing to work with other forces on the left in extra-parliamentary campaigns, the CPB declined invitations to join the Trotskyist-led Socialist Alliance (formed in 2001). Its anti-Labour electoralism was viewed as an unrealistic diversion from the union-based struggle to reclaim the Labour Party for the labour movement.

When the European Social Forum was held in London in October 2004, the CPB participated fully while also hosting another seminar for Communist and workers parties in Europe. The following year, the Party organised a full programme of meetings at the 'alternative' summit to that of the G8 capitalist powers in Edinburgh, one of them jointly with the Scottish Labour 'Campaign for Socialism'. At these events, Britain's Communists projected the concept of 'popular sovereignty', which embodies the struggle of the working class and its allies in each country to challenge neoliberal policies emanating from the European Union, the IMF, the World Trade Organisation or the World Bank, using industrial action, popular mobilisation and representative democracy to enforce the interests of the vast majority of the nation against those of transnational capital.

By this time, questions of energy, ecology and the environment had moved up the agenda at Social Forum and G8 summits. The United Nations panel on climate change was sounding the alarm about the impact of global warming, while the leading imperialist powers at UN heads-of-government COP summits were pretending to do something about it. As debate, controversy and campaigning grew in Britain and abroad, the Communist Party's science, environment and technology committee published *A World to Save* (2003), belatedly introducing a Marxist framework with which to analyse crucial issues for the future of humanity and its shared planet.

The Party's international work within Britain took a step forward with the formation of the Coordinating Committee of Communist Parties in Britain, bringing together the CPB, YCL and representatives of overseas parties domiciled here (including those from Bangladesh, Chile, Cyprus, Greece, India, Iran, Iraq and Sudan). Since then the CCCPB has organised a series of rallies and seminars on International Women's Day, the October Socialist Revolution, US strategy for the 'Greater Middle East', religious fundamentalism and Victory over Fascism in Europe. Some of these domiciled parties have also participated in a CPB-led electoral front, namely, Unity for Peace and Socialism, in London and the Midlands.

A CPB and *Morning Star* delegation to China in 2006 deepened a Marxist understanding of economic, social and political trends and developments there. The delegation's report, *China's Line of March*, proved influential in counteracting pro-capitalist and ultra-leftist misrepresentations back in Britain, particularly in the trade union and peace movements.

In order to lend shape and direction to popular and labour movement opposition to New Labour's neoliberal policies, the CPB executive committee in July 2008 proposed a People's Charter. The idea was taken up by left trade union leaders and Labour MPs and, after a battle the following year, the People's Charter for Change was endorsed by the Trades Union Congress.

Communists and left-led trade unions such as the Rail, Maritime and Transport (RMT) workers also continued the struggle to win the TUC away from a pro-EU, pro-'social partnership' position. The strike wave sparked by construction workers at Lindsey power station early in 2009 exposed the super-exploitation behind the European Union's 'free movement of capital and labour' mantra – and showed how united and militant action can overwhelm the anti-trade union laws. Strike leaders joined Communists and socialists in contesting that year's European parliamentary election on a Britain-wide 'No2EU – Yes to Democracy' platform, winning 153,236 votes.

By this time, too, the *Morning Star* had expanded in size and circulation, enjoying unprecedented levels of support in the trade union movement. A growing number of trade union activists and officials were coming to understand the valuable role of a daily paper which supports workers in dispute and acts as an educator and mobiliser across the labour and progressive movements.

The battle of ideas was also joined by a new publishing house, Manifesto Press, aligned politically with the Communist Party but also producing books in association with trade unions such as the RMT and the National Union of Teachers. At the annual TUC-sponsored Tolpuddle Martyrs festival in 2010, Communists and allies relaunched the *Country Standard* as a journal promoting the interests of workers and their communities in the countryside.

2010–2020 A new ruling-class offensive

Labour lost the May 2010 General Election with five million fewer votes and 160 fewer seats than in 1997. It had taken a perverse genius to turn hugely unpopular imperialist wars, followed by a spectacular collapse of the banking and monetary system in 2008, into an electoral defeat for the mass electoral party of the labour movement. But through their craven pro-big business, pro-imperialist policies, the New Labour faction had thrown away the biggest parliamentary majority in British history.

Throughout the previous period and during the election campaign, the Communist Party and its ten parliamentary candidates had warned that the Tory Party was regrouping. The ruling class did not want to risk a turn to the left in the labour movement as a new Tory leadership finally emerged under David Cameron and his staunchly pro-City chancellor George Osborne. Moreover, New Labour had prepared the way for a Tory victory with its 'one nation' appeal to bail out the banking sector with pledges totalling £1,350bn that would have to be financed from public spending cuts and regressive taxation. Osborne duly took up the cry that 'We're all in it together!'.

Having pronounced themselves the most consistent opponents of the City of London and fiscal austerity, the Liberal Democrats jumped into bed with the Tories within days of the election result. They proved cheap at the price. All Nick Clegg and the LibDems received in return for breaking their election pledges to oppose public spending cuts, privatisation and student tuition fees was a referendum on the Alternative Vote electoral system.

In January 2011, the CPB executive committee decided to oppose the measure because AV does not produce a representative result, favours centre-ground parties and would reduce the prospects for winning a genuine system of proportional representation (PR). Britain's Communists had long favoured the Single Transferable Vote in multi-member constituencies, which ensures that the political affiliation of those elected fairly reflects how people have voted.

LibDem attempts to use anti-Communism in the May 2011 AV referendum campaign failed to prevent a heavy defeat for the proposal. Nick Clegg and his party also paid the price for betraying their supporters, losing four million votes in the subsequent General Election.

Meanwhile, in the 2011-12 local elections, Communist Party and Unity for Peace and Socialism candidates – most of them members of the Association of Indian Communists in Britain – fought vigorous campaigns against local spending cuts, winning around 5 per cent of the votes in Leicester, up to 10 per cent in some Welsh and Scottish seats and almost one-quarter of the poll in Barnstaple. Welsh Communists gained more than 2,500 votes in the regional seats for the National Assembly, after a campaign which included radio and TV broadcasts in English and Welsh.

The CPB argued against the transfer of powers from local councils to directly-elected mayors in a series of referendums in May 2012, leafleting in cities such as Birmingham, Leeds, Sheffield, Bristol and Newcastle upon Tyne.

Nonetheless, much of the Party's work up to the 2015 General Election concentrated on the mass campaigns against austerity and the imperialist occupations of Iraq and Afghanistan.

The top domestic priority was to build the widest possible coalition to defend jobs, public services and the Welfare State, including the principle of non-means tested universal benefits. The ruling class had declared class war. In November 2011, in defence of their pay, pensions and public services, more than one million workers had launched the biggest wave of industrial action in Britain since the 1989 railway strike.

The CP argued that workers, the unemployed, single parents, people on incapacity benefit, pensioners, students and all who rely upon our public services had to be brought into a broad alliance, while recognising that the ruling-class and ConDem offensive would hit the working class, the poor, women and ethnic minorities disproportionately hard. In essence, this would be a popular, democratic anti-monopoly alliance in embryo, led by the working class movement and rooted in local communities, as envisaged in *Britain's Road to Socialism* (updated in 2011 and then promoted in public meetings across Britain).

However, lack of unity between public sector unions split the pensions campaign, strengthening the ruling-class offensive. Confronting a fresh barrage of anti-worker, anti-union measures, Communists and their allies brought together the United Campaign to Repeal the Anti-Trade Union Laws and the remnants of the LCDTU to set up the Campaign for Trade Union Freedom. It breathed new life into the struggle for workers' rights, although it could not keep more Tory measures from the statute book.

Nonetheless, with Communists prominent at every level, the People's Charter continued to win support and affiliations from the TUC, the Scottish, Welsh and Women's TUCs, the trade union councils and 16 national trade unions. Big CPB mobilisations took place to promote the charter, the *Morning Star* and the Communist Party at demonstrations in London and Glasgow. In 2013, a range of anti-cuts, political, trade union and progressive organisations came together to launch the People's Assembly against Austerity. More than one hundred local groups were formed, with Communists prominent at every level of the initiative. Large national and regional demonstrations followed, including 'Britain Needs a Pay Rise' marches called by the TUC.

This turn towards mass campaigning also included several CPB speaking tours, as well as major mobilisations to mark the Battle of Cable Street that brought together dozens of trade union, community and anti-racist bodies to celebrate the Communist-led defeat of the fascist Blackshirts in October 1936. Special issues of the *Unity!* broadsheet signified the Party's growing presence at annual labour movement events such as the Tolpuddle Martyrs festival, the Durham Miners Gala, the Burston school strike celebration and the Derby Chainmakers commemoration.

The CPB highlighted four particular fronts in the political class struggle.

Firstly, there was the need not only to resist the offensive waged by British state-monopoly capitalism; a positive, alternative left-wing programme had to win support within and beyond the labour movement. This meant generating a fresh wave of publications, public meetings, *Morning Star* editorials and feature articles setting out the case for public ownership

Secondly, and linked to this, the battle of ideas had to be stepped up within the labour and progressive movements. The stranglehold of big business-friendly class collaboration had to be broken. To this end, the Communist Party strengthened its own internal Marxist-Leninist education activities, reforged links with the Marx Memorial Library under its director John Callow, reinstituted an annual joint MML-CP Marx Oration, organised successful 21st Century Marxism events, held regional Communist University conferences for members and allies, republished a series of Marxist classics and produced quarterly issues of *Communist Review*. Closer collaboration with the *Morning Star* also expanded the paper's ideological content.

Third, the upsurge in mass campaigning and ideological work had to be translated into progress in the working-class movement. While the replacement of Gordon Brown by Ed Miliband represented a defeat for New Labour, most of the Blairite politicians and their views continued to dominate the Shadow Cabinet. Labour had to be reclaimed, at the very least, for social democracy if not for socialism. This meant, for instance, resisting the unrealistic calls to help launch or join any left-wing electoral alliance opposed to the Labour Party.

Finally, the Communist Party continued to challenge Labour's reactionary foreign and military policies, opposing the bombing of Libya, Britain's subservient alliance with the US, possession of nuclear weapons and membership of NATO – notably during that body's summit at Newport in Wales in August 2014. Various CP initiatives highlighted Israel's illegal occupation of Palestinian territories, supported the boycott and sanctions campaign in favour of a sovereign Palestine and demanded the freedom of political prisoners in Israeli prisons. The CPB and its international secretary John Foster continued to play a very active part in the international Communist movement at home and around the world, strengthening links with the Communist Party of China and working with the Communist Party of Ireland to issue a statement signed by 16 Communist and workers' parties in Europe, 'For Maximum Opposition to the EU'. The Coordinating Committee of Communist Parties in Britain, convened by the CPB, organised a series of successful meetings to celebrate International Women's Day and May 1.

In the European Parliament elections of 2014, the CPB and the RMT railway workers' union spearheaded a vigorous 'No2EU – Yes to Workers Rights' campaign in every regional constituency. Communists headed some of the alliance's regional lists and featured prominently in its election broadcasts and literature. However, the No2EU vote was hit by a media boycott, the well-publicised rise of the United Kingdom Independence Party (UKIP) – which topped the poll – and the sudden death of RMT general secretary Bob Crow, a former CP executive committee member who remained a close friend and ally of the Party.

At the 2015 General Election, the LibDem vote collapsed and the Scottish and Welsh nationalists advanced. The CP stood nine candidates and ran a high-profile billboard campaign, achieving more national publicity than usual. UKIP won almost four million votes, more than the Liberal Democrats, prompting the new majority Tory government to concede a referendum on Britain's membership of the EU.

In the meantime, Labour's defeat led to a change of leader in a ballot of all Labour Party members, registered supporters and affiliated unions. The election of Jeremy Corbyn, a *Morning Star* columnist and longstanding friend of the Communist Party, undoubtedly sent shockwaves through the British ruling class and its US and NATO allies, as well as through the right wing of the labour movement. The Communist Party and its allies in the extra-parliamentary movement had taken the lead in urging anti-austerity and anti-war campaigners to sign up to the Labour Party and vote for him.

The people of Britain administered an even bigger shock in the EU referendum in June 2016. On a higher turnout than in General Elections, people voted by a majority of 52 to 48 per cent to leave the European Union ('Brexit'). This despite the fact that the Conservative government and all the main political parties urged a vote to 'Remain', as did the CBI, the Institute of Directors, most City banks and employers' federations, the Country Landowners Association, the National Farmers Union, the TUC and many trade unions.

For its part, the CPB played a central role in the Left Leave ('Lexit') referendum campaign against continuing EU membership, with former RMT president Alex Gordon as convenor and Robert Griffiths in the chair. The Lexit committee worked closely with the RMT, ASLEF, the Bakers' Union, some Labour MPs, the Socialist Workers Party, the Socialist Party, the Indian Workers Association (GB), Counterfire and the Green Socialist Alliance.

The Lexit campaign put the left-wing, working-class, democratic and internationalist case against the pro-monopoly, pro-capitalist market EU and its 'Fortress Europe' policies. This was done without muddying the waters by jointly organising or sharing platforms with reactionary anti-EU campaigners. Predictably, neither the pro-EU nor the right-wing anti-EU media reported Lexit or CP arguments and activities.

The Communist Party's call for a boycott of the subsequent EU Parliament elections attracted media attention and some criticism in labour movement circles. The CP argued that the electorate had voted to leave the EU, MPs had spent three years obstructing that decision and, anyway, the European parliament was a largely powerless sham. As Communists predicted, UKIP were the chief beneficiaries of this pointless voting exercise at the expense of the Labour Party.

Where Communist candidates fought local elections, vigorous campaigning won support for left-wing policies as well as new members and friends. In the contest for West Midlands mayor, senior Unite the Union official Graham Stevenson attracted national publicity and almost 6,000 votes.

Had Corbyn's Labour Party won the 2017 General Election and carried out his pledge to implement the referendum result and take Britain out of the EU, his government would have had greater freedom to implement left and progressive policies for public ownership, progressive taxation, controls over trade and the movement of capital, conditional aid to industry and an end to compulsory competitive tendering and the high-price, wasteful and corrupt Common Agricultural Policy. As it was, the CPB refrained from standing its own candidates in 2017 and called for the maximum possible Labour vote, while emphasising the need to intensify mass campaigning and build the mass movements.

Although Corbyn did not win, Labour's advance at that election was enough for the British establishment and its pro-EU, pro-NATO allies inside the Labour Party to launch the most ferocious and disreputable campaign ever waged against a Labour leader. This went hand-in-hand with a campaign in the Westminster parliament, the law courts and on the streets to prevent Britain's exit from the EU.

In the midst of this turmoil, the Marx Memorial Library hosted a big conference at the TUC's Congress House to celebrate the centenary of the Bolshevik Revolution. Speakers came from Russia and Cuba, including Che's daughter Aleida Guevara. Six months later, in May 2018, the CP worked with the MML to organise a rally and break-out meetings to mark the bicentenary of Marx's birth, featuring Communist Party of India (Marxist) general secretary Sitaram Yechury and Labour Party deputy leader John McDonnell.

The internal and external attacks on Corbyn and the Labour leadership culminated in the sweeping victory of Boris Johnson and his Conservative Party at the December 2019 General Election. After three years of parliamentary sabotage by anti-Brexit MPs, Johnson had pledged to 'Get Brexit Done'. Labour's change of policy from respecting the EU result to promising a second referendum in order to overturn Brexit handed 52 Leave-voting Labour seats to the Tories. Again, the CPB stood no candidates and urged people to back Labour.

In 2021, however, 39 Communist Party candidates secured more than 13,000 votes in the elections for the Greater London Assembly, the Welsh Senedd, the Scottish Parliament and English local councils. Using different forms of mass propaganda, this was the Party's biggest election campaign since re-establishment.

On other fronts, the Communist Party consolidated and even strengthened its work in bodies as varied as the People's Assembly, the National Assembly of Women and the Cuba Solidarity Campaign. Trade union work concentrated on rebuilding 'broad left' networks in unions and at TUC conferences, while exposing the class nature of Johnson's Tory government and its so-called 'levelling up' agenda. Substantial Communist influence in the trades councils movement was used to promote the repeal of anti-union laws, public ownership, peace, arms diversification and closer links with the People's Assembly. Together with the *Morning Star*, the CP also warned that new Labour leader Keir Starmer's dilution of his party's policies would not enthuse the millions of electors who wanted a real alternative to pro-big business policies.

Ambitious plans were laid with allies and friends to celebrate the centenary of the Communist Party in Britain in 2020. But the programme of concerts, book launches, film, exhibitions and rallies had to be moved online where possible as the Covid-19 pandemic struck. Even so, these attracted large numbers of participants and compelled the CP to take its social media operations to a new, higher level under the leadership of communications director Phil Katz, Party chair Liz Payne and assistant secretary David Pettifor.

Within days of the first Covid-19 cases and deaths being reported in Britain in March 2020, the CP issued a detailed statement demanding emergency measures to combat the virus. This pointed to the impact of under-investment and privatisation on Britain's health, social care and civil emergency services, producing a shortage of staff, facilities and specialised equipment needed to meet the challenge. The CP called for all necessary private sector medical, pharmaceutical, research and manufacturing facilities to be requisitioned and deployed against Covid; the rapid construction of hospital units; full mobilisation of the armed forces; a rigorous testing and quarantine regime; strict controls on internal and external travel; the closure of schools and colleges; and full involvement of the trade unions in the planning and implementation of a comprehensive anti-Covid strategy.

Britain's Communists condemned the Conservative government's refusal to prioritise public health over corporate profit at every stage of the epidemic.

An updated edition of *Britain's Road to Socialism* (2020), gave fresh emphasis to capitalism's general crisis – not least on the environmental front – and to vital questions of imperialism and the European Union; working-class leadership; the oppression of women and racial minorities; strategic alliances against state-monopoly capitalism; state power and counter revolution; and the construction of socialism.

A 'Communist Renewal' process headed by former CP chair and ex-president of the National Union of Teachers Bill Greenshields aimed to strengthen the Party's organisational and campaigning capacity. Commissions on Trade Unions, Women, the Environment, Political Economy, Housing, Political Education, Anti-Racism Anti-Fascism, Progressive Federalism, and International affairs enhanced the Party's work in these and other areas.

The website 'Culture Matters' established by the CP's Culture Commission in 2015 has since grown into a cooperative promoting left-wing and progressive events and publications, supported by a range of labour movement bodies.

Yet more national trade unions invested in the cooperative society which owns the *Morning Star* and took seats on the PPPS management committee. A worthy successor to former editor John Haylett has been found in Ben Chacko. The involvement of leading Communists such as John Foster, Mary Davis and Alex Gordon has reinvigorated the Marx Memorial Library &

Workers' School as a vital resource for the working-class movement in Britain and internationally.

The victory over revisionism in the 1980s prevented the likely liquidation of the CP, the *Morning Star* and the MML. But it has taken the next 30 years to consolidate and rebuild their influence, in a period when the labour, left-wing movement in Britain and internationally experienced dashed hopes and severe defeats.

The torch of Marxism-Leninism still burns, ready to pass to the next generation of Communists. The working class and peoples of Britain need a strong, bold Communist Party and Young Communist League as much as ever, to fight capitalist crisis and imperialist war – and to put us on the road to socialist revolution.

Thora Silverthorne at International Brigade
memorial in Reading, May 1990

2

Thora Silverthorne and the 'new Nightingales' (1910-99)

Based on the text of my exhibition on 'The History of the Welsh Labour Movement' at Unison Wales headquarters, Cardiff, opened in 2022.

T hora Silverthorne was born on November 15, 1910, the daughter of Sarah Doyt and George Silverthorne of 170 Alma Street, Abertillery. Her father was a coal miner at Vivian and Six Bells collieries. A quiet but witty activist in the South Wales Miners Federation, jailed for refusing conscription in the 1914-18 'Great War', he was a founder member of the Communist Party in 1920.

One of eight children, Thora joined the Sunday School choir at Blaenau Gwent Baptist Chapel and so began her lifelong love of music. She also attended the Nantyglo Overflow School at Hafod-y-Ddol and then the Abertillery County School.She later recalled her 'very happy' childhood and the 'richness and solidarity' of working-class life in Abertillery, including at the feeding centre during the 1921 miners' strike. But there was also the poverty, made worse by the early death of her mother Sarah.

Aged 16, Thora joined the local Young Communist League and was soon chairing meetings at the Workmen's Institute where visiting speakers included the future Welsh and British miners' leader, Arthur Horner.

Victimised after the General Strike, George and family moved to Reading. There, Thora sold tickets in a local cinema and the *Daily Worker* at the railway depot. When babysitting for local Labour MP and president of the Socialist Medical Association (SMA), Somerville Hastings, he encouraged her to go into nursing. In 1931, she won a probationary place at the John Radcliffe Infirmary, Oxford, where sister Olive was already a senior nurse. There she resumed activity in the Communist Party and made life-long friendships with the likes of historian Christopher Hill. She also aided foot-sore hunger marchers as they passed through Oxford. Soon a theatre sister in Hammersmith Hospital, London, and a member of the National Union of County Officers' Guild of Nurses, she became very active in the SMA.

In 1936, backed by Nazi Germany and Fascist Italy, General Franco launched his military coup against the elected left-wing government in Spain. That August, Thora travelled with the Spanish Medical Aid Committee unit to assist the forces defending Spanish democracy. A band of several thousand saw the team off from Victoria Station and an even bigger crowd cheered them on their way in Paris.

The Communist International called for the formation of International Brigades. More than 3,000 members of the Communist, Labour and Independent Labour parties, went from Britain to fight in Spain. One in six are buried there.

On the Aragon front near Huesca, Thora was elected Matron and worked with Dr Alex Tudor Hart to turn an old farmhouse into an efficient 36-bed hospital. Many patients were German volunteers with the Thaelmann Battalion, but alongside Catalan surgeon Dr Moises Broggi she also tended to the women and children injured in fascist air-raids on local villages. The hospital was later destroyed by Nationalist shelling.

While on the Madrid front, Thora served time in the British ambulance unit with Chepstow-born doctor Kenneth Sinclair Loutit, Dr Archie Cochrane from Galashiels and Australian diarist, novelist, interpreter, medical volunteer and fellow Communist Aileen Palmer. According to newspaper reports, the unit had been bombed and shelled by Franco's insurgents on several occasions. Among the casualties was the promising young poet, Julian Bell.

While Matron of the British Medical Hospital in Madrid, she and Loutit were married in accordance with local custom. There, too, her friend and International Brigader Michael Livesay died in her arms.

Returning to England in August 1937 to sub-edit the *Nursing Illustrated*, Thora worked with Nancy Blackburn (Zinkin) and other comrades to form the Association of Nurses (AoN) in September as a real trade union to campaign for shorter hours (a maximum 96-hour fortnight instead of anywhere between 108 and 142) and better pay and conditions. As AoN general secretary, she told the press that her organisation aspired to the same position among nurses as the British Medical Association enjoyed among the doctors, while also supporting the TUC Charter for Nurses in a spirit of cooperation. Organised from her apartment in Great Ormond Street, the AoN grew quickly from its 24 founding members to 500 as discussions began with the TUC's Nursing Advisory Committee and the Federation of Health Unions.

In her official capacity, Thora Silverthorne bombarded local and national newspapers with letters setting out why nurses needed their own union, formed and controlled by nurses themselves. For instance, in response to an editorial column in the *Boston Mercury and Guardian* (Lincolnshire) asking 'What is there to attract the ambitious girl to the nursing profession?' Thora replied: 'The answer bluntly is nothing'. She pointed out that half of the work in the bigger hospitals was carried out by probationer nurses who are 'exploited in a most heartless manner', worse than in 'the meanest nineteenth century workshop'. Many such nurses were compelled to perform distasteful tasks in double-quick time; probationer hours were so long that the Nursing Charter's demand for a maximum and properly paid 96-hour fortnight was regarded as impossibly restrictive and unaffordable. Petty regulations even laid down the maximum number of items allowed on a nurse's dressing table and demanded that they spend leisure time under curfew in the hospital. Thus she wrote in the paper on October 22, 1937: 'Our ambassadors are forced to work secretly, but the news of a trade union for nurses is everywhere finding enthusiastic support'.

In December, the AoN presented evidence to a government inter-departmental inquiry into the shortage of nurses, Thora also making the point that the insistence on residence in scarce hospital quarters made no sense when it excluded young women who would like to enter the profession but preferred to live at home.

Early in the new year – and to the surprise of some newspapers – Thora came close to being elected to the General Nursing Council with the votes of more than 6,000 state registered nurses. According to the right-wing journal *Truth*, the AoN was being courted not only by the Trades Union Congress, but also by the British Union of Fascists. In her response, she explained the association's support for trade unionism but did not dignify the BUF claim with a mention.

When a young probationer told the *Leeds Mercury* that 'Florence Nightingale did not grumble about her conditions of work and neither do I', the AoN general secretary corrected her (March 11, 1938): 'Florence Nightingale swept away many abuses, not caring how strong was the opposition to her reforms, but abuses still remain in the nursing profession and they are seriously affecting the efficiency of the service ... by choking off possible recruits'. What was needed now was 'organised grumbling, not in a destructive but in a constructive spirit' to put things right.

With membership now rising to more than one thousand, the AoN claimed its share of the credit for breakthroughs made in London. After its branch approached the management, Hackney Hospital agreed to allow nurses light refreshments after an evening out and breakfast in bed on their days off. Soon afterwards, following further representations by the AoN and other health unions, the Labour leadership of London County Council extended these benefits to its hospitals across the city, also cutting the hours and petty restrictions imposed on nursing staff. Significantly, it was to Thora Silverthorne that national newspapers such as *Reynolds News*, owned by the Cooperative Movement, turned to for an approbatory comment. The paper's assistant editor, Gordon Schaffer, had promoted the

AoN from the outset.

The coverage was somewhat different in the *Nursing Times*. Reflecting the horror of Britain's medical and nursing establishment at this challenge to their authority and domination. A series of articles in the autumn of 1937 attacked the AoN and Thora Silverthorne personally. They were accused of dividing nurses and undermining their idealism for financial gain. It was claimed, falsely, that the AoN had registered as an independent trade union and that Thora might not be a state-registered nurse (her General Nursing Council certificate first recorded her SRN qualification on November 23, 1934). Her second husband, Nares Craig, later recalled her account of a meeting of nurses in a large London hospital around this time: from the chair, the hospital Matron repeated the common accusation from Royal College of Nursing sources that the AoN and its leaders were recipients of 'Moscow Gold'. Most of the nurses were persuaded more by Thora's militancy than by their matron's slanders.

Late in 1938, in order to enrol fully in the ranks of the trade union movement and its TUC, the Association of Nurses began negotiating a transfer into the National Union of Public Employees (NUPE), where it was reconstituted as the latter's National Association of Nurses section. Across the table during the unity negotiations sat NUPE's general secretary Bryn Roberts who, like Thora, hailed from Abertillery and advocated friendship with the Soviet Union.

She also continued to work for unity in action of Britain's nurses. As chair of the Nurses Emergency Committee, a coalition of professional and trade union bodies, she led a campaign for the employment of nurses in the early months of World War Two. The London 'blitz' had not yet begun, but Thora was already pointing out the absurdity of the situation whereby many nurses faced unemployment when they should be preparing for the casualties to come. Instead of employing trained nurses, 'untrained girls' were being taken on for auxiliary nursing work in the Air Raid Precautions service at a lower rate of pay. Other outstanding grievances included compulsory living-in and unreasonable transfers to different locations.

'This is not the way in which modern Nightingales are used to facing difficulties', she told the press after leading a deputation to the Ministry of Health on December 12. The following day, Thora reported back to a mass meeting because '30,000 nurses are determined to see that the wartime needs of the country are the first charge upon their profession'. She could only report plenty of sympathy, but no government plans for action.

In Personal File (no. 52773) opened by Britain's Security Service (MI5) in 1942 there is a 'character sketch' of 'Mrs Thora SINCLAIR-LOUTTIT' seemingly drawn by a Miss Ogilvie of F2 branch:

> She is reported to be very thin, about 5'2" in height, sallow complexion, thin pointed face, very long prominent nose

which is pointed. She has dark brown eyes, and dark brown hair cut in a long bob style and having a vague and natural wave. She is stated always to wear country tweed-type costume and woollen jumper, sandals and no stockings, although she occasionally wears ankle-length socks. She has been described to us as rather the Chelsea 'arty' type. She has a low-pitched and cultured speaking voice. She is stated to be very modern in her outlook, and always gives the impression of being extremely busy and efficient. This latter, however, is partly a bluff for others are apt to do the work for which she takes the credit.

The author's jaundice is evident, but the next two sentences also indicate that Thora's phone was tapped and her house and movements possibly subject to some level of state surveillance:

She always appears to be in a hurry, attending meetings and giving lectures every evening, etc., and is said to have no home life and appears to use her appartments [sic] just for sleeping in. It seems that people are always calling to ask her to go to a meeting or to discuss matters with her.

The 'character sketch' continues, with a little more care for accuracy:

She is a trained nurse herself, and considers the rights and wrongs of nurses to be her special problem. She also believes that both at school and in adult life everything should be co-educational. She loves discussion groups. She also believes that there ought to be clinics for everything, holiday centres for workers, nurseries for babies in every town and village, and co-ed schools. She is very fond of children and thoroughly approves of the way in which they are brought up in the USSR.

During the war, Thora and Kenneth Loutit grew apart (although he remained a lifelong admirer) and after a spell in High Wycombe she rented a mansion flat in Southampton Row, central London, with her daughter Tina and a few nursing friends. After the war, as organising secretary of the Socialist Medical Association, Thora lobbied Prime Minister Clement Attlee and Health Minister Aneurin Bevan about their plans to establish the National Health Service. In particular, the SMA was keen to ensure that hospital consultants be employed on NHS contracts rather than have their own private practices.

In November 1946, she married again, this time to architect, engineer and fellow comrade Cameron Nares Craig, and served as a full-time officer with the Civil Service Clerical Association (later the Civil and Public Services Association and then the Public and Commercial Services union).

An entry in one of her MI5/ Special Branch files notes that Thora and Nares provided hospitality for delegates to the annual conference of the International Brigades Association in July 1947, including 'an American Communist of some importance, who has been staying with Rebecca WEST, the novelist'. This oblique reference could be to Paul Robeson, a vigorous supporter of the International Brigades in the 1930s and a friend of West's since the 1920s (despite her anti-Communism). The same file notes that left-wing MP DN Pritt – 'Johnny' to Thora and Nares – used the their house in Bloomsbury 'quite a lot'.

Scribbled notes on this particular file ask for it to be cross-referenced with files on Thora's brother Reg, a trade union organiser who is 'quite a celebrity in Party circles', and their father George who has 'a long record in political circles' including close relations with a number of named Labour MPs.

Her own reputation on the left was such that she was invited to join the reception committee led by Joyce Smith of the British Peace Committee to meet 60 French delegates on their way to the World Peace Congress, scheduled to open in Sheffield on November 13, 1950. Only one of the visitors got as far as Victoria Station, as all the others were detained by border officials and Special Branch officers at Dover before being sent back to France. He was Spanish artist Pablo Picasso. Faced with a Labour government prepared to ban and deport hundreds of socialists, Communists, scientists, academics, trade unionists and cultural figures from around the world, the World Peace Council transferred the congress to Prague.

In the 1960s, Thora finished work at the Socialist Medical Association and she and Nares purchased the Glebelands Nursery School in Blackheath. She then played a major role in the school's management, a hugely popular figure with the children. In 1971, Thora retired with her husband to Llanfyllin, Powys, where they spent time enjoying the gardens and waterfalls of the surrounding countryside.

For many years, Nares Craig worked for the Building Research Station, a public sector body which specialised in the development of low-cost but highly safe processes and materials. He himself pioneered the Brecast building system, widely adopted in earthquake and hurricane zones. In September 1973, Nares had travelled to Santiago, Chile, where he held several long and friendly discussions with President Allende about a project for 200 Brecast-style apartments as part of a slum-clearance programme. On the day after their second meeting, Allende was overthrown in a bloody US-backed military coup. Nares' research station was privatised by the Thatcher government in 1997.

For her part, Thora never forgot her time in Spain which – as Nares recounted in his online memoirs – she often described as 'the most important decision of my life'. In 1975, the year of General Franco's death, she went back and was pictured in the bombed ruins of a hospital near Barcelona alongside two former colleagues: Dr Broggi and Hungarian doctor Johnny Kiszelly. Thora continued to address meetings, unveiling a memorial to local International Brigaders in Reading in 1990. Five years later, she and Nares reluctantly moved back to London so Thora could have easier access to medical facilities. That November, her life was celebrated at a reception in the House of Commons hosted by Unison general secretary Rodney Bickerstaffe.

After the onset of Alzheimer's Disease, Thora died of pneumonia on January 17, 1999, leaving two daughters and a son. Her devoted partner Nares survived her by 13 years.

3

Party crises, recovery and re-establishment, 1928-1988

First published in abridged form in Mary Davis ed., A Centenary for Socialism: Britain's Communist Party 1920-2020 *(1920).*

C rises are not uncommon in Communist parties. They arise from a wide range of external and internal circumstances with many different causes, courses and effects. Of course, history demonstrates that crises occur in other political parties, too. What differentiates communist party crises is that they often assume a more overt ideological character, reflecting the proper significance that such parties give to matters of theory, analysis, policy formulation and the battle of ideas in different spheres and on different fronts of revolutionary class struggle.

While differences between contesting forces in an inner-party crisis may appear to be ones of policy or of a personal character, in a communist party these usually reflect deeper differences of ideological and political outlook.

That different views exist within a party is, in itself, not unusual. For Communists, where these differences are openly debated and resolved in the interests of the working class and the struggle for socialism, they are often positively healthy. This can be true even when competing views precipitate an upheaval within the Party, obstructing its work, changing its leading personnel and – temporarily at least – reducing its membership.

For instance, Lenin welcomed the crises in the German and Russian social-democratic parties in the late 19th and early 20th centuries and then in the Russian Communist Party in the early 1920s. This was because they produced greater ideological clarity and organisational cohesion in the process of sometimes fierce and factionalised ideological struggle over organisational, tactical and strategic questions.

In that light, internal differences within the Communist Party in Britain, and their development at times into an identifiable crisis, should not be regarded as abnormal, let alone as automatically unnecessary and damaging to the Party itself.

The first crisis: 'Class against Class'

There have been, arguably, six major crises in the history of the CP in Britain. The first broke out into the open in early 1928, although skirmishes had been fought around some of the most significant matters of contention over the preceding few years. In fact, different views on those same issues had led to sharp debates at the founding conventions of the Party in 1920 and 1921. At the heart of the disputes lay the question of the Communist Party's attitude towards the Labour Party, which was then overtaking the Liberals as the main electoral expression of working class aspirations. The majority view within the CP was to regard Labour as the federal party of the labour movement, whose social-democratic and reformist leadership had to be replaced by a revolutionary one. At this time, Communist Party members were still permitted to participate in the Labour Party, whether as individual members or as representatives of an affiliated trade union. However, from the outset, applications from the Communist Party to affiliate in its own right were rebuffed by the Labour Party leadership on the grounds of 'insurmountable differences'. While a minority of Communists had argued that their party should adopt an uncompromisingly hostile stance towards the Labour Party and its leadership – even to the point of not supporting Labour election candidates or boycotting bourgeois parliamentary politics altogether – they abided by the majority resolutions.

However, the betrayal of the General Strike in May 1926 by trade union leaders on the TUC General Council, together with the irredeemably class collaborationist politics of Labour Party leaders, brought these differences to the surface once again. The CP had been united in its condemnation of the treachery of both the 'left' and right-wing union leaders, in line with the judgement of the Communist International. But the majority on the Party's central committee (CC) did not maintain a position of unremitting hostility to all the 'left' union leaders and their allies. The ruling class had launched a major reactionary offensive against trade union rights and freedoms in the wake of the General Strike. Trade union membership and industrial action had gone into decline, while at the same time more and more working people – and newly enfranchised young women – were turning from the Liberals and even the Tories towards Labour. In the these conditions, the CC majority concluded, the Communist Party would risk alienating not only its existing but also its potential new allies within the labour movement should it adopt a thoroughly hostile stance towards 'left' union leaders and the Labour Party as a whole.

For the CC minority and the Comintern executive, to varying degrees, the British Communist Party leadership was failing to adjust to the new circumstances. From the beginning of 1927, the TUC and Labour leaderships had launched a fresh purge of Communists and their allies in the National Minority Movement, excluding them and trades councils and local Labour parties under their influence from the 'official' apparatus of the labour movement wherever possible. With a growing body of trade union militants ready to take industrial action, march on demonstrations and abandon Labour Party politics, here was an opportunity for the Communist Party to assert its independence and leadership and thereby reverse the sudden downturn in membership that had followed the rapid growth of 1926.

For its part, the Comintern had already declared that in this period of intensifying class conflict in Britain, the CP should attack the 'bourgeois' leadership of the Labour Party, expose 'parliamentary cretinism', concentrate on building its own workplace organisation and as quickly as possible launch a daily paper. The conditions had matured for building a 'mass Communist party'.

Within the CP, arguments broke out about how and whether its CC and Political Bureau (PB) were acting in alignment with the Comintern's recommendations. These reached a head at meetings from the end of 1927. The majority – which included secretary Albert Inkpin together with Andrew Rothstein, JR Campbell, Willie Gallacher, Arthur Horner and National Unemployed Workers Movement leader Wal Hannington – did not wholly share the Comintern's positive assessment of the immediate prospects in Britain. Domestically, capitalism appeared to be relatively stable and the empire faced no mortal threat. Moreover, the Labour Party's trade union base still offered the possibility of CP affiliation and of radically changing Labour's policies and its 'completely putrified' leadership. Electorally, the CP should stand only a limited number of parliamentary candidates and express 'critical support' for Labour everywhere else, believing that a Labour victory was necessary if only to demonstrate the bankruptcy of social democracy and reformism.

The minority led by Harry Pollitt, Robin Page Arnot, Labour-Communist MP Shapurji Saklatvala and Helen Crawfurd – and backed by *Labour Monthly* editor Rajani Palme Dutt and the Party's Comintern representative JT Murphy – believed that many workers were already beginning to draw revolutionary conclusions from the feeble record and downfall of the short-lived Labour government in 1924, from the betrayal of the General Strike and lockout, the ruling class offensive, the anti-Communist and anti-socialist purge in the labour movement and now the class-collaboration talks led by TUC president Ben Turner and Sir Alfred Mond of ICI. Most of this CC minority wanted the CP to reconsider or forsake its goal of affiliation to the Labour Party, field many more parliamentary candidates on an anti-Labour manifesto – echoing the view of the Comintern executive – and review or abandon 'united front' projects with Labour allies such as the National Left-

Wing Movement, set up under CP direction in November 1925.

Both main sections of the Communist Party's CC took their case to a British Commission of the Comintern in February 1928. The subsequent resolution of the executive committee of the Communist International (ECCI) sided predominantly with the minority's position, insisting that a Labour government would be as reactionary as the Tory alternative, that the CP should therefore campaign with as many of its own candidates as possible for a 'revolutionary workers' government' – reinforcing a slogan provisionally agreed at the Party's PB in December 1927 – but without yet abandoning the fight within the Labour Party and the aim of CP affiliation. The Party CC accepted this line by a clear majority in March 1928, although substantial doubts and differences existed about how to apply it, not least in the CP's trade union work. Party district committees and branches responded to the Comintern's lead with greater enthusiasm, relieved to move at least some distance away from the previous policy.

In a foretaste of what was to come, battles in the PB and CC led to a reallocation of posts and responsibilities that summer. Secretary Inkpin was demoted to 'business manager', with Campbell narrowly defeating Pollitt for the new position of 'political secretary', Murphy replacing Pollitt in charge of trade union work and Rothstein taking Murphy's place as head of the parliamentary department. The central party apparatus and its secretariat remained firmly in the hands of the old CC 'majority'.

At its Sixth World Congress in July-August 1928, the Comintern deepened and amplified its attack on the social democrats across Europe who were propping up a capitalist system which could follow Italy and turn fascist. Having gone through a period of acute crisis (1917-23) and then of partial stabilisation (1924-1927), capitalism had now entered a 'third period' of monopolisation, state intervention and intensifying contradictions and deep destabilisation. In this clash of 'class against class' there could be no middle way between siding with the interests of the working class (which in every country could only mean supporting the Communist Party) or siding with those of the capitalist class, as the social democrats were doing. Left-wing social democrats were denounced as the 'most dangerous faction' who were 'essential for the subtle deception of the workers'. The congress warned that social democracy displayed 'fascist tendencies' and would play a 'fascist role in periods when the situation is critical for capitalism'.

The World Congress also reaffirmed the ECCI's previous criticisms of the CP in Britain, particularly the 'serious error' of its 9th congress in October 1927 to call for a Labour government under the control of the Labour Party's national executive committee. According to the Comintern: 'The marked shift of the leaders of the [TUC] General Council and the Labour Party to the right ... confronts the CP with tasks which require a much clearer class standpoint and a more decisive struggle against the Labour Party'. In a non-plenary session, the CP delegates from Britain came under attack for not having closed down the National Left-Wing Movement (NLWM).

Back in Britain, the Party leadership drew fire for not condemning the left-wing Cook-Maxton Manifesto for allegedly erecting an extra barrier in the way of disillusioned Labour supporters who might otherwise be heading directly into the Communist Party. When Labour's annual conference in October 1928 endorsed a total ban on Communist participation in the party's affairs, the CP leadership responded by dropping its goal of affiliation and calling upon unions to disaffiliate from the Labour Party. But the CP leadership executed an ambiguous retreat from this stance at the 10th congress in January 1929, while also condemning 'left sectarian' talk of forming breakaway 'red' unions. However, taking the line of Marjorie and Harry Pollitt, YCL general secretary Bill Rust, Murphy and Dutt, delegates defeated a CC recommendation to continue support for the NLWM. Within months, the project was liquidated from the top (something which the Comintern executive itself had argued against). Nonetheless, most of the Party leadership secured re-election to the CC (although Rust and Page Arnot were excluded on spuriously 'non-political' grounds), having expressed some self-criticism. At the subsequent CC, Campbell's previous post of 'political secretary' was abolished and he was elected 'general secretary' instead.

The 10th congress had also agreed that CP candidates would contest the forthcoming General Election on the slogan of a 'Revolutionary Workers Government'. The Party's election programme, Class Against Class, branded Labour as the 'third capitalist party' and – opposed on the CC by Campbell, Inkpin and Rothstein – urged electors not to vote Labour in other constituencies except where its candidates endorsed the CP's manifesto.

The Communist Party's electoral performance in May proved a big disappointment. Twenty-five candidates averaged 2,000 votes each, compared with 7,000 for the six candidates just five years earlier. Saklatvala lost his North Battersea seat to the official Labour candidate. For the CC majority, this result confirmed their doubts about the wisdom of applying the 'New Line' to Britain and its labour movement. For other CC members, it confirmed their view that the majority were holding back the Party by failing to implement the 'New Line' consistently and wholeheartedly. That, of course, was also the view of Comintern leadership, which had launched a ferocious campaign against 'social fascism' and its pro-capitalist governments in Germany (whose police chief had ordered a May Day massacre of Communist workers in Berlin) and Britain. This campaign chimed with Stalin's drive in the Soviet Union against Nikolai Bukharin – president at the Comintern's sixth world congress – and the 'right oppositionists' and 'deviationists' accused of blocking socialist construction and world revolution.

However, following discussions with the Comintern executive, a PB proposal that convinced New Line supporters should occupy half of its places was rejected by the CC. There was no room for Gallacher – now reconciled to the 'New Line' – and Murphy on the renewed PB, leaving 'organisation secretary' Pollitt a lone voice for the Comintern position. Gallacher was quickly added before a Comintern summit in Moscow in August, although this did not prevent a high-powered commission (which included Molotov, Togliatti, Ulbricht and Bela Kun) demanding the recomposition of the 'complacent' PB and the despatch of Inkpin and Rothstein to the districts for closer contact with the rank-and-file. In August 1929, the PB was altered to comprise Pollitt, Gallacher, Campbell, Arthur Horner, Tom Bell and Idris Cox, a rough balance between those convinced and unconvinced about the 'New Line'. More decisive was the replacement of Campbell by National Minority Movement (NMM) leader Pollitt as general secretary.

At the same time, the NMM conference that August adopted the 'New Line' in principle in its programme for industrial work, emphasising the need to form factory committees and councils of action of unionised and non-union workers. The NMM itself should be built to become a new trade union centre. With Horner now at the helm, all of this was to be carried out while bringing militancy and unorganised workers into the official movement and escalating the struggle against its ruling right-wing bureaucracy.

Not that Pollitt shared every aspect of the mood rapidly gaining ground in the CP. Encouraged by the Comintern and its publications, a series of district committee meetings and Party aggregates across Britain was generating a crescendo of denunciations of Ramsay MacDonald's minority Labour government and the continuing 'rightist danger' on the Party's own CC. In this atmosphere, and with the anti-Communist offensive in the labour movement going strong, Party militants and their allies had formed two 'breakaway' unions. In revolt against the refusal of right-wing officials in the National Union of Scottish Mineworkers to accept election results and stand down, the United Mineworkers of Scotland was set up in 1929. In London, around the same time, strikers formed the United Clothing Workers Union after their own union dismissed Communist officials leading the action. In those industries as elsewhere, Communists used their influence and positions to promote militancy, although unrealistic demands, intransigence or outside direction sometimes alienated local workforces. Pollitt shared Horner's concern that the mass of trade unionists would not be attracted to the CP and its 'united front from below' by strident attacks on their own established organisations as well as on their social-democratic and even left-wing leaders. The Comintern executive agreed that abandoning the struggle within existing unions was a very serious step, not be undertaken without thorough analysis.

In late October 1929, one month before a special Party congress, the 'Wall Street Crash' of stock exchange prices lent credibility to the thesis that a 'Third Period' of cataclysmic capitalist crisis was indeed on the way. The draft theses for the 11th CP congress announced the arrival of an 'acutely revolutionary situation'. At the congress itself, the turn to the 'New Line' was completed. Most of its critics except Campbell – who had swung leftwards – failed to get elected to the CC, while Hannington (who denied being on the right) succeeded independently. Whereas the Party's crisis now began to recede internally, the crisis in its external relations with the working class and the labour movement in Britain continued. The 'New Line' was implemented vigorously. The Comintern's insistence on the Party launching its own daily paper was heeded within weeks with the launch of the *Daily Worker* on the first day of 1930. The Labour government's fiscal orthodoxy was attacked relentlessly. Former allies in the Labour Party were denounced as 'sham lefts', with the ILP singled out for extra vituperation. Industrially, Party militants and their mostly ex-Labour allies in the NMM led or supported strikes and tried without great success to meet another challenge set by the Comintern, namely, to build CP workplace cells.

Even with an ostensibly united leadership supported by a large section of the membership, the Party could not make much ground between the end of 1929 and late 1931. A substantial share of its resources, including assistance from the Soviet Union and Moscow, was put into keeping the financially unviable *Daily Worker* afloat, a job made much more difficult by a wholesalers' boycott, police raids and the imprisonment of staff members. Daily sales of the paper slumped from an initial 44,000 to 25,000 over the first six months. In the battles in industry and the trade union movement, strikers were often grateful for CP and NMM support, but it did not win them to Party membership. The Red International of Labour Unions and a British Commission of the Comintern executive both intervened in August 1930, sharply criticising 'left sectarian' deviations in applying the 'New Line' in industry. The CP and NMM should drop the abstract and unrealistic slogans, the revolutionary phrase-mongering, the ideological preconditions on unity with other workers and the neglect of work in the 'reformist' unions. The British Commission also called upon the CC and PB to give real authority to Harry Pollitt.

All the while, trade union leaders, officials and the TUC were continuing to portray Communists and their allies as irresponsible, disloyal wreckers and splitters in the service of a foreign power. New as well as old divisions opened up on the Party's leading bodies as they discussed the Comintern and RILU criticisms, breakaway 'red' unions and how to respond to the expulsion of Communist-led organisations from the labour movement. Sometimes these were compounded rather than helped by contradictory Comintern interventions. Early in 1931, the arraignment of Arthur Horner in Moscow for opposing the unofficial continuation of a South Wales Miners Federation strike exposed the problems that could arise when applying the 'New Line'. He was accused by the South Wales district CP, the local Miners Minority Movement, its unofficial Central Strike Committee (which he chaired) and the Party PB of defeatism, 'trade union legalism' and attacking the 'New Line' and the Comintern because he understood that the strike was lost: he knew the Communists and their allies would alienate many rank-and-file miners and risk isolating themselves if they carried on the action in defiance of the SWMF leadership – as soon proved to be the case. Pollitt and Gallacher defended him as best they could, in the face of a campaign in the Party and facilitated by editor Bill Rust in the *Daily Worker* against 'the right danger' and 'Hornerism' that even Palme Dutt thought went too far. In the end, the Comintern executive distributed its criticism across the spectrum, from Horner's 'legalism' to the 'left sectarianism' of the South Wales CP and its district secretary Idris Cox. But the whole episode indicated that the Party crisis was still not over.

A more pragmatic intervention in the Lancashire textile dispute at the beginning of 1931, insisted upon by Pollitt, won the Party more friends than enemies. Local Communists such as Bessie and Harold Dickenson, Amy Hargreaves and Rose Smith organised picket lines and campaigned against the discriminatory dismissal of women weavers. With Pollitt and his closest allies exerting new-found authority, there were other impressive initiatives: the British Commission's proposal for a 'Workers' Charter' campaign with local committees and a national convention in 1931, promoted by the *Daily Worker*, won substantial support for its practical demands on unemployment benefit, a shorter working day, rights against dismissal, a statutory minimum wage and trade union law reform. A Women's Charter demanding equal pay and benefit rights inspired two national conferences that same year.

These were realistic responses to the reality of the 'Third Period' in capitalism's development since 1917. It had indeed turned into one of deep crisis, but it was also a period of political and trade union defence and retreat rather than one of revolutionary offensive. It is difficult to imagine how it might have been otherwise. Unemployment soared throughout most of the developed capitalist world, more than doubling in Britain in the two years after the Wall Street Crash to 3.4m (16 per cent but more than twice that level in older industrial regions). As industries such as coal, steel and shipbuilding went into steep recession, workers feared for their jobs and most would only contemplate industrial action when they had little left to lose and at least something they could win. These were not the conditions in which unions – let alone a communist party – could best hope to organise in the mines, factories, yards and mills. Previously, the CP had begun to build its base in the very industries – coal, textiles, docks and shipbuilding – and regions hit hardest by the Great Depression. From having a large majority of Party members employed in industry on the eve of the General Strike, that proportion had fallen to little more than one-third by autumn 1932. Unsurprisingly, therefore, CP membership had continued on its downward trajectory from a peak of 12,000 near the end of the 1926 lockout to 5,560 by the March 1928 CC which formally adopted the 'New Line', then 3,500 at the January 1929 10th congress, 3,170 at the December 1929 special 11th congress before reaching a low-point of 2,350 in August 1930.

In terms of prestige and influence in the working class, the CP's recovery began in 1931 and was reflected in membership growth to almost 4,000 by September. Although the NMM by then had been too weakened by industrial decline and sectarianism to drive the Workers' Charter movement forward, so that both began to peter out, the Party was breaking out of its semi-isolation in the labour movement. Mass unemployment had provided the basis for the National Unemployed Workers Movement, led by Wal Hannington, to take bold action against the Means Test, benefit cuts and house evictions, while providing advice to many thousands of unemployed workers and their families and organising 'hunger marches' to the TUC conference in Bristol (1931) and to London (1930 and 1932). Although boycotted by most trade union leaders and the TUC, opposed by the Labour leadership, infiltrated by state agents and violently attacked by police, the marches and more local demonstrations grabbed the public imagination and won growing support from trade union organisations, trades councils, local Labour parties and Labour MPs. Despite the criticism from some members of the CP's political bureau and subject to hasty proposals from the Comintern leadership, the NUWM leadership ensured that the movement concentrated on practical issues and attracted unemployed workers – including women who comprised a distinct contingent on the 1932 hunger march – regardless of their political outlook.

The Party's recovery was also assisted by the treachery of the Labour government. After implementing an austerity programme of drastic public spending cuts, Prime Minister MacDonald resigned in August 1931 only to re-emerge with Chancellor Philip Snowden and Dominions Secretary and railway union leader JH Thomas at the head of a 'National Government' stuffed with Tories and Liberals.

In the General Election which followed two months later, the CP fielded only one more candidate than previously, but their electoral support was significantly higher. Whereas the 25 candidates in 1929 had polled 50,634 votes and won an average of less than 6 per cent per constituency (although Alec Geddes obtained 25 per cent in Greenock and Gallacher 21 per cent in West Fife), the 26 candidates in October 1931 polled 74,338 votes with a constituency average of just over 8 per cent (with Horner winning 32 per cent in Rhondda East and Gallacher 22 per cent in West Fife). This last performance also represented an improvement on most of the intervening by-elections, although JR Campbell had secured 21 per cent in Ogmore in May 1931 (down to 8 per cent in October).

Together with the vigorous General Election campaign against MacDonald's betrayal, the Party's work among industrial workers and, in particular, the unemployed – of whom there were 3.4m by the autumn of 1931 – boosted membership to more than 7,000. Thousands of working-class people were turning to the Communists – but two million had stopped voting Labour. Even so, more than six million electors had supported Labour's new leadership as the trade unions set about rebuilding their party.

In January 1932, the PB decided to reorganise the Party and switch the emphasis of its industrial work from the Party-controlled and ailing NMM to broader, militant alliances within trades unions and workplaces. These 'January Resolutions' expressed conclusions already reached in a joint commission of the Comintern executive, the RILU and the CP. While denunciations of the Labour Party and especially the ILP would continue with even greater ferocity, the Party would turn to the masses in its four strongest districts. CC members and material resources were allocated to London, Scotland, South Wales and Lancashire and to specific unions and workplaces. There were criticisms that the Party was abandoning its claim to exclusive leadership of the working class, including the unemployed, but Pollitt and Hannington resisted any further turn to the left.

Support on the CC for the January Resolutions had been overwhelming. Nevertheless, there were difficulties in applying this reinterpretation of the 'New Line' to British conditions. Differences were expressed about the mechanics and deficiencies when doing so. Many new members proved to be merely passing through and some went back to the Labour Party or on to the left-turning ILP. Membership fell from a peak of around 9,000 to 5,600 at the 12th congress in November 1932, before levelling out and then growing steadily from the autumn of 1934 as the economy recovered, and employment levels and trade union membership grew.

Centrally and locally, Communists nurtured and supported a widening range of cultural and sporting initiatives which greatly strengthened the Party's cohesion, giving members a 'Party life' and rhythms of work way beyond political meetings and paper sales. Along with other news and analysis, these were reported in the *Daily Worker* which had seen its circulation stabilise at around 11,000 from mid-1930, thanks to the sacrifices of its army of unpaid distributors and sellers. By 1932, the paper's circulation reached 20,000 daily, with 30,000 on Fridays and 46,000 on Saturdays.

The first major crisis in the Communist Party's history was effectively over. Now the Party had to undertake another reorientation as the economy and the Labour Party began to recover, the National Government consolidated its rule and fascism came to power in Germany before taking root in Britain. By the time the CP issued its first strategic programme, *For Soviet Britain*, in 1935, the drive for a 'united front from below' for the insurrectionary overthrow of capitalism was already changing in practice to that of building a 'united front' of working-class organisations at the core of a wider 'people's front' against fascism and war.

The second crisis: 'A war on two fronts'?

On September 30, 1938, Prime Minister Chamberlain returned from a summit with Hitler at Munich waving a piece of paper and declaring, infamously, that it would guarantee 'peace in our time'. The Munich Agreement confirmed the understanding of Stalin and the Soviet leadership that Britain and the other capitalist democracies opposed collective security against the fascist powers. Instead, Britain had sacrificed Czechoslovakia to make a separate peace with Nazi Germany, leaving Hitler free to expand still further eastwards towards the Soviet Union. The Communist Party launched a massive 'Chamberlain must go!' campaign across Britain. Yet, uncomfortable as it became to admit later, many people were relieved that war had seemingly been averted.

As a direct consequence of this 'appeasement' policy of the British ruling class, the Soviet Union concluded a 'Non-Aggression Pact' with Nazi Germany in August 1939 (with its secret protocols to divide Poland and export Soviet oil to Germany). It came as a surprise to anti-fascists, Communists and anti-Communists alike. At the same time, many of them could see why the Soviet Union would not want to risk going to war alone against Nazi Germany and its Italian and Japanese allies. The Non-Aggression Pact would give it time to prepare economically and militarily for the inevitable mortal combat with Nazi Germany when it came.

When Britain declared war on Germany on September 3, 1939, following the latter's blitzkrieg on Poland, the Communist Party's CC had already agreed unanimously the day before to call for a 'war on two fronts – against Hitler abroad and against the imperialist Chamberlain Government at home'. This stance was echoed by the PB on September 15 (despite a Soviet press telegram opposing the 'robber war' between the imperialist powers) and on the first day of the CC on September 24 with only Palme Dutt and Bill Rust dissenting. On September 17, the Soviet Union had entered eastern Poland and prevented it falling into Nazi hands. However, within a month the Party's pro-war position was reversed. Dave Springhall had arrived from Moscow overnight and on September 25 reported the Soviet and Comintern analysis to the CC that this was an 'imperialist and unjust war for which the bourgeoisie of all the belligerent states bear equal responsibility. In no country can the working class or the Communist Parties support the war'. The overwhelming majority of the Party leadership backed the change of policy at an acrimonious reconvened meeting on October 2 and 3, while a minority – notably Harry Pollitt, JR Campbell and West Fife MP Willie Gallacher – maintained that the earlier position had been correct. In view of their differences, Pollitt was removed as general secretary to be replaced in all but name by Palme Dutt at the head of a three-person secretariat; Rust returned to his previous post as editor of the *Daily Worker* in place of Campbell; and Springhall was appointed national organiser.

The majority of Party members then expressed their support for the

Comintern position in a series of well-attended and lively meetings across Britain. Many had had doubts about the initial two-fronts policy, much though they had committed themselves to the anti-fascist struggle at home and abroad during the 1930s. Not only Stalin, at the head of socialist construction in the Soviet Union, but Comintern secretary Georgi Dimitrov – the hero of the 'Reichstag Fire' trial in 1933 – were held in the highest regard by Communists and many other socialists during the 1930s. They had a proven record in opposing fascism in Spain. In contrast, CP members in Britain had seen no evidence that their own country's ruling class would fight fascism, or that the Tory-National government could be swiftly replaced by a militant anti-fascist one. The British Empire belied all the fine phrases about defending freedom and democracy. The British government had stayed neutral as Spain and Albania succumbed to the fascists. In France, the Popular Front government had fallen and the country's 70 outlawed Communist deputies placed under arrest. Nowhere in Europe did the capitalist and landowning classes look like mounting a serious challenge to the fascist powers.

Pollitt and Rust recanted their mistaken positions in statements in the *Daily Worker* in mid-November, thus maintaining the semblance of Party unity at the top. In neither case did the recantation reflect a genuine change of view about the character of the war (Pollitt pleaded guilty only to an 'impermissible infraction' of party discipline), although the desire to help unite the Party was sincere enough. In fact, Stalin himself declared afterwards, in 1946, that the character of the Second World War had been an 'anti-fascist' one from the very outset, from the Nazi invasion of Poland.

In September 1939, Britain's declaration of war on Nazi Germany had fulfilled diplomatic obligations – but it produced no serious military offensive.

Whereas an ineffective British Expeditionary Force was sent to France to do very little, a 100,000-strong Franco-British army was despatched to assist the right-wing Finnish government in its anti-Soviet endeavours (it later joined forces with Nazi Germany against the Soviet Union). Meanwhile, in Britain, bunkers were built for the top bureaucrats, business leaders and politicians, while working-class people were left defenceless. Almost alone, the CP campaigned for proper Air Raid Precautions – especially deep underground shelters – for the general public.

A temporary, partial retreat from the Party line occurred when France surrendered to the Nazis in June 1940. A statement published in the *Daily Worker* from the French CP, calling upon the French people to resist their enslavement by a foreign imperialism, was followed by a PB manifesto which urged the British people to defend their 'independence and democratic institutions' against the danger of 'fascist invasion and tyranny'. No mention was made of the war being an imperialist one, while for the first time since October 1939 a clear distinction was drawn – and preference expressed – between bourgeois democracy and fascism, although it was still vital to clear out the 'guilty men of Munich' (a task not completed under Prime Minister Churchill until the departure of Lord Halifax in December 1940). Palme Dutt pushed back against his own PB in the *Daily Worker* and *Labour Monthly* soon afterwards, formally upholding the manifesto while disparaging the notion of national defence and insisting that the main enemy was still at home. In effect, there were two different, selective interpretations of the June manifesto voiced by Pollitt on the one side and by Palme Dutt and Rust on the other, with the Comintern not ruling in favour of either. Palme Dutt moved quickly as de facto general secretary to ensure that his prevailed.

The period of 'phoney war' came to end with the blitz on London and other cities and ports from September 1940. As dockside communities and those closest to the munitions factories sustained devastating damage, Communist councillors and community leaders such as Phil Piratin and Ted Bramley led mass invasions of the Mayfair and Savoy hotel shelters. They broke into Liverpool Street, Warren Street, Highgate and Goodge Street underground stations, leading thousands of people to safety, and forcing the government to open them to the public every night.

Above ground, the CP and allies such as independent left-wing MP DN Pritt convened a huge People's Convention in January 1941. More than two thousand labour movement delegates demanded a 'people's government' to secure a 'people's peace', an end to profiteering, nationalisation of key industries, democratic and trade union rights, friendship with the Soviet Union and freedom for Britain's colonies. One week later, the British coalition government headed by Winston Churchill decided not to outlaw the Communist Party. Labour home secretary Herbert Morrison banned the *Daily Worker* and *The Week* instead.

By this time, the whole character of the war was changing. With the Nazis occupying much of western and central Europe, Communists emerged at the head of armed resistance movements. Then, on June 22, 1941, the fascist powers attacked the Soviet Union. The Communist Party's PB met immediately and declared its solidarity with the Soviet Union and support for 'a people's victory over fascism and a People's Peace'. Palme Dutt and the PB – with Pollitt dissenting – also demanded that a 'people's government' replace the Tory-Labour-Liberal coalition government headed by Winston Churchill. On June 24, the Comintern executive's secretariat made clear its view that the British CP should not demand the downfall of the Churchill coalition, severely attacking the PB majority line. Privately, Pollitt supported the Comintern position and on July 4 the CC decided he should leave his shipyard job and resume the post of CP general secretary. He reaffirmed his belief that 'this is a People's War. One that only the common people can and will win'. Only the working class could be the driving force in building the national and international unity needed for victory. It had the most to contribute to the anti-fascist struggle, industrially and politically – and the most to lose from a Nazi victory.

Britain's Communists threw themselves into the fight for maximum production. While the Party continued to argue for higher pay, its policy was to establish joint production committees with shop-floor participation and settle industrial disputes as quickly as possible. Sometimes, notably in the coal industry, Party members found themselves representing strikers in heated disputes with their comrades in official full-time positions in the union. This occurred most often in the South Wales coalfield, which supplied much of the steam coal needed by the Royal Navy. The CP had gained substantial influence at every level of the South Wales Miners Federation, symbolised by the election of Arthur Horner as its president in 1936. Yet here as elsewhere, the Party came through its crisis of 1939-41 largely intact. Its membership actually grew through the first half of its 'imperialist war' policy, from just under 18,000 in July 1939 to 20,000 by early 1940. Palme Dutt's *Labour Monthly* doubled its sales to 21,000 over a slightly longer period. However, incomplete records indicate a likely fall of several thousand afterwards, as the 'Dunkirk spirit' grew and the blitzing of Britain's docks and cities brought the 'phoney war' to an end. The turn to the 'anti-fascist people's war' line in alliance with the Soviet Union reversed that decline. By the end of 1941, membership had climbed back up to reach a new peak of almost 23,000.

As the Party threw itself into the war effort and the Soviet people and Red Army defied the anti-Communist cynics with their heroic resistance, CP membership in Britain rocketed to 56,000 in the course of 1942. The number of Party workplace groups or branches headed towards a thousand. Aneurin Bevan, Pritt and other left-wing Labour figures joined the Communists in a big popular campaign in favour of the Allies opening a 'Second Front' against Hitler's forces in Western Europe. Although the military conscription of working-class young men took its toll on Party membership, the CP grew significantly in influence. Unbanned by the coalition government in August 1942 and by wholesalers and advertisers shortly afterwards, the *Daily Worker* had almost doubled its circulation to more than 100,000 by the end of the war.

The Communist Party's second major internal crisis had been resolved, external events and forces having created and helped resolve it. Maintaining at least the facade of unity at the top undoubtedly ensured that a recovery could take place in the most successful way. Had Pollitt and Campbell not publicly recanted in November 1939 and turned their energies to constructive Party work, their 'mistaken perspective' (as Campbell insincerely put it) almost certainly had enough support at the time to make possible a split in the Party.

The third crisis: 1956, Khrushchev and Hungary

The year that saw the erection of Laurence Bradshaw's powerful monument to Karl Marx in Highgate Cemetery, 1956, also shook the international Communist movement to its foundations.

In February, in his report to a closed session of the 20th congress of the Communist Party of the Soviet Union, general secretary Khrushchev denounced the 'cult of personality' and exposed some of the crimes and abuses of the Stalin period. Many Communists around the world were shocked to learn that violations of socialist democracy and human rights had taken place on such a scale. In fact – as CPSU and state archives were to confirm – millions of Soviet citizens had been incarcerated in the late 1930s for sabotage or subversion, hundreds of thousands executed and whole peoples accused of disloyalty and deported from their homelands. Anti-Communist propagandists in the mass media and academia quickly inflated the number of deaths to twenty or thirty million and more, adding the real or imagined casualties of war, famine, disease and anything else that could be blamed – rightly or wrongly – on the Soviet system.

In Britain, after brief discussion in the *Daily Worker* of some of the revelations, the CP leadership presented a resolution to the Party's 24th congress in March acknowledging past 'mistakes and weaknesses' in the Soviet Union, all of which had supposedly been corrected since. Weighed against this should be the undoubted economic, social and cultural advances being made in the Soviet Union, which were shifting the world balance of forces towards socialism and colonial liberation. The positive role and legacy of Stalin was emphasised, while criticisms were made of a 'cult of personality', also deemed to be safely in the past. This proved to be an inadequate response for the many members who, in a state of bewilderment and disbelief, sought a more searching analysis of why such criminal violations of socialist democracy had been able to occur. Why, they also wanted to know, had these been accepted at the time and subsequently upheld so uncritically by Britain's communist party? In May 1956, Palme Dutt attempted in *Labour Monthly* to dismiss the significance of the revelations about Stalin's rule, before being compelled to concede that 'criminal misdeeds' had occurred in the pre-war period. Harry Pollitt tried to provide some answers, but he was by this time an ill man, standing down as CP general secretary in the summer in favour of John Gollan.

As details of Khrushchev's revelations gained widespread circulation, a growing number of CP members demanded more information and debate. Those involved in producing the monthly *Jewish Clarion* reacted sharply to reports of anti-Semitic policies in the Soviet Union. Some of the staunchest opponents of Zionism in the Party's National Jewish Committee publicly criticised Soviet restrictions on Jewish cultural activities and the prosecution of Zionist campaigners.

In July, the CP executive committee (EC, formerly the Central Committee) acknowledged that 'serious mistakes and grave abuses' had occurred under Stalin and appointed a commission to consider how inner-party democracy might be improved, although pressure was resisted to adopt a looser, decentralised form of organisation in place of 'democratic centralism' (the organisational principle seeking to combine full and free democracy within the Party with complete unity in public policy and action). That same month, a number of academics led by historians EP Thompson and John Saville began publishing *The Reasoner*, a journal of dissent. They had already expressed their views at length in the Party's weekly journal *World News* and Thompson had written several abusive and deliberately provocative letters to district and central officials. *The Reasoner* duly echoed his condemnations of the CP leadership and argued for an end to democratic centralism. Following discussions with the two comrades concerned, both the Yorkshire district committee and the Party's political committee (PC, formerly the Political Bureau) asked Thompson and Saville in vain to close their journal, on the grounds that the journal breached democratic centralism, was superfluous to existing inner-party channels for dissent and debate, provided the basis for divisive factionalism and gave the publishers an advantage over other CP members who could not afford to produce their own materials.

Consequently, Thompson and Saville were summoned to the September EC, where assistant general secretary George Matthews proposed that they be instructed to cease publication, carrying the clear implication that disciplinary action would be taken if necessary. In the discussion which followed, EC members expressed a range of views about the best course of action. Former MP and now circulation manager at the *Daily Worker* Phil Piratin acknowledged that the journal's founders were in breach of Party rules, but proposed publication of an EC statement in *World News* and a response in *The Reasoner* before deciding on any further action. Leading National Union of Teachers activist (and future president) Max Morris urged greater freedom of expression – even a 'free-for-all' – in the Party press, although industrial organiser Peter Kerrigan condemned this approach as a suspension of democratic centralism and an 'abdication of leadership'. Arnold Kettle wanted a wider exchange of views across the Party, rather than dealing with two individuals. In the end, it was agreed without a vote to publish a statement in *World News* setting out the EC's views, including that *The Reasoner* was unnecessary and should cease publication, together with a record of the discussions held with the two dissidents.

But before the third issue of the *The Reasoner* could appear, the crisis in the international communist movement exploded in Hungary. There had already been mass demonstrations in Poland for higher living standards and greater freedom. In mid-October, the Soviet leadership travelled to Warsaw for talks, before the country's rehabilitated new leader Wladislaw Gomulka implemented a series of popular reforms. Towards the end of that month, students and workers sparked a wave of protest in Hungary. As in Poland, these signified substantial discontent with economic and social conditions in the 'People's Democracies', which reactionary elements intended to transform into a challenge to communist rule and the socialist system. As Soviet troops entered Budapest to suppress demonstrations at the invitation of the old regime, communist reformer Imre Nagy took office and negotiated their withdrawal on October 24. However, one week later, communist party buildings were attacked by armed mobs and officials brutally massacred. On the following day, Nagy announced Hungary's intention to leave the Warsaw Pact and a new struggle broke out within the communist party leadership. A section led by Janos Kadar called the Soviet tanks back on November 4 and fierce fighting ensued as insurgents fought against outside intervention. In the end, Kadar's pro-Soviet regime was secured.

In Britain, the *Daily Worker* reported these dramatic events – including the official pronouncements with all their denunciations, self-criticisms and contradictions – in a difficult process which created deep divisions among the staff. Different reporters in Budapest had conflicting sympathies and sent conflicting accounts. The paper's coverage reflected the divisions within the CP and the wider labour movement. Nevertheless, its editorial line under JR Campbell reflected the view of the Party leadership.

A special extended meeting of the Party EC took place on November 3 and 4, attended by district secretaries as well as EC members. General secretary Gollan spoke of the 'grave danger of reaction obtaining victory in Hungary'. He refuted the analysis set out in journalist Peter Fryer's unpublished reports for the *Daily Worker* and pointed to the problems caused for ruling communist parties by Khrushchev's revelations, emphasising the unfavourable conditions for building socialism in countries with a fascist past (as in Hungary), a strong Roman Catholic church (as in Poland), a largely peasant population and only small, previously illegal communist parties. The necessary but forced pace of development politically, ideologically and industrially in Poland and Hungary had created problems, including 'violations of socialist legality'. Consequently, the 'popular demands of the people' had provided the base on which reaction could act. Communists should be self-critical for not making it clear that 'People's Democracy' would be a long, protracted and step-by-step advance. The situation in Hungary had deteriorated because the initial rectification of mistakes had been 'too slow' and 'not sweeping enough'. The communist party (namely the Hungarian Socialist Workers Party) had lost control and cohesion, leading to collapse and a reliance on the use of force to maintain party leadership. The battle inside the Party had paid little heed to developments outside, notably to how these might be used for Cold War, anti-socialist ends. The Soviet troops in Hungary had been placed in a very difficult situation, according to Gollan. At first, they had withdrawn when requested to do so by the Nagy government, but who could deny that what happened next had amounted to counter-revolution? Gollan also asked the EC to bear in mind that the Warsaw Treaty had only come into existence in response to the US occupation of western Europe and West German president Adenauer's pledge to 'liberate' eastern Europe. If the Soviets withdrew now, the issue would be not only one of Hungarian independence but also of Western political and military intervention. The CP in Britain could not afford to lose its sense of class and political reality, even though socialism abroad had received a set-back. While facing up to problems, it had to preserve its cohesion (hence the discussion being organised around the Inner-Party Democracy commission) and fight all tendencies to dismantle the Party and its Marxist-Leninist character, to belittle the Party's role and question democratic centralism.

Palme Dutt urged the Party not to tear itself to pieces over Hungary, but to concentrate on present 'achievements' there rather than past problems – while also suggesting that critics of the British party's position were stirring up anti-communism instead of fighting for socialism. Piratin, who had deep misgivings about the Soviet leadership's political intervention in Poland, thought Palme Dutt's contribution would unite no-one. He broadly endorsed Gollan's analysis but thought that his draft statement for the EC contained 'almost no self-criticism' and was 'too general'. The communist leadership in Hungary had failed, splitting and disarming the Party. No-one on the EC underrated the strength of the counter-revolution, 'but you gain nothing by shouting the odds' about it. The Hungarian communist party had about one million members in a population of six million adults. In many of the great factories, 50 to 60 per cent of the workers were party members although many must have been 'band-waggoners or counter-revolutionaries'. Party comrades in Britain wanted to know what went wrong, Piratin insisted. For him, the answers being given were insufficient. When Communists in Britain were asked whether their own leaders would not meet the same fate as Matyas Rakosi – former leader of the Hungarian party removed from office and summoned to live in the Soviet Union after Khrushchev's denunciation of Stalin – what could be said in reply? It was necessary to have certainty as well as unity.

Responding to this discussion and then opening a more detailed consideration of the Soviet military intervention, Gollan argued that the Party was making an interim assessment only, although the basic factors in its analysis were correct. He conceded that publishing so many contributions in *World News* which, in effect, proposed liquidation of the CP in Britain had been a mistake. He also confirmed that the PC had been divided on whether to support the Soviet Union and Kadar in crushing the revolt. The majority favoured doing so, on the grounds that Nagy had gone over to counter-revolution and Cardinal Mindszenty, newly freed from house arrest, had indicated his desire to see the restoration of the kind of pre-war society ruled by the fascist Horthy and his Iron Guard. A minority on the PC had wanted to 'sit tight' at least for the time being, while standing with the Soviet Union against the return of capitalism in Hungary. Taking either position as an EC would cause 'great political problems' and divisions, Gollan concluded. Piratin expressed his 'reservations' about the decision of the Hungarian party leadership to call upon Soviet troops. Where did the 'good' party members' in Hungary stand? The Kadar government had voted 11-2 to ask for Soviet assistance on the second occasion, and in those circumstances he believed the EC should support Kadar and the Soviet Red Army. There had been chaos and, 'legalistically', no government at all, allowing others to climb into the saddle. He was sure that the United States would have intervened in Hungary had the Soviets not beaten them to it.

By the following weekend's EC meeting, it was clear that a deep divide had opened up across the Party at every level. While letters and resolutions from Party meetings were running at least two-to-one in favour of the EC line, many Party members were resigning in protest at the support given to the Soviet intervention. Among them were Thompson and Saville, who had just been suspended by the EC after publishing the third issue of their journal.

Divided within and under siege from ruling-class and right-wing enemies in the mass media and former friends in the labour movement, the impetus quickly developed across the Party to unite. This embraced EC agnostics such as Morris, Kettle and industrial organiser Peter Kerrigan as well as more convinced supporters of the Party line such as Palme Dutt and Idris Cox. An ideal opportunity for turning outwards in action presented itself with the invasion of the Suez Canal on November 5 by British forces acting in concert with France and Israel. The Party seized this opportunity to contribute to a mass anti-war movement alongside Aneurin Bevan and the Labour left. The CP organised hundreds of workplace and public meetings upholding the right of Egyptian president Nasser to nationalise the canal and demanding Britain's immediate withdrawal. The Party leadership also launched a series of other initiatives from the autumn of 1956 and into 1957. These highlighted the question of peace, exposed the madness of the H-bomb, attacked slum landlordism and extortionate rents, demanded higher state pensions and helped lead the battle in the labour movement to defend nationalisation and the goal of socialism.

The Party's special 25th congress in April 1957 reflected this mood for militancy and unity. The EC's position on Hungary received substantial endorsement and the report of the Inner-Party Democracy commission was adopted, with its commitment to opening up new avenues of internal discussion without violating the principles of democratic centralism. A new draft of the Party's programme, *The British Road to Socialism*, was also adopted, subject to final consultation with the branches. It differed significantly from the 1951 edition, its main amendments reflecting the impact of Khrushchev's revelations and the Hungarian uprising on the left and the wider public. These were to omit the repeated attacks on Labour's advocacy of 'democratic socialism', to drop 'People's Democracy' as the path to socialism in Britain and to elaborate and emphasise the role, breadth and active participation of the popular alliance – including a united labour movement – necessary to achieve and exercise power and to build and defend socialism. This new edition also emphasised how socialism must involve the expansion of democratic and personal freedoms and the participation of ordinary people and their organisations in the struggle against over-centralising and bureaucratic tendencies.

For thousands of CP members, however, this was all too little and too late. They were dismayed that the 25th congress had refused to condemn the Soviet intervention and the punitive measures now being pursued against Nagy and other government ministers soon to be executed. They did not trust the commitment of the CP leadership in Britain to greater democracy within the Party or under socialism. Despite the upsurge in the Party's mass activity, membership fell by more than one-quarter from 34,117 in June 1956 to 24,670 by February 1958. Among the leavers were Fire Brigades Union general secretary John Horner, Derbyshire Area NUM secretary Bert Wynn, leading Scottish NUM official Alex Moffat (who later returned), London bus workers' leader Bill Jones and Marxist historian Christopher Hill. One-third of the *Daily Worker* staff also resigned as the paper's daily sales fell in the course of 1956 from around 77,000 to 63,000, albeit with spikes at the height of the Hungary and Suez conflicts.

Yet the CP survived, old loyalties prevailed, Party and Young Communist League campaigns continued and the situation in Hungary stabilised. The Party switched its emphasis from international nuclear disarmament to unilateral renunciation of atomic weapons by Britain, as Communists joined the first march to Aldermaston in 1958 and supported the Campaign for Nuclear Disarmament. The political tide was turning against the Tories and the labour movement was debating what kind of Labour government it wanted. CP membership had turned upwards by early 1959 and on the threshold of the 1964 General Election stood at 34,281 – higher than at any point in 1956.

The fourth crisis: roads to socialism

Following protests by writers and students, Alexander Dubcek assumed the position of first secretary of the Communist Party of Czechoslovakia in January 1968, supported by Soviet president Leonid Brezhnev. The Czech CP and government published a popular ten-point 'Action Programme' to democratise political and economic life, carefully avoiding any talk of withdrawing from the Warsaw Pact. The *Morning Star* and CP in Britain welcomed 'the positive steps taken to tackle the wrongs of the past and strengthen socialist democracy'. But in the Communist Party of the Soviet Union (CPSU) and other ruling parties in eastern Europe, the 'Prague Spring' had come to be seen as a possible replay of the attempted counter-revolution of 1956 in Hungary.

When Soviet and other Warsaw Treaty forces entered Prague on August 20, 1968, they met overwhelming but passive, non-violent resistance. The next day, in the absence of general secretary John Gollan and international secretary Jack Woddis, industrial organiser Bert Ramelson was summoned to the Soviet embassy to receive a message from the CPSU, read out by the ambassador. This attempted to justify the steps taken to defeat imperialist-backed 'counter-revolution' in Czechoslovakia. It was challenged bluntly by Ramelson, echoing the unanimous support of the Party's EC in July for the Action Programme. Later on August 21, the CP political committee, along with many other communist parties in the developed capitalist countries, declared its total opposition to this military 'intervention'. The word 'invasion' was deliberately not used, in the hope that this would not antagonise Party members whose inclination would normally be to give the benefit of any doubt to the CPSU and Soviet leadership. A section of the CP membership in Britain could be expected to support the Soviet line as a matter of principle. On August 24, the Party EC overwhelmingly endorsed the PC's position and called for a peaceful resolution of differences, respect for Czechoslovakia's right to determine its own road to socialism, and the withdrawal of Warsaw Treaty forces from the country. While understanding Soviet security concerns, the CP leadership in Britain could not share the Soviet assessment that counter-revolution had been underway in Czechoslovakia. On September 12, the PC went so far as to accuse the CPSU of a serious breach of trust between communist parties, having 'misled' them about the degree of support among the Czech Communists and government for a military intervention. The YCL characterised the intervention as an 'invasion'. For some prominent members of the Party's national student committee and the Radical Students Alliance, such as young Party EC member Martin Jacques, the demolition of the Prague Spring instilled in them a life-long hostility to the Soviet Union and the international socialist system.

The debate taken into the rest of the Party – and into the *Morning Star* and the Party's weekly internal journal *Comment* – exposed stark differences that had found little expression in the EC or PC. Leading Communist trade unionists, academics, lawyers, journalists and cultural figures in Britain took up positions for the EC's line (Mick McGahey, Will Paynter, Dick Etheridge, GCT Giles, Isabel Brown, Bob Stewart, Eric Hobsbawm, Maurice Cornforth, Maurice Dobb) and against (Abe Moffat, George Guy, Bert Papworth, Dave Bowman, Mikki Doyle, Alan Bush). Nonetheless, when votes were taken at branches and district committees, a substantial majority endorsed the August 24 EC statement and only three district congresses (Surrey, Hants &

Dorset and North East England) out of 18 were opposed.

The most strident denunciations of the Soviet-led intervention came from a Maoist breakaway from the CP earlier that year, namely, the Communist Party of Britain (Marxist-Leninist). Chaired by Amalgamated Engineering Union full-time official and member of the AEU and CP executives Reg Birch, it condemned the 'Soviet revisionist clique' for committing a 'crime of imperialist aggression'. The politics of the CPB(ML) reflected China's opposition to the Soviet Union's policy of 'peaceful co-existence' with the imperialist powers for fear of nuclear conflict, which Mao Zedong regarded as a self-serving surrender. Although the departure of Birch and a small number of other Party members had little impact on the parent organisation, their orientation to the trade union movement enabled the split to survive the following decades, unlike a previous Maoist breakaway led by Michael McCreery.

An updated edition of *The British Road to Socialism* (*BRS*) was published in October 1968, incorporating what the EC regarded as lessons from the Czech experience. Intended to meet the challenges thrown down by social-democratic and Trotskyist critics, it emphasised the importance of a 'democratic advance to socialism', with a multi-party system including parties hostile to socialism continuing after working-class state power had been achieved. Instead of seeking to undermine, replace or split the Labour Party, the CP wanted to assist its left trends in the struggle to turn that party against reformism and capitalism and towards the construction of a socialist society. As 'state-monopoly capitalism' was the obstacle to progress on every front as well as to socialism itself – the capitalist state being 'intertwined' with the big banks and corporations – the immediate need was to construct a 'broad popular alliance around the leadership of the working class, fighting every aspect of the power of the monopolies'. Other Communists saw the programme as diluting the class basis of the Party's strategy to take and maintain state power, placing too much store by electoral work and capitulating to 'bourgeois' concepts of democracy. For some, such 'revisionism' also encompassed the alleged retreat from 'proletarian internationalism' as reflected in criticism of the CPSU and the Soviet Union.

The inner-party battle on the Czech crisis continued up to the Party's 31st congress in November 1969, with some veterans of previous crises supporting the Soviet intervention (notably Palme Dutt and Andrew Rothstein) or opposing (JR Campbell, Peter Kerrigan and Max Morris). Although a 292-118 vote settled the immediate argument in the Party leadership's favour, ideological differences arising from this question and changes in the *BRS* would resurface fully in the mid-1970s.

As things stood, there was no mass defection from the CP on the scale of the Hungary crisis. In reaction to criticism, the Soviet Union had cut its prepaid daily import of 12,000 copies of the *Morning Star* to 9,000, but editor

George Matthews managed to negotiate its restoration after little more than a year. In June 1969, the International Meeting of Communist and Workers' Parties in Moscow reinforced the call for unity in the international communist movement in the struggle against capitalism, imperialism, racism and fascism and for peace, national liberation and socialism.

Although the small but steady decline in CP membership in Britain continued, from 34,261 in 1964 and 30,607 in June 1968 to 28,803 twelve months later, it then levelled out. There was plenty of intense activity – and not a few successes – to keep the Party together over the post-1968 period. Party trade unionists played a leading part in national battles to block the Labour government's anti-strike plans, free the Pentonville dockers, bring down the Industrial Relations Act, save Upper Clyde Shipbuilders, end 'lump' labour on building sites and break Tory government pay limits with the 1972 miners' strike. Communists were prominent in the 'Broad Left' leadership of an increasingly militant and politicised students' movement, with Digby Jacks elected president of the National Union of Students in 1971. Internationally, CP members in Britain mobilised in solidarity with the peoples of Vietnam, South Africa, Chile and elsewhere. By mid-1973, Party membership had climbed back up to 29,903.

The fifth crisis: questions of class politics

Labour victories in the two General Elections of 1974, on the back of another successful miners' strike, created the conditions for a demobilisation of the labour movement. Following a settlement of the NUM dispute and speedy legislation restoring and expanding the rights of workers and their unions, the Labour government drew up a 'Social Contract' with the TUC. It promised further progressive reforms in return for wage restraint and a curb on workplace militancy. Hitherto valuable 'broad left' allies of the CP in the trade union and student movements failed to recognise the turn to class collaboration that lay behind the government's approach. This agenda could be seen in the decision of Prime Minister Harold Wilson and his closest allies to campaign to keep Britain in the European Economic Community in the 1975 referendum, whereas the CP and much of the Labour left wanted to get out of the monopoly capitalist free-market, anti-socialist bloc. Later that year, the TUC conference rejected the left's Alternative Economic Strategy (AES) pioneered by the Communist Party, left economists and trade union leaders such as Ken Gill of the engineering union's Technical and Supervisory Section (TASS).

Against this backdrop of trade union retreat and left defeat, the Party began the process of reviewing its strategy and any implications for *The British Road to Socialism*. This opportunity was seized upon by a network of younger Party intellectuals whose 'new thinking' had been exciting some interest in the CP's national student and economic committees and in the YCL. Driven by an organised faction calling itself the 'Smith Group' and then the 'Party Group', these 'modernisers' questioned the centrality and leading role of the working class in the struggle for socialism. They pointed to the diversity of the modern workforce as evidence that it could no longer be seen as a single force with one overriding identity or even one fundamental class interest. They believed the CP should move away from the organised working class and 'militant labourism' at the core of its strategy. The Party's overwhelming emphasis on 'class politics', and the antagonistic interests of the working class and the capitalist class, was outdated and narrow. The alleged result was an obsession with workers' pay, conditions and terms of employment and with industry and the wider economy which the reformers derided as 'economism'. Instead of opposing wage-control policies and denying that pay increases fuelled inflation, the faction argued, the CP and the labour movement should devise an anti-inflation incomes policy based on social solidarity, prioritising the needs of the low-paid at the expense of the higher-paid.

Most significantly, the faction's version of feminism viewed the oppression of women not as a function of exploitation and super-exploitation in class-based societies, rooted in the division of labour. Rather, it was a social, cultural and even psychological practice autonomous from – even independent of – the economic basis of capitalism and earlier modes of production. It was the product of male domination in a system – 'patriarchy' – which reproduces itself within every class and in every type of society. Women and other, misnamed, 'new social forces' based on gender, ethnicity and sexual orientation, or motivated chiefly by concerns for the environment and peace, could play (or at the very least share) the leading role which the working class and the labour movement were failing to fulfil. Such a 'broad democratic alliance' for change could only be built on the basis of autonomy, pluralism and equal status, which required the labour movement – and especially the CP – to move away from hierarchical, centralised and bureaucratic models of organisation and conduct.

Selecting and distorting concepts developed by the Italian Marxist-Leninist Antonio Gramsci, these latter-day and self-styled 'Gramscians' and 'revolutionary democrats' regarded traditional and orthodox Communists as 'left sectarians' who were guilty of 'class reductionism'. Capitalism's economic, social and in particular technological development was turning the philosophical and political outlook of the British and other communist parties, namely, Marxism-Leninism, into an anachronism. The Soviet-led intervention and subsequent moves to dismantle the reforms of the 'Prague Spring' had confirmed the inability of the Soviet-style model of socialism to reform and democratise itself. The faction emphasised the need to 'democratise' both capitalism and socialism.

By all outward appearances, this was an energetic new force in the YCL and the Party, raising fresh and interesting if uncomfortable questions. After the 34th Party congress in November 1975, they comprised a determined and coordinated group on the EC around Martin Jacques, newly appointed national organiser Dave Cook, student leader Sue Slipman, Judith Hunt and Pete Carter.

The first reaction of the CP leadership to this new trend had been to welcome and promote it within limits as a dynamic pole of attraction for young, educated, professional and women recruits. This reflected the 'pragmatist' politics of past and present general secretaries John Gollan and Gordon McLennan, successive *Morning Star* editors George Matthews and Tony Chater, industrial organiser Bert Ramelson and the others in the core leadership of the Party in the late 1960s and 1970s. Schooled in Marxism-Leninism, their pragmatism adapted it to conditions in Britain with its parliamentary system, a widespread public commitment to the freedoms extracted from the ruling class and the existence of a mass social-democratic Labour Party based on the trade union movement. Politically, this pragmatic approach was reflected in *The British Road to Socialism* with its strategy for the working class to win state power at the head of an alliance between the labour and progressive movements, through a combination of electoral and extra-parliamentary struggle. Unlike social democrats and most of the left in the Labour Party, they understood and condemned capitalism and British imperialism in class terms, placed much more emphasis on trade union militancy, the leading role of the working class and mass campaigning between elections and made clear the need for a left government and the revolutionary movement to take all necessary steps to defend itself against reaction and counter-revolution.

Unfortunately, the outward appearance of the emerging faction as a dynamic, effective and attractive force belied the reality. As it took control of the YCL and its publications from the late 1960s, against fierce opposition from more orthodox Marxist-Leninists, so the diversion into sex, drugs, rock 'n roll and identity and cultural politics failed to halt the advance of the ultra-leftist politics of various Trotskyist groups. By 1975, YCL membership had fallen from a peak of 6,031 in 1967 to 2,338 and the faction had been advancing on the Party's national students committee since the EC's imposition of Dave Cook as national student organiser in 1972, followed by Jon Bloomfield two years later.

Now, many of the same people whose politics had contributed to the decline of the YCL set about revising *The British Road to Socialism* and the Communist Party itself. The nine-person commission appointed by the EC in March 1976 to draft a new edition of the Party programme included four from the reformers' faction (Jacques, Hunt, Chris Myant and Pete Carter) as well as pragmatists such as Matthews and Gollan. As it conducted its consultative and drafting work, other revisionists waged an offensive against the *Morning Star* in the Party's fortnightly journal *Comment*. The daily paper had been losing sales since Labour's General Election victory in

February 1974 and the downturn in industrial militancy. Critics blamed the paper's 'narrow', 'boring' and 'economistic' obsession with trade unionism, economic issues and traditional class and labour movement politics. At the 35th CP congress in November 1977, some of those criticisms were repeated in a resolution proposed by ex-national students organiser Jon Bloomfield and passed despite opposition from the pragmatist section of the EC. Delegates decided that a sub-committee should review the *Morning Star*'s content. However, they overwhelmingly rejected the reference back from one of the chief factionalists, Geoff Roberts, of a resolution congratulating and praising the Soviet Union and the CPSU on the 60th anniversary of the Bolshevik Revolution. Dave Cook's subsequent failure to produce a more damning report on the content of the *Morning Star* reflected the unfavourable balance of forces against the Eurocommunists at the time, which prompted some of the faction's intellectuals to leave the CP in despair. His draft report conceded that the paper was doing a good job with limited resources, but doubted whether the Party had capacity in the current political situation to reverse its declining circulation. The report also reaffirmed the necessity to keep the management of the *Morning Star* separate from the Party.

The 35th CP congress also adopted a new edition of the *BRS*. Even before that event, as aggregate meetings debated its contents, opponents of the new draft had decided to leave the Party in protest. Led by Surrey District secretary Sid French, who had opposed the programme adopted in 1968, they rejected any implication that the Communist Party could rival or displace Labour as the main party of the working class, disagreed with the policy of standing candidates against Labour ones and accused the CP leadership of violating 'proletarian internationalism' with its criticism of the Soviet-led intervention in Czechoslovakia. Subsequently, French and some 700 supporters based mostly in southern England and parts of Lancashire formed the New Communist Party in July 1977. A much more significant breakaway than that under Reg Birch in 1968, they weakened the anti-revisionist front in the CP, while going on to have little impact on the campaigning capacity of the parent party and even less on the politics of the labour movement. As an alternative and within the Communist Party itself, Charlie Doyle's pamphlet *A Critique of the Draft British Road to Socialism: Revolutionary Path – or Diversion?* provided the basis for a series of meetings under the slogan 'Against the Draft: Against the Split'.

The main debate at the 35th congress centred on a reformulation in the new *BRS* draft, namely, that a 'broad democratic alliance' for progress and democracy must be built, led by the working class but also comprising movements arising from society's new or transformed 'social forces'. Previously, the programme had proposed a 'broad popular alliance' to challenge the capitalist monopolies and state-monopoly capitalism and open the road to socialism, led by the working class but also drawing in all people whose interests are threatened by state-monopoly capitalism.

The pragmatists downplayed the significance of the new 'broad democratic alliance' formulation, welcoming the greater prominence given in the proposed alliance to women, racial minorities and peace campaigners. On the other hand, the 'modernisers' presented it as a decisive shift away from 'narrow' class-bound politics. No longer was this an alliance in the class struggle against state-monopoly capitalism, as the pragmatists still believed it to be. Rather, this was henceforth an alliance for the ideals of democracy and freedom, as presented in *Marxism Today* and *Comment* by their new editors, respectively, Martin Jacques (from March 1977) and Sarah Benton (from 1978). By this time, they and their supporters had assumed a new identity as 'Eurocommunists', Britain's paler pink equivalents of the Spanish, Italian and – to a lesser extent – French Communist Party leaders who had declared their commitment to a constitutional, pluralistic and peaceful path to socialism. Britain's Eurocommunists, emboldened by what they claimed as their co-thinkers in Western Europe's biggest communist parties, opened up new fronts in the ideological struggle within the CP.

Thus, in September 1978, *Marxism Today* featured Eric Hobsbawm's Marx Memorial Lecture 'The Forward March of Labour Halted?' This marked a milestone in the Eurocommunist offensive against class politics, although at the time this was probably not the lecturer's intention. According to Hobsbawm, the British labour movement had ceased its political advance in the late 1940s or early 1950s and entered a long period of crisis. The structure of British capitalism had changed and along with it the composition and outlook of the working class. The decline of manual labour and of the skilled labour aristocrat had eroded traditional ways of working, living, organising and thinking politically. Women and immigrants now comprised a larger and growing proportion of the workforce. Modern technological innovation was blurring demarcations of work and status between different occupational groups, thereby reviving sectional rivalry. Within the working class, differentiations had increased between people on low pay or social security – and often beyond the reach of trade unionism – and those who could take advantage of the economic and social improvements made possible by the long post-war expansion. The overall result was a decline in class cohesion and consciousness, in trade unionism and in electoral support for the Labour Party. This had not been reversed by the radicalisation of students and intellectuals in the 1960s, nor by a period of workplace trade union militancy in the early 1970s. The task facing Marxists, therefore, was to analyse and understand why the labour movement had lost its dynamism and historical initiative in order to resume its forward march.

There was much to question and ponder in Hobsbawm's thesis. Leading CP trade unionists such as new industrial organiser Mick Costello, TASS general secretary Ken Gill and Liaison Committee for the Defence of Trades Unions chair Kevin Halpin challenged various aspects, pointing out that trade unionism had grown substantially among non-manual workers, militancy had always ebbed and flowed and that the unions, the CP and its allies were capable of developing the tactics, strategy and politics to overcome recent set-backs such as the 'Social Contract'.

For the Eurocommunists, on the other hand, Hobsbawm had shown that 'class politics' (as narrowly defined by they themselves) and its alleged 'economism' could no longer meet the challenges of new times. Indeed, Dave Cook and others insisted, it was debatable whether the labour movement any longer had the capacity to transform itself to understand, accommodate and champion the needs, demands and interests of the poor, women, gays, black and ethnic minorities, the self-employed, professional people and other social forces and their movements. These doubts and the necessity to shift the main focus of political struggle into the ideological and cultural spheres were then amplified in *Marxism Today*, *Comment* and at the annual Communist University of London (which had grown enormously since its launch in 1969). Eurocommunist control of these platforms ensured that they were mostly occupied by their co-thinkers from within and beyond the CP.

Up to that point, CP membership had fallen from 28,519 in 1975 to 20,599 by June 1979. The decline was even steeper in those sections of the Party already dominated by the politics of Eurocommunism. On the national students committee, the abandonment of class politics had undermined CP influence in the Broad Left and allowed Labour students to move to the right as they battled their own party's Trotskyists. Shortly after Eurocommunist Sue Slipman was elected president of the National Union of Students in 1977, the 'Broad Left' began to disintegrate as CP students forged a closer relationship with the Liberals in the 'Left Alliance'. The presidency of another Eurocommunist, Dave Aaronovitch, marked a further move to the right, opening the door to the National Organisation of Labour Students and its careerist leadership.

Slipman signalled her own political trajectory when, at the Party's EC in March 1979, she condemned industrial action in principle as 'divisive', especially when Communists could not control and terminate it. Furthermore, she claimed, supporting strikes alienated potential allies for the 'broad democratic alliance'. Within two years she had joined the Social Democratic Party – an anti-left, pro-European Community, pro-nuclear weapons breakaway from Labour which then formed an alliance with the Liberal Party.

Under the sway of Eurocommunist 'non-class' interpretations of youth culture and the oppressions of gender, race and sexual orientation, the YCL had suffered a steep fall in membership from 2,338 in 1975 to 1,021 by 1979. Its congress in that latter year dropped the YCL's commitment to 'Marxism-Leninism' in favour of the 'creative application of Marxism', ditched democratic-centralism to embrace 'internal democracy' and a semi-federal leadership and adopted a new programme, *Our Future*, which largely avoided any mention of capitalism.

A poor turnout at the 1979 Communist University of London indicated that the vacuous and sterile orthodoxies of British-style Eurocommunism were losing a little of their lustre. At just 517, this was well below the attendances of previous years. Only the rising sales of *Marxism Today* provided a candle in the gloom, rising under the editorship of Martin Jacques from 3,000 to 4,500 inside a year or so. Yet, within the CP and among its pragmatist leadership, there was increasing irritation at the growing tendency of the journal to carry interviews, features and reviews by or with politicians, journalists and other personalities who had never shown any commitment to socialism, communism or the labour movement.

The Eurocommunists then overplayed their hand in a review of the Party's internal structures and processes. Charged by the 35th congress in 1977 to consider and make recommendations to improve them where desirable, the EC had appointed a 16-person commission on Inner-Party Democracy. Its first draft report provoked national organiser Dave Cook and five other Eurocommunists on the IPD commission to issue their 'Alternative Proposals' in summer 1979. These included recognising the right of CP members to form groups of individuals and Party organisations to promote their collective positions during pre-congress discussion periods. This was something, of course, that the Eurocommunists had already been doing all year around, every year, along with a group of Marxist-Leninists behind the journal *Straight Left*. Aware that the formation of platforms, tendencies or factions had long been a major factor in the Trotskyist movement's chronic history of prolific splits, EC pragmatists and the 36th congress in November 1979 rejected it. Instead, the majority IPD report was adopted which proposed mostly minor enhancements of internal discussion, reporting and accountability while reaffirming the supreme organisational principle of democratic centralism.

In the period immediately before and after the congress, the EC majority attempted to rein in the Eurocommunist faction. Although Dave Cook paid more lip-service than most to trade unionism and class politics, he was relieved of some political responsibilities as national organiser and then demoted to the post of national election agent. Martin Jacques was not subsequently re-elected to the PC. There were criticisms that too much of *Marxism Today*'s content tended to mystify or demoralise Party loyalists rather than inspire them. Most of the features and reviews were written by Eurocommunists and non-Party intellectuals, to the almost total exclusion of mainstream and Marxist-Leninist party members. In truth, most of the world's communist parties – and certainly the French – would have removed Jacques long before had he been the editor of their 'theoretical and discussion journal'. In November 1980, Sarah Benton resigned her editorship of *Comment* and her membership of the CP, complaining of both 'bureaucratic inertia' and political interference by the Party leadership.

She found it intolerable that the elected national officers of the elected EC should insist that an official CP journal should pay more attention to the official policies of the Party as decided democratically by the membership.

This might have been the juncture at which the leadership could have resolved the gathering party crisis without much of the damage that would come later. There was still a majority in the Party, the congress and the EC who did not share the core 'non-class', anti-Leninist and anti-Soviet politics of the Eurocommunist faction. Yet there was a fatal reluctance to act more decisively against what was, undeniably, a significant and still relatively dynamic if destructive force in the Party. Moreover, Margaret Thatcher's General Election victory in May 1979 had created the conditions in which the Eurocommunists and *Marxism Today* could acquire a new lease of life. The election result had demoralised the labour movement, which was then hit by a barrage of Tory government policies. Had Hobsbawm been right all along? How could the Thatcher regime's popularity among some categories of working people – particularly professional, managerial, supervisory, self-employed and skilled workers – be explained?

As early as February 1980, *Marxism Today* was suggesting that the labour movement and the left now faced an unprecedented enemy with its own unique characteristics. According to non-CP sociologist professor Stuart Hall, 'Thatcherism' represented a radical, powerful fusion of economic, political, cultural and ideological strategies that could not be directly reduced to class. From then onwards, this became a central, recurring theme of Britain's Eurocommunists and their publications. In fact, in the first of his articles on 'Thatcherism', Hall had taken the interests of capital and the balance of class forces as its starting point. Unfortunately, as the decade wore on, the notion of 'Thatcherism' headed into a swamp of introspection, confusion, pessimism and capitulation, increasingly expressed in sub-Gramscian sociological jargon which excluded all but the more intellectual and academic of readers. The central, more comprehensible message for the labour and progressive movements – including for the Communist Party and its possible alliances – was that they all needed to totally 'transform' themselves in order to combat a 'Thatcherism' which, anyway, was making itself all but invincible. The more orthodox, Marxist-Leninist analysis was that state-monopoly capitalism was entering a new phase of development, namely neoliberalism, which sought to combine monetarist economics with a populist ideological and authoritarian offensive that was anti-collectivist, anti-trade union, anti-socialist and anti-communist. This reinforced the necessity for the labour movement to politicise itself, fight the battle of ideas and build a broad alliance behind the left's AES of all those left and potentially progressive forces whose interests were contradicted by those of the capitalist monopolies and their state apparatus. Of course, this alternative analysis received very little coverage in *Marxism Today*, other than to be consistently misrepresented and attacked.

Boosted by its own novel analysis and approach to the changing political circumstances in Britain, *Marxism Today*'s circulation continued to rise as the *Morning Star*'s continued to fall. Ostensibly, at least, the journal and the Communist University of London were winning some new friends and a higher profile for the CP, while more traditional allies in the labour movement orientated themselves almost exclusively to the left-wing resurgence inside the Labour Party around Tony Benn and Ken Livingstone. In these circumstances, the Communist Party's pragmatist leadership feared the impact a forced exodus of Eurocommunists might have on the size, resources and prestige of a party whose membership decline was already accelerating.

In this brief hiatus, differences within the non-Eurocommunist section of the leadership began to grow, with the Eurocommunists aligning enthusiastically with one side against the other. Early in 1980, the CP executive committee came out against the Soviet Union's military intervention to back one faction of the revolutionary-democratic government in Afghanistan against another and to help the regime resist CIA-backed Islamic fundamentalist terrorism. The *Morning Star*, its editors and EC members Tony Chater and David Whitfield and many other Communists took a different view. At the end of the following year, the paper made clear its sympathies for the declaration of martial law in Poland, whereas the sympathies of most EC pragmatists, the Eurocommunists, almost all Trotskyist organisations, US president Ronald Reagan and Tory prime minister Margaret Thatcher lay with the Solidarnosc workers' movement and its anti-communist leaders.

Yet, as in previous Party crises, there were other external developments which provided opportunities for united CP campaigning. The Tory government's anti-working class, anti-trade union offensive provoked a series of industrial confrontations in the early 1980s, notably in the steel industry, although the Party was no longer capable of playing the substantial role in them it once could. As unemployment soared towards three million, however, the CP drew on its alliances and resources across the spectrum to initiate a 'People's March for Jobs' from Liverpool to London in 1981. It received support from the Scottish, Welsh and English regional TUCs and, writing in the *Morning Star*, Labour MP Neil Kinnock. More than 100,000 supporters accompanied the marchers on their entry to Trafalgar Square on May 30.

Existential crisis: from Eurocommunism to re-establishment

This proved to be an Indian summer for the Communist Party. The autumn bombshell was dropped by *Marxism Today* in September 1982 in an article by sociology lecturer Tony Lane, 'The Unions: caught on the ebb tide'. After a wide-ranging survey of changes in Britain's industrial and residential patterns and their implications for trade unionism, he struck the journal's usual note of pessimism – invariably dressed up as 'realism' – about the prospects. Lane then portrayed what he called 'a new working class elite' among shop stewards who were abusing expenses, engaging in a widening range of 'perks and fiddles' and using their union position as a stepping stone to supervisory jobs, with convenors and full-time officers switching sides to become personnel managers and even industrial relations directors. Other stewards took advantage of their office in order to have an 'easy life', getting off the job and out of the workplace 'with spurious excuses of "union business"'. It would not have come as a great revelation to Communists on the factory and office floor that abuses of facility time occur or that some poachers turn gamekeepers. But they would also have known a far bigger reality, namely, the selfless, dedicated work done by many thousands of shop stewards who daily ran the very real danger of victimisation at the hands of the employer. This risk had hugely increased since Thatcher's election in 1979 with the sacking of British Leyland senior convenor at Longbridge Derek Robinson ('Red Robbo') and the first in a barrage of anti-union laws. Lane's article, which chimed with *Marxism Today*'s ceaseless assault on 'narrow class politics', 'economism', 'workerism' and 'macho' attitudes in the trade union movement, caused uproar in the Party.

The first shots in retaliation were fired by the Communist Party's industrial organiser Mick Costello on the front page of the *Morning Star* on August 26. Having previously defended the Party's view of trade unionism and free collective bargaining as being in the front line of the class struggle, he called Lane's article an insult to trade unionism and a 'gross slander on the labour movement'. Many of the best known and most respected Communists in the trade union movement protested likewise in letters to CP general secretary Gordon McLennan, including Ken Gill, Derek Robinson, Kevin Halpin, Kent NUM leader Malcolm Pitt, London printworker Mike Hicks, leading construction union militant Bill Jones on Merseyside and Brent trades council president Tom Durkin, together with the Party's national women's organiser Maggie Bowden, *Marxism Today* editorial board members John Foster and Mike Seifert and numerous CP district committees and workplace and residential branches. Lane himself complained to the Party leadership about Costello and the *Morning Star* while Jacques called the latter's response 'outrageous' in its distortions and lack of consultation. Dave Cook condemned what he said 'stinks as a set-up job' and George Matthews wrote to Chater demanding that Lane be given a right of reply in the paper.

At the PC on September 1, Kevin Halpin's proposal to dismiss Jacques as *Marxism Today* editor and not to sell the offending issue of the journal at the TUC conference was defeated by eight votes (McLennan, international secretary Gerry Pocock, national organiser Ian McKay, Vishnu Sharma and

Party chair and engineer Ron Halverson; plus Eurocommunists Jacques, Pete Carter and Nina Temple) to six (Halpin, Chater, Costello, London secretary Gerry Cohen, civil liberties lawyer Tess Gill and Scottish secretary Jack Ashton). The battle lines were being drawn for the final, decisive conflict to come.

Later in September 1982, the EC reaffirmed its belief in the integrity of the shop stewards' movement, rebuked Jacques for publishing the article without wider consultation, but disagreed with Costello's characterisation of it as 'slander'. The EC reserved its sharpest criticism for Tony Chater, David Whitfield and Mick Costello for colluding in an attack on a Party journal – *Marxism Today* – and misrepresenting the industrial organiser's views as an official statement of the Party's position. Soon afterwards, the *Morning Star* carried a feature by labour historian Vic Allen arguing that Eurocommunism in the Communist Party had been allowed to go too far. Mick Costello resigned from his CP post only to re-emerge as the paper's industrial correspondent, having been appointed by Chater without the customary consultation with the Party leadership.

A *Morning Star* circulation campaign at the beginning of 1983 made little headway before ending in mutual recriminations between the CP leadership and those in charge of the paper. At 15,000, average daily sales were only half of those ten years previously. *Marxism Today*'s monthly circulation, on the other hand, had more than doubled to 11,500 under the editorship of Martin Jacques. Most of the new readers were students, academics, media and culture workers and – to the admitted satisfaction of its editor – liberal right-wing intellectuals in business, think-tank and political circles.

In preparation for that summer's regional AGMs of the People's Press Printing Society (PPPS), the cooperative which owns the *Morning Star*, the Party EC put forward a recommended list of candidates for election to the PPPS management committee. Most were not Eurocommunists but veteran full-time Party officials such as former editor George Matthews, Welsh secretary Bert Pearce and Yorkshire secretary Dave Priscott, alongside Chater. In response, the management committee protested that a 'body outside the PPPS' was seeking to take control of the paper, a description of the EC's status that may have been technically correct but was also unprecedented in its hostility. PPPS shareholders – most of them Communists – preferred to elect the management committee's own list at the meetings. By then, CP membership had dropped to 15,691 on paper, although fewer than 500 of them had turned out to support their own executive committee's candidates.

The 38th congress in November 1983 was one of the stormiest in the Party's history. On one side of the main division stood the Eurocommunists and their allies among the Party leadership pragmatists, although there were tensions between them over the centrality or otherwise of the trade union movement and other 'social forces', over specific policies such as public ownership and a 'progressive' incomes policy and in their attitudes towards the European Community and the Soviet Union. More philosophically, the Eurocommunists believed that culture, broadly defined, and the state apparatus were sufficiently autonomous from monopoly capitalism to make them major and even favourable – as well as necessary – sites of ideological struggle.

On the other side stood those in the Party who had more orthodox Marxist-Leninist views on such questions, ranging from pragmatists around Tony Chater and Mick Costello to the more doctrinaire faction which had not left the CP in protest at the 1978 *BRS* and had since published *Straight Left* as a pro-Soviet paper orientated to the Labour Party and the peace and anti-imperialist movements. A tiny sect around a monthly journal, *The Leninist*, also made its appearance led by individuals expelled from the New Communist Party's youth section. While proclaiming its own integrity and consistency, this grouplet switched sides several times over the coming period as it denounced everyone else as opportunists, revisionists, liquidationists and anti-Party traitors.

At the 38th congress itself, pro-leadership delegates outnumbered pro-*Morning Star* ones by a ratio of around three-to-two. Widespread allegations that this representation had been gerrymandered by leading Party committees and officials were dismissed. Delegates were watched and searched for illicit literature in the form of Straight Left pamphlets, unofficial congress bulletins and alternative lists of anti-Eurocommunist candidates for leadership elections. Chater, Whitfield, Costello and most of their allies lost their seats on the EC and opposition amendments characterising peace as a class question and supporting martial law in Poland to defeat the anti-socialist Solidarnosc movement were also defeated. The EC meeting in January 1984 expelled four Straight Left supporters for factional activity and demanded – with six votes against – the replacement of *Morning Star* editors Chater and Whitfield by Eurocommunists Chris Myant, the paper's diplomatic editor, and editorial assistant Frank Chalmers.

The Soviet government and party indicated their preferred side by paying £800,000 in advance for their daily importation of 9,000 copies of the paper. A buoyant PPPS management committee pressed ahead with its appeal to buy a cost-saving new press to print the *Morning Star* in its Farringdon Road premises.

Despite a growing revolt by branches and district committees – notably the East Midlands and West Middlesex – against expulsions, the Party EC partly succeeded in an all-out mobilisation for the PPPS AGM in June 1984. Two Eurocommunist supporters – Myant and Scottish NUM vice-president George Bolton – were elected to the management committee, enabled by a split in the opposition as the Straight Left faction submitted its own last-minute list. Nonetheless, Ken Gill and Labour MP Ernie Roberts were among the victorious pro-*Morning Star* candidates. That said, had the Scottish sectional meeting not turned violent and been terminated early, the Party EC might have taken most of the six seats up for election. As it was, a slight majority of the 2,700 voting shareholders refused to give unqualified support to either the editor or the management committee, or to welcome the much trumpeted new printing machine. Hoping to build on these successes, the Party leadership then tried and failed to force the PPPS management committee to hold a special AGM within the next few months, before organising its own in October. Not surprisingly, this attracted only half of the number attending in June and its resolution to remove Chater as editor was ruled out of order by the management committee.

Meanwhile, the national strike called by the NUM against pit closures was turning into the biggest, most militant clash between organised labour and the state for two generations, drawing whole working class communities into a life-and-death struggle against organised strike-breaking, police violence, the courts, the social benefits system and the mass media. Active solidarity extended across wives and families, the gay community and other unions. Every section of the CP and YCL mobilised on the ground in support of the cause. This was class warfare in its broadest, deepest and most political manifestation. Every day, the *Morning Star* reflected this fully, on occasions even handing control of its front-page to the NUM leadership. Tony Chater met NUM president Arthur Scargill six times over the course of the strike to coordinate the paper's coverage. Yet the CP leadership produced more leaflets and bulletins attacking the *Morning Star*'s editors and management committee than supporting the miners. Two meetings between Scargill and McLennan and CP industrial organiser Pete Carter satisfied neither side.

Differences over the conduct of the strike between the CP leaders and Communist miners' leaders in the Scottish and South Wales coalfields on the one side, and the NUM leadership and Kent Communist miners' leaders on the other, became well known within the Party and across the left. These mainly concerned the NUM's refusal to hold a national ballot, the 'invasion' of Nottinghamshire by flying pickets at the beginning of the action, the subsequent emphasis on mass picketing and Scargill's intransigence in negotiations with the National Coal Board. The differences also soured relationships between prominent Communist women and leading militants in the Women Against Pit Closures movement such as Ann Scargill and Betty Heathfield. To the extent that NUM vice-president Mick McGahey shared some of his Party leadership's criticisms, he voiced them only at the highest level within his union and the CP while staunchly supporting the NUM's policy and its leader in public.

Throughout the whole twelve months of the strike, *Marxism Today* carried just five articles on different aspects of the struggle, none of them involving the central leadership of the NUM. Otherwise, it was the usual diet of features on 'Thatcherism', Eurocommunism, the weaknesses and failures of the left, bleak post-industrial futures, 'non-class' feminism and the perils facing trade unionism, as well as articles attacking or undermining class politics, 'state' socialism, the AES and the 'hard' or 'fundamentalist' left in the Labour and Communist parties. Among the few permitted notes of ideological dissent were struck by Tony Benn, whose speech at the journal's 'Left Alive' event was reprinted. In it, the acknowledged leader of the left in the labour movement demolished the personalisation of ruling class policy as 'Thatcherism'. His Marxist analysis of the state, the European Community, NATO and class struggle could have come straight out of *The British Road to Socialism*. For Benn, 'our road to victory does not lie in coaxing back half a dozen *Guardian* readers from their flirtation with the SDP, but in mobilising the 10 million people who don't vote but ... who are repressed by our society'. Whereas the *Morning Star* regarded the Bennite movement as the natural and closest allies of the Communists, the Eurocommunists and their journal preferred to promote Labour's new leadership and the likes of Neil Kinnock, David Blunkett, Roy Hattersley and Peter Hain.

In response, the political and theoretical case against the Eurocommunists and their pragmatist allies was set out clearly at the end of 1984 in the pamphlet *Class Politics: An Answer to its Critics* by Ben Fine, Marj Mayo, Elizabeth Wilson and others. Refuting 'non-class' theories of the state, feminism and racism and duly serialised in the *Morning Star*, their analysis met with crude caricature and patronising ridicule in the pages of *Marxism Today*.

Against the backdrop of ferocious political class struggle in the mining communities and beyond, drawing in other sections of the labour and progressive movements, evidence that the tide might be turning in favour of the left in the CP came at the North West district congress in mid-November 1984. Delegates voted to sweep most Eurocommunist and pragmatist members off the district committee. Fearing a similar result in London, the EC imposed national organiser Ian McKay on the district party and used the pretext of minor membership irregularities to restrict discussion and ban the election of a new district committee at the forthcoming district congress. General secretary McLennan had initially wanted a less drastic course of action, but he was later overruled by the PC and an emergency EC. His attempt to dictate EC terms to the London delegates on November 24, including the election ban and the continuation of McKay as acting district secretary, failed spectacularly. The majority of delegates refused to join McLennan's walkout of pragmatists and Straight Leftists. Chaired by Mike Hicks, the congress went on to elect a new district committee devoid of EC followers. Six days later, a special EC suspended 22 of the London rebels for 'factionalism'.

In January 1985, with McLennan rather than the Eurocommunists leading the charge, the EC expelled Chater, Whitfield and four of the 'London 22', namely Mike Hicks, leading NALGO EC member Ivan Beavis, Tom Durkin and *Morning Star* foreign editor Roger Trask. Others were suspended or banned from office, although many of their local Party branch and industrial organisations refused to exclude them from subsequent meetings. Measures were also taken to police the North West district committee to prevent unidentified 'factional activity'.

Furthermore, the EC decided not to wait until November to convene the Party's 39th congress, bringing it forward to May 1985. In the meantime, the Party's monthly journal *Focus*, edited by leading Eurocommunist Frank Chalmers, would be turned into a weekly tabloid paper and sent free to all Party members, promoting the EC and its political and disciplinary positions. On its side, the *Morning Star* launched a fresh drive to revive or establish readers and supporters groups. Writing in the paper, a host of widely respected Party members challenged the political and authoritarian direction of the leadership. These included former assistant general secretary and International Brigades battalion commander and political commissar Bill Alexander, ex-industrial organiser Bert Ramelson, sacked London District secretary Gerry Cohen and veterans Andrew Rothstein and Robin Page Arnot (dismissed by Eric Hobsbawm in *Marxism Today* as 'rather ancient members'). As branches and industrial advisory committees were being suspended, closed or reorganised in London, Scotland and elsewhere, expelled members such as Tom Durkin and Ivan Beavis addressed a series of 'Calling All Communists' meetings across Britain.

In the run-up to the special congress, while giving some space to dissidents such as John Foster and Marxist political economist Ben Fine, *Marxism Today* waged a major offensive against the 'impossibilist', 'fundamentalist' and 'hard' left – Stuart Hall was fond of all three labels – in the Labour Party, the the NUM and CP. Eurocommunist intellectuals such as Alan Hunt pinned the label of 'Stalinist' on Chater, Costello, Foster and other *Morning Star* supporters, while Hobsbawm also tried to draw parallels with the 'Class Against Class' crisis.

The hundreds of delegates to the 39th congress faced unprecedented scenes as they entered Hammersmith Town Hall on Saturday, May 18. They were lobbied by expelled members and their supporters demanding an end to the inner-party purge. Inside, by a two-to-one ratio, delegates endorsed the expulsions in London and elsewhere of 42 Communists including TUC general council member Ken Gill and eleven other members of the PPPS management committee. On the congress floor, Tony Chater delivered an unapologetic and defiant speech in which he warned that Gordon McLennan would be next on the Eurocommunist hit-list. In the main debates, delegates called for 'the broadest movement against Thatcherism', stretching from the Labour Party and the Liberals to the SDP and Thatcher's critics in the Tory Party. In essence, this type of 'broad democratic alliance' would replace the one aimed at state-monopoly capitalism (which speaker after speaker derided as narrow and out of date 'class politics'). Pete Carter repeated his criticism of the NUM leadership for its reliance on mass picketing during the defeated miners' strike, while also condemning all picket-line violence (including that of miners resisting police attacks and fighting for their jobs and communities). The congress also instructed the incoming EC to launch a Party discussion on the AES.

For the first time, the Eurocommunists emerged from a Party congress with a clear majority on the 45-member EC. Nina Temple announced the new leadership's intention to build a 'tolerant party', with no 'political expulsions' and full freedom to debate different views with no labelling and victimisation of comrades.

The following weekend, the *Morning Star* held a festival in Alexandra Palace to celebrate the 40th anniversary of the defeat of fascism in World War Two. Numerous campaigning, international friendship and solidarity organisations booked stalls and renowned economist Victor Perlo of the CPUSA was among the international speakers.

At the PPPS AGM in early June 1985, the five EC-backed candidates were heavily defeated by a margin of more than one thousand votes out of almost 5,000 in the management committee elections. Despite bussing shareholders – some very recent – to the sectional meetings, the Eurcommunists and their pragmatist allies were outnumbered by *Morning Star*, NCP and Straight Left supporters in the labour movement. Transport & General Workers Union general secretary Moss Evans had already thrown his weight behind the paper and its 'survival plan', with the £680,000 web-offset printing press now installed in Farringdon Road. At the Manchester meeting, NUM president Arthur Scargill turned up to support the *Morning Star* and its leadership, expressing his gratitude for the paper's unstinting support throughout the 1984-85 miners' strike. He told shareholders: 'The *Morning Star* is guilty of one act, it supports working class politics and socialism'. Fire Brigades Union general secretary and management committee member Ken Cameron voiced his dismay that divisions in the CP had spilled over into the broad left paper of the labour movement. He had no problem with the editorial line of the *Morning Star* being based on the Party's programme *The British Road to Socialism*, nor with the political affiliations of the paper's editors and the majority of management committee members. His objection was to a Communist Party leadership that had abandoned the class-based politics of the *BRS*.

On its side, the Eurocommunist-dominated EC had the support of *The Leninist* sect, whose two dozen members proclaimed themselves the only possible saviours of the Communist Party from liquidationism.

The die was now well and truly cast. Later that month, a number of those expelled – notably Tony Chater, PPPS secretary Mary Rosser, Robinson, Hicks, Costello and economist Photis Lysandrou – formed the Communist Campaign Group. Politically, the overriding objective of the CCG was spelt out in a founding pamphlet, *The Crisis in the the Communist Party and the Way Forward*, namely: 'the re-establishment of the Communist Party as a leading force in the fight against capitalist oppression and for socialism'.

Strategically, the CCG affirmed its commitment to, firstly, the leading role of the organised working class in a broad democratic alliance directed against state-monopoly capitalism; secondly, socialism as the primary objective of class struggle, with the working class and its allies taking state power; and thirdly, the development of international working-class solidarity, including with national liberation movements and 'with the socialist countries where the working class has state power'. Arguing that the Communist Party would not be rescued from liquidation by futile attempts to fight within the rules and structures captured and abused by the Eurocommunists, the CCG called for mass defiance and resistance from Party members and organisations. The aim would be to block and nullify anti-Party measures at every level of the party. This would create a situation of dual authority and organisation. Who would prevail? The CCG would prove by its rallies, meetings and other activities that the Eurocommunists represented a 'minority clique'. The CCG's priorities would be to support the *Morning Star* and carry forward communist work in the trade union, peace and other broad movements.

How would the conflict in the Party be resolved? There could be no recourse either to a bourgeois court of law nor – in the face of EC gerrymandering and victimisation – to the usual supreme court for Communists, namely, the Party congress. Thus, it remained to be determined precisely how the existence of the Communist Party would be secured. For now, the CCG would cooperate with and coordinate other Communists – whether members, expelled or suspended – to defend the rules, constitution and programme of the CP. This meant, however, that the CCG would not accept support from factions within the Party – such as Straight Left – which did not accept those rules, constitution or programme.

Organisationally, a national steering committee was set up and within months a full-time organiser, Ray Colvin, had been appointed to work initially from the *Morning Star*'s office block in Farringdon Road. In most regions of England and in Scotland and Wales, CCG committees of past and present Communist Party members were established.

This process of construction contrasted sharply with that of destruction going on inside the CP itself. By November 1985, resignations and yet more expulsions had reduced Party membership by almost 20 per cent over the previous two and a half years to 12,711. The North West district committee had been dissolved by executive decree and replaced by a list of approved nominees. Disciplinary action was being taken against Party organisations which refused to operate expulsions or suspensions of their members. In addition, the EC and its district officials used the annual issue of new membership cards to purge the Party of hundreds of *Morning Star* and CCG supporters. Refusing to re-card dissident members deprived them of their right of appeal under rule. In London, in particular, whole branches and industrial advisory committees were being merged, suspended or closed down as some 35 members were expelled. One result was that a dozen or so CP branches and advisories reconstituted themselves as CCG bodies.

Not surprisingly, therefore, the January 1986 EC recorded major re-carding shortfalls in many districts, notably the North West, South East Midlands, Sussex and Wales. Even so, the Eurocommunist majority decided to push ahead with the purge in London and the North West, besides investigating the work of the East Midlands district committee with its large Straight Left faction. The only bright spot appeared to be a rise in the circulation of a new weekly paper, *7 Days*, edited by former *Morning Star* assistant editor Chris Myant and launched in the wake of the PPPS defeat. Sales had risen from 7,000 to 9,000, although this was to prove a short-lived advance.

When leading Party economist Sam Aaronovitch made the case in February's *Marxism Today* for dumping the Alternative Economic Strategy, backed by other members of the Party's economic committee in a two-day seminar, defence of the AES was left to Monty Johnstone, pro-*Morning Star* economists such Ben Fine and Laurence Harris and to Ron Bellamy and Photis Lysandrou of the CCG. In March 1986, the Party's EC received an extraordinary report from industrial organiser Pete Carter which insisted the Party had to change its old 'broad left' alliances and methods of work. Published in May as a pamphlet, the report argued that the CP must turn away from the 'hard left' (militant trade union leaders, Benn and the Campaign Group of Labour MPs) whose 'ill-conceived strategies will assist the Tories' by alienating potential sympathisers; and towards what Carter misleadingly called a new 'broad left', naming the pro-Kinnock Labour Coordinating Committee and the likes of David Blunkett, Tom Sawyer (moving rightwards as deputy general secretary of NUPE) and, more surprisingly, Rodney Bickerstaffe (NUPE's more left-inclined general secretary) and NUR general secretary Jimmy Knapp. In concrete terms, Carter proposed little to which many on the so-called 'hard left' would object: that unions should avoid sectionalism, take more account of the interests of women, ethnic minorities and local communities and – a little more controversially – pursue trade union statutory rights instead of returning to pre-1979 'immunities' from common law. The main purpose of his report and the Party's subsequent pamphlet, *Trade Unions: the New Reality*, appears to have been to attack trade union militancy and ingratiate the CP with Labour's new regime under Neil Kinnock.

Partly in response to Sam Aaronovitch and Carter, the CCG published a pamphlet written mostly by Photis Lysandrou, *Which Way for Labour? A Communist Perspective for the Labour Movement*. It provided the basis for a series of public meetings across Britain explaining why the labour movement should unite around the AES and resist any realignment to the right. More specifically, it opposed moves by Eurocommunists and the Labour Coordinating Committee to drop such key AES policies as nationalisation, free collective bargaining and Britain's withdrawal from the European Community. Like Carter's original EC report, the pamphlet and meetings took place against the background of a ferocious struggle at Wapping and Kinning Park, Glasgow, between the print unions and Rupert Murdoch's News International empire. Almost 6,000 striking workers had been sacked and production facilities moved to the new plants in a deception involving the anti-strike electricians union. CCG members Ann Field, Mike Hicks and Bill Freeman played major parts as national and branch officials in the frontline of the year-long dispute.

That same spring, representatives from CCG local and industrial organisations met in an aggregate to discuss political perspectives and future plans. These included launching a new journal, the *Communist Campaign Review*, in the autumn. The contents of its first few issues demonstrated the political and ideological gulf between the CCG with its allies on one side and the Eurocommunists on the other, with Max Aderath writing on the leading role of the working class, Mary Davis and Ann Field on women and class struggle, John Foster on so-called 'Thatcherism', Ron Bellamy on revisionism, John Gray on the AES and John Hoffman on the state. Alongside the last two, other non-CCG contributors included Tony Benn on nuclear energy. Particularly significant were contributions featuring CPUSA general secretary Gus Hall on racism and senior members of the South African and Soviet communist parties. *Morning Star* editorial staff members Roger Trask and John Haylett led the CCG's difficult work of developing relations with overseas parties, most of which observed the long-established protocol of not recognising factions, breakaways or alternatives to those already in existence in states such as Britain.

The PPPS AGM in June 1986 saw a clean sweep for the management committee in elections against a slate of EC-approved Eurocommunists. A motion calling upon the *Morning Star* to cease supporting the CCG was defeated by 1,995 votes to 722. Following the meetings, the Party's East Midlands and West Middlesex district committees declared that the overwhelming support for the management committee and the new tabloid *Morning Star* showed that, by departing from the Party's Marxist-Leninist principles and rules, the EC had lost the confidence of the Party membership. As a consequence, it should either change its approach or resign. The EC decided instead to launch an investigation into the West Middlesex district committee.

At an aggregate of London CCG supporters the following month, Photis Lysandrou raised the problems both of trying to defeat the Eurocommunists inside the CPGB and of having to establish a separate party should this prove impossible. Mary Rosser warned that *Morning Star* backing for the political offspring of a split could not be guaranteed (not least because there were many *Morning Star* supporters inside the CCG and outside – such as Ken Gill, Bert Ramelson, Bill Alexander, Jack Gaster and many on the East Midlands and West Middlesex CP district committees – who did not, thus far, agree with any such strategy). Mike Hicks feared the risk of a breakaway party ending up in the same marginalised position as the New Communist Party. Then there was the challenge of securing recognition by the ruling parties in the Soviet Union and other socialist countries. At the same time, many CCG supporters in London shared Lysandrou's preference for abandoning the commitment to remove the Eurocommunist leadership and, instead, actively preparing to rebuild the Communist Party. This was also the predominant view in the CCG in the North West, Wales and the Midlands. A similar inclination could be seen in a series of *Morning Star* articles by Mick Costello in early 1987, when he suggested that it would not be possible to resolve the crisis in the CP by defeating the Eurocommunist EC from within the 'remains' of the Party. By then, the CCG was engaged in the second of its major campaigns, leading up to the publication of a pamphlet on peace drafted mainly by Tony Chater. Communists were also demanding the release from Brixton prison of Wapping strike leader Mike Hicks – newly elected along with Bill Freeman to the SOGAT national executive – who had been convicted on a trumped-up charge of assaulting a senior police chief on the picket line. His incarceration made it easier for the union leadership to capitulate to News International and the Metropolitan Police. Hicks was released in time to attend the May Day celebrations in Moscow as an honoured guest.

Meanwhile, on the Eurocommunist party's political committee, it was beginning to dawn that they were now facing an existential crisis. At the first meeting in February 1987, Yorkshire district secretary and *Marxism Today* editorial board member Dave Priscott had declared: 'As a party of socialist revolution we may have had hard times (nothing particularly new in that) but we can survive and fight our way forward. As a party of radical democratic left reformism there is absolutely no future at all for us'. Party theoretician Monty Johnstone agreed.

In the second PC that month, Nina Temple indicated in a written contribution that she had gone over fully to the idea of the Party transforming itself into a broad left party in a nexus of alliances. She recognised that Party membership was falling (in fact by more than one hundred a month), that weekly sales of *7 Days* had almost halved and that the CP's capacity to engage in struggle had been 'greatly hindered' by the loss of the *Morning Star* and by weaknesses in its trade union, youth and electoral activity. What she did not acknowledge, however, was that most of these areas were those in which the Eurocommunists had succeeded in reorientating the strategy of the Party or the YCL. They had insisted on the most confrontational attitude to the *Morning Star* editor and management committee; they had led the drive to promote *Focus* and *7 Days* as an alternative; Eurocommunists such as John Grahl and Bill Warren had denounced 'economism' in the trade union movement, undermining such key AES objectives and policies as public ownership, free collective bargaining and full employment, while Tony Lane and Pete Carter had alienated many militant trade unionists including the leadership of the NUM and supporters of the Liaison Committee for the Defence of Trade Unions. YCL membership had plummeted under its former national secretary Temple and her successor and fellow Eurocommunist Doug Chalmers from 1,021 in 1979 to 439 in 1985. By the time of the February 1987 PC, it stood at less than 218.

On the positive side of the balance sheet, Temple pointed to the Party's 'wider political agenda' of recent years embracing feminism, anti-racism, alliances and the ideological influence exercised by *Marxism Today*. In reality, however inadequately or ineffectively at times, the Party had always been active on these fronts, sometimes with considerable success; the difference now was that its impact in workplaces, trades unions, local elections and among young people – which at times had been of some significance – was plunging to new lows. As for *Marxism Today*, its confused and confusing meanderings through culture, theory and politics featuring a host of middle-of-the-road and liberal academics, pollsters, journalists and politicians could only have spread doubt and despair among readers who genuinely cared about the future of the Labour Party, the labour movement and socialism.

Not that the Party leadership's coalition of pragmatists and Eurocommunists could be held wholly and directly responsible for a resumption of the Party's decline from the mid-1970s. For instance, the rise of the Third World manufacturing nations, the impact of European Economic Community free-market trade and investment and the consequent restructuring of the British economy from mining, shipbuilding, engineering and manufacturing towards services, part-time work and self-employment had eaten deeply into the Party's own industrial base.

Throughout the 1970s and into the 1980s, Trotskyist groups and campaigning organisations inside and outside the Labour Party – unencumbered by any commitment to solidarity with the Soviet Union and other socialist countries – outflanked the CP with their leftist slogans and bold initiatives, attracting new and young recruits who in the past might have gone to the YCL and the Communist Party. Moreover, the election and re-election of the Tories in 1979 and 1983 had shown that a significant section of the working class as well as the middle strata and big business could be attracted to a radical financial, economic, social and ideological agenda based on monetarism, economic deregulation, privatisation, private home ownership, lower income tax, anti-collectivism, anti-trade unionism, anti-socialism and British nationalism.

The lesson that Nina Temple drew from all of this was that reorientation of the CP towards the approach proposed by the Eurocommunists – whose projects in very different conditions were already running out of steam in Spain and Italy – was proving correct. It would, she contended, enable the Party to face the new realities, forge fresh alliances and regain relevance on the political scene.

Meanwhile, a consensus was emerging within the CCG on the necessity to break the inner-party stalemate and staunch the outflow of members from the CP and from organised Communist politics altogether. Successive issues of the *Communist Campaign Review* in the first half of 1987 set out the urgent need to restore the existence of a properly functioning communist party, re-establishing its role as a force capable of organising and leading the fight for the AES and socialist revolution. With a General Election approaching, the Labour Party was moving rightwards under leader Neil Kinnock and deputy leader Roy Hattersley. They were running scared of the SDP now in alliance with the Liberals. *Marxism Today* contributors applauded Labour's retreat from what the journal described as the 'hard left' manifesto of 1983 and its policies to extend nationalisation, repeal anti-trade union laws, introduce a wealth tax and withdraw from the European Community.

On the eve of the June 1987 election, the front cover of *Marxism Today* trailed its lead feature by Eric Hobsbawm arguing for tactical voting in favour of Labour and Liberal-SDP Alliance candidates. In the same pre-election issue, *Guardian* leader writer Martin Kettle made the case for treating the Liberals and SDP as 'part of the British reformist left' and therefore 'natural allies' of the Labour Party.

As things turned out, quite widespread tactical voting against the Tories did not prevent Margaret Thatcher winning a third term of office with only slightly fewer votes and seats and still only a minority (42 per cent) of the poll. The single biggest factor in Labour's defeat was the three million votes (10 per cent of the total) won by the SDP renegades. In an election when leadership image and professional communications counted more than ever, Kinnock was more attractive to swing voters than his predecessor Michael Foot, with Labour's rightwards shift contributing little to the party's modest increase in votes and seats.

Subsequent discussions on the Communist Party's EC revealed a rift within Eurocommunist ranks. One section led by Martin Jacques wanted to liquidate the CP as a party (a view he had held secretly since 1982) and turn it into a *Marxism Today* intellectual support group close to the Kinnockites; on the other side, Nina Temple, Monty Johnstone, Pete Carter and Chris Myant, in alliance with McLennan and other pragmatists, wanted to transform it into a broad left party working in alliances with the Greens and 'new social forces' on the basis of a revised *BRS*. As for *Marxism Today*, the EC agreed to new printing and editorial board arrangements which, in effect, cut it adrift from any Party control. Having already given up the battle for control of the *Morning Star*, this left the EC with *7 Days* as its only regular voice to the outside world. Yet the paper was losing around £1,000 a week as sales sank to well below 5,000.

The *Morning Star* had also gone into a major crisis. Its 'Survival Plan' had failed to secure enough commercial work – notably from the trade unions – for the new press. The Farringdon Road building had been sold and the CCG had decamped to a cramped office in Luke Street near the paper's temporary new premises. PPPS secretary Rosser and editor Chater addressed six well-attended meetings of shareholders and supporters across Britain in the autumn, explaining the problems and intended solutions.

The Communist Party's 40th congress in November 1987 opened a new phase in its disintegration. Membership had declined to 10,350. Nonetheless, delegates rejected by a ratio of three-to-one a West Middlesex resolution to revoke the expulsions and suspensions. In the wake of the Single European Act signed by Prime Minister Thatcher, which accelerated the political and economic integration of the European Community, delegates also declined to launch a campaign for Britain's withdrawal. However, they gave qualified support to one of the Tory government's flagship policies, namely, the sale of council houses to tenants and into the private housing market. The congress mandated the incoming EC to produce a revised new draft of the *BRS*. For their part, the Eurocommunist 'transformers' and their pragmatist allies proclaimed the 40th congress as their final victory over the forces of fundamentalism and sectarianism in the CP, by which they meant over the *Morning Star* and Straight Left supporters.

Immediately afterwards, the CCG issued a broadsheet asking 'Which way for the Communist Party?' Assessing the congress, it argued that this constituted something more fundamental than a 'setback' or the 'hardening of a temporary aberration'. No, the event 'marked a decisive turning point in the affairs of the Party', demonstrating that it was no longer possible to overturn the revisionist policies of the leadership from within. Through gerrymandering, 101 expulsions and in London more than 600 exclusions, a congress grossly unrepresentative of Britain's Communists had been manufactured. Whereas the EC candidates had been defeated by a ratio of three-to-one in a vote of 3,000 PPPS shareholders – the overwhelming majority of them Communists – at the 1986 AGM, the ratio had been reversed in the 175-55 vote at congress to dismiss 21 appeals against expulsions from the Party. The vote to abolish Rule 15(b) committing members to buy, sell and support the *Morning Star* had been carried by 180 votes to 46. Moreover, the decision to review the Party's structures and procedures, together with the collapse of the YCL to just 44 members and the imminent financial bankruptcy that would probably force the sale of Party centre at St John's Street, central London, were the organisational counterparts to the abandonment of the Party's principles. During the congress itself, there had been minimal discussion of moves away from such fundamental policies as support for the AES, withdrawal from the European Community and opposition to wage controls. The majority of delegates fully embraced the 'Thatcherism' thesis and, in effect, cancelled the Party's election-time disavowal of Hobsbawm's call for tactical voting and electoral pacts with the SDP-Liberal Alliance. Here, according to the CCG, was the intended culmination of all the organisational measures: 'the official transformation, at this Congress, of the Communist Party into a social democratic party'. What is more, the undemocratic, administrative measures made the transformation irreversible.

This was the message propagated in public meetings and the *Morning Star* over the following weeks by Hicks, Robinson, Lysandrou, new national organiser Nidge Tovey and other CCG speakers. The CCG issued a press statement on January 8, 1988, taking on the responsibility of working with other Communists and their Party and ex-Party organisations in regions across Britain to elect a congress preparations committee (CPC). The latter would then organise a 're-establishment congress' at which a new executive committee would be elected. The Communist Campaign Group would place all its resources at the disposal of the CPC and dissolve itself at the opening of the congress. A £25,000 congress appeal was launched by treasurer Monty Goldman to this end. The CCG's position – initially resisted by Robinson and others – was that the Communist Party could only be re-established on the basis of its existing democratic-centralist rules, Marxist-Leninist principles and programme, *The British Road to Socialism*. Hence the CCG's unwillingness to accept an offer of talks from the New Communist Party, which had opposed the *BRS* since its own foundation in 1977. As far as the CCG was concerned, the programme was not negotiable because it could only be amended after re-establishment, once the Party's democratic structures and processes had been restored.

Responding to these plans, the Straight Left faction saw no major political differences between the CCG 'splitters' and the party leadership, viewing any attempt to set up an alternative party as an irrelevant exercise in disruption that would not re-unite Marxist-Leninists. Once again, the tiny band of interlopers behind *The Leninist* proclaimed their unique fitness to 'reforge' the party, while continuing to predict the imminent demise of the *Morning Star*, the CCG and any re-established communist party. True to its own pretensions, the grouplet later renamed itself the 'Communist Party of Great Britain', changed its organ to the *Weekly Worker* and thereafter devoted itself to infiltrating, disrupting and attacking almost every genuinely communist and socialist party and alliance in Britain.

With the formation of the preparations committee and its production of a 'Perspectives' discussion paper, the 'Re-establishment Congress' was set for April 23-24 in London. CCG and CP branches and advisories applied for representation, together with the majority sections of the West Middlesex and East Midlands district committees and a CCG Youth Section led by Kenny Coyle which began publishing the *Young Communist* journal. On the opening day, 145 voting delegates attended representing 1,591 people who had signed the petition in support of re-establishment. Opening the congress from the chair, Mike Hicks saluted the three forces which, united, could and would defeat imperialism: the socialist countries, the national liberation movements and the international working class. He cited the recent battles of the miners, the printworkers and the nurses, the fight for peace and against unemployment, racism and sexism. The ruling class and its Tory government were conducting the class struggle on these and other fronts, but with no effective opposition from the Labour Party. What was missing was any input or influence from a communist party. Ten years of 'inept and reformist' leadership had slashed the Party's membership from 30,000 to 7,000, on paper. After five successive Eurocommunist general secretaries, the YCL had now been 'totally liquidated'. After a long period of gerrymandering, the 'reformists' and 'liquidationists' were in control of the St John Street headquarters and 'want to destroy the *Morning Star* and turn the Party into another reformist group'. He predicted: 'When the assets run out they will liquidate the Communist Party'. But the Party was neither its name nor its assets, 'it is its policies and principles and people prepared to fight for it'. This re-establishment congress was the living proof that the Marxist-Leninist Communist Party was alive 'to take on the enormous historic struggle facing us in Britain today'.

Delivering the main political report, Tony Chater welcomed the Soviet Union's proposals for nuclear disarmament and the policies for *perestroika* (restructuring) and *glasnost* (openness) which were breaking down hostile stereotypes of the socialist system. He wanted to see a mass movement throughout the world 'to force the dominant sections of the ruling class to accept a new system of international relations based on peaceful co-existence and cooperation'. Alongside the struggles against imperialism in South Africa, Palestine and Nicaragua, Communists should not forget Northern Ireland. The Party had a responsibility to involve the British labour movement in the campaign for a democratic solution which 'respects the national rights of the Irish people, ends sectarian divisions, and leads to the ending of partition'. His class-based analysis of so-called 'Thatcherism' in the midst of the international crisis of capitalism highlighted its authoritarian as well as its economic and social aspects. The material basis of reformism was being removed, opening up opportunities for the left as reformists promoted a 'new realism' which fully accepted capitalism in words as well as deeds.

Significantly, the *Morning Star* editor expressed regret that some forces prominent in the inner-party battle against revisionism had not joined the re-establishment process. He did not name them, but he had in mind the likes of former industrial organiser Bert Ramelson, PPPS chair and TASS general secretary Ken Gill (who had just served a term as the first-ever Communist president of the TUC) and former deputy general secretary of the Tobacco Workers Union Terry Marsland, a champion of women's rights in the trade union movement. They had judged the move to be 'premature' in a series of discussions with the CCG, where joint work had also been planned. Gill eventually joined the re-established party.

Talks to create wider communist unity would continue, Chater told the congress, but there would no place for factions within the re-established Communist Party. They created division. His recommendations from the congress preparations committee that the Party should drop the word 'Great' from its name, to avoid legal complications, and that the incoming EC should appoint a commission to prepare an updated draft of the *BRS*, were agreed by delegates after a brief discussion. Derek Robinson concluded the main political session before Photis Lysandrou and Tom Durkin opened and closed a discussion on peace and internationalism. Scottish TUC assistant general secretary Doug Harrison and Peter Ritman introduced sessions on the labour movement and 'Building the Party', respectively, while Ron Bellamy and Kevin Halpin responded. Andrew Clark and Mary Rosser opened and closed on the *Morning Star* which the congress declared to be 'the Party's number one priority'. Rule 15(b) requiring members to support the paper was restored to the Party's constitution. The emotional high-point of the proceedings was a special presentation by Mike Hicks to 'our number one Bolshevik', Andrew Rothstein, a founder member of the Communist Party in 1920 and former president of the Marx Memorial Library and the British-Soviet Friendship Society.

The Re-establishment Congress ended traditionally, with the singing of *The Internationale* and a brief meeting of the newly elected EC. Among its 33 members, besides the main speakers at the congress, were leading trade union activists such as Judy Cotter, Richard Maybin and Ivan Beavis (all NALGO), Jan Warhust and Jack Evans (NUT), Mike McLoughlin (TASS), unemployment and anti-fascist campaigner Alec McFadden, Scottish CND leader Alan Mackinnon, unemployment marcher Alan Millington, historians Mary Davis and John Foster and – signifying the intention to re-establish the Young Communist League – Kath Campbell.

At the first meeting of the Communist Party of Britain (CPB) executive committee, Mike Hicks defeated Derek Robinson by 17 votes to 14 to become the general secretary. Hugely admired and an almost legendary figure in the labour movement, 'Red Robbo' had worked tirelessly to build support for the CCG and re-establishment in meetings across Britain. Hicks had marshalled and inspired thousands of pickets at Wapping before being detained at her majesty's pleasure. He had the support of key CCG figures such as Tony Chater and Mary Rosser. Subsequently, Robinson was elected unopposed as the Party's chair and Kevin Halpin as industrial organiser.

Over the following period, the CPB rebuilt branch, district and advisory organisation at local, district and national levels and the YCL was re-established along with its journal *Challenge*. Campaigning materials were produced on the Poll Tax, peace, equal pay for women and South African apartheid and pamphlets published on *Women and Class* (by Mary Davis) and *70 Years of Struggle: Britain's Communist Party* (by Joe Berry).

Having refused to recognise the legitimacy of the 40th congress gerrymandered by the Eurocommunists, the re-established CPB held its own 40th congress in November 1989. Left-wing Labour MP Jeremy Corbyn welcomed delegates to his north London constituency. On this occasion, 30 communist parties, national liberation movements and embassies from around the world – notably from Vietnam, South Africa, Namibia, India, Iran, Egypt, Nicaragua, the USA, Korea and Finland – attended or sent messages of solidarity. A representative of the African National Congress received a thunderous reception. An updated draft of *The British Road to Socialism* (renamed *Britain's Road to Socialism* in 2001) was amended and adopted by the 170 voting delegates representing 1,681 members. This new edition removed much of the reformist or ambiguous content of the previous one. It was made clear that the Party was proposing a 'democratic anti-monopoly alliance' in which the organised working class would be the leading force in the struggle to open the way to socialism. An organised mass movement outside parliament would create and combine with a socialist parliamentary majority and a Labour government of a 'completely new type' to implement and enforce an Alternative Economic and Political Strategy (whose new name repudiated the accusation against the AES of 'economism'). The formulation was changed later to that of a parliamentary majority of Labour, socialist and communist MPs and a 'left government' rather than a 'new type' of Labour government.

The CPB 40th congress also decided to launch a party-wide discussion on energy and the environment and the upheavals in the Soviet Union and the eastern European socialist countries. These upheavals were such that the Soviet authorities halved their 12,000 daily import of the *Morning Star* from the following January. More controversially, delegates voted – against the recommendation of the EC – by 99 to 59 to hold a 'consultative conference on communist unity' with communists outside the CPB. This eventually took place in January 1991 following a series of joint leadership meetings with the NCP. The conference emphasised the value of joint work which might create the basis for more formal means of coordination, but proved inconsequential. The differences of 1977-78 over the *BRS*, Communist Party electoral policy and an uncritical attitude towards the socialist countries were never far from the surface. A more fruitful unity process took place four years later, when a breakaway group from Straight Left calling itself Communist Liaison, together with other communists involved along with CPB members in 'Communist Trade Unionists', made individual applications to join the CPB by collective agreement with the latter's EC. Although initially resisted by general secretary Hicks and his closest allies in the CPB leadership, the influx of Nick Wright, Andrew Murray, Anita Wright, Graham Stevenson and others enormously strengthened vital aspects of the Party's work.

By then, the Eurocommunist party had come to end. The final descent began soon after the CPB's re-establishment congress. Ignoring their own congress mandate to revise the *BRS*, the drafting group appointed by the Eurocommunist EC produced an entirely different document, 'Facing Up to the Future'. Published as a *Marxism Today* supplement in September 1988, it was primarily the work of *Financial Times* journalist Charlie Leadbeater assisted by Martin Jacques and Beatrix Campbell. Three of the other drafters – Bill Innes, Marian Darke and Monty Johnstone – dissociated themselves from it because of the document's 'failure to recognise the centrality of the class struggle in capitalist Britain today' and its meagre mention of the socialist alternative in just two paragraphs. An amended version was published as *A Manifesto for New Times* in March 1989. This, in essence, disowned the legacy of the Bolshevik Revolution and the Soviet Union and, ironically, largely adopted economism's narrow interpretation of 'class politics' so these had no more significance than the politics of gender, race and the environment. Indeed, the *Manifesto* itself was shot through with another form of 'economism', namely, the notion that 'post-Fordist' technological development in itself – almost divorced from class exploitation and political power – drives economic, social, political and ideological change. No longer was the working class seen as the force which could and must take control of the present, lead a revolutionary transition to socialism and so determine the future.

On the eve of the Eurocommunist party's congress in November 1989, *Marxism Today* editor Martin Jacques published the writing on the wall in a typically provocative editorial. Adopting the terminology of the Communist Party's sworn enemies on the right and the far left, he welcomed the systemic crisis in the Soviet Union and eastern Europe: 'The stalinist system has finally floundered. It has reached the point of no return. But it is not simply the end of stalinism. In an important sense it is the end of leninism'. Out of the collapse, he claimed, would come 'real gains' in a 'socialist renaissance' for the Western left and its intellectuals. Presenting the main political report to the congress on behalf of the EC, he elaborated: 'Leninism – its theory of the state, its concept of the party, the absence of civil society, its notion of revolution – has also had its day'. The party in Britain would have to undertake a 'no-holds-barred' public discussion about its own future, with all options open including mergers, a name change, abandoning democratic centralism, adopting different forms of membership and even creating a loose association in place of a party because 'we have no future as we are'.

Having postponed his retirement as general secretary, Gordon McLennan led the pragmatists, residual Marxist-Leninists and a section of the Eurocommunists to a final Pyrrhic victory over the more revisionist Eurocommunists. By a slight majority, they amended *A Manifesto for New Times* to affirm the centrality of class struggle and the role of the Communist Party. The Labour Party was still the 'central force' to defeat 'Thatcherism', but should form electoral alliances with others such as the Liberal Democrats and the Greens. An attempt by West Lewisham delegate Bert Ramelson to refer back the *Manifesto* and carry out the mandate from the previous congress to update the *BRS* instead was heavily defeated. An attempt by five districts to adopt only those parts of the *Manifesto* explicitly discussed and agreed – leaving the *BRS* more or less intact as the party's programme – was rejected 112 votes to 86. Thus, the Manifesto officially became the new programme of the Eurocommunist party. But the 'liquidationists' suffered a defeat at the hands of the 'transformers' and the pragmatists in a debate on *Marxism Today*. Its contents and distance from the party were heavily criticised, especially when the journal and its promotional events had received a subsidy of more than £68,000 over the previous two years, driving the treasurer to resign. After its spectacular increases in circulation to reach 15,600 a month, the figures were now falling. Somewhat pointedly, delegates agreed to renew the sales drive for *7 Days* as a 'communist newspaper'.

Within weeks of the congress, the 'transformers' and pragmatists used their enhanced position on the new EC to elect Nina Temple as general secretary. She inherited a summer membership figure of 7,615. Within two years it had shrunk to 4,742. As communist party rule and the socialist systems in the Soviet Union and eastern Europe disintegrated, so did the Eurocommunist party in Britain. Unable to have any impact on mass campaigning or industrial action, the EC decided in January 1990 to launch a debate about the party's future. The September meeting decided by 19 votes to 13 to 'transform' their party and build broad alliances rather than simply dissolve it. A special congress at the end of 1990 abandoned the formal commitment to Marxism-Leninism and proposed a possible change of name to one of 21 other titles. By the summer of 1991, almost 3,000 members from across the ideological spectrum had left the rudderless and sinking ship.

The EC recommended the adoption of a new name – the 'Democratic Left' – and a constitution based on decentralism and federalism instead of democratic centralism. In November 1991, shortly before another congress to agree these proposals, the *Sunday Times* threatened to publish sparse details from a file in the Kremlin archives about funds given by the CPSU to the CP in Britain. Former assistant general secretary Reuben Falber was then persuaded by Nina Temple and former *Daily Worker* and *Morning Star* editor George Matthews to provide further details in the Party's fortnightly journal *Changes*. Unknown to most Party members and officers, cash had been received via the Soviet embassy since 1958, reaching £100,000 at one point in the 1960s and dropping to around £14,000 during the following decade before ending in 1979. Much of the money had been distributed between the *Morning Star*, clandestine parties overseas and pensions for retired Party and Comintern officials. Horrified that British Communists had, like other parties and national liberation movements around the world, accepted financial solidarity from the Soviet Union, Jacques and Beatrix

Campbell were among those Eurocommunists who promptly resigned from the CP as it lay on its death-bed.

At the congress itself, delegates voted by a ratio of two-to-one to adopt the EC's proposals, thereby embracing 'a politics drawing from creative Marxism, feminism, anti-racism, ecology and other progressive traditions'. Scottish members unhappy with the name change and influenced by developments in their own country set up the Communist Party of Scotland. Supported by Mick McGahey and Gordon McLennan, it joined the movement for Scottish independence and eventually dissolved itself into the Scottish Socialist Party. Having briefly floated free from the Party several years before, *Marxism Today* folded the following month. Its ideological legacy soon resurfaced – albeit in a distorted form – in the anti-working class, anti-socialist and pro-European Union politics of 'New Labour'. Over the next two years, membership of the Democratic Left slumped to 1,234. Subsequently, the organisation mutated into the New Times Network and then the New Politics Network, taking with it most of the Communist Party's financial and property assets before vanishing along with them into a myriad of non-party initiatives.

As for the re-established Communist Party, it took more than a decade to rebuild its basic organisational and campaigning capacity to even a small fraction of what it had been at the beginning of the long, existential crisis in the early 1980s. At the top of the CPB, Mike Hicks was re-elected general secretary until 1998, while Richard Maybin succeeded Derek Robinson in the chair. *Communist Review* became the Party's theoretical journal and *Communist News* was launched as an internal paper.

By the late 1990s, the Communist Party was ready to play a bigger part in the labour and progressive movements, building old and new alliances, regaining some of the ground it had lost in the trade unions. The *Morning Star* had survived – despite a 3,000 cut in the Soviet order in 1991 and its total cancellation by the Boris Yeltsin regime in 1992 – and was poised to transform itself under editor John Haylett and his deputy Bill Benfield into a paper in which trade unions would want to play a direct role, based on a large financial commitment, while also respecting the editorial line based on *Britain's Road to Socialism* agreed at successive PPPS AGMs. As the international Communist movement was reconstructed, the CPB participated fully in bilateral relations and the annual meeting of Communist and workers' parties from around the world.

But recovery from the crisis of 1982-88 took far longer than many of those involved in the Party's re-establishment would ever have imagined at the time. That is because the crisis was the most serious and damaging in the history of the Communist Party in Britain. While having its own, ultimately decisive internal characteristics, including the accumulation of differences going back to the late 1960s, it also reflected – and was related to – a wider crisis in the British labour movement and an historic crisis in the international Communist movement. What distinguished it more than anything else from previous crises in the Party's history was that one of the contending forces in the inner-party struggle had lost any commitment it may once have had to the existence of a Marxist-Leninist communist party in Britain; the leading Eurocommunists actively sought the transformation of the Party into a fundamentally different kind of organisation and, if that could not be achieved, its destruction. In the end, they failed on both counts.

4

'Red Robbo': Derek Robinson – a giant of the labour movement (1927-2017)

Funeral oration, 22 November, 2017

Derek was a 20th century giant of the labour movement. He led the car workers of Longbridge in hundreds of battles to win dignity and a share of the value they produced by what was often their arduous, intensive and soul-destroying work. But he also recognised that advances and reforms won under capitalism could be clawed back by greedy and ruthless employers. That's why he joined the Communist Party and argued the necessity for revolutionary change and socialism.

Derek also played a central role in the struggle to safeguard the *Morning Star* and the existence of Britain's Communist Party. He worked tirelessly to build the Communist Campaign Group of party members expelled or excluded by the CPGB's revisionist leadership in the 1980s. His contribution made him the obvious choice to chair the re-established Communist Party of Britain in 1988.

How the ruling class and its media hated 'Red Robbo' – and how they feared him as well! He was always clear that it was the Communist Party that made him a working class fighter, a Marxist and a Communist. We are as proud of him as he was of his party.

What drove workers in their hundreds and thousands – many with family and financial responsibilities – to down tools and leave their benches, desks and assembly lines? Not once, but reputedly 523 times.

Not the power of one man, not even if that man was Derek Robinson, labelled 'Red Robbo' by the hostile mass media – a badge, incidentally, that he wore with pride.

No, it was the deep human desire for dignity, respect, recognition and reward, in the face of what Karl Marx called the 'alien and dominating force' of the machine.

Derek Robinson led those workers because he had earned their loyalty. He had inspired them to fight for decent pay and working conditions. And when he was sacked for putting forward an alternative to a misnamed 'Rescue Plan' that would sink 25,000 jobs at the British Leyland factory, more than 30,000 car workers walked out or barricaded themselves inside the factories.

That's not mentioned in Derek's obituary on the BBC website.

But we know it happened. It was even reported in a secret telegram sent by the US embassy in London to the Department of State in Washington DC on November 23, 1979.

Of course, the Americans knew all about the collusion between BL management, right-wing trade union leaders, the Thatcher government and the Security Service, MI5, to sack Derek Robinson, to undermine the mass resistance and so send a message to shop stewards across Britain: 'If we can get rid of "Red Robbo", we can get rid of you'.

One US embassy telegram refers to Derek as a 'shrewd, calculating, determined tactician'.

Those were indeed some of the qualities with which he served the working class. But we know that he was much more than that.

I have many fond personal memories of Derek, who came to south Wales on numerous occasions to address Communist Campaign Group, Communist Party of Britain, *Morning Star* and Liaison Committee for the Defence of Trades Unions meetings. When TUC tutor Pete Foley and I arranged for him to speak at a packed meeting of shop stewards in Bridgend, the right-wing district leadership of the engineering workers tried to ban union officials and stewards from attending. Some hope! The stewards loved his talk, in which he linked their industrial lives with the vision of socialism.

But my abiding memory of Derek was meeting him in the Social Club before we went together to march with the Party against the proposed closure of Longbridge. Everywhere we went, he was mobbed by workers who told him he had been proved right after all. Some were crying as they apologised for not having fought harder to save his job in 1979, when the Thatcher government, British Leyland bosses, MI5, Special Branch and the right-wing AEU leadership colluded in his sacking. He had put his name to an alternative plan to make new models, find new markets and save the thousands of jobs at Longbridge.

For thousands of his fellow workers, comrades, friends and family members, he was a warm, considerate, courageous and inspirational man. His was no vain or wasted life.

He went on to work for the *Morning Star* and played a leading role in the struggles to save the existence of our movement's precious daily paper, and to re-establish the Communist Party in Britain, becoming the Party's chair in 1988.

Derek Robinson was a giant of the labour movement. He was proud of his party – and his party will forever be proud of him.

Derek Robinson addressing a mass meeting

5

Not our history

Review of Geoff Andrews, Endgames and New Times: The Final Years of British Communism 1964-1991 *(2004).* Morning Star, *23 August 2004*

This is the sixth – and by far the worst – volume of Lawrence and Wishart's history of the Communist Party in Britain. It is partial in every sense of the word: a narrow-minded exercise in vanity publishing.

Coverage of the Party's central role in such momentous battles as the defeat of the Industrial Relations Act, the release of the jailed Pentonville Five dockers, the workers occupation of the Upper Clyde Shipbuilders, the 1972 and 1974 miners' strikes and the heroic strike by Asian women workers at Grunwick is either sketchy, shallow or non-existent.

The work, some of it clandestine, of party organisations and leading communists in CND, the Anti-Apartheid Movement, the Chile Solidarity Campaign and elsewhere does not feature at all.

The Communist-led struggle to defeat Enoch Powell's racist support among London dockers likewise goes unmentioned.

Communist organisation and influence in the trade union movement – out of all proportion to the Party's numerical size – is depicted mostly in terms of inner-party division and crisis. Any advances and victories are treated as fleeting exceptions to the rule of 'militant labourism' in decline.

The party's effective industrial organisers Bert Ramelson and Mick Costello are portrayed as slightly sinister Svengali-like figures, fighting a rearguard action for 'Stalinism'.

The heroes of Geoff Andrews's unfolding saga are those to whom he refers on almost every page of the book as the 'British Gramscians'. Organised as a faction in the Party from the late 1960s as the 'Smith Group' and then the 'Party Group,' so we are informed, they promoted ideas which bore little or no relation to those of the 1920s Italian Communist leader Antonio Gramsci.

Through their bulletins and other factional publications, in party organisations and alternative resolutions, they championed wage restraint, social partnership and an anti-Marxist variety of feminism.

In this, they were assisted by objective developments in the economy, society and in the composition of the working class which posed new challenges to the trades unions, the left and the Communist Party.

A party leadership unable to apply Marxism-Leninism to changing conditions opened the door to the 'Eurocommunists' who were asking important questions – but who were also proposing disastrously wrong answers.

Andrews reports the ensuing debates and controversies in a wholly one-eyed way.

The case of those who insisted that Britain's class-divided society must remain the context for the Party's policies and strategy has to be deduced from the extensive coverage given to the Gramscians and a supporting cast of non-party sociology academics.

Communists who defended any positive achievement or feature of the Soviet Union are dismissed as reciting 'the Soviet Mantra' – a politically illiterate term which even finds its way into the book's index.

In their struggle to control the daily *Morning Star* newspaper and liquidate the Communist Party, the Eurocommunists and their revisionist patrons carried out the biggest purge in the party's history, closing down entire organisations, expelling 101 members and deregistering another 600 or more.

The Communist Campaign Group provided a vital focus for the fight-back which guaranteed the continuation of the Party and paper.

Andrews compresses these events into a single short paragraph, referring to the 'irony' that 'the leadership was using democratic centralism to its full capacities in dealing with dissidents'.

Whole chapters are devoted, on the other hand, to the forward march of the British Gramscians and what became their house journal, *Marxism Today*.

Perhaps it is post-modern Whiggishness, but the consequent destruction of the Young Communist League, the Party's once-powerful national students' organisation, the Communist University and, eventually, of a section of the Party and of *Marxism Today* itself is presented as an onward and upward vindication of their ideas.

The author appears to have interviewed only those protagonists with whom he agreed at the time.

Although such 'dissidents' as Kevin Halpin, Ken Gill, John Foster, John Kelly, Jean Styles, Derek Robinson, Marj Mayo and Charlie Wolfson are mentioned – some frequently – in the book, none of them were similarly consulted. But, then, as current members of the Communist Party of Britain, they have, like the Party, apparently ceased to exist.

That the most mentioned name of all is that of Antonio Gramsci is bitterly ironic. It is only a footnote of history, but I was expelled from the Party in 1986 for publishing a lecture asking 'Was Gramsci a Eurocommunist?'

Gramsci lived and died a Marxist and a Communist. Today, not a single one of Andrews' Gramscian heroes would even want to claim the same

6

Gordon McLennan: 'A heavy responsibility' (1924-2011)

Morning Star, 25 May 2011

Gordon McLennan, former Communist Party of Great Britain general secretary died of cancer on Saturday May 21 at the age of 87.

He was born in Glasgow on May 12 1924, shortly after the very first Labour government took office.

He joined the Young Communist League as a 15-year-old, serving on its executive committee from 1942 to 1947. During this period, as McLennan became an engineering draughtsman, he was reputedly involved in strike action by the engineering and shipbuilding apprentices on Clydeside.

His skills as a capable organiser and an expressive public speaker soon marked him out for full-time Communist Party work. Those talents flourished as he became the party's Glasgow city organiser, then city secretary, Scottish organiser and, in 1956, Scottish secretary. The following year, McLennan was elected to the executive committee at British level.

Always a keen advocate of independent Communist Party participation in elections, he contested Glasgow Govan in the 1959, 1964 and 1966 general elections, the West Lothian by-election in 1962 and St Pancras North in the general elections of 1970 and February 1974.

As the Party's national organiser between 1966 and 1975, he contributed to an upturn in membership and influence inside the labour movement.

However, his responsibilities also included relations with the Young Communist League, where he failed to caution the new revisionist leadership of the YCL against its enthusiasm for unelecting, suspending and expelling political critics.

He succeeded John Gollan as Communist Party general secretary in 1975, continuing the party's tendency to elect leaders from a skilled working class background.

Initially, McLennan's reputation was as a force for party unity. He had not been prominent in the inner-party debate about such contentious issues as the 1968 Soviet intervention in Czechoslovakia. He agreed with the Party in opposing it, albeit with reservations, but had said little while Bert Ramelson sharply condemned the Soviets and Rajani Palme Dutt condemned the condemners.

Upon learning from Gollan that the Soviet party provided its British counterpart with secret funding, McLennan claimed to have asked for it to cease, although assistant general secretary Reuben Falber continued to take annual delivery for another four years.

Nonetheless, and under McLennan's leadership, Britain's Communist Party aligned itself with declarations from the Spanish, French and Italian communists about the necessity of a democratic, constitutional transition to a socialism that would bear little if any relation to the Soviet model.

At the same time, he disavowed the term Eurocommunism, insisting that it was neither accurate nor useful. Rather, it was 'intended to create differences in the communist movement'.

But with McLennan's patronage, the doors to senior positions in the Party were thrown open to the self-styled Gramscians, Eurocommunists and revolutionary democrats.

Certainly, changes in the economy, society, the working class and the labour movement were throwing up new questions and challenges or older ones in new forms. But instead of making a Marxist wysis of new realities, the leadership majority headed by McLennan handed the intellectual baton to a faction congealing around *Marxism Today*, nominally the Party's theoretical and discussion journal.

Like many good orators, McLennan himself wrote very little of any analytical quality.

The Eurocommunists launched a concerted offensive against class-based conceptions of political struggle, democracy and state power. Trade union militants and working class intellectuals were marginalised or excluded from the Party's intellectual work.

When CPGB members, especially in the trade unions and at the *Morning Star*, mobilised to defend class politics and the Soviet Union, the self-proclaimed 'anti-Stalinists' led the call for disciplinary action.

Tragically, McLennan sided with those he regarded as bringing fresh ideas and dynamism into the Party, while basing his stance selectively on party rules rather than on Marxist-Leninist politics.

Yet the evidence was there – in the sharp decline of the YCL and the disintegration of the once powerful national students committee – that the Eurocommunists were driving the Party towards the swamp.

Nevertheless, as general secretary, McLennan presided over the biggest purge in the history of the Communist Party in Britain.

At the London district congress in November 1984, he intervened personally to oppose the election of a new district committee, leading a minority walkout with the words 'All those who support the Communist Party of Great Britain, follow me'.

Elected district committees were dissolved. Hundreds of party members, including *Morning Star* editor Tony Chater, PPPS secretary Mary Rosser and leading trade unionists Ken Gill, Derek Robinson, Terry Marsland and Ken Brett were expelled, deregistered or excluded.

As more communists and their left allies came to realise the extent of the liquidationist danger, the *Morning Star* was kept out of Eurocommunist clutches.

McLennan came under heavy fire from Soviet communist officials about articles in *Marxism Today*. In March 1985, Boris Ponomarev, head of the CPSU international department, accused him in Moscow of breaching proper relations between communist parties by allowing ill-informed, one-sided attacks on the Soviet Union.

The diaries of deputy head Anatoly Chernyaev recount his own efforts to 'discipline' McLennan, claiming that the latter was 'confused' and 'no expert in debate', before concluding that 'he is too weak as a leader to make internationalist sentiments prevail at the CPGB'.

Yet many longstanding communists stayed with McLennan and the leadership majority, sure that he would steer a middle course between the "left sectarians" and the *Marxism Today* faction. In 1987, he was persuaded to continue holding the ring as general secretary of the CPGB.

It proved to be of no avail. The following year, many of the expelled and excluded comrades convened a congress to re-establish the Communist Party of Britain on the basis of its existing Marxist-Leninist principles and programme.

When McLennan eventually stood down in 1989, the liquidationists took full control of the remaining section of the CPGB. They officially renounced Marxism-Leninism in 1990 and changed its name to Democratic Left in 1991, as counter-revolution spread across eastern Europe and the Soviet Union.

A few years later, Democratic Left dissolved itself into the now defunct New Politics Network. Few noticed the death of the heavily subsidised *Marxism Today*.

By then, many in the previous leadership had abandoned ship, having allowed others to occupy the bridge and set course for the rocks.

As an emigre in London, McLennan aligned himself with the Communist Party of Scotland, which had sailed away from the wreckage. He undertook a short speaking tour under its auspices in 1992.

He had long championed the national, democratic rights of the Scottish and Welsh peoples, urging the Party to redouble its efforts after 1979 to help convince the labour movement of the case for devolution.

His main post-CPGB political activity was carried out in the Lambeth Pensioners Action Group. He was still able to deliver a stirring speech and once led a lie-down protest near Westminster Bridge in protest at New Labour's betrayal of pensioners.

Also active in the anti-war movement, he supported Respect candidate George Galloway in Bethnal Green and Bow in the 2005 general election, posing for photographs with Galloway and veteran anti-fascist Harold Rosen in front of the Cable Street mural.

McLennan remained a keen *Morning Star* reader to the end, which followed a long battle against cancer. His last word in the paper was in February 2008, when he had a letter published congratulating PCS general secretary Mark Serwotka on his support for fair voting.

'At last, at last! A leader of our present-day labour movement comes out publicly for "proportional representation in all elections," as William Gallacher Communist MP for West Fife advocated over 60 years ago in his evidence to the speakers conference on electoral reform. Well done Mark Serwotka', he wrote.

He is survived by wife Mary – with whom he often shared a memorable duet at social events, singing Rabbie Burns' 'My Love is like a Red, Red Rose' – sons Tom, Gregor and Johnny, and daughter Fran.

Gordon McLennan will be remembered by many as a modest, polite comrade with a lively sense of humour.

Critics will also recall his heavy, personal responsibility for the liquidation of the old CPGB in a period when the British and US ruling classes were intensifying their anti-working class, anti-people offensive on a global scale.

7

A great editor and comrade: John Haylett (1945-2019)

Morning Star, 17 October 2019

John Haylett was born on June 8, 1945, on the eve of a General Election that would sweep away wartime Prime Minister Winston Churchill in a landslide victory for Labour.

Liverpool, his home city, was as united in this turn to the left politically as it was divided over religion and football. Born in a pub and brought up in a pre-fab, John like his younger brother Steve and their father Doug was an Everton supporter, while mam Marie followed Liverpool.

John's sister June helped keep the peace when their dad was away at sea. As the brightest boy in the class, he passed the 11-plus exam to go to the Liverpool Institute, a prestigious grammar school.

His contemporaries there included Paul McCartney, future newsreader John Sissons and Stephen Norris – later to become a Tory MP best known for his nocturnal exertions of the mostly horizontal kind. John was on chatting terms with Paul and his mate John before they went on to form the Beatles.

Football became one of young Haylett's abiding passions. He also tried his hands at boxing, but found it difficult to accept that the hostilities should end inside the ring, not outside the gym afterwards.

Some teachers and quite a few of the older, posher chaps at 'The Inny' looked down on those rough-and-ready pupils with the heavy Scouse accents. Unapologetic about his egalitarian views, John's early experiences of the class struggle often brought him home black-and-blue from the schoolyard.

But in the classroom, he learnt French and Russian. He also joined the Young Communist League and in 1963 the Communist Party. In what was still the era of the Cold War between the Soviet Union and US imperialism, he also enrolled in the Territorial Army. His motivation might have differed from that of his senior officers.

John's headteacher bridled at the prospect of sending this articulate, pugnacious young rebel to university, refusing to write him a reference until he stayed at school a little longer and moderated his attitude.

John drew upon his fluency in Anglo-Saxon English to tell the headmaster what he could do with his reference. Then it was out of the school gates with him and into the wider world.

He briefly took a job in a bank and spent much of his money on politicking and – more like normal young men in that city at that time – bevvying to the Merseybeat music and the gritty, witty rhythms of the Mersey Sound poets. This was the Liverpool of ex- and now anti-Communist Bessie Braddock – who showed a 'No Vacancies' notice to left-wing applicants for Labour Party membership, but also of ex-International Brigader and dockers' champion Jack Jones and Communist building workers' leader Bill Jones

At the age of 19, John left Liverpool never to live there again, although his love for that proletarian city and its people never left him.

For the next year or so, Monsieur Haylett travelled around France – not for the last time – before arriving in 'that London'. He worked as a grave-digger and then a croupier, quickly discovering that young women in the 'Swinging Sixties' found his Scouse accent somewhat alluring.

It was there he met his first wife, Anne, with whom he had his much-loved daughter Marianne. The marriage broke down as the couple grew apart.

Later, he married Cherry, whose beloved son Leroy joined them from Jamaica. A whole world of West Indian music, food, cricket and card-games in the pub opened up in John's wide new circle of relatives and friends.

His deep and militant opposition to racism sprang from a personal passion as well as political principle.

By this time, he had dug himself into the world's first International Telephone Exchange in Faraday House in the City, where his Russian came in handy. He quickly gained a reputation as a dedicated, well-organised and fearless fighter for his fellow members of the Union of Post Office Workers.

As secretary of the telecomms branch, local strike leader and a delegate to union conferences, he came across the rather more headstrong Bernie Grant, later the Labour MP for Tottenham. They remained friends despite some political differences.

In this period, too, John's commitment to the Anti-Apartheid Movement almost took a dramatic turn. He had come to know Ronnie Kasrils, who was recruiting young communists and socialists in Britain for clandestine work in South Africa for the African National Congress.

John duly acquired a passport in the name of 'John Lloyd', although the word never came from Ronnie or the ANC to use it. After the fall of apartheid, Kasrils subsequently became South Africa's Defence Minister.

After a stint at the ITE, John fulfilled his ambition to attend university and study Russian, French and economics. Newcastle obliged without a reference from his old headteacher. While there, he threw himself into the party locally and was elected to its Northern district committee. With Cherry choosing to remain in London, his second marriage suffered.

Returning to London, John he began what became a life-long commitment to solidarity with the revolutionary people of Grenada, working closely with Jacqui Mackenzie and other New Jewel Movement representatives in Britain and with one of his favourite people, the legendary Ivan Beavis.

In 1983, after a stint painting and decorating for Hackney Council, Haylett the news-hound was born. He joined the staff of the *Morning Star*, capable of writing and telling a story, but without any training in the noble and ignoble arts of the trade.

His appointment was controversial. Pressed by the so-called 'Eurocommunist' trend, the revisionist leadership of the Communist Party under Gordon McLennan wanted to liquidate the class-based and pro-Soviet politics of the 'daily paper for peace and socialism'. Now it was rumoured in the newsroom that editor Tony Chater was hitting back by – in the words of the then news editor Roger Bagley – 'putting this hard-man in'.

Bagley Sr. remembers the cub reporter as a fast and enthusiastic learner.

'We got a lot of graduates who felt they would "do two years at the paper" as a sort of contribution to the movement, but weren't really interested in learning journalism. But John picked up on everything', Roger recalled later, 'One day I said to him: "You never know when a story might drop – it pays to have an overnight bag ready in case you need to dash off somewhere". The very next day he came in with a bag with essentials. He was ready to be sent anywhere at any notice'.

That immediately meant a trek alongside the People's March for Jobs from Glasgow to London. His next big assignment was covering the 1984-85 miners' strike, not from an office in London but from the picket-lines and pit villages of the coalfields.

John went onto other, higher posts in the *Morning Star* – although his pay stayed the same. True to his roots, he and his close colleagues had little time for the pretentious, gossipy cliques of media intellectuals. 'We drank with the production workers', he once remarked.

In the Communist Party, his political judgment and tireless activism earned him an elected seat on the London district committee. Fearful that its position would be weakened at the forthcoming London district congress in November 1984, the party leadership suspended and – in John Haylett's case – expelled some leading London members and demanded that no new district committee be elected.

On November 24, McLennan in person called upon everyone present at the congress to follow him out of the hall. Most of the 250 delegates stayed put.

The most prominent dissidents – the 'London 22' – were quickly suspended from party membership. In January, the executive committee expelled Tony Chater, deputy editor David Whitfield, London district congress chair Mike Hicks and leading trade unionists Ivan Beavis and Tom Durkin. Others of the 22 were further suspended or expelled, including John's close comrade Mary Davis.

Soon afterwards, John gravitated towards the Communist Campaign Group set up by Chater, Hicks, victimised British Leyland convenor Derek Robinson and the secretary of the PPPS cooperative which owns the *Morning Star*, Mary Rosser.

But the main focus of his work remained the *Morning Star*. On the foreign desk, he cultivated his connections with leading South African Communists such as Jeremy Cronin and future president Thabo Mbeki.

After the CCG helped re-establish the Communist Party of Britain in 1988, he used his extensive knowledge and network to good effect as its international secretary. Bridges had to be repaired with communist parties and national liberation movements around the world, many of which were in retreat and disarray after the collapse and counter-revolution in the Soviet Union and Eastern Europe from 1991. John helped ensure the re-established party's swift recognition by parties and movements in the USA, North Korea, Ireland, South Africa, India and Russia.

At home, the rise of the neo-fascist British National Party and in violent racist attacks on our streets prompted the birth of the Anti-Racist Alliance. Its distinguishing features were a predominantly black leadership and a capacity to mobilise Britain's black and minority ethnic communities. But leading lights such as Marc Wadsworth also welcomed John Haylett onto its national committee as one of its most trusted members.

As the efficient and respected deputy editor of the *Morning Star*, it was widely assumed that John would be appointed to the top job in 1994 when Tony Chater announced his wish to retire. Mary Rosser and husband Mike Hicks preferred her news editor and son-in-law, which explained an insidious whispering campaign that had begun some time previously. A decision was postponed. Everything was then done to prevent the Communist Party's political and executive committees from making a recommendation – including the falsification of minutes and a claim that one entire meeting had been a figment in the imagination of Haylett's supporters!

Nevertheless, by the narrowest majority, the PPPS management committee appointed John Haylett the paper's editor the following year.

In 1997, John travelled with CPB general secretary Mike Hicks, Mary Rosser and chair Richard Maybin in a delegation to China in 1997. His series of articles in the *Morning Star* broke through many of the myths and distortions peddled from the right and the far-left about that country's phenomenal development.

The visit also confirmed John's view that his party desperately needed a change of leadership. Supported by Richard Maybin, he nominated me and rallied the discontented to win a 17-13 majority at the January 1998 executive committee.

Retribution was swift. Within weeks, Haylett was suspended by Mary Rosser for 'gross industrial misconduct'. For possibly the first and only time in the history of the national press in Britain, most of the staff went on strike to demand the reinstatement of their editor.

Local MP Jeremy Corbyn was one of many to turn up on the NUJ picket line in Ardleigh Rd, complete with bicycle. The journos decamped to nearby premises to produce editions of the *Workers' Morning Star*.

Settlement terms agreed between Rosser's supporters in the Socialist Action faction and me – known only to John Haylett – were rejected out of hand by the PPPS secretary. With her support draining away as the strikers stood solid for six weeks, the dispute went to mediation which found in favour of John Haylett on every count.

Back in post, John embarked upon an ambitious strategy to rescue the paper from financial collapse, soon backed by a new PPPS secretary Jenny Williams (followed by Richard Maybin), a newly elected management committee and the existing CPB executive. Henceforth the paper would seek to grow rather than cut its way out of permanent crisis.

John continued with his political work, particularly in the anti-war movement. He worked closely with Halifax MP Alice Mahon in the Committee Against War in the Gulf and campaigned against the US invasion of Afghanistan.

In November 2001, as he was addressing a 500-strong meeting in Oxford town hall, ex-US president Bill Clinton's daughter Chelsea made a noisy entrance with her security service bodyguards. Backed by a barracking chorus of aggressive Americans, she interrupted the *Morning Star* editor as he was condemning the lack of media coverage of the thousands of civilian casualties in Afghanistan.

'You should remember the victims of the 9/11 terrorist attacks in New York', she shouted out.

'That's why we hold meetings like this, so that alternative viewpoints can be heard', John replied, his paper having promptly and prominently condemned the mass murder of several thousand office workers on that day.

Ms Clinton reportedly bought a copy of the *Morning Star* shortly afterwards, on her way out of the meeting.

John's go-for-growth approach culminated in a complete relaunch of the paper in June 2009 as a 16-pager with extra colour and also online, overseen by John's loyal deputy and now successor Bill Benfield. John moved into the new post of political editor, which better suited his new life in Cardiff.

In the early 1990s, he had met Sian Cartwright at the Wales TUC conference in Llandudno. She had then moved to London to be with him, eventually securing a high-level position in the train drivers' union ASLEF, responsible for political education and industrial relations.

The union's dynamic left-wing general secretary Mick Rix, together with RMT general secretary Bob Crow, were opening up vital new areas of practical and political support for the *Morning Star* in the labour movement. Tony Benn and John Pilger wrote regular columns.

After Sian was appointed head of education with the Wales TUC in Cardiff, she moved back to the city and John happily went with her. They were comrades in arms, sharing a passion for good food, wine, European travel and political argument.

He learned to love rugby, while she never learned to stop hating football.

As the love of his life, Sian brought John a new family of children and grandchildren to cherish alongside his other much-loved tribes and two recent great-grandchildren.

Their wedding in a country manor near Cardigan, at which I was honoured to be the 'best man', brought colour to that locality in every way possible. Never had the good people of that Welsh-speaking town seen so many Caribbean faces all at once – and never had those wedding guests experienced such a warm welcome anywhere else in Britain.

John spent his last years helping to build the Communist Party, as a member of its Welsh Committee, and winning new friends for the *Morning Star*. He interviewed political leaders including Plaid Cymru's Leanne Wood and Welsh First Minister Mark Drakeford. He made the *Morning Star* the partner paper of the annual Merthyr Rising festival.

He remained as alert, incisive and knowledgable as ever. *Morning Star* editor Ben Chacko could always count on John for wise advice and the occasional barbed or congratulatory email.

Warm, witty and always ready to reconsider his views in the face of evidence and reasoned argument, the end came quickly after a superficially mild stroke.

On September 28, 2019, he died in Sian's arms, holding Marianne's hand – another giant of the labour and communist movement at rest after a lifetime of struggle, tribulations and the many joys of love and comradeship.

8

In defence of Palme Dutt

Review of John Callaghan, *Cold War, Crisis and Conflict: the CPGB 1951-1968* (2003) *Morning Star*, 27 December 2003

John Callaghan comes not to praise the Communist Party, but to bury it. His recent volume on the history of the Communist Party of Great Britain (CPGB) from 1951 to 1968 has the air of a funeral director who sneers at the corpse he is preparing.

This book is the fifth in the series commissioned by Lawrence and Wishart, itself a publishing house set up by the Communist Party and which has since floated free into the hands of its directors.

The first two volumes by James Klugmann, written in the late 1960s, chronicled the party's development up to and during the 1926 General Strike. Klugmann's work is that of a communist partisan, where most published histories of the Communist Party in Britain are partisanly anti-communist. While this makes for a refreshing change. it need not have excluded a more critical approach.

Noreen Branson's two contributions in 1985 and 1998 took the story up to 1951.

Unlike his predecessors, Callaghan cites internal party documents – especially where these can demonstrate division, dissent or duplicity.

He creates a negative impression of the Party from the beginning and reinforces it ad nauseam thereafter. Thus, the British party is introduced as one which is in 'subordination' and 'tutelage' to the Communist Party of the Soviet Union, with 'Moscow Gold' helping to establish a relationship of 'dependency'.

But the bulk of the evidence, even in this book, as elsewhere, is that British communists voluntarily accepted the leading role of the CPSU in the world revolutionary process, sincerely believed in mutual solidarity between communists and did not automatically parrot the Kremlin line.

From the early 1950s, Rajani Palme Dutt and then Idris Cox led the

CPGB's international work. Their international department orchestrated an impressive network of sections, committees and publications involving several hundred party members.

It provided information, advice and assistance – and participated in many clandestine operations which do not feature in this book – to the benefit of communist and workers' parties and national liberation movements across the world.

That is why, decades later, the names of Dutt and Cox are revered by numerous foreign communists and their parties. But Professor Callaghan knows or cares little of this. Instead, in this area of work as in every other, he prefers to dwell upon the weaknesses, failures, shortcomings and mistakes.

In particular, as the author of an antagonistic biography of Dutt subtitled *A Study in British Stalinism*, Callaghan is keen to add to his charge sheet against this 'factionalist' and 'opportunist'.

Dutt's 'formidable list of mistaken assumptions' about the international situation, the 'incoherence' of his economic analysis and his 'Leninist-Stalinist' perceptions are held chiefly responsible for the party's anachronistic post-war world-view. His book *Britain's Crisis of Empire* (1949) is singled out for a fearsome kicking.

Among Dutt's 'completely wrong' propositions are that the Soviet-led socialist bloc was going from strength to strength. Callaghan provides no proof or argument to the contrary because 'it is easy to see now'. Yet it is also indisputable that economic development. technological progress and military capacity increased at a faster rate in the socialist countries than in the West between the late 1940s and the early 1960s.

Second, Dutt believed that Soviet-style socialism could overcome racism, national chauvinism and economic backwardness. Again, the wrongness of this belief is merely asserted by Callaghan.

Were there not real achievements in these areas, especially in Czechoslovakia, Hungary and the Soviet Union itself? After all, the record compares favourably with that of capitalism there before and since the socialist period.

Third, Dutt supposedly claimed that Britain and the West depended on colonial possessions for their prosperity. In truth. Dutt made no such claim for the main Western imperialist power – the United States.

His claim in relation to Britain and western Europe up to World War Two is well argued and substantiated with official figures relating to trade, investment and profits. It was a claim voiced widely by the British ruling class itself.

Dutt also argued that the continuation of direct colonial rule would prove increasingly expensive, unpopular and unsustainable.

Against all this, our smiter of dead Stalinists triumphally poses the fatal contradiction at the heart of Dutt's anti-empire case.

How could 'the majority of the workers in an imperialist country share unconsciously in the exploitation ... of the colonial peoples' – Dutt's words – while at the same time the cost of this exploitation 'is imposing on the masses of the British people ever heavier burdens of taxation, higher prices and lowered standards?'

Let me explain this non-contradiction to our erudite professor. Dutt makes it clear that the working class – and then mainly the upper layers – receive only crumbs from imperialist exploitation.

In that sense and to that extent only do workers share in the exploitation, enjoying cheap imports and the cyclical job security made possible by cheap raw material inputs.

But they also bear a disproportionate share of the burden – paying taxes to finance the foreign and military costs of imperial exploitation, supplying the troops to fight the wars and suffering the consequences of domestic under-investment as capital is diverted into arms production or exported overseas.

There comes a point – if Callaghan can follow this – where the 'ever heavier burdens' outweigh the crumbs. Dutt provides figures to demonstrate that this point was arriving.

Britain's subsequent abandonment of direct colonial rule east of Suez and in Africa proved the perspicacity of what Callaghan loftily calls the 'somewhat strained communist argument' advanced by Dutt and others.

So we come to another of Dutt's 'completely wrong' propositions – that right-wing leaders dominate the British labour movement because of imperialist super-profits and the associated financial corruption of a layer of the working class.

Clearly, Callaghan must have an alternative explanation for the enthusiastic advocacy of empire, imperial exploitation and imperialist war by Labour Party and trade union leaders who are well rewarded politically and financially. We shall look forward to reading it.

A fifth 'completely wrong' proposition was that the revolt of the colonial and dependent peoples is 'the most powerful driving force, in unity with the revolt of the working class in the capitalist countries, in the transition from capitalism to socialism'.

Wherever Callaghan has found this quotation, it does not feature in *Britain's Crisis of Empire*, even though that is what the reader is likely to assume.

Dutt's position in his 1949 book is that the colonial peoples and their national liberation movements should be seen as important allies in the fight against imperialism and – by extension rather than immediately – against capitalism and for socialism. Nowhere does Dutt suggest that they are the most powerful driving force in the transition to socialism, with or without anyone else.

Dutt's 'completely wrong' proposition number six is that the surplus for British overseas investment derived historically – note, historically – from

Britain's manufacturing exports and so British imperialism is doomed as this source dries up.

Wolverhampton University's professor of politics corrects him: Britain's financial and commercial sector generated the surplus for overseas investment.

A footnote refers us for proof to a book published in New York nine years after Dutt's death which, sinisterly in Callaghan's view, was not reviewed in the CPGB press.

But wait, here is Dutt on pages 15 to 20 of *Britain's Crisis of Empire* (at least in my copy) showing how the surplus was at first generated by merchant capitalism through slavery, plunder and trade – in other words through the financial and commercial sectors – with minimal exports from Britain and then, only later, by manufacturing and exports.

Callaghan's desperation to discredit everything said and done by Dutt disfigures this volume of Communist Party history. He is markedly more unbalanced here than in his biography of Dutt, who was – whatever his faults – a consistent, principled and outstanding champion of colonial freedom.

Of course, Dutt and the British party could have acknowledged that British imperialism might survive the forthcoming collapse of empire, not only by retaining economic domination there, which they anticipated was a danger, but by diversifying foreign investment into western Europe and north America.

But they were – how can this be said without shocking Professor Callaghan – revolutionary communists who chose to advocate a fundamentally different course instead, namely a radical restructuring of the British economy and economic as well as political self-government for the colonies.

In 1956, Khrushchev's denunciation of Stalin at the 20th CPSU congress and the Soviet military intervention in Hungary shook the international communist movement to its foundations.

In response, Britain's Communist Party established a commission on inner-party democracy and, the following year, convened a special 25th congress. Some 11,000 members left the Party during this period – nearly one-third of the membership.

No proper history of the Party could fail to deal with this crisis in detail. But Callaghan is obsessed with it.

Not only does it have a deserved chapter of its own in what is a thematic book, rather than a chronological narrative, but it overshadows most other chapters and is frequently conjured up as a reference point for some setback or deficiency.

Yet the Party had recovered its membership loss by 1962. Throughout that decade, it retained around 30,000 members – twice the level of the successful pre-war Popular Front period.

9

Botched Autopsy

Review of John Callaghan, *Cold War, Crisis and Conflict: the CPGB 1951-1968* (2003) *Morning Star*, 29 December 2003

John Callaghan's new history of the Communist Party of Great Britain 1951-68 proclaims in its preface and on the back cover that the party is dead. From this false premise, our professor of politics proceeds to carry out an autopsy with evident pleasure.

Had he or his research staff consulted any of those named in the book who are still members of Britain's Communist Party today. they could have told him that rumours of the Party's demise are greatly exaggerated.

The Communist Party of Britain was re-established in 1988 on the basis of the existing rules, principles and programme of the CPGB. It is the heir and successor of the CPGB.

The revisionist leadership of the old CPGB succeeded only in liquidating their own section of the Party a few years later, having failed to take over and destroy the *Morning Star*.

It is inconceivable that Callaghan is unaware of the *Morning Star* and Communist Party's survival, the latter recognised by the UK Election Commission as the only party legitimately entitled to use the name and symbols of communism.

Perhaps Callaghan's ideological affinity with the *Marxism Today* clique which tried to shut down the paper and the Party has blinded him to the continuing existence of both. In any event, he is keen to demonstrate that the Party deserved to die.

Thus, almost every achievement of the CP between 1951 and 1968 is downplayed and then buried under a landslide of qualifications and criticisms. Every silver lining has a giant dark cloud.

For example, Callaghan reports the programme of campaigning activities undertaken by the Party's not untypical – his judgment – Lancashire and Cheshire District during 1952. Twelve marches on local, national and international issues and two May Day demonstrations mobilising 60,000 people in total. 200 factory gate meetings and 484 open-air meetings.

Not a bad record for one district in just 12 months, *Morning Star* readers may think. But they would be wrong. Our demanding professor – no doubt used to a higher level of political activism – notes that 'attracting support was often difficult' and that the demonstrations 'sometimes mustered thousands, but never tens of thousands'.

Nationally, writes Callaghan, much of the Party's mobilisation, its tens of thousands of marches, rallies and public meetings, had an 'air of routine' about it. Many of the Party's campaigns were conducted 'in splendid isolation'.

When the Communist Party held very big, popular factory gate and public meetings against the Anglo-Israeli invasion of Suez, Callaghan ignores them and sneers that those members who attended a Trafalgar Square demonstration 'were easy to dismiss as hypocrites' – it's 1956 and the Hungary crisis again.

He refers several times to the Communist Party's 'takeover' of CND in the 1960s, amid frequent mentions of the campaign's decline. Yet no such takeover is established by evidence. Hints at communist skulduggery are not substantiated.

Of course, it would be optimistic to expect the professor to credit, as Bruce Kent later did at a Communist Party congress, the open and non-sectarian role played by Communists in sustaining CND, ensuring that it could mobilise the mass demonstrations of the 1980s.

Callaghan stirs his own vituperative comments – often with little or no attempt at substantiation – into the cauldron of criticisms and condemnations from contemporary anti-Communists.

A chapter on 'The Cultural Front' begins by characterising the Party as 'a conservative organisation' and a 'living fossil' whose activities were often 'futile' when not not downright 'dangerous'.

The views of prominent British Communists on US imperialist mass culture are quoted in the hope of provoking ridicule, peppered with Callaghan's own opinions of them as 'parochial,' 'nationalistic,' 'lurid,' 'fabricated,' 'unconvincing' and 'synthetic'.

The Party's cultural policies were peddled in order to promote 'Stalin's Cominform agenda,' naturally.

Yet, shorn of its Cold War hyperbole, that communist critique anticipated today's concerns about comics, books, films and television programmes which revel in violence, social and sexual degradation, hedonism, military aggression and US or Western moral 'superiority'.

The Communist Party's many initiatives in the cultural sphere, from making films to organising the Edinburgh People's Festival (the forerunner of today's fringe), from launching music and theatre clubs to inspiring the South Wales miners' annual gala and eisteddfod – huge cultural extravaganzas which completely escape Callaghan's attention – give the lie to charges of 'conservatism'.

Callaghan does give the Party some credit for its work among, for and by women. But, while the criticism (and CP self-criticism) are reasonable, the coverage is sketchy. In so many other vital fields, such as in the tenants' movement, communist activity receives virtually no mention.

In the 1960s and 1970s, the Communist Party almost alone on the left championed the national rights of the Scottish and Welsh – as well as the Irish – peoples, but this principled stance is relegated to a single sentence.

However, not even the Party's worst enemy would deny its influence in the trade union movement. Yet, here again, Callaghan dwells on shortcomings and failures such as the decline of workplace branches.

The strategically planned struggle from 1949 until 1968 to reverse the ban on Communist officials in the Transport and General Workers Union, for instance, receives little attention.

There are also factual inaccuracies. Ford's Dagenham workers did not take action, but were laid off in the Briggs' Bodies dispute of 1952. Leading Communists like Jack Dash did not oppose the 1954 docks strikes, but fought against the exodus from the TGWU to the 'Blue' stevedores' union.

However, Callaghan's treatment of the 1956-61 war against the Communist leadership of the ETU electricians' union is unexpectedly balanced.

In his discussion of the Party's economic policies, our politics professor gives undue prominence to minority views which accord with his own. Thus, the misconceived case for a 'progressive' incomes policy receives generous coverage, while the Party's deepening analysis of the role played by the City of London and transnational corporations is neglected. His digs at the annual predictions of capitalist slump merely echo the Party's self-criticism in 1965.

Communist economists were nevertheless correct to argue that postwar expansion did not abolish the economic cycle, that the state and employers would attack public spending and wages and that the international monetary system would break up, even if they under-estimated state monopoly capitalism's ability to sustain the expansion until the reassertion of general crisis from the late 1960s.

Long-standing CP opposition to British membership of the European Common Market is reported with incredulity – although many of the Party's forecasts of political union, militarisation, the incorporation of eastern Europe and economic policies which favour the European monopolies have since materialised in front of our eyes.

Callaghan's own political sympathies for the pro-incomes policy, pro-EU, anti-class struggle stance of the genuinely deceased *Marxism Today* clique are displayed even more openly in his book *Socialism in Britain Since 1884* (1990). He is too hostile to the Marxist-Leninist and democratic-centralist principles of the Communist Party – which he describes as the 'rehashed Leninism' and 'vanguardist mentality' of a party perpetually 'in a state of denial about the true extent of its marginality' – to write a balanced, insightful and analytical history of it.

The reader would be forgiven for thinking that the Communist Party had reached an advanced stage of disintegration by 1968 – whereas it stood on the brink of a major expansion of membership and influence.

The task of producing an alternative history of the post-war period must now fall to a team of better qualified authors, Party and non-Party. And a subject index, together with a record of CP executive committee members, should accompany the fruits of their labours.

10

'Worth a warrant': Dora Cox (1904-2000)

First published as a chapter in Meddick, Payne & Katz eds., *Red Lives – Communists and the Struggle for Socialism* (2020)

Dora Roberts was born in London on July 24, 1904. Her grandfather had left Yorkshire to work on the Russian railways, but her father had been forced to flee the country after participating in a series of strikes there at the turn of the century. In London, he met and married Dora's mother, a Lithuanian Jewish refugee. Young Dora left school at 15 and trained for secretarial work. After attending a Socialist Sunday School, she joined the CPGB and the Young Communist League as a founder member in 1920 and 1921, respectively, volunteering for typing work with the Party.

After helping to organise two youth delegations to the Soviet Union and celebrating the tenth anniversary of the October 1917 Socialist Revolution there, Dora spent several years attending a trade union college in Moscow, also assisting the Communist International with secretarial duties.

On her return to London, where she helped the Party with translation work, she met and married Idris Cox in March 1931. He was by this time a member of the CP's central committee and political bureau, with particular organising and propaganda responsibilities in the National Minority Movement. Dora Cox edited the Women's Page of the NMM's paper, *The Worker*, and was already being described by the Security Service (MI5) as 'one of the more important members' of the CPGB and 'worth a warrant'. Her mail was being intercepted ... when the intelligence services could keep up with her changes of address. This attention to her may well be explained by MI5's belief – based on information from 'an entirely reliable source' – that Dora Robbins [sic] or Roberts or Cox is 'employed in shadowing Arcos employees who are engaged on work of a secret nature'. Arcos was the Anglo-Russian Cooperative Society in London raided by police in 1927 on the pretext of searching for stolen War Office documents that were never found.

In mid-1932, Dora was described in the first of her two Security Service files as: 'age 28/30, height medium, complexion pale, hair dark, longish face, straight nose, slim build, Jewish appearance, wears pince-nez'. Later that year, in accordance with NMM strategy, she began work in a woollen mill in Burnley where she was reported as 'taking a keen interest in all that affected her fellow workers and playing a leading part in recruiting them into the United Clothing Workers' Union'.

After a brief spell back in London, Dora and Idris moved to his native south Wales in mid-1933, first to Pontyclun and then to Cardiff. They also spent time in Tonypandy, where Dora worked closely with National Unemployed Workers Movement organiser, county councillor and novelist Lewis Jones before leading a 15-strong Welsh women's contingent on the 1934 Hunger March to London. An iconic photograph in Wal Hannington's book *Unemployed Struggles* (1936) showed Dora and women comrades on route, sitting on a grass verge resting their tired feet. When Idris was appointed editor of the *Daily Worker* in 1935, she stayed behind in Cardiff with their first child John before joining him in Highbury and then a ground-floor flat in Balham. Within a year, the family was back in Cardiff where Idris had been assigned to the post of organising secretary for the South Wales district of the CPGB. The campaign against the Means Test and unemployment benefit levels continued, with Dora as one of the speakers alongside local MP George Daggar at a rally organised by the Abertillery Trades and Labour Council.

In the great 'Aid for Spain' campaign to support the Spanish Republic and the International Brigades against General Franco's fascist-backed rebellion, Dora took John in his pram to collect on the streets of Cardiff. She also assumed the terrible responsibility of visiting the families of International Brigade volunteers to inform them that their husband, son or brother had been killed in Spain.

After a brief period in London again where Dora helped out in the Party's King Street headquarters, the Cox family were back in Cardiff after the outbreak of World War Two. The contents of her MI5 file, gleaned from mail interceptions and telephone taps, testify to her very active role in the Gabalfa group of the Party. An informant at a Cardiff CP branch meeting reported her as saying that 'the Communist Party was not out for a bloody revolution, and that the Russian Revolution was only made brutal and bloody through the counter-revolutions'. Dora volunteered at the Party's Cardiff office and bookshop and campaigned locally for the provision of Haldane shelters and other air-raid protection measures. Seven months pregnant with daughter Judith, she addressed a women's emergency conference in London in October 1940, warning Londoners that there was no adequate protection for evacuees sent to south Wales.

This was probably the busiest period in Dora's political life, even though she had two young children and Idris was frequently at meetings in London and many other places besides. In Cardiff, she helped organise political education classes, a People's Convention event and a big rally featuring the 'Red Dean' of Canterbury after Nazi Germany attacked the Soviet Union in June 1941. But she did not agree with comrades that the mass of local people were now in sympathy with the British CP: they supported Russian resistance because many were simply 'anxious that the war should stay where it is' – on the Eastern front – 'and so save their own skins'. There followed public meetings with Pollitt, Palme Dutt and Willie Gallacher and leafleting to establish a group of CP members and supporters – to which Dora would be attached – at the local Royal Ordnance Factory in Llanishen, north Cardiff. In particular, she worked closely with Annie Powell of the Rhondda to campaign across south Wales for women to join the armed forces or go into essential war industries, which required the provision of childcare facilities in schools and big workplaces. Dora participated in the call for a 'second front' in Western Europe and insisted that it be explained to workers why they should support Churchill as war leader despite his many mistakes.

By 1943, the Cardiff branch had grown to a membership of 300 and Dora was heading the propaganda and political education work for the South Wales CP district. According to an MI5 assessment that July: 'Although still only in her early thirties, Dora COX has given more years to the trade union and labour movement of this country than many twice her age ... Despite family responsibilities – Dora COX is the proud mother of two children – she is, today, as ever, most active in the fight against fascism'.

After the war, the family continued to live in the Welsh capital, where Dora led the Welsh Committee's work among women from the Party office and reported regularly to Tamara Rust in King Street. The mail at all three premises was routinely intercepted. Checks revealed the good news, including successful fund-raising bazaars and International Women's Day initiatives; but there was also the negative impact of anti-Soviet Cold War propaganda and widespread working-class resentment at the CP's criticisms of the 1945-51 Labour government.

A letter from Dora to Rose Smith – a comrade in arms from the Lancashire days and herself a leading Communist – in May 1951 sheds some light on the real reasons for the decision of the Party's political committee to remove Idris Cox from his post as Welsh secretary. According to Dora at the time: 'The main criticism is that he has not succeeded in building a collective leadership and developing new cadres'. She and her husband both accepted the stricture, which he had then reported back to Welsh committee in a 'magnificent Bolshevik manner'; otherwise, Dora wrote, there might have been a divisive battle and he could easily have blamed others.

Idris was transferred to work in the Party's international department.

Times were difficult as Dora tried to sell the house and Idris looked for a new family home in London. She told one correspondent that the rising cost of living 'is sending me nearly dotty' and ended up working as the office manager for a local building contractor. Still, she supported the campaign of her friend and comrade Betty Ambatielos (formerly Bartlett) against the imprisonment of family members in Greece and met the request from future Labour MP Leo Abse (described as a 'communist' in a Special Branch phone tap report) to arrange a meeting with Idris. Abse's proposal that they visit an ill comrade was rejected as 'too dangerous'.

Before joining Idris in Brixton Hill in March 1952, Dora wrote to him at Party centre about very successful British-Soviet Friendship Society events to welcome back a delegation from the Soviet Union. The Cardiff meeting was addressed by expelled Labour MP John Platts-Mills and Soviet journalist and novelist Boris Polevoi, while NUM general secretary Arthur Horner spoke in his hometown of Merthyr Tydfil. In other intercepted correspondence, she expressed disappointment to Tamara Rust about having to miss the founding conference of the National Assembly of Women.

With the family reunited in London, Dora found work as a medical secretary for Lambeth Hospital management committee, joining NUPE. Son John escaped the permanent Special Branch surveillance of their home with a working farm holiday in Bucharest, while daughter Judith and sometimes the rest of the family spent summer holidays in Cornwall. Their mother wrote fondly to an old friend and comrade, Andrew Rothstein, of her tiredness from housework and full-time employment, leaving her only enough energy to attend meetings of the local Co-operative Guild.

In 1970, Idris retired from Party work having been in the leadership for almost 40 years, with senior international responsibilities for half that time. Dora always gave her unstinting support, meeting many renowned Communists and national liberation leaders along the way. The family retired to Talywaun, near Pontypool, where Dora remained active with CND – John became vice-president in the 1970s – and took part in the local miners support group during the 1984-85 strike. She died in January 2000, leaving behind John, Judith and their own personal MI5 files.

Press ahead: the *Daily Worker* was launched in 1930 and continues in the form of the *Morning Star* to this day.

Willie Gallacher: Red Clydesider, MP for West Fife (1935-1950) and foundation member of the Communist Party

Mick McGahey: legendary miners' leader shares a platform with Labour MP Tony Benn, on the far right is Kevin Halpin, CPB industrial organiser

Harry Pollitt addressing workers during the Second World War, sharp disagreements over the nature of the war in 1939 led to his temporary resignation but he returned to lead the party until 1956

Welsh-language version of the *Communist Manifesto*, the importance of the national question has long been stressed by communists in Britain

'Communism is the youth of the world': a new generation of communists has emerged to take forward the struggle for peace and socialism

YOUTH CHARTER

Building a brighter future for Britain's youth

11

The new imperialist offensive: CP international policy 1977-88

First published in Communist Review *no. 97 (Autumn 2020)*

In November 1977, the CPGB's 35th congress approved a revised edition of the Party's programme, *The British Road to Socialism* (*BRS*). On the international front, this prescribed little change from the strategic approaches outlined in the previous 1968 edition.

Published in March 1978, the new *BRS* pointed to environmental degradation and the development of weapons of mass destruction as aspects of capitalism's all-round political, economic, social, cultural and moral crisis. This 'general crisis' was worsening as the balance of world forces tilted decisively against capitalism and imperialism and in favour of progress and socialism. Aided by international solidarity, liberation struggles had been won in Vietnam, Laos, Cambodia, Angola, Mozambique and Guinea-Bissau and were now intensifying in Zimbabwe, Namibia and South Africa.

According to the new edition of the programme:

> The existence and support of the socialist countries have been crucial factors in helping the national liberation movements to achieve and consolidate their victories.

Having lost large parts of their formal empires during the post-war period, the imperialist powers had turned to neo-colonialist policies, although these were meeting strong resistance including growing support for the 'Non-Aligned Movement' of liberated countries.

The *BRS* paid tribute to the domestic achievements of the socialist countries with their consistent, superior record of economic growth, full employment and low prices. It was equally complimentary about the strength and policies of the socialist states which – together with the international peace movement – had forced the NATO powers to accept arms limitation treaties and the Helsinki Agreement in favour of mutual recognition, common security and international cooperation. Sections of the Trotskyist and Maoist movements in the West, on the other hand, denounced the Soviet commitment to detente and peaceful co-existence as a betrayal of 'proletarian internationalism'.

In fact, the *BRS* recognised that powerful forces in the imperialist countries wanted to continue driving an arms race by developing new means of mass destruction such as Cruise missiles and the neutron bomb. World peace was not yet guaranteed and so the peace movement had to be strengthened.

The Party's policies were clear: Britain should adopt an independent foreign policy based on the principles of peaceful co-existence; cooperation with progressive forces in the capitalist world and with the socialist states; British withdrawal from NATO; replacement of both NATO and the Warsaw Pact by an all-inclusive European Security System; unilateral nuclear disarmament and the closure of all foreign and nuclear bases in Britain; immediate independence for Britain's remaining colonies and the withdrawal of British armed forces overseas; an international treaty to abolish nuclear, chemical and biological weapons; a lasting peace in the Middle East based on UN resolutions including a homeland for the Palestinian people; active support for national liberation struggles particularly in Southern Africa; and a substantial increase in aid to Third World anti-imperialist countries.

Within a year or two of the new *BRS* appearing, a series of major conflicts on the world stage would throw up formidable challenges to the CPGB, its programme and its internal cohesion. A faction within the Party would exploit these in order to undermine long-standing positions. Since the 1970s, a group of intellectuals and some trade unionists had been organising to turn the Communist Party into a liberal-left network drawing its ideas from a range of social movements and non-Marxist ideologies. They identified themselves with the pluralist, constitutionalist and non-Leninist 'Eurocommunism' proclaimed by the mass communist parties of Spain, Italy and to a lesser extent France.

This tendency had been represented at the European Conference of Communist and Workers' Parties in Berlin in June 1976, where general secretary Gordon McLennan was among the critics of the Soviet political system.

Britain's own Eurocommunists had strengthened their position on the CPGB executive committee and in various official posts as a result of the Party's 34th congress in 1975. They comprised half of the committee appointed the following year to redraft the Party programme.

Initially, they concentrated more on changing the CPGB's domestic policies and strategy than its international ones. The 35th Party congress had indicated how difficult it might prove to alter the CPGB's fundamental alignment with the socialist countries, even in the aftermath of the 1968 crisis in Czechoslovakia. By a substantial majority, congress delegates passed a resolution on the 60th anniversary of the October Revolution thanking the Soviet Union and the CPSU for their 'great example and inspiration' and celebrating the 'triumphs of socialism' in peace and war. In vain, some Eurocommunists tried to prevent the matter being put to a vote.

Undaunted, they recommended their advance with the appointment of Martin Jacques as editor of *Marxism Today* in late 1977. Within months, the journal carried articles promoting the three main communist parties associated with Eurocommunism.

The election of Margaret Thatcher's Tory government in 1979 signalled a set-back for detente and the revival of Cold War rhetoric. This was confirmed by Western responses to the Soviet Union's military intervention in Afghanistan that December. The Brezhnev government's intention was to consolidate the victory of one faction within the ruling People's Democratic Party of Afghanistan over the other, while also defending the progressive and democratic policies of the Afghan revolution against feudal reaction and Islamic fundamentalist terrorism. The CPGB leadership criticised what it regarded as unacceptable interference by one country and its communist party in the internal affairs of another, a view repeated by McLennan at the CPSU congress in Moscow. The 37th CPGB congress in November 1981 narrowly endorsed this criticism, although more than one-third of the delegates supported an amendment condemning the deposed faction in Afghanistan and welcoming the Soviet Union's military intervention.

As the war against the mujahideen and their CIA, SAS and Middle Eastern backers escalated, the *Morning Star* came out clearly in support of the those Afghan and Soviet forces fighting to defend social progress, women's rights, free healthcare and universal education. The paper's Foreign Editor Roger Trask produced an eye-witness report, *Afghanistan: Grasping the Nettle of Peace*, in January 1987. By then, the Communist Campaign Group of expelled and excluded CPGB members, the majority of Britain's Communists and even the Militant faction in the Labour Party had aligned themselves with the Kabul regime and the Soviet Red Army against the Afghan warlords and the founders of Al Qaeda.

The previous six years had also witnessed a catastrophic war in the Middle East, following the decision of the US-backed dictatorship of Saddam Hussein in Iraq to attack the Ayatollah Khomeini's theocratic dictatorship and Iran in 1980. Britain's Communists and their labour movement allies established CODIR (the Committee for the Defence of the Iranian People's Rights) and CARDRI (the Campaign against Repression and for Democratic

Rights in Iraq). Together with exiled communists and progressives from those countries, they campaigned against the brutal reactionary regimes in Baghdad and Tehran, marching side-by-side against the war and winning wide support in the British labour movement.

The CP in Britain continued to support the national and democratic rights of the Palestinian people represented by the PLO, while opposing military attacks on civilian targets. Communists worked closely in Trade Union Friends of Palestine with allies such as Fire Brigades Union leader Ken Cameron.

The prospect of a nuclear conflagration drew nearer when the Thatcher government announced its intention to expand Britain's atomic weapons arsenal with Trident submarines and Cruise missiles from the US. CND grew rapidly from 1980, mobilising marchers in their hundreds of thousands. Communists played a significant role at every level of the peace movement and were involved in the women's peace camp at the Greenham Common US Air Force base.

Although CND took no official position on which side bore most or full responsibility for the Cold War and the arms race, most of its campaigning was aimed at Britain's nuclear weapons, NATO membership and US bases. On the other hand, a new body – European Nuclear Disarmament (END) – was forthright in its view that the US and the Soviet Union were equally to blame and equally guilty of acts of aggression.

It was as though the superpower which had been first to manufacture the atom and hydrogen bombs, the only one to use them in war, the first to establish an international military alliance and the first to develop Inter-Continental Ballistic Missiles was no more to blame than the superpower which had not; that the list of countries bombed and invaded by the US at the cost of millions of lives was no worse than any list that could be pinned on the Soviet Union. Furthermore, END courted support from dissident groups and intellectuals in the socialist countries, while repudiating the established peace movements there, and called for the destruction of both European blocs from below rather than any defence of the socialist one. In Western Europe, it drew support from social-democratic parties and the Eurocommunist leaderships of the Italian and Spanish CPs.

Although the CPGB executive committee affiliated to END 'with reservations', some of the Party's Eurocommunists enthusiastically promoted the new body because its outlook repudiated solidarity with the Soviet Union and the socialist countries. Others such as CND vice-chair John Cox were more cautious. In *Marxism Today* (September 1980), he rejected alignment with Soviet foreign policy as an outmoded basis for peace movement campaigning, while still holding the US chiefly responsible for stoking the arms race, sustaining repressive regimes and undermining detente. He rejected the tendency of leaders of the newly founded World Disarmament Campaign (WDC) to favour multilateral measures in place of demands for unilateral disarmament. Most of all, Cox emphasised the need for CND to maintain its position of non-alignment, while recognising in reality that the bulk of its campaigning would continue to target the policies of Britain, the US and NATO. At the same time, he said of both the US and the Soviet Union that 'neither, in practice, has shown much respect for the independence and traditions even of its allies during the past two decades'.

The influence of Communists in CND was judged sufficient for the Tory government to make it an issue on the eve of the June 1983 General Election, in the hope of smearing Labour leader Michael Foot and his anti-nuclear weapons manifesto. Utilising information from Special Branch and MI5, there was a coordinated drive by Defence Secretary Michael Heseltine, the *Daily Mail* and the big business outfit Common Cause to paint CND as a 'Communist front', with up to half of its executive members in the CPGB. A telephone tap was placed on John Cox but no evidence could be found of Communist manipulation of the peace movement.

At the 38th CPGB congress in November 1983, CND general secretary Bruce Kent thanked the *Morning Star* for its 'steady, honest and generous coverage' of the case for nuclear disarmament and referred to the Communist Party and CND as 'partners in the cause for peace in this world'. As things turned out, mass campaigning by CND and other peace organisations against Cruise and the Trident nuclear weapon system rendered END and the WDC irrelevant in Britain.

Thatcher and the Tories returned to office in 1983 on a wave of British nationalistic feeling having won the Falklands War. When Argentinian forces invaded the islands in April 1982, the CPGB had condemned the US-backed military junta in Buenos Aires for using force in an effort to decide the future status of the disputed islands. Likewise, the Party opposed the Thatcher government's decision to send a taskforce, organising public meetings to demand its immediate return and the withdrawal of all belligerent forces from the region. Some far left groups advocated a military defeat for British imperialism (and therefore a victory for the mass murderers of Argentinian socialists and communists), while *Militant* demanded a Labour government that would 'continue the war on socialist lines'. The CPGB political committee proposed 'a negotiated settlement through the United Nations which takes into account that Britain's claim to sovereignty is a hangover from this country's colonial past and should be ended'.

The Falklands War soon ceased to have much political significance in Britain. For most of the 1980s, it was overshadowed by the struggle in Poland. Discontented workers at the Gdansk shipyards had protested against government economic policies and formed an unofficial trade union, Solidarnosc ('Solidarity'). It rapidly turned into a political movement in league with liberal intellectuals and the reactionary Roman Catholic church to challenge communist rule. In the face of mass mobilisations and fearing Soviet intervention, General Jaruzelski and the military took control of the country at the end of 1981.

The CP political committee in Britain opposed martial law, demanded the release of detained Solidarnosc leaders and called for a return to civilian rule. At least five of the Party's 20 districts thought the Party leadership's criticisms of Solidarnosc – that it contained 'provocative' and 'anti-socialist' elements and was being used by imperialism to undermine detente – were inadequate. The *Morning Star* opposed imperialist interference in Polish affairs and called for compromise between the Warsaw government and the Polish United Workers Party, on the one side, and Solidarnosc on the other. Unlike most Trotskyist organisations, many CPGB members quickly came to understand that the real aim of Solidarnosc, with its material and financial support from the CIA-inspired 'National Endowment for Democracy', was to bring down Poland's socialist system. Some left-wing MPs and trade union leaders in Britain such as Arthur Scargill adopted a similar stance, Tony Benn noting that the Labour Party and TUC leaderships were 'supporting Polish Thatcherism'. Following the counter-revolution in Poland after 1989, most workers in the Gdansk shipyards – the birthplace of Solidarnosc – lost their jobs following the privatisation decreed by the EU Commission in return for state aid.

The much-vaunted 'Soviet invasion of Poland' never materialised and, indeed, was never planned.

Mikhail Gorbachev assumed the leadership of the CPSU and the Soviet Union in 1985 and, like most communist parties around the world, the CPGB welcomed his accession. He had recently visited the Marx Memorial Library, knowing its close alignment with the CPGB and the *Morning Star*. Gorbachev's plans for *glasnost* (openness) and *perestroika* (reconstruction) promised to reinvigorate Soviet society and modernise its faltering economy. His proposals for comprehensive multilateral disarmament challenged the West and threw its political leaders into confusion. The Intermediate Nuclear Forces Treaty (1987) committed the US and Soviet Union to significant arms control and disarmament measures.

In his political report to the Communist Party's re-establishment congress in 1988, *Morning Star* editor Tony Chater warmly welcomed these developments. Only later did it become evident that neither the CPSU nor Soviet society had been properly prepared to withstand the spread of nationalist and anti-communist ideas unleashed under *glasnost*, while *perestroika* turned into a strategy for dismantling the planned, socialist basis of the economy.

Closer to home, the conflict in northern Ireland appeared no nearer to resolution. The IRA concentrated its attacks on the security forces as Loyalist murder squads operated in collusion with agencies of the British state. The CPGB called for a 'democratic solution' based on a Bill of Rights to end discrimination against the nationalist and Catholic community; an end to the British state's repressive measures; the withdrawal of British troops to barracks; and policies to address severe problems of poverty and unemployment. According to the 1978 *BRS*: 'These steps would create conditions in which sectarian strife could be ended and British troops withdrawn completely'. Moreover, Britain should recognise the right of the people of Ireland to rule the whole of their country and work with their representatives to bring this about by consent.

Many Communists in Britain and Ireland were unhappy with aspects of this policy. They believed that partition and British occupation of the north of Ireland – rather than sectarianism as such – were at the root of the conflict. British troops were there to enforce the union with Britain and any withdrawal to barracks would either be made impossible by paramilitary violence or prove to be short-lived, so best call for their complete withdrawal as part of an end to British rule at the earliest possible time. The Northern Ireland unionists must not be allowed to exercise a veto on reunification indefinitely and should face up to the inevitable.

The 'back to barracks' policy, promoted by the CPGB's Irish Advisory, divided the Troops Out Movement as well as the Party. Nevertheless, the *Morning Star* and the majority of the Party leadership had been unequivocal in their support for the restoration of political ('Special Category') status to new Irish Republican prisoners, which culminated in the hunger-strike campaigns of the Armagh women and H-Block 'blanket' protestors of 1980 and 1981. This was in stark contrast to the silence of Party journals *Comment* and *Marxism Today*, both effectively under Eurocommunist control, on the question of Irish prisoners and their heroic sacrifices for 'political status'. Likewise, Eurocommunists in the National Union of Students argued against policies and initiatives which could be identified with 'Troops Out' and 'pro-hunger strike' positions.

In his 1988 congress address, Chater emphasised the responsibility of the re-established party to involve the British labour movement in the campaign for a democratic solution which 'respects the national rights of the Irish people, ends sectarian divisions, and leads to the ending of partition'. The CP in Britain reforged a closer bond with the Communist Party of Ireland, supporting the latter's dialogue with IRA supporters on the alternatives to armed struggle.

In Chile, the US and British-backed dictatorship of General Pinochet permitted no open, legal and democratic forms of protest. In 1986, the Manuel Rodriguez Patriotic Front linked to the Chilean Communist Party had attacked a convoy carrying the dictator, shooting dead five of his armed bodyguards and wounding eleven others. Pinochet survived his injuries. Communists from Britain subsequently assisted in the international effort to help the militants escape and find refuge in other countries. Other CPGB clandestine activities included the provision of financial, printing and other assistance to the ANC, the South African Communist Party and other movements experiencing illegality and repression.

Naturally, Britain's Communists condemned the US-led invasion of Grenada in 1983 to snuff out the revolution led by the New Jewel Movement. Divisions within the NJM complicated the work of the CP in Britain and its allies in Caribbean Labour Solidarity.

The final years of the decade saw a sea-change in the British labour movement's stance on membership of the European Economic Community (the EEC or 'Common Market'). In the 1983 General Election, the Labour Party led by Michael Foot pledged to withdraw Britain. The Communist Party's basic standpoint had been set out in the 1978 *BRS*: 'The Common Market was originally encouraged by the US, not only as an economic grouping directed against socialism, but as the political counterpart of NATO. Despite the subsequent efforts of the EEC countries to develop it also as a counter to the US and Japan, deep-rooted differences within it impeded the efforts to integrate Western Europe economically and politically'.

However, the latter part of this analysis looked as though it might be overtaken by the Single European Act (1987), signed by Prime Minister Thatcher, with its timetable for far-reaching measures of economic, financial and political integration by the end of 1992.

By 1988, after years of mass unemployment and industrial and electoral defeats, Britain's trade unions were ready to embrace the EEC and the mirage of a 'social market' safety-net offered to the TUC conference by EEC Commission president Jacques Delors. The Communist Party leadership had long ceased publishing pamphlets exposing the capitalist and imperialist character of the Common Market.

Tony Benn, Transport & General Workers Union leader Ron Todd, AUEW-TASS and its Communist general secretary Ken Gill and the leadership of NALGO tried in vain to hold back the tide. On the other side, most Labour MPs and the centre and right-wing of the trade union movement pressed home their advantage. *Marxism Today*'s numerous Eurocommunist and *Financial Times* contributors argued that the CPGB's longstanding opposition to the EEC was narrow-minded, nationalistic and out-of-date.

This revisionism found no echo in the re-established Communist Party of Britain in 1988. From that point onwards, the CPB would join the *Morning Star* in making the working-class and anti-imperialist case against the European Union and its 'European single market' designed to benefit the Western European monopolies.

12

'Ideological Grave-robbing'

Review of Nina Fishman, *Arthur Horner: A Political Biography* vols I & II (2010). *Morning Star*, 14 September 2010

Arthur Horner was elected president of the South Wales Miners Federation (the 'Fed') in 1936, and served as general secretary of National Union of Mineworkers from 1946 until 1959.

He was one of the most prominent Communists in 20th century Britain.

Horner abandoned an earlier calling as a lay preacher to embrace militant trade unionism, the Unofficial Reform Committee, the Rhondda Socialist Society and then the Communist Party.

To evade conscription during the 1914-18 imperialist war, he escaped to Dublin to join James Connolly's Irish Citizens Army. Arrested on his return to Holyhead, he was sentenced to six months' jail in Wormwood Scrubs.

Horner should have done another two years for continuing to refuse military service with the British armed forces, but his election as checkweighman at Mardy colliery secured an early release.

He was rational, decisive, a persuasive orator and a diligent administrator. Loved by union staff and a wide circle of friends, he also wrestled for much of his adult life with alcoholism, causing his wife Ethel to join forces with Communist Party leader Harry Pollitt in an effort to keep it under control.

When Horner opposed futile attempts at providing 'revolutionary alternative leadership' outside the Fed's official structures in the early 1930s, the CP considered expelling him for 'Hornerism' – but the Communist International decided that his prestige among the miners was too great to waste.

This much is indisputable fact. Indeed, the late Professor Fishman mines a rich vein of sources to recount Horner's early history.

But the warning lights flash – the canary starts to choke – after only a few pages of volume one.

Horner's father 'perhaps' took out a Co-op loan to buy a house (we don't know), Arthur's sister Mabel 'probably' depended on her brother for emotional and financial support (no evidence), young Arthur 'probably' remained absorbed by boxing and football, he 'may' have imbibed his father's preference for white-collar work (we have no idea), he was 'likely' to have found Birmingham exhilarating (who wouldn't?) – all this and more in just one early chapter, and on it goes for 1,000 pages.

Such speculation and supposition would be of less consequence if the author didn't extend it into the most significant aspects of Horner's trade union and political life.

He joined the Communist Party in 1920. He remained in it until he died in 1968, through thick and thin.

Yet Fishman claims at almost every turn that Horner seriously considered leaving the Party, not least because his politics were those of a social democrat.

Time after time, she returns to these propositions like a dog to its vomit, failing to provide one jot of evidence in 827 pages of narrative and 1,369 reference notes spanning an additional 189 pages.

And this despite access to the most intimate thoughts of Horner himself, expressed in private correspondence and countless transcripts provided by two decades of MI5 bugging, phone tapping and mail interception.

All of Horner's pro-Communist sentiments expressed in private and public, in hundreds of pro-Communist and pro-Soviet speeches and articles for the Communist Party, the *Daily Worker* and the NUM apparently counted for nothing.

For instance, we are informed that 'it is likely he considered leaving the party' in 1931. But Ethel and his best friends in the Rhondda were 'likely to have urged him to remain loyal'. Pollitt and and other comrades in London 'may have induced him to consider' a token act of conciliation with the Party.

Then Horner 'resolved his doubts' before throwing himself anew into party activity. Nowhere does Fishman substantiate any of these speculations.

Fishman later reminds her readers that, previously, 'we observed that he had seriously considered leaving the CPGB in 1938' when president of the Fed and a member of the Party's central committee.

Except that we had observed no such thing. In volume one, Fishman had reproduced an MI5 note indicating Horner's response to receiving instructions from the CP secretariat on all matters of policy: 'Horner resents this and has made it clear that, while the party can rely on him to follow its line, he insists on the right to form his own judgement on questions connected with the conduct of the miners' problems, as he is much better qualified in that respect than are the other party leaders, who have no personal knowledge of the subject'.

According to MI5, some comrades believed that Horner might resign from the CP rather than accept diktats. But, once again, nothing confirms that Horner himself considered or threatened to do so.

In late 1946, he was pressed to replace former NUM president Will Lawther at the National Coal Board but declined.

Fishman adds that 'Horner may also have reflected that joining the NCB would provide him with a non-personal reason for leaving the CPGB', thereby avoiding terrible rows with Communist friends and family. Moreover, his right-wing NUM colleagues are 'likely' to have appreciated the appeal of such circumstances to him, and 'may also have suggested' etc.

There is no evidence that such considerations were going through anybody's mind except Fishman's. Around that time, Horner was making several high-profile appearances at CP and *Daily Worker* events.

In May 1947, he spoke at a CP press briefing on the eve of the Labour Party conference. When the NUM executive committee subsequently tried to carpet him, Horner told his critics: 'You object to this not because of what I've said, but because I've said it as a Communist. Yes I am a Communist. Was there any doubt of that, when you elected me? ... No inducement, and no threat, will ever make me into anything different'.

Undeterred by facts, Fishman goes on to claim that by 1951 Horner 'felt he could no longer square his party membership with either his conscience or his union position'.

He was in conflict with party leaders centrally and in Wales because he refused to support unofficial pit strikes. Horner had long argued that the left should win control of the official union machinery rather than undermine it.

But here again, Fishman provides no evidence that this stance led him to reconsider his party membership.

Horner wrote and spoke clearly about the limitations of public ownership under capitalism. Nonetheless, he tried hard to make coal nationalisation work for the benefit of the miners, the working class and the people of Britain.

Under his leadership all the demands of the 1946 Miners' Charter, which went far wider than wages, were achieved by 1955 without a national strike. During this period he did not regard wage militancy as the top or sole priority for Britain's miners.

Fishman attributes this approach to what she approvingly calls Horner's 'conception of social democratic responsibility'. This theoretically illiterate phrase recurs *ad nauseam*, even making it into the index.

Yet Horner unfailingly made clear his opposition to pay controls under capitalism, sometimes finding himself in a minority on the NUM executive, at others leading the charge against post-war Labour government and TUC policy.

Fishman even tries at one point to misrepresent Horner's deep and unshakeable alignment with the Soviet Union. She utterly misinterprets a 1951 speech to suggest that he 'apparently' did not rule out the possibility that the Soviet Union might start a war.

With her obsessive use and misuse of words and concepts such as Clausewitzianism, 'Young Turks,' *demarches*, *apparat* and the like, the author severely mangles both the art of writing and the science of political understanding.

But her greatest disservice is to the life and outlook of Horner himself, a devout and practical Communist who deserves better than Fishman's ideological grave-robbing.

13

Man of anthracite: Dai Dan Evans (1898-1973)

Co-authored with Roger Jones, first published as a chapter in Meddick, Payne & Katz eds., *Red Lives – Communists and the Struggle for Socialism* (2020), and now extended.

'A person of great enthusiasm and tremendous physical strength – sort of Tolstoyan figure of a man – used to play rugger for Swansea at one period and with all the blue in his face that shows a man has been cutting coal all his life – little bits of coal fly off, and embed themselves in the skin'.

This was the description of Dai Dan Evans given by documentary film-maker Humphrey Jennings in 1942, when making the anti-fascist film 'The Silent Village'. Evans, the local miners' agent, appeared in the film which was set in the village of Cwmgiedd in the Swansea Valley and told the story of the Nazis' destruction of the Czech mining village of Lidice. So who was this 'Tolstoyan figure' who so impressed the man from the Crown Film Unit?

David Daniel Evans was born in 1898 in Abercraf at the very top of the Swansea valley, on the edge of the Breacon Beacons. He shared the year of his birth with the organisation which subsequently absorbed his time and effort for nearly all of his working life – the South Wales Miners Federation, better known as the 'Fed'. Like most of the young boys and men of his area, he began work at the age of 14 in Waunclawdd colliery as a collier's assistant. The area at the time was part of the Anthracite coalfield, which had been expanding rapidly with the development of British imperialism and increased access to markets in Europe, firstly, and then across the world. According to the 1911 census, over 80 per cent of the population spoke Welsh in his part-industrial, part-rural locality of small towns and villages.

The outbreak of war in 1914 transformed the world and village life. 'Dai

Dan', as he quickly became known, attempted to enlist in the British Army in early 1915 but was turned down due to his age. The following year, he joined the Independent Labour Party and registered as a conscientious objector on political grounds rather than as a pacifist. Such was the flux of ideas swirling around the world, even in relatively isolated Welsh villages, points of view could rapidly develop and change. The Bolshevik Revolution and the development of independent working class education through classes run by Nun Nicholas for the National Council of Labour Colleges made him a convinced Marxist.

Subsequently, he joined the Communist Party. In his own words, 'I would say the three books that have affected me mostly, that have given me the character of my philosophy, my economic understanding, my political understanding are *The Communist Manifesto*; *Wage, Labour and Capital*; and *Value, Price and Profit*, all by Marx'. Such was his commitment to political education that throughout the inter-war period he continued to lead education classes in the Swansea and Dulais valleys while still working for the 'Fed' as a full-time official.

In 1923, after ending his rugby days as a front-row forward with Swansea RFC, he emigrated to Canada to work in the lignite mines of Alberta. During this period he attempted to enter the USA illegally, only to be imprisoned and deported in 1926. Returning home, he began to work again at the Gurnos pit, later taking part in the 1926 strike committee. The subsequent six-month lockout, he recalled decades later, 'taught us to know our enemies'. He then started as a faceworker in the International Colliery, Abercraf, and remained there until 1937. During this period, he was elected Fed lodge chairman and then secretary, becoming known as one of the quartet of 'Anthracite Evanses'. They re-established the Amalgamated Anthracite Combine Committee which secured the minimum wage for all anthracite miners as of right. In 1936, Dai Dan was elected to the SWMF executive council. Thus, he went from rank-and-file member to the South Wales leadership within ten years. However, this was an era of decline for the coal industry as a whole, the South Wales coalfield alone losing 241 pits between 1921 and 1936 and, consequently, the Fed losing almost half its membership which fell to 113,000.

Even so, the International and Abercrave collieries won a reprieve in 1939, when two of the 'Anthracite Evanses' – Dai Dan and Jim – persuaded the miners to invest in a part-ownership cooperative scheme to save their pits. These survived as going concerns until the mid-1960s.

Dai Dan was part of the collective effort which broke company unionism in the South Wales coalfield to stabilise and increase Fed membership. In particular, he was one of those selected by the executive to lead the campaign against the South Wales Miners Industrial Union (SWMIU) at Bedwas colliery in the summer and autumn of 1936. He later recalled getting up at 5 o'clock in the mornings to go and meet the miners coming off shift to wait for the train to take them away. There would be around 15 minutes when the opportunity arose to make a speech to the Bedwas men, who were the 'hard core of the scab union' in south Wales. Through a combination of skilful propaganda, clandestine recruitment, a small but significant 'stay-down' strike and negotiations in which the Fed made 'no-strike' concessions to the colliery company, a majority of the Bedwas miners were won over in a ballot.

When Fed president Horner signed an agreement incorporating the SWMIU in Taff-Merthyr colliery, the company union's debts could not be fully revealed to his general secretary Oliver Harris. As Dai Dan explained decades later: 'Old Ollie wouldn't think of compensating the buggers'.

Thereafter, Dai Dan's activities could be simply gauged by his progress onwards and upwards in the ranks of the South Wales Area, from his appointment as the miners' agent for the Anthracite District to his stint as area's chief administrative officer, where he played a vital role in bringing non-manual colliery officials and staff in South Wales into the COSA section of the NUM. When South Wales general secretary Will Arthur retired with ill-health, Dai Dan stepped into the breach as acting secretary. But he was narrowly defeated for the permanent position in April 1953 by vice-president Will Crews, by just 375 votes in a poll of 75,835. Communist Will Paynter having beaten Crews for the area presidency shortly before, a victory for Dai Dan would have upset the preference of many Welsh miners for their top elected posts to be shared between CP and Labour Party members. His consolation was the vice-presidency.

Following the events in Hungary in 1956, a couple of miners' lodges wanted Communists banned from all South Wales posts. The area's Executive Council unanimously rejected the proposal on December 4, defending freedom of speech and the right of political association. 'It will be a bad day for the trade unions and Labour Movement when this is denied', the press was told; officials are elected 'on their record of trade union activity and work', including their readiness to carry out union policy.

That policy included opposing the hundreds of unofficial stoppages that broke out across Britain's coalfields in the first half of 1957. Many had only minority support and achieved no improvement in pay or conditions. They also cost the miners large wage losses, provoking a backlash even in areas heavily influenced by the Communist Party such as Scotland and South Wales. Dai Dan declared that his executive council had 'consistently condemned' the actions, which should be dealt with at lodge level.

Neither this stance nor his Communism prevented his election to the post of South Wales Area general secretary in September 1958.

Three months later, Dai Dan led a small South Wales NUM delegation to Hungary for two weeks, at the invitation of the miners' union there who wished to discuss the battle against pneumoconiosis. On his return, he told the *Western Mail* (December 16) that he 'found the Hungarians extremely joyous people'. He denied that his politics were colouring his judgment, adding:

> We had ample opportunities of seeing the people, and talking to them about their society, their standard of living and how they were treated. There was no difference between their standards of dress and ours. Without exception they said that standards and conditions had improved since the old days. I said to myself that if these people were sullen and working under a cruel, coercive regime, then there would be a real decline in output. The miners would be the most conscious of all the workers in that respect. But although last year's output was originally estimated to be 12½ million tons, the miners actually produced 22½ million tons.

What reactions had he found to the 1956 revolt? What about the resolution of the UN General Assembly condemning its suppression?

> Everyone I spoke to called it the counter-revolution. They included executives of industry. union leaders, rank-and-file members, miners. In Budapest I could see some of the effects of the damage. I went through the streets where the fighting took place, but they had been practically completely reconstructed. I prefer to believe what I saw and heard rather than Mr Cabot Lodge [the US representative at the UN]. I believe the working class of Hungary before anyone else.

During his period of office as general secretary, Dai Dan faced an acceleration of the National Coal Board's programme to close loss-making pits. With 36 collieries on the condemned list – six of them in south Wales – he told the South Wales Area annual conference in May 1959 that all-Britain strike action may be necessary in order to maintain production and jobs. Supported by oil companies cutting their prices, the Tory government was pressing the major nationalised industries – electricity, gas, rail, steel – to switch from coal, despite the instability of oil supplies from the Middle East.

With coal stocks high and the NUM leadership rejecting any possibility of united industrial action, the South Wales executive council and an unofficial movement of lodge activists fell back on a campaign of public meetings, marches and lobbies of Parliament in a bid to alert MPs and public opinion to the dangers of a new energy strategy. Locally, miners vented their anger and frustration through a fresh series of stoppages over safety and pay, even bringing Dai Dan and president Will Whitehead back early from the TUC conference to meet lodge committees.

Before retiring in 1963, Dai Dan played an important role in improving services at the Talygarn Miners Rehabilitation Centre and introducing the house-coal pooling scheme for miners' widows. He oversaw pioneering initiatives to identify and counteract the horrendous impact of coal dust on the health of his members, including his own detailed survey of the progressive nature of pneumoconiosis published in 1963.

Yet it was after the key political aim of the union had been achieved with the nationalisation of the coal industry that he made a unique contribution to working-class life in Wales, beyond 'straightforward' political and economic objectives.

He instituted the bilingual South Wales Miners' Eisteddfod in 1948, giving new expression to a Welsh cultural tradition going back to the 12th century. His aim was to satisfy the collective need for cultural activities, but based on working-class self-organisation. Almost every year for the next four decades, miners and their families would flock to Porthcawl to enjoy competitions in music, poetry and prose. Despite the end of the deep coal mines in South Wales, the initiative still lives on as the annual Welsh Open Brass Band Championship.

His second major achievement in the political, cultural and social sphere was the establishment of the South Wales Miners Gala. Comprising a march, rally and musical competitions, the first took place in 1953 and was addressed by Aneurin Bevan, Horner and Paynter. Most years brought delegations of miners from around the world, many of them from pro-Communist union federations and countries such as the Soviet Union, Poland, Romania and China. This became the major outdoor fixture in the trade union calendar and survived until the last event in Swansea, in 1988.

These two institutions alone would be enough to testify to the breadth and depth of Dai Dan's political vision. There are other illustrations, too numerous to mention. His service to the working class in his own community included spells as president of the Ystradgynlais Welfare Hall and chair of the Abercraf Library.

As a Communist educated in those NCLC classes in the Swansea Valley, and in his own modest way, he put into practice Marx's edict to the trade unions: 'Apart from their original purposes, they must now learn to act deliberately as organising centres of the working class in the broad interest of its *complete emancipation*'. In his own modest way, this was a principle he attempted to follow and implement.

At Dai Dan's memorial meeting in 1974, the orations were delivered by his friend and comrade Dai Francis, Will Paynter, Welsh CP secretary Bert Pearce and Labour MP Caerwyn Roderick. Francis declared: 'Dai Dan does not need a stone memorial. He will be remembered as one of the many of his generation who made enormous personal sacrifices so as to make the South Wales miners' union one of the most politically and intellectually advanced sections of the British working class'.

Ystradgynlais Male Voice Choir sang the hymn 'Blaenwern', beginning with the verse:

Dyma gariad fel y moroedd,
Tosturiaethau fel y lli:
Tywysog Bywyd pur yn marw -
Marw i brynu'n bywyd ni.
Pwy all beidio a chofio amdano?
Pwy all beidio a thraethu'i glod?
Dyma gariad nad a'n angof
Tra fo nefoedd wen yn bod.

Behold the oceans of love,
Behold the floods of kindliness:
A pure Prince of Life is dying –
Dying after buying life for us.
Who will fail to remember him?
Who will not sing his praise?
Here is love not forgotten
In the heavens of future days.

14

The Communist Party and the national question

First published in abridged form in Mary Davis ed., *A Centenary for Socialism: the Communist Party 1920-2020* (2020).

During the first two decades of the 20th century, large parts of the labour movement in Scotland and Wales supported the principle of 'Home Rule All Round'. The Scottish sections of the Labour Party and the Independent Labour Party (ILP), and the Scottish Trades Union Congress (STUC), all passed resolutions in favour of a Scottish Parliament. This reflected patriotic sentiment, a need to right the wrong done by the 1707 Act of Union, a belief in the principle of national self-determination and a preference for more local policy-making especially in a period of post-war reconstruction.

Likewise in Wales, the ILP north and south, the North Wales Labour Council and the South Wales Labour Federation all favoured Home Rule, and even a federal system in the case of the SWLF. In the absence of a Welsh TUC, trade union sentiment was primarily represented by the South Wales Miners Federation (SWMF), whose less militant leaders supported devolution, and the North Wales Quarrymen's Union which was enthusiastically in favour. There was also the view that a Welsh Parliament could soon become a vehicle for Labour's progressive policies, while also lightening the burden of work on the Westminster parliament.

1920-1938 Discovering the Question

In Scotland, the industrial militancy concentrated on 'Red Clydeside' had an anti-imperialist political character that Marxists such as John Maclean believed they could recruit to the cause of a 'Scottish Workers Republic'. When he and his followers failed to win Lenin's agreement to the establishment of a separate Scottish communist party, affiliated to the Communist International, they stayed out of the British CP and formed the short-lived Scottish Workers Republican Party. The militants in the Clyde Workers Committee (CWC) who joined the British CP from 1920, swiftly dominating the Party's Scottish section, had little interest in any kind of nationalism. They feared its negative impact on all-Britain working class unity and on the priority that should be given to solidarity with the anti-colonial movements fighting for liberation from the British Empire. The likes of CWC chair Willie Gallacher did not share Maclean's assessment that the class struggle was so much more advanced in Scotland that a breakaway republic could bring the empire crashing down. In any case, many of the CWC and Socialist Labour Party militants who came to the CP had previously been influenced by anti-parliamentarian syndicalist ideas. They saw no particular role for nationality and parliaments in the class struggle against exploitation and for socialism. On the other hand, the most significant forces which attached political significance to the national question in Scotland – those following John Maclean or the ILP – did not join the Communist Party.

Anti-parliamentary syndicalism had also been gaining influence in the SWMF. The miners who mostly constituted the South Wales Socialist Society (renamed the South Wales Communist Council during the CP unity process) rejected bourgeois parliaments regardless of nationality or location. That the Liberal Party played such a prominent role in pre- and post-war 'Home Rule' initiatives confirmed suspicions that the national question was a diversion from working class and socialist politics. For the Marxist left in south Wales, Ireland had a far bigger claim on their attention as an oppressed nation fighting for its freedom. Leading syndicalists in Wales such as Noah Ablett and WF Hay joined neither the CP nor a Maclean-style alternative. Others ended up as Labour MPs. As in Scotland, support for devolution in Wales was strongest in the ILP, in the tradition of former Merthyr Tydfil MP Keir Hardie; many ILPers such as SO Davies, Minnie Pallister and David Thomas stayed in the Labour Party, while the likes of celebrated poet TE Nicholas became foundation members of the CP without forsaking their commitment to Welsh self-government and the Welsh language.

From the outset, therefore, there was little or no interest among Britain's Communists in the national question as far as Wales and Scotland were concerned. The Labour Party advocated parliaments for the two nations from 1918 onwards, but with declining enthusiasm once the 1923 General Election showed that it could form a government for the whole of Britain. The CP had other priorities as far as the national question was concerned, namely Irish unity and independence and freedom for the colonial peoples.

Nor was there a substantial body of Marxist theory to guide the CP in cases such as Scotland and Wales. The Irish had demonstrated time and again a desire to exercise their right to national self-determination, thereby attracting the attention of Marx, Engels and Lenin. To the extent that the national question in Scotland and Wales – as distinct from specific events in their histories – had featured at all in the seminal texts of Marxism, the references were fragmentary and insubstantial. True, in *The State and Revolution* (1916), Lenin had referred approvingly to Engels' suggestion that a federal republic 'would be a step forward in Britain where the two islands are peopled by four nations and in spite of a single Parliament three different systems of legislation already exist side by side', but there was no other reference of that kind elsewhere in the writings of Lenin, Engels or Marx.

At its Second congress in 1920, the Communist International (the 'Comintern') adopted 'Theses on the National and Colonial Question' drafted by Lenin which might have provided the basis for the development of CP policy in Britain. For instance, they called upon communist parties to make a precise analysis of the economic and historical conditions of each national question in their own territory, identifying the class interests within each nation, emphasising working class unity, opposing all forms of national antagonism, and proposing federalism as the most appropriate – if only transitional – way to recognise national rights, promote unity, and secure equality between nations with guaranteed rights for national minorities.

During the 1920s, the CP in Britain made no such analysis in relation to Scotland and Wales. This was the decade of building a young party and the world's first workers' state in the most hostile conditions; these were years of momentous battles in industry, of 'Red Friday' and 'Black Friday', the General Strike and lock-out, mass unemployment, the Wall Street Crash and the first hunger marches. Scottish Home Rule Bills proposed by ILP and Liberal MPs at Westminster, backed by the Scottish Home Rule Association, kept the issue alive; the Labour Party's programme *Labour and the Nation* (1928) advocated 'separate legislative assemblies in Scotland, Wales and England'. But for most Communists, the devolution question faded into obscurity and the CP kept aloof from the intermittent campaigning. Scotland and Wales were not mentioned in the CP's *Draft Programme to the Comintern* (1924), nor in its General Election manifestos of 1922-24 and 1929 (*Class Against Class*).

The 'Bolshevisation' of communist parties meant in Britain the centralisation of power in the Party's central committee (CC), political bureau (PB) and professional apparatus. District organisation at Scottish and South Wales levels experienced a loss of autonomy in deciding local priorities and approaches to policy and action. That said, there is no evidence in the written or oral archives of a groundswell of desire among Welsh and Scottish Communists to discuss or develop policy on their own national question. Indeed, so strong was the impetus for centralised working-class unity during the ferocious battles of the 1920s that not only did hitherto separate Scottish and English trade unions amalgamate on an industrial basis; in the wake of the General Strike, those sections in Scotland under CP influence proposed that the Scottish TUC should forsake its independence to become an advisory council of the TUC in London.

It took the advance of nationalist movements in the Great Depression of 1929-32 to prick the consciousness of Communists that their party, too, might need a policy on the national question within Britain.

In Scotland, the labour movement's alliance with the Home Rule movement had disintegrated. In 1931, the STUC renounced its formal policy of Scottish self-government within a British commonwealth and the ILP disaffiliated from the Labour Party in 1932. This strengthened the hand of Labour's social-democrats who increasingly saw the future in terms of bureaucratic reforms imposed from Westminster and Whitehall. This created a minor political vacuum in Scotland where the labour movement's Home Rule policy used to be. In a period of mass unemployment, home evictions and poverty enforced by the Means Test, some nationalists insisted that the solution to capitalist crisis was a Scottish parliament and independence.

When a Scottish nationalist candidate won 13 per cent of the vote in the 1932 Dunbartonshire by-election – almost twice that of the CP – Willie Gallacher urged the Party to 'make a thorough study of all the problems that confront the Scottish workers'. Otherwise, he wrote in the *Communist Review* (May 1932), more people – especially in the universities and professions – would blame English rule and see a Scottish Parliament as the answer to their problems. The CP needed to 'effectively deal with the Fascist demagogy of the Scottish Nationalists'. Robert Maclennan warned that pandering to nationalist sentiment was a reactionary diversion which would undermine British working-class unity. Helen Crawfurd showed how levels of government spending on economic and social assistance were far higher in England than in Scotland. She feared that very real grievances would be exploited by some big landowners and capitalists; they could see in Scottish nationalism its 'potentialities as the basis of a fascist movement ... attracting the youth of Scotland away from the class struggle'. She wanted the CP to clarify its position on Home Rule.

However, the predominant view on the Scottish CP district committee was that in Scotland there was no national question as such. While retaining elements of autonomy, Scottish landowners, capitalists and the middle class had participated fully and profitably in the British state and empire. Communists still looked upon Scottish nationalism and 'Tartan culture' as the province of upper- and middle-class romantics or reactionaries. The Scottish working class, on the other hand, faced the same exploitation and class enemy as workers in England. The creation of a breakaway United Mineworkers of Scotland in 1929, under Communist leadership and outside the Miners Federation of Great Britain, had nothing to do with political separatism or nationalism. Rather, it reflected the intensity of the conflict between left-wing militants and a corrupt, anti-democratic right-wing leadership.

The sea-change in Wales and Scotland began with the Communist Party's turn to a united front of working-class organisations within a broader 'People's Front' against fascism and imperialist war. Led by Georgi Dimitrov from 1934, the Comintern also committed communist parties to seize the flag of patriotism from the fascist parties and their right-wing allies. Communists should embrace Lenin's dictum in 'On the National Pride of the Great Russians' (1915) to uphold and celebrate everything progressive in their own nation's history, in particular the struggles of working people against exploitation and oppression. Failure to do so allowed the forces of reaction to present themselves as the champions of the nation and its people.

However, the Party's new programme, *For Soviet Britain* (1935), came out too soon to reflect this new approach, making no mention of the national question except for Ireland and the colonies of the British Empire. The reference in an early draft to the aim of 'a federal republic of Soviet Britain' had been removed at the insistence of the Comintern in Moscow in August 1934.

On the heels of the Comintern's Seventh congress, Tom Wintringham in *The Left Review* (September 1935) expressed his hope that embracing patriotic 'liberty' and 'freedom' might lead to a better understanding of the literary works of Communist poets Hugh MacDiarmid and TE Nicholas, champions of Scots and Welsh-language culture. The following February, the same journal hosted a discussion on the national question in Scotland. CP supporter Jimmy Barke agreed with some nationalists that the country's cultural heritage was more progressive than England's and – because it resided mainly in Scotland's working people – would only be safeguarded under socialism. Rather than the working class adopting nationalism, therefore, the Scottish nationalists should themselves embrace the CP and socialism.

In autumn 1936, exasperated by the lack of progress, the Party's central committee (CC) and political bureau (PB) instructed the Scottish Committee to cease prevaricating and draft a policy statement and plan of action on the national question. Differences within the Scottish Committee rendered it impotent for more than a year, although secretary Peter Kerrigan and his committee were critical of their own failure to recognise the Scottish people's strong sense of nationhood. They now accepted that there should be 'some form' of self-government but were reluctant to raise the concrete demand for a Scottish Parliament. There was no great appetite for resurrecting an institution dissolved by its own 'parcel o' rogues' in 1707. Nor did many have strong feelings about equal status in law for Gaelic – already regarded by many Scots as doomed – or Scots and 'Lallans'. Industrial workers and small farmers were more concerned about their livelihoods, even at the tail-end of the Great Depression.

When Scottish organiser Aitken Ferguson eventually presented the Scottish Committee's report to the central PB in January 1938, it was agreed that the Party's immediate priority in Scotland should be to build a mass movement with Labour and the Scottish Nationalists on economic and social issues. Scotland had the right to national self-determination, including independence, but any campaign for a Scottish Parliament should be an all-party initiative prepared carefully beforehand by Ferguson and SNP secretary John MacCormick. In the meantime, emphasis should be placed on the call for Scottish MPs to meet regularly in Edinburgh in a Scottish grand commission with representatives of local government. In the House of Commons the following month, Communist MP for West Fife Willie Gallacher recommended this initiative to the Secretary of State for Scotland in view of the 'strong desire for a measure of devolution' in the country.

Belatedly, the Scottish Committee and local CP branches now went into action behind the Comintern's new line to embrace progressive patriotism. In spring 1938, a 'Pageant of Scottish History' was held through the streets of Edinburgh, Aberdeen and Dundee where 500 marchers carried more than 200 banners. Other pageants were banned by local authorities. Communists joined the Glasgow May Day procession with portraits of Robert the Bruce, William Wallace and Rabbie Burns alongside those of Marx, Engels, Lenin, Stalin and Dimitrov. They were following the example set by the Party's London district committee and organiser Ted Bramley, whose misnamed 'March of English History' in September 1936 had featured tableaux of the Magna Carta, the Peasants Revolt, the General Strike, Robbie Burns, the Dublin Easter Rising and the stay-down strike at Taff-Merthyr colliery.

This was not enough for Hugh MacDiarmid, who preferred to advocate the late John Maclean's slogan of a 'Scottish Workers' Republic'. A champion of the Scots Renaissance, the Scots and Gaelic languages and the national rights of Celtic Cornwall, he had joined the CP in 1934, having been expelled from the National Party of Scotland. After clashing publicly with Kerrigan he was expelled by the Scottish Committee in November 1936, before being readmitted the following May. In 1939, he was ejected again (and not readmitted until 1957), after calling for campaigns to promote separatism, republicanism and militant atheism, all of which were at odds with Party strategy.

In the South Wales coalfield, CP membership had collapsed along with coal exports in the wake of the General Strike and lockout. Working-class communities struggled to survive, weakened by the mass emigration of young people. CP activity confined itself largely to the National Unemployed Workers Movement and the miners' lodges. The Welsh National Party, rooted in the Welsh-speaking intelligentsia and more concerned with the future of the Welsh language and culture than constitutional issues, had made almost no political headway since its formation in 1925. Thus, there was little pressure on the CP to develop policy on the national question as the first-ever South Wales district pamphlet concentrated on economic and social policy. Even so, emboldened by the Comintern's anti-fascist patriotic turn, *The People Can Save South Wales* (1936) by district secretary Idris Cox invoked the spirit of centuries-old Welsh revolt against English kings and invaders, urging the people to unite against not only 'English masters' but also today's capitalist employers, bankers and landlords of every nationality.

In March 1937, the Party organised a 'South Wales in the March of History' parade through Tonypandy. Its brochure recounted the struggles of the common people from the Scotch Cattle, the Merthyr Rising and the Chartists in the 19th century to the Cambrian dispute, the General Strike, the huge anti-Means Test demonstrations and the election of Communist Arthur Horner as president of the SWMF in the 20th. The early wars against the 'tyranny of English oppressors' had now given way to the fight against fascism which, too, was 'alien and hated by the freedom-loving people of South Wales'.

With local CP membership trebling to 3,000 as a result of its work in the SWMF and the National Unemployed Workers Movement, South Wales district secretary Glyn Jones believed more could be done to 'pay attention to the national characteristics, prejudices and traditions of Wales'. In the Party journal Discussion (December 1937), he suggested the CP should publish more materials in Welsh, support linguistic rights and call for administrative autonomy for Wales. Despite support at the February 1938 CC from Rajani Palme Dutt and Gallacher, his request for regular Welsh-language content in the *Daily Worker* went unheeded except during National Eisteddfod week.

In north Wales, John Roose Williams had left the Welsh National Party (WNP) and was building the CP in Welsh-speaking industrial communities. His pamphlet *Llwybr Rhyddid y Werin* (1936) ['The People's Path to Freedom'] placed communism in the Welsh radical tradition of popular revolt. He proclaimed the CP's support for Welsh self-determination and the development of the Welsh language and culture. But real freedom could only be achieved by ending capitalist exploitation. Williams accused the WNP leadership of deploying 'Hitler's methods' with its 'Dinner Clubs' for the unemployed and poured scorn on Welsh Nationalist policy that South Wales should be 'de-industrialised' to save the moral and physical health of its people. At the same time, he drew a distinction between the anti-working class, anti-communist and backward-looking leaders of the WNP and the party's rank-and-file.

In the progressive journal *Heddiw* (February 1937) ['Today'], Williams confessed that his love for his birthplace and the working people, language and literature of his native Wales made him, too, a Welsh nationalist. But from a class and Communist standpoint, he could not separate his nation's fate from that of humanity as a whole. Workers across the world faced unemployment, poverty, fascism and war under capitalism because of their class, not their nationality, and the struggle against capitalism and its state power was at its fiercest in South Wales. Like TE Nicholas in his weekly newspaper column in *Y Cymro* ['The Welshman'], Williams supported campaigns for equal status for the Welsh language and against the removal of three acquitted Welsh Nationalists to an English court for re-trial. But for both Communists, these issues paled into insignificance beside the desperate problems of unemployment, poverty, fascism and war faced by peoples across the world. On every front, the pro-fascist National Government was the biggest enemy of the Welsh people. Only Communist leadership and a victorious working class could overcome capitalism and through socialism secure peace, civilisation and the language and culture of small nations. Russia and Republican Spain were showing how small nations and minorities could enjoy real freedom. The WNP should join the 'People's Front' and link the Welsh fight for national rights to the working class struggle for freedom and democracy against poverty, war and fascism.

By 1937, a new North Wales district committee of CP was contributing to the South Wales district committee's 'Draft Statement on Welsh Nationalism' (February 1938). It analysed the reasons for the WNP's recent growth and the CP's relative weakness. Again, a clear distinction was drawn between those nationalists who worked with Communists in local campaigns and the 'fascist elements' at the top of the WNP (whose sympathies indeed lay with Portugal's fascist dictatorship, Action Francaise, Nazi Germany's foreign policy and Franco's Nationalist rebels in Spain). Progressive Welsh nationalists should be won to the People's Front and to CP economic programmes for south and north Wales (where WNP policies were backward in comparison with the SNP). Welsh Communists now proposed a Secretary of State for Wales as in Scotland and a National Advisory Council, as steps towards the longer-term goal of a Welsh Parliament in a federal Britain.

After liaison with the North Wales committee, the South Wales district submitted a paper on 'The National Problem in Wales' to the Party's PB in July 1938. It struggled to define Wales as a nation in accordance with Stalin's definition in *Marxism and the National Question* (1913), newly published for the first time in English: 'A nation is a historically constituted, stable community of people, formed on the basis of a common language, territory, economic life, and psychological make-up manifested in a common culture'. It was difficult to argue that Wales had a community of economic life (or 'economic cohesion' as Stalin also put it), given the separate development and orientation of north and south. The paper's rejection of 'rigid rules and definitions' and its alternative proposition that the Welsh people are 'bound together by economic ties' found little favour with the PB. The demand for a Welsh Parliament within a federal system was also struck out, probably reflecting fears that it might contradict working-class unity.

A final 'Statement on the National Question in Wales' analysed Welsh history and society in class terms, pointing out that the Welsh landowners and capitalists had merged with their 'blood brothers of the English ruling class' to build up and share in the spoils of the British Empire. The Welsh language and its culture had been mostly left in the hands of the working people. Therefore, full and equal legal status for Welsh should be supported along with the establishment of an independent judiciary and a Broadcasting Council for Wales. But the nationalist thesis that Wales remained a colony of England, exploited by an 'English' rather than a British capitalist class, was rejected. Instead, the statement called upon all democratic and liberal forces – including the WNP – to join the 'People's Front' against Britain's National Government that was preparing the way for fascism.

At that summer's National Eisteddfod, a bilingual pamphlet produced by the two Welsh committees of the CP, *Llên y Werin/ Lore of the People*, praised the festival as a treasured expression of the common people's progressive and democratic unity, culture and aspirations. Fascism threatened the language and culture of small nations – as the 'valiant Basque people' could testify – whereas only socialism could secure their future.

1938-1966 Answering the Question

No mention was made of Britain's national question in the resolutions adopted at the 15th Party congress in September 1938. However, under the heading 'Work among the Middle Class and Professional Sections', the CC reported to delegates:

> For many years the Party has under-estimated the
> importance of the Scottish Nationalist Movement and the
> Welsh Nationalists ... our Party stands for a policy which
> preserves the best traditions of the Scottish people and the
> Welsh people, resists every attempt to encroach upon their
> national rights, and demands the fullest opportunities for the
> development of self-government.

The CC promised that popular pamphlets would be published in Scotland and Wales before the end of the year, setting out in more detail the CP's attitude on the national question.

Aitken Ferguson's subsequent pamphlet *Scotland* (1938) analysed the impact of the capitalist Depression on Scottish industry and the plight of the Highlands. A wide-ranging 'Plan to Save Scotland' put forward economic and social policies to benefit the unemployed, industrial and rural workers, smallholders and fishermen. Its constitutional proposals culminated in the case for a 'new legislative body in Scotland, with a Socialist and democratic majority elected on a basis of full joint suffrage'. The legislature would exercise extensive financial powers devolved from Westminster and have the capacity to 'compel reactionary elements to toe the line'. In a foreword to the pamphlet, John MacCormick welcomed it as a 'contribution to the fight for Scottish Freedom'. He joined Ferguson on public platforms to promote a plan for a Scottish constitutional convention to map out the country's future. Yet such was the lack of enthusiasm for this new line among the Party's 2,800 members in Scotland – more than half of them on industrial Clydeside – that a Scottish congress resolution in 1939 criticised the 'unsympathetic approach' of comrades to the 'nationalist aspirations of the Scottish people'.

The outbreak of war in September 1939 aborted the 16th CP congress and the adoption of a new Party programme. The CC's draft had set the framework for the Party's policy on the national question in Britain for the following decades. A section on 'Safeguarding and Extending Democracy' called for 'self-government for Scotland', preceded by regular meetings between Scottish MPs and representatives of local authorities and 'democratic organisations' to formulate economic and social policies for the country. Similarly, self-government was the aim for Wales with, as the first steps, equal status for the Welsh language and the appointment of a Secretary of State and Council of Education for Wales.

Although the Party had yet to discuss any constitutional reforms for England, Party publications and events were defining and celebrating a distinctive, progressive English identity and patriotism. Articles in *Labour Monthly* by the likes of Robin Page Arnot and books such as AL Morton's *A People's History of England* (1938), Jack Lindsay's *England, My England* (1939) and Christopher Hill's *The English Revolution* (1940) uncovered the 'history from below' of the struggles of England's working people against ruling class exploitation and repression. In Wales, the works of Islwyn Nicholas and the SWMF 'Pageant of Welsh History' (1939) were performing a similar function.

As attention turned to the challenges of post-war reconstruction, Idris Cox declared in *Forward to a New Life for South Wales* (1944): 'It is not enough to fight for the freedom of all other nations, and refuse to fight for our own. In the new world after the war, Wales must take a positive part as a free country in building the new family of democratic nations'. His immediate, practical proposals for a Secretary of State and National Administrative Council for Wales, the nationalisation of basic industries with all-Wales administration, improved north-south transport links, economic development in mid-Wales, agricultural support and a major housebuilding programme formed the basis for the Party's submission to the Welsh Reconstruction Advisory Council. The overriding need was to rebuild an industrial base in every part of Wales that would retain future generations of workers, thereby providing the only viable basis on which local communities, their culture and the Welsh language could survive.

In Scotland, the prospect of post-war reorganisation stimulated some sections of the labour movement to revive the call for devolution. However, a contrary perspective was growing even more strongly on the left of the Labour Party and in the ILP, that socialism would be achieved through reforms decided at Westminster; a Scottish Parliament could play only a minor role, if any at all. Secretary of State for Scotland Tom Johnston had come to this view, as had Welsh ex-home rulers and future government ministers Jim Griffiths and Dai Grenfell. Administrative devolution and social reform at the all-Britain level could achieve radical change without resorting to 'divisive' nationalism. Thus, the CP was almost alone when its policy document 'Britain for the People' – drawn up by a committee chaired by Gallacher – was published in May 1944, calling for Scottish and Welsh parliaments as well as a proportional representation (PR) voting system and more powers for local government.

The Party's outlook in Wales was strengthened still further in July 1944 by the unification of the South Wales and North Wales districts. Within months the Welsh Committee had published a statement on 'Communists and Welsh Self-Government' and a pamphlet for that year's National Eisteddfod, *The Flame of Welsh Freedom/ Fflam Rhyddid Cymru*. These linked the economic interests of the Welsh working class with the need for administrative devolution, leading to a Welsh Parliament in a federal Britain. The offensive against the WNP leadership's 'blend of semi-Fascist ideology and Roman Catholicism' was maintained, while the labour movement was urged to organise in a Welsh Trades Union Congress and an all-Wales Regional Council of Labour.

A more comprehensive programme, *Wales in the New World* (August 1944), drew together previous proposals for post-war reconstruction and emphasised cultural needs such as more Welsh-language education and the founding of a Welsh national theatre and orchestra. It saw a Welsh Parliament as an integral part of a federal Britain that would also improve parliamentary efficiency at Westminster. The first all-Wales congress of the CP endorsed the new programme in January 1945 – but not before Arthur Horner in the chair had contradicted Idris Cox and expressed his opposition to a Welsh Parliament as a concession to nationalism that would threaten working-class unity.

Meanwhile, in Scotland, the SNP had been making major inroads into the industrial working-class vote in a number of parliamentary by-elections. In 1943, the CP's Scottish Congress had urged the labour movement to lead a campaign for a Scottish Parliament with powers over industrial and social policy. Assistant editor of the *Daily Worker*, JR Campbell, went even further in *Labour Monthly* (May 1945), suggesting that Labour should consider an electoral pact with the SNP, instead of bringing in speakers – as in the Motherwell by-election – whose ignorant attacks on national sentiment drove away middle-class people while perpetuating divisions within the working class.

Partly in response to the nationalist resurgence, the Labour Party in Scotland campaigned for 'a Scottish Parliament for Scottish Affairs' in the 1945 General Election. Some Labour candidates also endorsed the all-party

Scottish Convention's call for a law-making Scottish Parliament. Willie Gallacher did likewise, although the Communist campaign in Scotland as elsewhere highlighted policies of nationalisation, planning, the Welfare State, colonial freedom and a peaceful new world order. In Rhondda East, CP general secretary Harry Pollitt almost defeated ex-Marxist Bill Mainwaring to join Gallacher and Phil Piratin at Westminster. Idris Cox believed that Pollitt's campaign should have shown more sympathy for Welsh patriotic aspirations, although it's doubtful this would have enticed enough of the 2,123 Welsh Nationalist votes needed for victory.

The CP welcomed Labour's General Election triumph, but without illusions about the incoming government. At the 18th Party congress in November 1945, a resolution on Wales called for the whole country to be scheduled as a Development Area qualifying for economic assistance. The government should switch munitions factories to civilian production and direct the location of industry. A Secretary of State for Wales should be appointed immediately and measures prepared for the establishment of Welsh and Scottish parliaments. A much longer resolution on Scotland dealt in more detail with the fate of specific companies and industries and demanded more administrative devolution, a Scottish Planning Commission, an economic plan for Scotland and regular meetings of Scottish MPs. But the congress declined to endorse the Scottish Committee's recently published pamphlet, *Whither Scotland?*, because of differences over the powers and top priority it proposed for a Scottish Parliament.

Having trounced the SNP at the polls, Labour in Scotland and at Westminster felt no pressure to concede a Scottish legislature of any sort. In response, the Scottish Covenant for a law-making Scottish Parliament was launched in the late 1940s with some labour movement involvement. Communists worked energetically with MacCormick and others to win two million signatures for the covenant. Former Scottish CP secretary John Gollan's book *Scottish Prospect* (1948) left no doubt about the Party's support for a Scottish Parliament and the vital role it could play in promoting economic development as the working class advanced towards political power. Yet there was less hostility to 'London government' now that it was a Labour one introducing the Welfare State, building council houses and nationalising key industries. With no electoral clout and no support from the increasingly anti-nationalist, anti-Communist Scottish TUC, the Scottish Covenant Association met with failure.

Nor would the post-war Labour government offer anything of substance to Wales, rejecting even a Secretary of State while setting up a powerless Advisory Council for Wales. This prompted a major debate within the CP's Welsh Committee and congress. In *The Fight for Socialism in Wales* (March 1948), Idris Cox rejected the 'narrow nationalism and economic separation' of Plaid Cymru and its policy of self-government within the British Commonwealth; instead, he proposed a 'Welsh Parliament within a

British federal system' as part of a united working-class struggle to abolish capitalism and establish a socialist Britain.

However, a Welsh Committee recommendation to put a Welsh Parliament at the top of the Party's devolution agenda was rejected by the Welsh Congress a few months later. Reports to the central PC and in *Party News* confirmed that many CP members, especially in south Wales, remained indifferent or even hostile towards devolution. With Welsh now spoken by only one-third of the population, the national question was seen as a diversion from the class struggle and a potential source of division in the labour movement. This outlook was not shared by the likes of Dai Dan Evans, administrative head and later the vice-president and general secretary of the South Wales Area NUM, and prime mover behind the establishment of the bilingual South Wales Miners Eisteddfod in 1948. The Party also identified itself with the Welsh language through the centennial translation of the Communist Manifesto from the original German into Welsh by WJ Rees, published as *Y Maniffesto Comiwnyddol* in 1948. All the while, TE Nicholas was winning eisteddfod chairs as his sonnets celebrated Welsh workers, nature, Lenin and the Soviet Union and condemned capitalism, racism and the Cold War mongers.

Differences within the CP, combined with efforts to maintain left unity as the Labour government and the TUC launched an anti-Communist offensive in the civil service and trade union movement, probably explain the absence of the national question from the main reports and resolutions of the 19th and 20th Party congresses in 1946 and 1948. However, this changed abruptly as the leadership searched for a strategic way forward for the CP and the wider labour movement in the new political, economic, social and international conditions of the late 1940s. With a General Election looming, the EC issued a draft election manifesto, *The Socialist Road for Britain* (August 1949). Its section on 'Democracy in Britain' proposed measures to extend working-class democratic rights and secure a united Ireland, before making the most expansive statement to date on the national question from the CP centrally:

> It is essential that the Scots and Welsh be given self-government in their domestic affairs at the earliest possible moment. The refusal of the Labour Party to honour its pledges on self-government has aroused justifiable indignation among the Scots and Welsh people, who are determined to fight against the danger of their countries returning to the depressed conditions of the interwar period and who regard a national legislature as essential to their national development. Scottish and Welsh Parliaments should be set up, with power to deal with education, town planning, agriculture, land, trade and industry (other than foreign

trade), transport, fuel, and broadcasting. The people must
fight for legislation on these proposals without delay.

Introducing this manifesto to the 21st congress in November 1949, Palme
Dutt drew attention to the 'national claims of Scotland and Wales' – the only
mention of the issue in any of the main platform speeches at the congress.

Yet this position was abbreviated to a single, timid sentence in the first
edition of the Party's new programme, *The British Road to Socialism* (*BRS*),
unveiled by the EC in January 1951: 'There must be full recognition of the
national claims of the Scottish and Welsh peoples, to be settled according
to the wishes of these peoples'. Even this looked out of place in a section
calling for 'National Independence of the British People and of All Peoples
of the British Empire', which condemned US imperialism in Britain and
British imperialism in the colonies. Early drafts drawn up by Palme Dutt,
Emile Burns and George Matthews had explicitly proposed parliaments
for Wales and Scotland. It is not clear from surviving records who caused
the reference to be dropped and why, although it did not arise in the prior
discussions between general secretary Pollitt and Soviet leader Stalin.
Dutt's position is implied in his article 'The Fight for British Independence'
in the *Communist Review* (February 1951), where he argued that the British
ruling class had crushed and distorted all 'traditional sentiments of national
pride and patriotism' in order to replace with them with jingoism, notions
of racial superiority and pride in the British Empire. This had made the
left suspicious of patriotism, deleted the terms 'England' and 'English' from
imperialism's official vocabulary, and could also be seen in the 'parallel
contemptuous blindness to Scottish national feeling or Welsh national
feeling'.

Certainly, there continued to be a lack of enthusiasm for legislative
devolution from the top of the CP down to rank-and-file members in south
Wales and – to a lesser extent – industrial Scotland. Nevertheless, the Welsh
Committee accepted an invitation from Undeb Cymru Fydd (the 'New
Wales Union') to participate in a 'Parliament for Wales' campaign. The
Party's Welsh Secretary Idris Cox addressed the launch conference in July
1950 and joined its executive committee. Predictably, some anti-devolution
newspapers and politicians attempted to paint the initiative as Communist-
inspired although, in reality, Plaid Cymru members were far more numerous
at every level of the campaign. Half a dozen Welsh Labour MPs were also
actively involved along with the Welsh Liberals. The hostility of the Welsh
Regional Council of Labour (WRCL) and a few Labour MPs was palpable,
adding to the reluctance of many CP members to take part in a campaign
that divided the left and the labour movement.

The campaign suffered a fatal reverse at the South Wales Area NUM's
annual conference in May 1954. Two Communist lodge officials, Cyril Parry
and Hywel Davy Williams, moved the motion to support a parliament for

Wales. But the WRCL had successfully lobbied the NUM area executive to ensure that only NUM-sponsored MPs who opposed the motion were allowed to address the conference, which voted by a substantial majority to reject a Welsh Parliament in the belief that it could jeopardise the future of the Welsh coal industry, strengthen Welsh nationalism and divide the NUM and the labour movement. A few weeks later, the WRCL conference opted instead for more administrative devolution and a dedicated minister for Welsh affairs.

Despite the failure to deliver the support of the South Wales NUM – although both its president Will Paynter and future general secretary Dai Dan Evans were Party members – Communists such as Onllwyn lodge official Dai Francis and Annie Powell (later the mayor of the Rhondda) made a significant contribution to the campaign. Plaid Cymru leader Gwynfor Evans paid fulsome tribute to the CP's work in the coalfield communities of south-west Wales.

More might have been done but for the removal of Cox as Welsh organiser in June 1951, followed by another change of leadership when his successor Alun Thomas was replaced by Bill Alexander in 1953. Ostensibly, Cox had been transferred to the Party centre and then to international duties because of organisational weaknesses in Wales. Claims that the real or main reason was an alleged inclination towards Welsh nationalism have proved difficult to substantiate, although his ardent support for a Welsh Parliament and Welsh language rights was not shared by such leading Communists as Paynter, general secretary Pollitt and NUM president Arthur Horner. Cox himself offered no definitive view on the issue, although he expressed regret that the lack of CP involvement had allowed Plaid Cymru to exert growing influence over the campaign's organisation. As the Welsh Committee reported to the PB in April 1951, many Party members were indifferent where not hostile towards the campaign because they did not want to work with religious and 'middle class' elements, feared that such a parliament would lead to economic and political separation and saw the issue as a distraction from class politics and the struggle for socialism. A Welsh Committee report in January 1954 identified the consequence: nationalist and separatist sentiments were coming to dominate the campaign, divorcing it from any perspective of a 'People's Democracy' and socialism in Britain.

Although the CP in Wales continued to put the case for administrative and democratic devolution, including a Welsh National Planning Commission, correspondents in *World News* complained that the Welsh Committee was failing to project the case in publications or at events such as the National Eisteddfod. More positively, the Welsh Committee began to develop policy to promote the Welsh language in the law, education and broadcasting.

In Scotland, the failure of the Labour government and the Scottish Covenant to produce any constitutional change had knocked some of the stuffing out of the movement for devolution. Throughout the 1950s, the

Scottish TUC supported only greater administrative devolution, rejecting calls from the Communist-led Glasgow, Clydebank and Greenock trades councils and Scottish Area NUM for greater 'self-government' or a Scottish Parliament. In its submission to the Royal Commission on Scottish Affairs in 1953, the CP's Scottish Committee had reiterated its case for administrative devolution and a Scottish Parliament with economic powers, but with a constitutional safeguard that would prevent future Scottish legislation under-cutting UK standards in industrial and social matters.

Centrally, CP policy on the national question had reached relative equilibrium, between a concrete measure of self-government for Scotland and Wales in the form of their own subordinate parliaments and the Party's strategy for socialist revolution in Britain as a whole. The CP's 1955 General Election manifesto contained a sub-section on Scotland and Wales calling for parliaments to safeguard their economic health and 'great cultural traditions'. In 1958, the debate in *World News* around a new draft of the *British Road to Socialism* helped prepare the way for a more concrete formulation than the previous anodyne reference to the 'national claims' of the Scottish and Welsh peoples. In a chapter outlining the measures to be taken by a socialist government in Britain, the updated programme declared: 'Scotland and Wales need to have their own Parliaments, with powers to ensure the balanced development of their economies within the general plan for Britain, as well as to satisfy the wider aspirations of their peoples'. Desmond Greaves had been more ambitious, having argued for an explicit commitment in the programme to a federal system for Britain and to protecting the Welsh and Gaelic languages.

Conversely, by the late 1950s the Labour Party had hardened its stance against any kind of elected assembly or parliament for Scotland or Wales, fearing such bodies might suck powers upwards from the many Labour-controlled local councils.

Following the 1964 General Election, the Labour government's alternatives were to establish a Secretary of State for Wales and the Highland and Islands Development Board in Scotland. But Prime Minister Harold Wilson's plans to redistribute wealth and modernise the British economy were soon knocked off course by the financial markets in league with the Bank of England. Unemployment grew in the older industrial areas of England, Scotland and Wales as regional development policies failed to absorb an upsurge of redundancies in the coal, rail, shipbuilding and textile industries. Disillusionment with Labour in office, centrally and locally, grew although – as another General Election win in 1966 demonstrated – for many workers there appeared to be no acceptable electoral alternative ... at least in England.

1966-1998 Refining the Answer

The result of the Carmarthen parliamentary by-election in July 1966 sent shock-waves around the world. Gwynfor Evans had taken the seat from Labour, overturning that party's majority of 11,000 over the Liberals in the March General Election. A religious pacifist with less conservative social views than the previous WNP leadership, and vigorously opposed to nuclear weapons and the US war in Vietnam, he had drawn support from the farming, small business and self-employed sections of the electorate together with elements of the Welsh-speaking working class on the western edge of the South Wales coalfield.

Four more spectacular by-elections were to follow over the next two years: Plaid Cymru took almost 7,000 votes from Labour in Rhondda East, to come within a whisker of victory; the Scottish Nationalists in Glasgow Pollok won half of their 10,000 votes from Labour who lost the seat to the Tories; in November 1967, the SNP came from nowhere in Hamilton to take 9,000 votes from Labour and send Winnie Ewing to Westminster; then Plaid Cymru attracted 10,000 votes from Labour and almost captured Caerffili.

In response, the CP's Welsh Committee and congress in 1966 reaffirmed support for a Welsh TUC, proposed a 'National Convention' of political and civic bodies to draw up a programme for Wales and praised the 'courageous efforts' of young Cymdeithas yr Iaith Gymraeg (Welsh Language Society) activists in their mass campaign of non-violent civil disobedience. The influx of people into the nationalist movement included many with 'socialist and communist convictions' with whom the CP should cooperate. At the same time, the Welsh CP leadership was critical of the Party centrally and the Labour Party and labour movement at every level for their failure to take national aspirations seriously (the CP General Election manifesto had devoted just six words to them). A Welsh Parliament could be achieved under capitalism; the key question was whether it would be fought for and won by a broad national movement – including Plaid Cymru and the CP – allied to an all-Britain anti-monopoly alliance, or fought for and lost by a narrow and divisive nationalist movement. In a paper to the Party's central PC in April 1967, the Welsh Committee also proposed a semi-federal system of Welsh and Scottish parliaments with the Westminster central parliament reformed to counteract the numerical preponderance of English MPs. The economic resources of Britain and as a whole should be shared to equalise development and prosperity.

At the April 1967 PC, general secretary Gordon McLennan and industrial organiser Bert Ramelson urged caution, given the anti-devolution attitudes of the Labour Party and TUC. The July EC responded more positively and a statement – endorsed by the 30th Party congress in November 1967 – proclaimed the urgency of establishing Welsh and Scottish parliaments with substantial economic powers and elected by a system of proportional representation (PR). The British labour movement needed to break the conservative resistance of the Labour government and party to the way forward.

That said, the Welsh Council of Labour had moved forward a little in 1966, adopting the policy of an elected Council for Wales, albeit with limited executive powers. In 1967, the Labour government had secured the Welsh Language Act, giving Welsh equal validity in law with English but doing little to promote equal use or status in practice. The Scottish Council of Labour and Secretary of State Willie Ross, on the other hand, remained adamantly opposed to any elected national body for Scotland. Their chief concern was to secure the regionalisation of local government and the appointment of Scotland-wide bodies to promote economic development including tourism.

Following the Communist Party's July 1967 EC meeting, Welsh secretary Bert Pearce sparked an 18-month debate with an article in *Marxism Today* (November 1967) calling upon the Party to adopt a much bolder approach to the national question in Scotland and Wales. Their peoples wanted economic, social and cultural issues to be treated on a national and not just an all-Britain level. Drawing upon the work of John Gollan and pan-Celtic scholars George Thomson and WJ Rees, Pearce set out a Marxist analysis of how classes in Scotland and Wales had merged into an all-Britain class structure, while retaining distinctive national characteristics that could express themselves politically in economic, social and cultural matters. The crisis of British imperialism and widespread disillusionment with Labour's record in local and central government was driving people towards the nationalist parties as an acceptable alternative to Labour. Yet the problem, at root, for workers in Scotland and Wales as everywhere was capitalism. The solution, therefore, lay in a united class struggle for socialism, part of which must entail the recognition and expression of national aspirations. The CP and the labour movement must campaign energetically for the maximum devolution of economic, financial and other powers to Welsh and Scottish Parliaments elected by PR, combined with extensive administrative devolution, the establishment of a Welsh TUC and measures to secure a fully bilingual Wales. Labour and the nationalist parties should forsake their divisive standpoints and unite in broad-based national movements in both countries to fight for these and other democratic and progressive policies.

Writing in *Labour Monthly*, Gwynfor Evans (December 1967) and Winnie Ewing (February 1968) made it clear that their parties were single-minded in their pursuit of 'national freedom' from English domination, and nothing less. Editor Palme Dutt reaffirmed his view that the working-class and socialist movement should 'understand with sympathy the aspirations and outlook of the Scottish and Welsh Nationalist movements'.

In June 1968, in response to Pearce, Idris Cox cited Stalin's definition of a nation and – challenging a *Morning Star* article by Scottish CP secretary Jimmy Reid – declared that the Welsh and Scots were, rather, 'nationalities who can become nations'. A Welsh-speaker himself, Cox pointed to the complex and changing circumstances of Welsh and Gaelic, reinforcing the case for far-reaching policies in their support. But he also raised the question of England and its national future. The draft new edition of *The British Road to Socialism* (1968) had repeated the call for devolved parliaments, but without proposing how that might affect the Westminster parliament. That could mean Scottish and Welsh MPs being able to influence policies for England in devolved areas, while English MPs could not decide them for Wales or Scotland.

Thus Cox anticipated anti-devolution Labour MP Tam Dalyell's 'West Lothian question' by almost a decade. To strengthen the all-round fight for devolution, therefore, he proposed that the demand should also be raised for a separate English Parliament, within a federal system for the whole of Britain. In an article in the *Morning Star* (February 1968), Gwynfor Evans had opposed federalism on practical as well as political grounds, pointing to the imbalance in size between the three nations and the complicating factor of English regionalism. Cox believed that the proposal in the *BRS* for elected regional councils in England to counteract administrative centralism should not have been considered in isolation from the question of an English Parliament and federalism. He also wanted the Communist Party to reorganise its own internal structures to reflect the position of Wales and Scotland as nations; they were not merely the equivalents of the Party districts in England. This position had been rejected by McLennan at the April 1967 PC (but was eventually conceded two years later).

In any event, the debate reflected and energised a major development of the CP's policy on the national question centrally. Following debate at the Party's 30th congress in November 1967, and further discussion around an amended draft, the EC published a new edition of the *BRS* in October 1968.

In an unprecedented section on 'National Rights', the programme proposed as an immediate priority single-chamber parliaments for Wales and Scotland elected by PR, with adequate powers and finances to deal with trade, industry, agricultural planning, social security and broadcasting. Although not relying upon socialism to deliver Scottish and Welsh parliaments, it presented the fight to achieve and direct them in the interests of the people as part of the common struggle to defeat British capitalism. Moreover, such reforms would also meet the 'urgent need for increased popular control and democratic effectiveness in the whole structure of government in England as well'. In a section on 'Socialist democracy', the *BRS* declared: 'The Welsh and Scottish peoples would need to develop the most effective, democratic forms of self-government in the process of the common effort to build socialism. The peoples of Britain together would work out the best forms of association to fulfil their national, democratic and social aspirations'. Although this was in the spirit of self-determination, recognising that the peoples of self-governing nations must decide their own future, critics suggested it was nonetheless an abdication of leadership by the CP not to express a preference – for or against federalism, for instance

– and argue for it.

In Scotland, the CP was making substantial ground in the trade union movement, from the factories and shipyards to the Scottish TUC general council. At the STUC conference in 1968, Communist president of the Scottish Area NUM Mick McGahey proposed support for a Scottish Parliament. Facing strong opposition, including a pro-unionist composite motion from the engineering union and NALGO, he agreed to remit his motion to the STUC general council for further consideration. At the following year's conference, delegates unanimously adopted a motion again moved by McGahey – but this time with support from the general council and its new assistant general secretary and CP member Jimmy Milne – in favour of a legislative assembly for Scotland.

In Wales, the national question had taken a more militant turn, with hundreds of Welsh Language Society members going to prison for their campaign against English-only road signs. A Welsh republican group MAC, Mudiad Amddiffyn Cymru ('Movement for the Defence of Wales') was carrying out a spectacular bombing campaign against public buildings and installations. The Welsh CP condemned MAC's tactics, while telling the anti-devolution Secretary of State for Wales George Thomas that his proposed all-party summit against terrorism should consider Welsh economic development and self-government instead. At the 1968 Welsh congress, the Party called for a Welsh TUC, an Economic Plan for Wales and a broad campaign for a Welsh Parliament. It also condemned the investiture of Charles Windsor as 'Prince of Wales' planned for 1969 and which provoked TE Nicholas to compose one of his most savage sonnets ('Syrcas '69') against the English monarchy and its reign in Wales. The congress also approved plans to publish a journal, *Cyffro/ Change*, which went on to promote a broad discussion of political and cultural issues across the left and into the nationalist movement. A short while later, the Scottish Committee launched its own journal, *Scottish Marxist*, which performed a similar educational and unifying function.

At the CP's 31st congress in November 1969, Glasgow trades council secretary Hugh Wyper proposed a resolution on behalf of the EC which represented the Party's most extensive central policy statement to date. Incorporating many of the points already being promoted in Scotland, Wales and the *BRS*, it broke new ground in some important respects: firstly, it highlighted the impact of British imperialism on the peoples and resources of the two countries, notably the presence of military bases and NATO forces and the diversion of funds into armaments expenditure and overseas investment; secondly, the resolution called for a 'Wales Trade Union Congress'; thirdly, it demanded not only equal status with English for the Welsh language, but also that 'the Gaelic language too, where it is in use, should be fostered as part of Scotland's cultural heritage'; and fourth, that future relations between the Scottish, Welsh and English peoples might require a 'separate English Parliament', or at least an alternative way of handling specifically English affairs in the central parliament at Westminster. The 31st congress also considered the possibility of elected regional assemblies in England, but rejected an amendment committing the Party to the immediate demand for an English national parliament.

This resolution formed the basis for more detailed submissions from the party's EC and Welsh and Scottish committees to the Royal Commission on the Constitution set up by the Labour government in 1969. When the Scottish TUC presented its evidence in March 1970 for a diluted Scottish Assembly with executive-only powers, the commissioners could barely conceal their scorn for what they said would be little more than a 'talking-shop'. The proposals presented by the Labour Party's Scottish Council in a pamphlet, *The Government of Scotland* (1970), were so feeble that Royal Commission chair Lord Crowther enquired why they weren't asking for more. The party's representatives replied that a Scottish Assembly could prove economically divisive, take powers from local government and undermine the work done by Scottish MPs and their Select Committee at Westminster.

The Jersey Communist Party, on the other hand, demanded sweeping reforms of the island's corrupt and 'semi-feudal' parliamentary system which was based on a low-wage and low taxation economy.

In Wales, Communists such as South Wales NUM general secretary Dai Francis and former NUPE president and Glamorgan trades councils leader D Ivor Davies worked closely with T&GWU Welsh regional secretary Tom Jones (a former International Brigader) and his successor George Wright to promote the establishment of a Welsh TUC. The TUC regional advisory committee system had proved unable to coordinate industrial and solidarity action across Wales during the 1972 miners strike. But the first conference of the new body in May 1973 was not recognised by the TUC and some trade union leaderships. Eventually, agreement was reached which inserted what became the Wales Trades Union Council (WTUC) into a reformed framework of regional TUCs across England and Wales, with a much enhanced role for Welsh trades councils. Moreover, much to the annoyance of his civil service advisors and the TUC in London, Secretary of State for Industry Tony Benn provided the Welsh TUC with the funds to produce a series of high-profile research and policy papers. It came as little surprise when the first official conference of the Wales TUC, with Dai Francis as chair, called for an 'elected Legislative Assembly' for Wales. This went further than the Royal Commission's majority recommendation the following year for a Welsh Assembly with executive powers only, alongside a legislative assembly for Scotland.

Meanwhile, the SNP was reaping the political benefit of the discovery of North Sea or 'Scottish' oil. The CP and an expanding 'Home Rule' wing in the Labour Party were also beginning to win sections of the labour movement – in particular the Scottish TUC – back to a position of support for a Scottish assembly or parliament. The SNP's by-election victory in Glasgow Govan in October 1973 laid bare Labour's electoral vulnerability, which was confirmed when the SNP took seven and then eleven seats in the two General Elections of 1974.

The Labour government's Scotland and Wales Bill to enact the Royal Commission's findings was finally withdrawn in early 1977, following a hostile campaign orchestrated by south Wales Labour MPs such as Neil Kinnock reneging on their previous pledges. Labour rebels in the north of England were worried that their regions would be disadvantaged in competition with Welsh and Scottish Assemblies for public and private sector investment. Portraying devolution as a recipe for 'dictatorship' in which only Welsh-speakers would be permitted to sit in the Welsh Assembly, Leo Abse accused a 'bunch of Communists' on the WTUC general council of browbeating others into supporting it. Bert Pearce attacked the Pontypool MP for chasing a 'few cheap headlines' and pointed out that the WTUC policy had been devised by socialists with real experience in the working-class movement, seeking answers to people's real problems. In *Marxism Today* (December 1977) he criticised the failed Bill for putting forward a Welsh Assembly too powerless to inspire much enthusiasm and a Scottish Assembly with no substantial economic powers. Furthermore, the government's White Paper on *The English Dimension* had offered nothing by way of powers or resources to the English regions as part of a comprehensive post-devolution settlement. The intransigence of anti-devolution English and Welsh Labour MPs, in turn, reflected the British labour movement's retreat into regionalism and 'left-sectarian socialism'.

In Scotland and Wales, the CP organised schools and conferences to draw more socialists and trade unionists into pro-devolution discussion and campaigning. In *Labour Monthly* (February 1976), Royston Green highlighted the distinctive Celtic identity of Cornwall and its own native language, urging socialists and the labour movement to come to the fore in the battles to promote balanced economic and cultural development in Cornwall.

Separate devolution Bills for Wales and Scotland were eventually passed in 1978, although their weaknesses remained and dissident Labour MPs and their Tory allies inserted clauses requiring a referendum in both countries. In an updated *BRS* (1978), supporters of national rights for Scotland and Wales were included among the 'social forces and movements' that can be mobilised for radical change along the road to socialism. The programme also argued that 'the people of England should have similar rights in relation to their affairs' as part of a restructuring and decentralisation of government. The unity of Britain could only be based on the principle of 'voluntary cooperation between the three nations'.

Despite criticisms of Labour's devolution proposals, the CP in Scotland

and Wales campaigned vigorously for them in the March 1979 referendum, as part of the broad but non-Labour 'Scotland Says Yes' campaign and with the Wales TUC, Labour Party and Plaid Cymru in the 'Wales for the Assembly' campaign. Neil Kinnock repeated the anti-Communist jibes aimed at the WTUC and miners' leader Dai Francis. Although a majority voted narrowly in favour of a Scottish legislative assembly, it was not enough to fulfil a threshold clause introduced by hostile Labour and Tory MPs. In Wales, the proposed executive assembly was heavily defeated on a low turnout. The 11-strong body of SNP MPs then supported a Tory 'no confidence' motion in the Commons, bringing down the Labour government and opening the way to Margaret Thatcher's General Election victory and 18 years of Tory rule. The SNP lost all but two of its seats in May and the devolution issue lay dormant until the mid-1980s.

The experience of an unyielding Tory government in London imposing mass coal and steel redundancies, the Poll Tax and other right-wing policies on Labour-voting Scotland and Wales revived the case for devolution and even full independence. Labour leader Neil Kinnock pledged support for a Scottish Assembly in 1986 and his party later introduced a Scotland Bill in the Commons. Communists participated with Labour members, the STUC and many civic organisations in the Campaign for a Scottish Assembly – boycotted by the SNP leadership – which gave rise to the Scottish Constitutional Convention and its blueprint for a Scottish Parliament. These developments encouraged the Wales TUC to propose a Welsh Constitutional Convention, although Welsh Labour hostility to cross-party initiatives strangled the idea at birth. The re-established Communist Party launched an ambitious series of initiatives in the early 1990s for 'A People's Parliament for Wales'. When the 'New Labour' government submitted its plans for a Welsh Assembly and a Scottish Parliament to fresh referendums in 1997, the CP played a leading role in the broad 'Socialists Say Yes' campaign, recognising the need to shore up support for devolution in the labour movement where anti-devolutionists had done so much damage in the 1970s. In Scotland, the Communists made a similar left-wing and democratic case in favour of a Scottish Parliament, while also participating in the official 'Scotland Forward' campaign.

Recent history has vindicated the positions taken by the Communist Party on the national question since the 1940s. The CP argued that the labour movement and the left should not only take full account of national feelings and aspirations, but also understand the democratic necessity and the progressive potential in Welsh and Scottish self-government. For decades, large sections of the Labour Party across the spectrum and, until very recently, almost all of the far left were hostile to devolution. The CP insisted that without the left and labour movement taking a leading role in broad movements for devolved parliaments, these would not be achieved, although nationalist parties would gain ground at the Labour's expense.

Communists also pointed out that there was an 'English question' to be resolved in a progressive way, or else it would act as a barrier to devolution and could lead to an upsurge of reactionary forms of English or British nationalism.

1998-2020 'Progressive Federalism'

Since 1998, the Party's programme *Britain's Road to Socialism* has been updated to take account of changing realities. The accumulation of greater powers for the Welsh and Scottish legislatures – which should include powers repatriated from the European Union – has led the CP to propose a federal system for Britain based on equal status for the three nations, a fair distribution of wealth, an English Parliament and – where the demand exists – English regional assemblies. Such a system should include the legislatures of the Isle of Man and the Channel Islands so that their peoples can break free from the archaic and anti-democratic structures used to protect British and international tax avoidance. Cornwall has its own national characteristics and the programme proposes an autonomous assembly to address the democratic, cultural and economic needs of its people. In fact, the CP has recently published the first-ever edition of the *Communist Manifesto* in Cornish, *Deryvadow Party an Gemynwer* (2016), translated by Heather Penruth with assistance from the Agan Tavas ('Our Language') campaign; a commission including the former Welsh Language Society chair Gareth Miles and pan-Celtic scholar Gwyn Griffiths has also updated the 1948 translation in *Maniffesto'r Blaid Gomiwnyddol* (2008).

Britain's Road to Socialism (2020) explains why the barrier to progress on every economic, social, cultural and democratic front is British state-monopoly capitalism and the largely integrated British capitalist class. This will only be overthrown by a united working-class movement at the head of a popular, democratic anti-monopoly alliance of forces. Therefore, the CP opposes national separatism in current conditions, not as a matter of principle but of revolutionary strategy. Nonetheless, this alliance of forces should include those many people in the Scottish and Welsh national movements whose progressive and socialist outlook makes them allies in the fight for many of the policies set out in the Left-Wing Programme proposed by the CP and others on the left across Britain.

15

The worlds of TE Nicholas (1879-1981)

Delivered in Welsh as the TE Nicholas annual memorial lecture at the National Eisteddfod, Cardiff 2018, subsequently published as a pamphlet in 2018 and in a new and extended edition in 2023.

It's not possible to talk about one single world of Thomas Evan Nicholas, one of the most famous Welsh-language poets of the 20th century. He lived and worked through three distinct ages of world history, different enough from one another to each to comprise a distinct world, each one inheriting characteristics from the one before which are then destroyed or transformed in order to create the new world in its turn.

The world of hearth and valleys

Nicholas was born in 1879 into an age in which imperialism was spreading across much of the world, led by British monopoly capitalism but with American and German capitalism demanding their place in the sun. This was the first world of TE Nicholas. The British Raj was approaching its peak, while the British subjugation of Africa was on the verge of completion.

Nicholas began his life in Crymych, north Pembrokeshire, a little north-west of the South Wales coalfield which by then almost alone powered the British imperial navy. The coalfield reached its peak in 1913, with almost a quarter of a million miners working in more than 600 collieries. Those miners came to play a significant role in the rise of the British labour movement, especially after the establishment of the South Wales Miners Federation – the 'Fed' – in 1898.

They formed part of the bedrock of so much in their political, social and cultural world, including the institutes and libraries, the Independent

Labour Party, the Plebs League, the Central Labour College in London and weekly newspapers such *Llais Llafur* ('Labour Voice') and the *Rhondda Socialist*.

Socialist and trade union leaders from around the world came to visit. Among them were 'Big' Bill Haywood from the United States to address meetings across the valleys, Jim Larkin and James Connolly from Ireland, John Maclean from Scotland and Tom Mann and Sylvia Pankhurst from England.

The young Nicholas threw himself into this turbulent world.

In the beginning, he worked briefly in Treherbert before studying for the ministry at the Gwynfryn Academy in Ammanford. There he came into contact with the Christian socialist ideas of the Rev RJ Campbell, the communist cooperatism of Robert Owen – which chimed with the tradition of cooperative working between the smallholders of his native *bro* – and the progressive Welsh patriotism, poetry and socialism of Robert Jones Derfel. There, too, he met and formed a lifelong friendship with future miners' leader and MP for Merthyr Tydfil SO Davies.

After a brief stint as the minister of Welsh chapels in Llandeilo and Wisconsin, USA, Nicholas arrived at the coal mining village of Glais in the Swansea valley. There, and even more so in Merthyr Tydfil as the editor of the Welsh-language columns of Keir Hardie's paper, *The Pioneer*, Nicholas encountered class warfare in all its naked cruelty.

He enrolled unequivocally as a soldier in the working-class army, shoulder to shoulder with Keir Hardie. The two men understood that the class struggle had to be fought until the working class triumphed over the capitalist class, capitalism and imperialism.

In this first of the worlds of 'Niclas y Glais' ('Nicholas of Glais' as he became known), he began to realise also that '*Mae'r Byd yn Fwy na Chymru*' ('The World is Bigger than Wales') and endeavoured to provide some kind of divine justification (as in '*Weithwyr Fy Ngwlad*' – 'Workers of My Country') for the labour movement's struggle for social justice. However, within a few years of the publication of *Salmau'r Werin* ('Salms of the Common People') in 1909, Nicholas was mocking the national narrowness and sense of superiority of patriotic poets. In '*Gorwel*' ('Horizon'), he tells them and us:

> Gwell caru'r byd na chanu'r cwmwd tawel,
> Mae 'dyn yr un ar bum cyfandir' maith:
> Mae'n werth i enaid Cymro ddryllio'r Gorwel,
> A chroesi weithiau dros derfynau'r Iaith.

> Better to love the world than sing of the quiet spot
> 'Man is the same on five continents' world-wide:
> Breaching the Horizon is a Welsh soul's worthy lot
> Crossing the bounds of Language to the outside.

Previously, RJ Derfel had likewise cooled in his Welsh patriotic ardour in favour of a more internationalist socialist outlook. In the case of Nicholas, of course, he continued to compose patriotic and parochial verse, while adding much more class-based and outward-looking poetry and prose to it.

Although Nicholas turned away at least a little from non-political patriotism, he espoused a fundamentally political Welsh nationalism. There were the polemics with the Rev. WF Phillips who denounced notions such as class politics and socialism as the evil and anti-Welsh doctrine of godless foreigners. Nicholas argued – echoing Keir Hardie – for a Welsh nationalism that rejected class collaboration, the British Empire and the English monarchy in favour of official status for the Welsh language, home rule and socialism.

Against the background of violent clashes during the national railway, Powell Duffryn and Cambrian coal mining strikes of 1910-1912, he heaped scorn upon the poetry that merely sang the praises of a God who doesn't need them, or sought to win prizes at *eisteddfodau* for a few pennies.

Where once, the poet confesses in *Cerddi Gwerin* ('Poems of the Common People', 1910), 'I would rhyme for praise and profit/ and for fame throughout the land', these days 'I rhyme in the night-time of my shame/ Poems of the common people – they are everything'.

In 'Y Streic', Nicholas is full of anger and class hatred following the clashes between miners and imported police in Tonypandy and other towns and villages in 1910, in a south Wales under military occupation. The poet flays the idle landowners, the wealthy, the peacekeepers who 'beat down old women', the soldiers who 'walk the streets/ Their guns terrorising the valley', before promising:

Ni soniaf am hawliau Duw
Nes cael bara ar fyrddau'r byd,
Ni soniaf am nefoedd tu hwnt i'r bedd
Nes cael y bythynnod yn glyd.

Ofer yw sôn am Iawn,
A chanu am Galfari,
Tra bryniau'r Rhondda yn goch dan waed
Diniwed fy mrodyr i.

I won't speak of the claims of God
Till all the world's tables have bread
I won't speak of heaven beyond the grave
Till the cottages have warmth ahead.

It's futile to speak of Justice,

And sing of Calvary,
While Rhondda's hills are red
With my brothers' blood, guilt-free.

Behold his message from this time onward:

Anadlaf chwyldroad i mewn
I galon dyn ymhob man;

I breathe revolution into
The hearts of men everywhere;

The Great War between the imperialist powers created the conditions in which the first of the worlds of Niclas y Glais would vanish forever. He raged against the slaughter which threatened to abort the new world carried in the womb of the British labour and international socialist movements. Surely the most powerful of all his poems was '*Dros Eich Gwlad*' ('For Your Country'), which makes savage mockery of the pernicious British jingoism used to recruit the young workers of Wales to the King's colours.

Cerddwch i'r rhengoedd, fechgyn,
Mae pris ar lofruddion yn awr:
Cerddwch i'r rhengoedd i daro brawd
Ar archiad swyddog i lawr;
Ni feddwch un fodfedd o ddaear,
Ni feddwch eich taid na'ch tad;
Ond cerddwch i'r rhengoedd yn dyrfa fawr,
Cerddwch yn ddewr dros eich gwlad.

March to the ranks, boys,
There's payment now for murder:
March to the ranks at the officer's command
To strike down a brother;
You own not a square-inch of land,
Nor did your father or grandfather;
But march to the ranks in a mighty band,
March bravely for your country.

This was written within two months of the outbreak of the 1914-18 war. Already, Nicholas clearly understood the barbarism that lurked behind the civilised mask of imperialism.

The world of the common people

The second world of Niclas y Glais – 'Byd y Werin' ('The World of the Common People') – was born in the carnage of the Great War and the outbreak of the socialist revolution in Russia.

The betrayal by most social-democratic and labour parties of their previous pledges to oppose an inter-imperialist war split the international socialist movement. The collapse of the Tsarist dictatorship and the treachery of the pro-war regime that followed created the conditions in which Lenin, the Bolsheviks and their allies could take state power.

Nicholas welcomed the Russian revolutions of 1917. He helped organise the first trade union for farm workers and build the Labour Party in west Wales, but was defeated as the ILP candidate for Merthyr Tydfil in the General Election of 1918, after the death of Keir Hardie. He was physically attacked in a brutal campaign won by a demagogic working-class jingo who had the enthusiastic support of the local Tory press.

Nicholas understood that the working class had not yet completed its political transition from Liberalism to Labourism, but also knew that the labour movement needed a bold, visionary and uncompromising vanguard. He belonged on the footplate at the front of the train, shovelling the coal in the heat and the sweat – not in the guards' van in the rear.

There was, therefore, nothing 'accidental' – as Ithel Davies once claimed – about his decision to answer the call of Lenin and the Communist International to form Communist parties in every country. As a result, the Communist Party was founded in Britain and Wales in 1920.

From that time on, the commitment of TE Nicholas to the international communist movement and the Soviet Union was the central defining characteristic of his politics, his poetry and his journalism. He took his political message to the people in terms they might best understand, especially in the rural areas, using the imagery and metaphors with which many were most familiar.

Although thousands of workers were leaving the chapels in the south Wales valleys, just as Nicholas himself was abandoning the pulpit, he expressed the ideas of socialism and communism in the vocabulary and metaphors of Christianity. For instance, Keir Hardie and Lenin were portrayed as Christ-like figures; they had come to lead the lost souls out of the wilderness and so had drawn the wrath of Mammon upon their heads.

His visit to the Soviet Union in 1935 confirmed his belief that workers could build a new world of solidarity, cooperation and social justice; there was no need to wait for the next world after death. As Nicholas put it in a letter to the weekly newspaper Y Cymro, the Russian system 'reflects the religion of Christ more thoroughly than our own system does'.

Nicholas used the most evocative of Christian imagery to end his sonnet 'Rwsia', where 'the pure hands of the finest people of the age / Are pulling Jesus free from the wooden cross'. What is significant about this work, though, is his happy acceptance that so many Russian people had no need of prayers, worship, priests, altars, alms, icons or scriptural disputes.

And whereas his earlier poem 'Rwsia, 1917' had preached peace as the only pathway that could preserve the ideals of a newly-born revolution, even though surrounded by its enemies, ('weapons of war are not the weapons of man's Freedom; the Truth will overcome arms ... You cannot keep your costly freedom with War'), his elegy for Lenin two decades later referred to 'home-made armaments – the device of countryside's common people'.

Certainly, Niclas y Glais could not remain a pacifist in this, the second of his worlds, 'the World of the Common People'. More than any other single issue, the war in Spain against international fascism compelled him to accept that there were times when military force was necessary in a just cause. He remained a lover of peace ('*heddgarwr*') but ceased being a pacifist ('*heddychwr*'). He played a leading role in the great popular crusade to send food, clothing and the volunteer fighters and medical staff of the International Brigades to defend the democratic Spanish Republic against the forces of General Franco, Adolf Hitler and Benito Mussolini. After the fascist victory, he acted as treasurer of a committee which successfully raised funds to place a memorial in a new Stalingrad hospital to the slain International Brigaders from Wales.

In his weekly column in *Y Cymro*, 'O Fyd y Werin' ('From the World of the Common People'), Nicholas argued for the vast superiority of Stalin's socialist system over Western capitalism. He mercilessly attacked Welsh Nonconformist denominations, the Roman Catholic Church ('*Pabyddiaeth*' – Papism), the Labour Party and its treacherous ex-leader Ramsay MacDonald: why weren't they standing up for the interests of the common people of Wales and of those under fascist attack in Spain, China (Manchuria) and Abyssinia? Even more provocatively, he accused Gandhi of blocking the real struggle for freedom in India – freedom from its foreign, British capitalists.

Nicholas thought the national petition for equal status for Welsh in the courts was relatively unimportant and had little to do with the daily needs of the working class, although he had happily signed the petition himself.

He did not accept for a moment that fascist aggression would long be appeased by the Munich Agreement. He could see that the character of the next age would be decided by what would be the ultimate, decisive military struggle to come – that between Nazi Germany and the Soviet Union. He understood that the Molotov-Ribbentrop Non-Aggression Pact merely postponed that final confrontation, allowing the Soviet Union to reorganise and expand its capacity. But Nicholas could not support what he regarded as British imperialism's bogus declaration of war against German imperialism in September 1939, which cost him his column in *Y Cymro*.

He spent three months in Swansea and Brixton prisons in 1940 on bogus charges of pro-fascism! There he composed some of his finest work, published in the volumes: *Llygad y Drws: Sonedau'r Carchar* ('Spy-hole: the Prison Sonnets' 1940) a *Canu'r Carchar* ('Prison Songs', 1942).

He applauded the Soviet Union's military occupation of a strip of southern Finland in order to create an anti-fascist defensive shield in front of Leningrad. In line with Britain's Communist Party, he believed that Nazi Germany's invasion of the Soviet Union in 1941, together with the emergence of Communist-led resistance movements against the Nazis in France, Belgium, Italy and other European countries, had turned an imperialist war into a people's war against fascism.

The Second World World War certainly brought his own second world – 'Byd y Werin' – to an end. The third of the worlds of TE Nicholas would arise from the ruins.

The world of the 'Cold War'

After the war, the new Communist governments had to rebuild extensive parts of the Soviet Union, Poland, Czechoslovakia and eastern Germany. This was done in cities such as Leningrad (or St Petersburg as it is once more) and Warsaw with a quality that has never been acknowledged in the West.

Great Britain was replaced by the USA as the world's main imperialist power economically, politically, culturally and militarily. As mass Communist parties grew out of the anti-fascist resistance movements in France, Italy, the Netherlands and Belgium, the first steps were taken to construct a European Defence Community and a European Political Community in the west, as an anti-socialist, capitalist bloc sponsored by US imperialism and NATO.

National liberation movements had begun to challenge imperial rule in Asia, Africa and South America, many of them supported by the Soviet Union and other socialist countries. The People's Republic of China was founded in 1949 and British, French and US imperialism were prepared to fight rather than allow Malaya, Korea, Vietnam and other countries to achieve national unity and freedom under Communist leadership.

In the 'Cold War' between the two nuclear super-powers, TE Nicholas had no hesitation in standing on the side of the Soviet Union and the other socialist countries. He contrasted the flagrant, provocative war-mongering to be seen in the USA with the declarations and proposals of the Soviet Union in favour of peace, multilateral disarmament and 'peaceful co-existence' between the different social systems.

Thus he lent his voice to the campaign against turning large tracts of land in his native Pembrokeshire into a military training ground.

When the US and British governments – not for the last time – manipulated the United Nations to go to war against Communist North Korea, Nicholas sprang to the defence of his fellow former student at Gwynfryn Academy, SO Davies, and Keir Hardie's son-in-law Emrys Hughes. They had challenged

Labour Prime Minister Clement Attlee in the Westminster parliament. As news of their stand against the Korean War travelled around the world, Nicholas wrote to SO, in Welsh as usual:

Annwyl SO,

Llongyfarchiadau i chwi ac Emrys. Dim ond eich dau ar y cychwyn. 'Llef UN yn llefain', ond fe ddaw'r lleill. Y mae eich enw wedi mynd i wefusau'r werin bobl mewn noswaith, a disgwylir pethau mawr oddi wrthych yn y frwydr hon. Dinistrir y Blaid Lafur gan Attlee fel y gwnaethpwyd gan MacDonald, yr ychydig weddill fydd yn cyfrif. Carwn i chwi ac Emrys sylweddoli fod cefnogaeth unol y werin gennych yn hyn o beth. Nid oes gwasg heddiw i ddweud gair, gwasg Cymru yn ail-adrodd celwyddau'r wasg Seisnig. Rhoddwyd taw llwyr arnom ni sydd yn heddychwyr erioed; ac yr wyf yn rhy hen i fynd drwy'r wlad i siarad; nid oes ond aros yn dawel a darllen celwyddau'r wasg a gwrando ar gelwyddau'r radio, a disgwyl ambell air gennych chwi a'ch bath yn erbyn y trychineb mawr.

Dinistrio'r UNO yw un amcan, fel y gwnaethpwyd yn helynt Sbaen ac Abyssinia, a dinistrio gwaith Sosialaeth yn Korea er dangos i'r byd fod Sosialaeth yn fethiant.

'Ond na bai fy mhen yn ddyfroedd a'm llygaid yn ffynhonnau dagrau', dros y trueniaid bach yn eu gwlad. Daliwch ati, chwi biau'r dyfodol, ac nid rhaid i chwi ofni am eich sedd fel llawer ohonynt.

Cofion at Seph.

Yn gywir,

T.E. Nicholas

Dear SO,

Congratulations to you and Emrys. The two of you stand alone at the start. 'ONE voice crying ...', but the others will come. Your name has sprung to the lips of the common people in a single evening, and great things are expected of you in this battle. Attlee is destroying the Labour Party just as MacDonald did, but it is those who remain that will count. I want you and Emrys to realise that you have the unanimous support of the working class in all this. There is no press today where one can say anything; the Welsh press merely repeats the lies of the English press. We who are pacifists have always been gagged; and I am too old to travel the country and speak; there is nothing for it but to stay quiet, read the lies in the press and listen to the lies on the radio, waiting for the occasional word from you and your kind against the holocaust.

Their objectives are to destroy the United Nations Organisation, as was done in the troubles over Spain and Abyssinia, and to destroy Socialism's achievements in Korea in order to show the world that Socialism is a failure.

'Oh that my head were waters, and mine eyes a fountain of tears', for those poor souls in their small country. Keep at it, you will inherit the future, and you don't have to worry about keeping your seat like so many of the others have to.

Regards to Seph.

Yours truly,

T. E. Nicholas

The reference to 'Seph' is to Sephora, SO's wife. She was about to be elected to the presidium of the newly-formed World Peace Council alongside Pablo Picasso, Paul Robeson, French writer Louis Aragon, Chilean poet Pablo Neruda and the 'Red Dean' of Canterbury, Hewlett Johnson.

Nicholas sat with her on the general body of the council and its British Peace Committee. Three Security Service (MI5) files on him – now in the National Archives – contain copies of intercepted letters and internal peace movement documents. One such letter mentions his unavailability to attend the World Congress of People for Peace in Vienna in January 1952. His mail to the British Peace Committee was regularly opened (including a letter in June 1953 in which Nicholas hoped that a peace settlement in Korea would give China 'a little time to build up her new life)'; his phone calls to the Communist Party headquarters in King Street, London, were recorded, as was his involvement in the World Peace Council by the Secret Intelligence Service (MI6).

The files contain much else on Nicholas over various periods between 1915 and 1954. They include the photostat of a letter to the Communist Party's Central Propaganda Department in April 1954 from the Party branch in Ystradgynlais, requesting support for its activities during the forthcoming National Eisteddfod, when it intended to hold a public meeting with Nicholas and either Harry Pollitt or Willie Gallacher as the speakers. A Special Branch 'history sheet and registration form' from 1949 described Nicholas as 'probably the most dangerous C.P. member in Cardiganshire' – which, obviously, is far less recognition than he deserved.

Unlike the 1940s, the 1950s was not a fertile decade for Nicholas the poet. But with NATO and West German tanks exercising in Pembrokeshire and a US-trained anti-communist army invading Cuba in the Bay of Pigs, he composed the sonnet 'Cuba and Wales' in 1961. It ended:

Yn Cuba draw, milwyr y fall a'r Ianc,
Yng Nghymru fach Hitler a'i leng a'i dranc.

In Cuba afar, the Yankee death-soldiers
In Cymru so small, the death-troops are Hitler's

Nicholas also opposed the plans to build a nuclear power station at Wylfa on Anglesey. In the sonnet 'Atomfa Môn', he feared that it would blight the island, its economy and the Welsh language and culture there, poisoning the land, sea and sky.

One of his last sonnets, in 1969, was to mark the investiture in Caernarfon castle of the son of the queen of England as 'prince of Wales'. 'Syrcas Caernarfon' represents Nicholas at his coruscating best. Fifty eight years previously, he had mocked those Liberal 'Welsh nationalists' who had attended an investiture in Caernarfon to 'commemorate England's supremacy over the Welsh' and 'glorify a foreign prince'.

Now, at the age of 89, he gave full vent to his Welsh republicanism:

Ail-blennir y faner estron ar gestyll Cymru,
A phlyg pendefigion i'r Sais fel brwyn yn y gwynt,
A gwerin y graith – etifeddion y cawl a'r llymru
Yn anghofio slogan pont a chraig Eryri gynt;
Yng nghymanfa gwallgofiaid Cymru cyhoeddaf yn groch
Fod ystafelloedd y Castell yn dylcau moch.

The foreign flag re-planted on the castles of Cymru,
Worthies bow like rushes in the wind to the Englishman,
As the scarred common people – heirs to gruel and flummery
Forget the slogan on the crags and bridges of Snowdon;
In this chorus of Welsh lunatics, I defiantly cry
The Castle and its chambers are now a pig-sty.

Yet, as Hefin Wyn points out in his biography *Ar Drywydd Niclas y Glais* (2017), ('On the Trail of Niclas y Glais'), Nicholas never contemplated joining the Welsh National Party. Much though he treasured Wales, its working class and its language, he believed that these could only be safeguarded in a socialist system, and thus the most important objective is a revolution to overthrow capitalism.

Nor did he have any time for the nationalist party's interpretation of Welsh history, heavily influenced in the 1920s and 1930s by the 'Catholic Reaction' in France. This deeply counter-revolutionary school of thought despised the Protestant Reformation and the Enlightenment, and regretted the end of the Middle Ages. According to Catholic Reaction mythology, the medieval period had been one in which the benevolent nobility patronised and protected a cultured peasantry in an orderly, civilised society – until its overthrow by industrialisation in the age of capital. Nicholas had no time, either, for nobles, princes, kings and their system of exploitation and oppression.

When Saunders Lewis and the Welsh National Party proposed the deindustrialisation of south Wales in their 'Ten Points of Policy' in 1934, Nicholas could hardly contain his contempt for such romantic, defeatist nonsense. His sonnet 'Symud y Glofeydd' ('Moving the Coalmines') ended:

Symud y dur a'r glo i wlad y myllt?
Dad-ddiwydiannu Merthyr? Yffach wyllt!

Shift steel and coal to the mutton's land?
De-industrialise Merthyr? Madness be damned!

Eventually, Merthyr Tydfil triumphed over the schemes to shut down the town and move the entire population to Canada or the banks of the River Usk. Like other communities in the valleys, it was re-industrialised in the post-war decades, although not enough to avoid substantial unemployment from the 1960s onward.

Nicholas also rejected Gwynfor Evans' choice of Ireland and Denmark as excellent examples of how small self-governing nations are almost bound to prosper. The former was a poor country, under the narrow, conservative and cruel influence of the Catholic Church; a land whose native language was in rapid retreat despite 'independence'. The second example, Denmark, was the country that yielded to Hitler without firing a bullet; later, it was a base for British and American airplanes, part of NATO strategy to bomb the very country – the Soviet Union – that had liberated much of Europe from fascism.

The 'New World Order'
TE Nicholas died in 1971 and the world has certainly undergone another transformation since then.

The Soviet Union and the socialist systems of central and eastern Europe are no more. Just as Nicholas used to describe the United States as a land of capitalist 'gangsters' – he said some of the gangsters were in prison but most of them were in the government – much the same could be said about countries such as capitalist Russia and others in eastern Europe today.

Perhaps Czechoslovakia's Prague Spring in 1968 was the final opportunity to reform and save socialism on the basis of genuine mass support – something the Czech Communist Party had undoubtedly enjoyed in the 1946 election and the revolution of 1948.

Yet Nicholas saw those moves towards 'socialism with a human face' as the beginning of capitalist counter-revolution. In a television debate in August 1968 about the crisis in Czechoslovakia, he discussed the crisis with other Welsh-speaking Communists Annie Powell, South Wales miners' leader Dai Dan Evans, Will Rees and John Roose Williams. Only Annie Powell, the future mayor of the Rhondda, staunchly defended the party line and condemned the Soviet military intervention. The others were either equivocal or accepted the inevitability of events in the name of '*realpolitik*'. Nicholas agreed with the Soviet case for intervention:

Rwy'n falch iawn ei fod e wedi digwydd am fy mod yn credu ein bod ni wedi arbed y trydydd rhyfel byd ... Dynion wedi mynd i fewn i'r Blaid Gomiwnyddol [yn Tsiecoslofacia] er mwyn cael swyddi, ac wedi cael swyddi, yr hyn mae'r Sais yn ei alw yn key positions, wedi cael gafael yn y peiriant gwleidyddol ac yn lle ei ddefnyddio i amcanion sosialaidd a gwerinol, yn ei ddefnyddio i bwrpas yr hen drefn oedd yno cyn i'r chwyldro [ym 1948 – RG] ddigwydd.

I'm very pleased that it has happened because I believe we have avoided the third world war ... Men have gone into the Communist Party [of Czechoslovakia] in order to get jobs, have obtained jobs – those that the English would call 'key positions' – and have taken over the political apparatus and instead of using it for socialist purposes have used it for the purposes of the old order that was there before the revolution [of 1948] happened.

In the same way, Nicholas suggested, a socialist government had been elected in Britain but with no intention of using its position in order to introduce a socialist society.

He thought there was something wrong in the socialist movement in Wales and Britain when Labour MPs such Goronwy Roberts in Caernarfon took the same view of the Czech events as US president Lyndon B Johnson and former Tory Prime Minister Alec Douglas Home. The US military were destroying a small country, Vietnam, thousands of miles away; Home it was who – together with Prime Minister Neville Chamberlain – had betrayed world peace in Munich in 1938.

Since the demise of the Soviet Union and its allies, monopoly capitalism and the main imperialist powers have strengthened their economic, political and military grip on large parts of the world, especially as the European Union and NATO have expanded eastwards and war has, once again, become a normal way of removing regimes that do not comply with US and the West's plans.

Nicholas would understand more than most why organisations such as CND, Stop the War, the British Peace Assembly and the World Peace Council are still needed as much as ever.

He would also rejoice at the rise of China as a major economic and political power in the 'New World Order'. Key sectors of its economy – land, energy, transport, banking – remain largely in public ownership as do the overwhelming majority of Chinese multinational corporations. Domestic development is directed by a central plan to meet social as well as economic objectives. Rapid economic growth has not come without its problems but, even so, China under Communist Party rule has succeeded in lifting 700m of its people out of absolute poverty since the 'Reform and Opening Up' process began in 1978 – a feat unequalled in human history, as the World Bank points out.

Nicholas would welcome these developments, albeit with some misgivings about the risks associated with the use of private capital and market mechanisms. After all, towards the end of his life, he welcomed Mao's 'Great Proletarian Cultural Revolution' – an episode that most of its witnesses and the current Chinese leadership today view as a disastrous aberration.

Nicholas didn't live long enough to suffer the shame of his own nation voting against itself in the Welsh Assembly referendum of 1979. More than likely, he would have welcomed the referendum victory in 1998 and the subsequent establishment of the National Assembly, just as he would welcome the advances in Welsh-medium education. It's likely that his view of S4C would be decided by the extent to which the channel's news and current affairs merely repeat the lies of English television.

Yet he would surely be savaging the absence of any socialist vision on the part of the National Assembly, the Welsh government, and much of the labour movement including Welsh Labour. He would be insisting that the future of Wales, its communities, identity and Welsh language will never be secure on the basis of capitalism and its market forces. He would urge us to look beyond our national boundaries, too, for socialist unity and working-class solidarity against imperialism, NATO and the European Union.

In his second volume of autobiography, *The Company I've Kept* (1966), Scottish communist, republican and poet of distinction Hugh MacDiarmid recalled one of his poems where Lenin and John Maclean are described by the Russian word *kravissy* – which means both 'beautiful' and 'red'. After addressing the students in Aberystwyth, McDiarmid visited Nicholas who he thought was, indeed, one of those very few who – alongside Lenin, John Maclean and Rabbie Burns – deserve that description: *kravissy*.

The big question for Welsh poets, therefore, in the dangerous 'New World Order', is this: is there a new TE Nicholas today – a new 'voice of the common people' – someone who deserves the description *kravissy*?

16

Annie Powell and 'Red Rhondda' (1906-1986)

First published as a chapter in Meddick, Payne & Katz eds., Red Lives – Communists and the Struggle for Socialism *(2020).*

When Annie Powell died in August 1986, at the age of 79, the news was even thought worth reporting by the *New York Times*. The death of the former Mayor of the Borough of Rhondda appeared to signify the end of the era. Communist mayors had always been rare in Britain, with only Joe Vaughan to the Party's credit in Bethnal Green in the early 1920s and Finlay Hart as provost of Clydebank in the 1960s. Women mayors of any party have been almost as scarce and, certainly, Annie Powell is the only Communist one so far.

She was born into a Welsh-speaking home in Ystrad, halfway up the Rhondda Fawr – the bigger of the Rhondda valleys – in the heart of the South Wales coalfield. The great revival of Welsh preacher Evan Roberts had just come to an end and the Thomas family were devout members of the local Bodringallt Annibynwyr (Independents or Congregationalists) chapel.

The local MP was the legendary Lib-Lab president of the South Wales Miners Federation, William Abraham ('Mabon').

Young Annie Thomas went from Bodringallt Primary School to Pentre Grammar School whose motto echoed the battle-cry of Owain Glyndwr to his trusted lieutenant Cadwgan in the fight for Welsh freedom, 'Hoga dy fwyell' ('Sharpen your battle-axe'). But it was only when a student teacher at Glamorgan Training College in Barry that she began taking an interest in politics. It was 1926, the year of the General Strike and the six-month lock-out of Britain's miners. More than half of her fellow trainees came from the homes of unemployed workers.

Annie began her teaching career in Trealaw, just down the valley from her home. As a volunteer with the Methodist Central Hall, Tonypandy, and Trealaw Community House, raising money to buy food and clothes for the unemployed and their families, she was shocked by what she saw: 'The poverty of the people and of the children was something that hit me really hard', she still remembered half a century later.

She joined the Labour Party and became active in the National Union of Teachers. In September 1936, she married Trevor Evan Powell. An outfitter since leaving school, he was a warm-hearted, popular man who enjoyed a laugh, a joke and a game of whist. He also shared her left-wing views.

In the course of the Great Depression, Annie Powell could not help but notice that the most active campaigners against unemployment, poverty, the Means Test and house evictions were the Communists. Her disappointment with the Labour Party grew: 'They didn't discuss theory, in the sense that the Communists discussed theory, and neither did they organise events and put themselves at the disposal of the people in the same way as the Communists did. And it was because the Communists were doing something, I think, that attracted me in the first instance to know more about them'.

She was swept up in the huge CP-led campaign throughout the Rhondda valleys to build the Popular Front against fascism and war. In particular, she remembered the day when thousands of protestors broke up a rally held by Sir Oswald Mosley and his Blackshirts on De Winton Field in Tonypandy. The intention had been, in her words, that 'not even the ears of the sheep on the mountain shall be defiled by the words of Mosley'.

Her religious background prevented her from making an emotional or overnight decision to join the Communist Party. She eventually did so in 1938, and later commented: 'It was a decision taken after I'd done a terrific amount of reading and given an awful lot of thought to it'.

After joining the CP she soon met the likes of the Party's general secretary Harry Pollitt, SWMF president and future NUM general secretary Arthur Horner, future NUM president Will Paynter and Jack Davies, chair of the Cambrian Combine joint lodges committee. Although they had never been to college, she thought their broader experience and sharper brains taught her some 'very valuable lessons'.

During the Second World War, she carried out organising work for the Party with Dora Cox, encouraging women join the amed forces or enter essential wartime production industries. This meant campaigning for employers and local authorities to make provision for childcare. In March 1946, Annie contested the Gelli ward in the Glamorgan County Council elections, polling one-third of the votes against the victorious Labour candidate and an Independent. Throughout this period, Labour and Communist were the only parties with the capacity to fight seats in the Rhondda valleys. By now, Annie was also a delegate to CP congresses. At the 20th congress in 1948, she pointed out that for all the Labour government's fine words about opening new factories in Wales, only one had been started so far and employed just 20 workers. She was also elected by delegates to the CP executive committee for the first time, albeit briefly.

An MI5 file on Dora Cox records a report from Annie Powell of her adverse experiences when canvassing in the Rhondda during the 1949 local elections. Many Labour voters had been turned against Russia by the incessant Cold War propaganda and resented all Communist criticism of the post-war Labour government. One consequence was the CP's loss of three county council seats on that occasion.

Nevertheless, Trevor and Annie Powell contested the 1950 borough council elections, attracting press attention as a husband and wife team standing in the neighbouring wards of Penygraig and Ystrad. By this time, the Communist Party had lost all five seats on the Rhondda borough council, although it remained the only political force capable of challenging Labour. The heroic defeats continued.

Nonetheless, Annie was a rising star in the Party, frequently invited to speak at public events beyond the mining valleys. During the July bank holiday in 1951, for instance, she addressed an open-air meeting in the market place in Wells. Given a fair hearing by all accounts, she stressed the need for world peace and supported a Five Power Pact between Britain, the US, France, the Soviet Union and China to solve all major international problems by negotiation instead of war.

This, too, was her theme in the May 1955 General Election, when she took over from Idris Cox as the CP's candidate in Rhondda East. The Labour incumbent was Bill Mainwaring, ex-miner, ex-lecturer at the Central Labour College and ex-Marxist. Annie was the first-ever woman candidate in the constituency and one of only five on behalf of all the parties in Wales at that election. Her campaign literature highlighted the main issue:

'The Tories have announced they are producing the Hydrogen Bomb and will use it. The right-wing Labour leaders, to their eternal shame, support them. Famous scientists warn us that the H-Bomb will cause not only a torturing death for millions, but mass poisoning by atomic radiation for children yet unborn. Last time we escaped heavy raids, but with one H-Bomb in South Wales there will be no escape. Death and destruction would come to every street in the Rhondda'.

Every day, Annie informed the electors, she taught 36 'fine lively youngsters, bigger, stronger and better dressed than ever before'. She wanted them to grow up in a Rhondda of secure employment through peace, East-West trade and higher living standards which would only come about as the result of united working-class action.

Like every election since 1945, when Pollitt had come within a thousand votes of winning the seat, it was a Labour landslide. But Annie had increased the Communist vote by 50 per cent, finished ahead of the Tory and made a big impact on the electors.

Two months later, she narrowly beat the Labour and Independent candidates in a Penygraig ward by-election to win the Party's first seat on Rhondda borough council for six years. Already active in the Cooperative movement, the NUT and on the CP's Welsh Committee, she now took on her extra duties with gusto.

In September 1955, for example, Councillor Powell and local CP branch secretary Richard Jones lobbied the management committee of the Judge's Hall, Trealaw, with a petition demanding that its newly imposed 'colour bar' for local dances be lifted. They were joined in the protest by a committee of black youths from Cardiff, the intended victims of the ban. Victory was swift as the management climbed down.

Annie was less successful when trying to save a local GP from eviction after she had overstaying a temporary council-house tenancy. The borough council rejected a 1,146-signature petition and nobody would second Councillor Powell's motion to reconsider the matter, even though she pointed out how difficult it would be to attract another doctor to the area. Fiercely protective of the Rhondda's image, Annie was among the councillors who protested when Wilfred Pickles brought his television request show to Ferndale and failed to 'attain the cultural and intellectual standards that the history of the Rhondda calls for'.

In 1956, Annie Powell returned to the CP executive committee at the 24th congress. Having taken part in the 'Parliament for Wales' campaign earlier in the decade, collecting signatures for its petition, Annie continued to press for measures of devolution. In 1957, she presented the Welsh Committee's evidence to the advisory Council for Wales, calling for the appointment of a Secretary of State, a Welsh National Planning Commission and regular summits of Welsh MPs and local authority representatives. As chair of the Party's Welsh Committee, she ensured that its meetings were strictly punctual and highly disciplined.

All the while, 'Mrs Powell' was still teaching, moving on to Trefforest Central School where former pupils remembered her as effective, strict but fair. Her most trusted charges were sent to the shops to buy her favourite Capstan Full Strength cigarettes. Her commitment to the profession was such that she once had to miss a ceremony welcoming a deputation from the Soviet embassy who were visiting the Rhondda as guests of the mayor. However, following the Soviet Union's military intervention in Hungary, a fierce anti-Communist campaign enabled Labour to capture her seat in the May 1957 local elections.

Stung by defeat, Annie and her large and enthusiastic team threw everything into their 1959 General Election campaign. One of only five women candidates in Wales yet again, she took part in a loudspeaker pit-head debate with Labour candidate G Elfed Davies and a Tory at Maerdy colliery. Although excluded from television and radio coverage, she was given space in the *Western Mail* to propose Soviet-style rapid industrial expansion, accusing the Tory government of siding with the oil monopolies in their 'cut-throat war' against the coal industry. She argued that higher wages and East-West trade would boost economic growth. Industrial diversification could be based on coal derivatives; compensation to the former coalowners should be cut; the miners should be granted a seven-hour day; and no pit should be closed until alternative work had been found for all those facing redundancy. In the midst of the Cold War, Annie won 4,580 votes – little more than previously, but enough to finish ahead of the Tories and Plaid Cymru.

Re-elected to the EC, she represented Britain's Communists at the international meeting of 81 parties in Moscow in 1960. She later told of how she had charmed Soviet leader Nikita Khrushchev at a reception by singing the Welsh national anthem, '*Mae Hen Wlad Fy Nhadau*' ('Ancient Land of My Fathers') to him, in her mother-tongue, naturally. In great demand as a speaker, Annie's engagements included a BBC Home Service radio debate on the student grants system and a public meeting in Abertillery on the CP's programme *The British Road to Socialism*.

In May 1961, she addressed a conference called by the South Wales Area NUM and the Glamorgan Federation of Trades Councils protesting against NATO plans to train German Panzer regiments in Pembrokeshire. 'German troops should not be allowed to soil the land of Wales', Annie told delegates, urging coal miners, factory workers and teachers to stop work should they arrive. When Scottish secretary of the CPGB Gordon McLennan contested the West Lothian by-election in 1962, she spoke at his eve-of-poll rallies alongside general secretary John Gollan, Willie Gallacher and miners' leaders Mick McGahey and Abe and Alex Moffat. The meetings called for higher wages and pensions, no more pit and rail closures and cancellation of the Tory government's plans to buy Polaris nuclear missiles from the US.

In 1961, Annie regained her seat on Rhondda borough council, reflecting her ongoing concern for the locality and especially its severe housing problems. Writing in *Marxism Today* (February 1962), she condemned Minister of Health Enoch Powell for wanting 'a way back from sanity', from rent controls and the alleged 'indiscriminate subsidy' of council tenants. She pointed to the severe shortage of dwellings, the slow pace of slum clearance and the reluctance of private landlords to invest their higher rental incomes in property improvement. She also criticised Labour's refusal to deal with the speculators and advocate public ownership of urban land. The next Labour government should set itself a definite housebuilding target, nationalise the construction companies and extend low interest rates to local authorities and home-buyers. The article also defended the NHS against proposals for a European-style social insurance model, called for a substantial increase in the basic state pension and benefits and demanded comprehensive social provision for the elderly.

As a member of the EC, Annie Powell was also heavily involved in the Party's consideration of foreign affairs. Especially difficult was the Soviet-led military intervention in August 1968 to snuff out the 'Prague Spring' led by reforming Czech CP prime minister Alexander Dubcek. Four days later, she took part in a Welsh-language television discussion with comrades TE Nicholas, the celebrated poet, former South Wales miners general secretary Dai Dan Evans, translator of the original *Manifesto of the Communist Party* (1848) into Welsh WJ Rees and north Wales pioneer John Roose Williams. After Nicholas had supported the intervention, Evans thought it might be justified and Rees believed that military force was as vital to the world Communist movement's survival as unity; it was left to Powell to stand by CPGB policy. She reminded the forum that the Party in Britain had condemned the intervention. Answering a question from presenter Gwyn Erfyl, she said she had never taken her lead from the Soviet Union, where conditions were different. Now she feared what West Germany might do. Even if the Czech CP had failed to abide by decisions of the Bratislava summit of ruling communist parties, they should all have got back together to 'talk and talk and talk' instead of resorting to tanks and guns.

After a spell as deputy mayor of the Rhondda, her Labour colleagues elevated Annie to the mayorship in May 1979, shortly after the election of Margaret Thatcher as Tory prime minister. It was a rare departure from the tribal politics of the south Wales valleys for Labour councillors to bestow such an honour on a non-member. On assuming office, she told the BBC – in Welsh, of course – that her chief ambition was to instil 'new faith' in the people of the Rhondda that their communities would live. They were not dying, even though mass unemployment had returned.

Annie Powell stood down from the council in 1983 and laid down the red flag three years later. Husband Trevor lived on at 12 Railway View, Llwynypia, for another 20 years to reach his century. He was a much-loved regular in the Ynyscynon Hotel and the Llwynypia Workingmen's Club to the end.

17

The Communist Party 1920-2020: A thematic summary

First published in an abbreviated form in Communist Review *no. 96 (Summer 2020) and extended here, including useful points proposed by editor Martin Levy.*

One hundred years ago, on July 8 1920, Lenin replied to a letter he had received from the 'Joint Provisional Committee for the Communist Party of Britain' (JPC).

The leader of the revolutionary Russian state welcomed the JPC's plans to forge a single Communist Party from the British Socialist Party, the Communist Unity Group of the Socialist Labour Party, the South Wales Communist Council (formerly the South Wales Socialist Society) and other socialist and working-class bodies.

These revolutionary socialists were responding to the call from Lenin and the Bolsheviks to form communist parties and affiliate to a third, Communist International. They had opposed the slaughter of the 1914-18 Great War between the imperialist powers and were inspired by the workers' revolutions in Russia, Germany and Hungary. Repelled by the capitulation of almost all of Europe's social-democratic parties to the war-mongering of their own country's ruling class, including the Labour Party's decision to join the War Cabinet, they now intended to break with social democracy and its rotten Socialist International. They wanted to be part of the Third International, in the finest tradition of the first, the International Working Men's Association of Karl Marx.

The JPC had set out the fundamental basis for establishing the 'Communist Party of Great Britain' at a Unity Convention on July 31 and August 1, namely, to support: (1) 'The Dictatorship of the working class'; (2) 'The Soviet System'; and (3) 'The Third International'.

In his favourable reply to the JPC, Lenin set out four imperatives for the new party, already expressed in discussion and correspondence with Sylvia Pankhurst. Britain's Communists should: (1) unite in a single Communist party; (2) fight elections and seek parliamentary representation; (3) support the election of Labour governments and seek affiliation to the Labour Party; and (4) forge the closest links with militant trade union organisations.

These three founding principles and Lenin's four strategic policies form a useful framework for reviewing and assessing the first 100 years of the Communist Party in Britain.

Working-class political power

The general policy resolution proposed to the Unity Convention by the JPC declared its support for the 'dictatorship of the proletariat as a necessary means for combating the counter-revolution during the transition period between capitalism and communism'.

By 'dictatorship of the proletariat', Marx and Engels had usually meant the conquest of political power by the working class and the use of its own state apparatus to abolish capitalism, enter the lower stage of communist society (which Engels and Lenin later referred to as 'socialism') and defend the new regime against counter-revolutionary violence. In the 19th century, the term 'dictatorship' meant 'rule', the capacity to dictate the course of events, rather than its common usage since the 1930s and fascism to mean the oppressive and anti-democratic abuse of state power by a small minority or even a single ruler. For Marx, on the other hand, the embryonic 'dictatorship of the proletariat' of the Paris Commune meant the introduction of real democracy for the mass of the people. The overthrow of the Commune by Prussian invaders with the approval of the French bourgeoisie also demonstrated the necessity for the working class to break up the old capitalist state apparatus and build its own – one capable of defending the revolution.

Many delegates to the Unity Convention would have been aware of Lenin's insistence on the essential function of the workers' state to 'suppress the resistance of the exploiters', especially in the era of imperialism when the capitalists can use new forms of resistance and join forces with foreign powers anxious to protect their own interests.

Since its foundation, the Communist Party in Britain has proclaimed socialist revolution as its primary goal, with working class and its allies taking state power in order to dismantle capitalism and construct a socialist society. The question of how this is to be achieved is one of the definitive tests for any revolutionary party to answer. In Britain, only the Communist Party has proposed strategies for this. However, its first real programme, *For Soviet Britain* (1935), was quickly overtaken by the Communist International's turn to a 'United Front' of left-wing and working-class organisations at the core of a wider 'People's Front' against fascism and imperialist war. A new *Draft Programme* (1939) was not adopted because the CPGB's 16th congress was aborted by the outbreak of war. Since 1951, *The British Road to Socialism* (*BRS*, now *Britain's Road to Socialism*) has set out the Party's perspectives for winning revolutionary change, as a focus for discussion and a guide to action for communists and socialists.

This strategic approach has enabled the Communist Party to avoid many of the errors, diversions and somersaults of social-democratic and far-left critics who base their political activity on short-term election manifestos or a list of abstract or unrealistic slogans.

The CP has always drawn a sharp distinction between achieving a Labour or left government in office under capitalism, and establishing a socialist government when the working class has won state power once capitalist rule has been overthrown.

In Britain, we have experienced Labour governments in 1923-24, 1929-31, 1945-51, 1964-70, 1974-79 and 1997-2010. They were always in office, but never in power. The state apparatus remained one designed – with some modified relics of feudalism – and deployed to maintain capitalism and imperialism, staffed at the head of all essential departments by personnel devoted to that purpose. With some honourable exceptions, most senior Labour ministers had no ambition to turn office into power; nor would they have been allowed to do so by those with real power – Britain's monopoly capitalists, whose interests are served by the state apparatus.

While identifying the opportunities created by the election of a Labour government – especially one under constant pressure from the labour movement – Britain's CP has never fostered the illusion that socialism would arrive 'by a royal decree countersigned by two ministers', as Lenin mockingly put it. However, all references to a 'dictatorship of the working class' as the Party's aim were dropped after 1945. The term had become so closely associated with fascism that its use was regarded as misleading and counter-productive, especially when the Party's immediate aims included extensive measures to expand democratic rights under capitalism, democratise the capitalist state apparatus and place these on a new basis – free from capitalist restrictions – under socialism. Indeed, the 1968 edition of the *BRS* pledged to respect the freedom of political parties hostile to socialism after the revolution, providing they did not engage in subversion or armed rebellion.

The massive turn of workers and their families to Labour and its progressive manifesto of 1945 led *The British Road to Socialism* between 1951 and 1978 to put a 'Labour government of a new type' – followed by successive left governments – at the centre of its perspective for achieving socialism. While the *BRS* upheld the importance of extra-parliamentary struggle and the leading role of the organised working-class movement and the Communist Party, the programme implied that the road to socialism would be a largely constitutional one. The overwhelming strength of the movement for socialism would also make possible a transition without civil war (as envisaged initially if fleetingly by Marx but never by Lenin), although Labour and left governments must have the means to defeat armed rebellion and counter-revolution.

For the Communist Party's far-left detractors, these all-important caveats have always been ignored in order to misrepresent the *BRS* as merely a reformist 'parliamentary road to socialism'. At the same time, it should be conceded that weaknesses of emphasis and formulation reflected the growth of a reformist outlook in the CP, mostly from the top downwards, during the post-war period until the re-established Communist Party of Britain (CPB) published new or updated editions of *Britain's Road to Socialism* in 2001, 2011 and 2020.

Working-class self-organisation

The workers' councils or soviets advocated at the Unity Convention were conceived according to the Russian model and as replicated in Munich and Budapest in the revolutionary upsurges of 1918-19. In Britain, these were to be the means by which the workers would seize and exercise power, led by the Communist Party. Indeed, such bodies had already arisen, at least in embryo, in the miners' Unofficial Reform Committee in south Wales, the Workers and Soldiers Councils of 1917 and the Clyde Workers Committee – all of which involved activists who helped form the CPGB.

Immediately after the Unity Convention, these same Communists and others later threw themselves into the Councils of Action which sprang up in 1920 to campaign against renewed British military intervention in Russia to aid the 'White' insurgents and Polish invaders. The councils brought together local trade union, socialist and Labour Party organisations, but soon faded as the 'Reds' overcame the 'Whites' in Russia and Ukraine, as the Poles retreated and as Britain's military plans were put into cold storage.

The Party's commitment to working-class self-organisation found new expression in 1921, when Wal Hannington and other Communists set up the National Unemployed Workers Committee Movement. Local committees mobilised against Boards of Guardians, the workhouse system and later the Means Test, organising regional and national Hunger Marches from the late 1920s. During the 1926 General Strike, local Councils of Action enforce solidarity and organised local picketing, food supplies and emergency cover for the sick and vulnerable. CPGB members were tireless in their participation in these and other initiatives. During the strike and the seven-month mining lockout, more than a thousand CP militants were arrested, convicted and in numerous cases – including Communist-Labour MP Shapurji Saklatvala – imprisoned, the central leadership of the Party having already been jailed for sedition and conspiracy some months before the strike.

Admittedly, these were defensive battles and the Councils of Action secured participation and support far beyond the ranks of the relatively small Communist Party. Yet it was the CP – and certainly not the Labour Party nor the TUC leadership – which saw in such working-class self-organisation the potential for the creation of organs of revolution and state power.

Nevertheless, the perspective of workers councils or soviets as organs of political power during and after socialist revolution did not appear in the first editions of the *BRS*. Indeed, *The British Road to Socialism* (1951) explicitly rejected the Soviet model as a prototype for Britain. This raises the question of how the working class – the only force capable of paralysing and overthrowing capitalism – was to exercise its leading role in the revolutionary process other than through the institutions of the labour movement – including its Communist Party – and the state.

Not until 1978 did the *BRS* step outside the framework of existing structures. In the chapter 'Towards socialist revolution', it anticipated that 'new forms of popular organisation and new forms of struggle' would emerge as left governments and the mass movement battled to make real inroads into monopoly capital's wealth and power. These would 'probably include factory councils, neighbourhood committees and tenants committees, linked to more representative trades councils and helping to organise and mobilise the people and resist the sabotage of the ruling class'. They would constitute 'an element of the new state power by which the working class and its allies will eventually govern the country'. The 2011 and 2020 editions of *Britain's Road to Socialism* cite historical examples of such self-organisation in Britain, including the Working Men's Associations, the National and Female Charter Associations, workers' and consumers' cooperatives, workers' and soldiers' councils, councils of action, the People's Convention, the Campaign for Nuclear Disarmament, the Liaison Committee for the Defence of Trade Unions, miners' support groups and Women Against Pit Closures, anti-poll tax unions, the Stop the War Coalition and the People's Charter and People's Assembly.

In a sub-section on 'Taking state power and defeating counter-revolution', the 2020 *BRS* foresees trades unions participating in the left government's transformational military policy and suggests that 'new bodies of working class and popular power are likely to be necessary to monitor or take over state functions and ensure implementation of the Left-Wing Programme'. According to a sub-section on 'Building a socialist society', these would also be necessary to 'counteract any tendencies to over-centralisation, elitism, careerism and bureaucratic control'. Furthermore, the state apparatus at every level should be 'directed by the elected representatives of the people and monitored by non-state bodies appointed by working class and popular organisations'.

Communist internationalism

From its foundation, the CPGB staunchly supported the state power exercised by communist parties in the Soviet Union and, later, the People's Democracies of central and eastern Europe, the People's Republic of China and in the other socialist countries. As a constituent 'section' of the Communist International – the 'world party of socialist revolution' – the CPGB participated in its structures and was bound by its central decisions.

The most important of these decisions was that taken in 1924 for the 'Bolshevisation' of the Comintern and its parties, centralising their internal regimes and in effect enhancing the domination of the international movement by the Communist Party of the Soviet Union (CPSU). Yet, as British and Comintern archives now confirm, the CPGB had already established its own 'Bolshevisation Commission' in 1922, which began the work of reorganising the Party on the lines of the Russian model.

The Comintern and its executive committee (ECCI) had a more substantial impact on the CPGB in 1927-29, with the launch of their new 'Third Period' line. Following periods of revolutionary crisis and relative stabilisation, capitalism was heading for a slump in which more ruling classes – supported by the social-democratic parties – would turn to fascism. Communists in Britain should therefore break their links with the Labour left whose 'fake' left-wing posture misled workers away from the Communist Party and socialist revolution.

There was plenty of support for this 'Class against Class' line within the ranks of the CPGB itself, as TUC leaders entered talks with business chiefs and together with the Labour Party leadership launched an anti-Communist purge in the labour movement. However, at the same time the ECCI intervention also opened up debate in the CPGB about the nature of the Party itself: was it to be a disciplined Marxist-Leninist party organised to lead workers in struggle, or to remain at the level of a propaganda group isolated from the factories? The outcome, the victory of the former position, brought in Harry Pollitt as general secretary and led directly to the establishment in 1930 of the *Daily Worker*, subsequently sustained in the teeth of state persecution and a universal boycott by the big wholesalers, but still going today under the name of the *Morning Star*.

While the 'Third Period' analysis accurately foresaw the international capitalist slump which followed the 1929 Wall Street Crash, it overestimated the immediate revolutionary possibilities, causing the CP to turn too far to the left and alienate many of its left-wing allies. However, when the Comintern turned to the United Front, and a broader People's Front endorsed at its Seventh World Congress in 1935, the CPGB had already been moving in that direction.

The fact that some Liberals and even the odd Tory supported the Popular Front alliance against fascism in Britain did not signify the abandonment of class struggle and socialism by the Communist Party or its left allies. Even the most cursory glance at CP propaganda and congress proceedings in the latter half of the 1930s, and the briefest study of trade union struggles of the period, will demonstrate the Communist Party's continuing commitment to class struggle, socialism and communism. Only the most shameless far-left falsifiers of history can pretend otherwise.

Comintern leader Georgi Dimitrov – the hero of the Reichstag Fire trial in Nazi Germany in 1933 – impressed on the communist parties the imperative of seizing the banner of national freedom and sovereignty from the right-wing nationalists and fascists, embracing the progressive patriotism outlined by Lenin and celebrating the struggles of their own people against tyranny. This inspired Communists to uncover and celebrate the history of the common people and their struggles in England, Scotland and Wales and to propose measures of self-determination for the Celtic nations.

Throughout the inter-war period, the CPGB strove to fulfil its internationalist duty. This meant, firstly, defending the world's first socialist state, promoting its achievements, and countering imperialism's lies and scares. Spying for the Soviet state was neither organised nor explicitly endorsed by the CPGB, for whom the real 'traitors' were the ruling class which exploited and oppressed the peoples of the British Empire, readily making deals with the fascist leaders of Italy, Portugal, Germany and Spain.

Secondly, the CPGB willingly carried out clandestine missions for the Comintern to assist the development of Communist parties, trade unions and national liberation movements in Ireland and the colonies. Numerous files in British state and Comintern archives attest to the extent of this work and of ruling-class efforts to monitor and disrupt it. CPGB emissaries and Comintern agents were sometimes caught, such as those charged in the 1929-33 Meerut Conspiracy Trial with spreading trade unionism in India.

Until the early 1930s, the Party directed most of its efforts in support of the anti-colonial movements through the League Against Imperialism, although this did not survive the 'Third Period' divisions between the CPGB, the Labour left and the ILP. The main focus of the Party's international work shifted to anti-fascism and the war in Spain from 1936. On the initiative of the Comintern, the CPGB recruited more than 2,300 volunteers to serve in the International Brigades and medical teams fighting General Franco's nationalist rebellion – backed militarily by the fascist powers – against the elected Popular Front government. The Republican government had begun far-reaching reforms in education, healthcare, social security, labour relations and land tenure and granted autonomy to the Basques and other peoples. But now, for most socialists and communists, the overriding priority was to defeat the barbarians at the gates. More than 500 volunteers from Britain gave their lives for Spanish democracy and their memory has been honoured in Spain ever since.

The Comintern's most decisive intervention in CPGB affairs took place in 1939. On September 2, the day before Britain's declaration of war on Nazi

Germany, the Party had called for 'war on two fronts – against Hitler abroad and against the imperialist Chamberlain Government at home'. This was not an unpopular policy among Party members, although some believed that Chamberlain's phoney declaration should be flatly opposed. On September 24, during the Party's two-day central committee (CC) meeting, Dave Springhall arrived from Moscow to report that the CPSU and the Comintern characterised the war as 'imperialist and unjust ... for which the bourgeoisie of all the belligerent states bear equal responsibility'.

After years of appeasing fascism, the British ruling class and government had refused and then delayed signing a collective security pact with the Soviet Union, leaving the Soviets with no option but to agree a non-aggression pact with Germany and so buy time to prepare for the inevitable war against the Nazis.

By the following weekend, the Party's CC had swung over to support for the Comintern line. Harry Pollitt was removed as general secretary and JR Campbell as editor of the *Daily Worker*, replaced by a triumvirate of Rajani Palme Dutt, Bill Rust and Springhall (with Dutt as the first among equals). Debates across the Party and its publications revealed a clear division of opinion with a substantial minority unconvinced by the change of line, outweighed by those who had doubts originally or had been persuaded by the prestige and arguments of Georgi Dimitrov and the Comintern.

The CPGB pursued the new line vigorously, working with allies to convene a large People's Convention in January 1941 attended by 2,000 delegates on behalf of 1,300 labour movement organisations. The blitz of London, Coventry and other cities had begun and Communists had led occupations of London underground stations and luxury hotel shelters. The conference proposed the immediate formation of a 'People's Government' to deliver a 'People's Peace' and measures to protect workers' rights and people's safety and to end profiteering. Just nine days after that, the Labour home secretary Herbert Morrison banned the *Daily Worker*.

Following the fall of France in June 1940, the character of the war was already changing. Hitler's forces were occupying northern Europe as communist parties organised anti-fascist resistance movements. When Nazi Germany and its allies invaded the Soviet Union in June 1941, it confirmed that this was now a 'People's War against Fascism'.

Many CP members and supporters embraced the changed policy with relief. Communist shop stewards and union officials led the drive for workplace production committees to boost the war effort. Unfortunately, the Tory-Labour coalition government resorted to authoritarian laws and methods in its treatment of workers in crucial industries. Unofficial strikes broke out in coalfields such as South Wales and Kent and strike leaders were jailed. Prominent CP members led many of the actions while others – as regional or national union officials – tried to persuade miners to return to work. Despite ultra-left criticisms then and ever since, the Party was right to prioritise the fight against fascism above all else; most miners thought so, too, and elected Communists to many national and coalfield positions in the post-war National Union of Mineworkers (including Arthur Horner as president in 1946).

In May 1943, recognising that 'the national upsurge and mobilisation of the masses for the speediest victory over the enemy can best and most fruitfully be realised by the vanguard of the working-class movement of each country within the framework of its own state', the ECCI Presidium proposed the dissolution of the Comintern. Not a single communist party objected to it. An important factor in the decision was the desire to promote trust between the 'Big Three' allied powers – the Soviet Union, Britain and the United States.

The ruling communist parties of the Soviet Union and eastern Europe founded the Communist Information Bureau (Cominform) in 1947, together with the mass parties of France and Italy expelled from post-war coalition governments. Like the other smaller parties in western Europe, the CPGB did not participate in the Cominform but promoted its views and initiatives.

In the socialist countries, policies of industrialisation, workers' rights, women's emancipation, national equality, universal education and health provision, scientific advance, wealth redistribution, land reform and much else besides were implemented in the interests of working people and their families. However, flagrant abuses of socialist state power also took place, some of them attributable to the immense difficulties of building socialism in a world initially dominated by the imperialist powers. With the benefit of hindsight, it should be admitted that for long periods the CPGB – like other parties, and in the context of the sharp international class struggle, when the existence of the Soviet Union appeared to be under military threat – suspended its critical faculties in relation to these abuses and mistakes. In particular, the purges and show trials of late 1930s and late 1940s were accepted and reported at face value, despite the absurdity of much of the 'evidence' and the proceedings. The deportations of whole peoples in the wake of the 'Great Patriotic War' were denied, downplayed or otherwise endorsed.

The plans revealed in US and British state archives to launch unprovoked military attacks on the Soviet Union from 1945 onwards, to foment terrorist subversion in the German Democratic Republic and to assist the well-armed anti-communist mobs in Hungary in 1956 throw new light on the litany of 'the crimes of Stalinism' so beloved of the ruling class and the anti-Soviet far left. The CPGB supported – with misgivings and regret – the Soviet military intervention in Budapest, while recognising serious deficiencies in the ruling party and some of its policies; but it condemned the Soviet and Warsaw Treaty intervention in Czechoslovakia to reverse the reforms of 1968, urging a peaceful resolution through dialogue that would broadly retain the democratisation measures of the 'Prague Spring'.

Like communist parties and national liberation movements around the world, the CPGB did support many other aspects of the foreign policy of the Soviet Union and other socialist states, in a spirit of solidarity and mutual assistance. Crude anti-communist accounts of these relationships have been exploded by recent access to the Moscow and Amsterdam archives of the CPSU, the Comintern, the KGB, the Red International of Labour Unions (RILU) and the League Against Imperialism. They make nonsense of Trotskyist and Maoist claims that the ruling communist parties abandoned socialist internationalism, or that the policy of 'peaceful co-existence' imposed on the imperialist powers by the Soviet Union and its allies represented some kind of international class collaboration.

There have been many sensationalist revelations in recent decades of 'Moscow Gold' paid by the Comintern and the CPSU to parties in Britain and elsewhere. Three points should be made: firstly, the payments were regarded by the few CPGB officials who knew about them as acts of solidarity between Communists, in a world where imperialist governments offered each other all forms of assistance – including military support – in order to combat left-wing parties and national liberation movements; indeed, much of the money received in Britain was passed on secretly to parties and movements in other countries as well as going to the *Daily Worker* and funding Comintern pensions. Secondly, while these funds were valuable, in Britain for example they rarely formed more than one-tenth of the Party's income. Thirdly, they did not buy obedience to the Comintern or CPSU line, which anyway carried its own prestige.

The need to contain US imperialism's aggressive, expansionist foreign policy and avoid the catastrophe of nuclear war motivated Communists and their allies to establish the British Peace Assembly (BPA) in 1949 as an affiliate of what became the World Peace Council. Such was ruling-class hostility that in 1950 the World Peace Congress in Sheffield was sabotaged by the Labour government, which refused entry visas to numerous eminent scientists and artists. The event was reconvened in Prague. Although the CPGB along with the international communist movement initially prioritised the call for multilateral talks leading to all-round nuclear disarmament, Communists supported the first march to the Aldermaston atomic weapons research station in 1958. The contribution of Party members to the growth of the Campaign for Nuclear Disarmament (CND) earned condemnation from Tory defence secretary Michael Heseltine and praise at a CP congress from CND leader Bruce Kent. In every war of British imperialism, from Korea and Malaya to the Falklands and Iraq, Communists have stepped forward to take leading positions in broad-based peace movements. Recently, the CPB has cooperated with other socialists to re-establish the BPA as an affiliate of the anti-imperialist World Peace Council.

Moreover, Communists and their allies maintained a range of friendship societies to strengthen the social, trade union and cultural links between the peoples of Britain and the socialist countries, with many Labour members participating in defiance of their own party's bans and proscriptions against 'communist-front' organisations.

Britain's Communists also campaigned ceaselessly in solidarity with parties facing repression from the US, West Germany and Cyprus to Iraq, Indonesia and most recently the Ukraine. Over decades, the CP worked in broad alliances to organise big solidarity movements for the peoples of South Africa and Vietnam in their long struggles for liberation. Clandestine work was also carried out when requested, for instance in support of South African and Chilean communists and freedom fighters.

The CPGB played a full part in the international conferences of communist and workers' parties in Moscow in 1957, 1960 and 1969. The Party did not agree with the Communist Party of China's (CPC) characterisation of the Soviet Union as a 'social imperialist' power, nor with its assessment of the possibilities arising from nuclear conflict. Nonetheless, the Party in Britain urged polemical restraint on both sides and an end to the Sino-Soviet split in the international communist movement.

The collapse of the socialist systems in the Soviet Union and eastern Europe in the late 1980s and early 1990s dealt an enormous blow to the international communist movement and all those who received its assistance. Following its own re-establishment in 1988 after a debilitating fight against revisionism and liquidationism (see below), the CPB has played a very active part in the movement's reconstruction. This included participation in the international seminar on 'The Contemporary World Situation and Marxism' organised by the Communist Party of India (Marxist) in 1993 and then the annual International Meeting of Communist and Workers Parties that has taken place since the Communist Party of Greece hosted the first in 1998. In recent years, the CPB has established the Coordinating Committee of Communist Parties in Britain, bringing together exiled Communists from the Middle East, India, Cyprus, Sudan, Chile and other countries overseas to take part in anti-racist initiatives, seminars and commemorations including a major event every year to mark International Women's Day.

Communist unity

In his letter of July 8 1920 and subsequently, Lenin criticised the tactics of 'Comrade Sylvia Pankhurst' and the Workers' Socialist Federation (WSF) for pulling out of the unification process. He did not believe that different positions on questions such as electoral participation or support for the Labour Party justified standing aside from the formation of a single Communist Party in Britain.

The young CPGB maintained negotiations with other socialist and communist groups to bring them into the Party. A second Unity Convention, in January 1921, embraced more elements of the ILP – a process repeated in 1935 – and Sylvia Pankhurst's WSF. Having failed in his effort to win

Lenin's support for a separate party in Scotland, Marxist revolutionary John Maclean went on the establish his own Scottish Workers Republican Party. The Scottish section of the Socialist Labour Party also remained outside the CPGB.

Thereafter, the Party organised most of the Marxist left in Britain outside the Labour Party and the ILP until the 1980s. The CPGB remained organisationally united, despite the temporary loss of almost one-in-three of its 34,000 members after the Khrushchev revelations and Hungarian crisis of 1956. The defection of engineering union leader Reg Birch to form his own pro-CPC, anti-CPSU party in 1968 had little impact. More significant was the breakaway led by Surrey district secretary Sid French in 1977 to form the New Communist Party (NCP) after denouncing the new draft of *The British Road to Socialism* as revisionist and a departure from 'proletarian internationalism'.

Divisions in the CPGB in the 1980s did far more to damage communist unity. A faction of self-styled 'revolutionary democrats' or 'Gramscians' – later more widely referred to as 'Eurocommunists' – believed that the Party and formulations in its programme exhibited tendencies to 'class reductionism' and 'economism': too much time and resources were allegedly devoted to the economic aspects of the class struggle. As a consequence, the CPGB was neglecting the social, cultural and ideological fronts, neglecting vital issues issues and social forces that could not simply be analysed in terms of 'class'. This was itself a narrow interpretation of class politics and a total misrepresentation of the work of the Party. Nonetheless, the Eurocommunists – assisted by the core leadership of the CPGB – used their control of the Young Communist League, the Party's national student committee, the theoretical and discussion journal *Marxism Today*, the Communist University of London and then a succession of internal journals to systematically question and then attack the militant class-based Marxist-Leninist politics of the Party and its programme. Their embrace of a defeatist cocktail of liberalism, 'non-class' feminism, anti-Sovietism, anti-Leninism and ultimately anti-socialism destroyed the YCL and Broad Left domination of the National Union Students, turned *Marxism Today* into a house journal for anti-Communist intellectuals, severed the political relationship between the CPGB and the *Morning Star*, and undermined the Party's alliances in the trade union movement – at a time when the National Union of Mineworkers was being subjected to the full force of the state – and paved the way for the rise of New Labour.

Between them, the Eurocommunists and their allies carried out the biggest purge in the Party's history, liquidating district committees, branches and industrial advisories and expelling or excluding more than 700 CPGB members between 1985 and 1987.

Communists inside and outside the Party established the Communist Campaign Group to challenge revisionism and rebuild communist unity around the Party's existing rules, principles and programme. A congress subsequently re-established the Communist Party of Britain (CPB) in 1988. The Eurocommunists, on the other hand, renounced Marxism-Leninism, turned the CPGB into the 'Democratic Left' in 1991 and then finally liquidated *Marxism Today* and a succession of political organisations and networks.

During the early 1990s, the CPB engaged in successful communist unity initiatives with the Communist Trade Unionists network of former CPGB members and the Communist Liaison group which emerged from the old party's *Straight Left* faction. An attempt to begin a similar process with the NCP proved unproductive, despite the CPB's revision of *Britain's Road to Socialism* to remove its problematic formulations. Although differences with the NCP remain over electoral policy and a number of international and historical questions, these do not constitute sufficient grounds for contradicting Lenin's call for unity.

Today, the CPB is growing once more and organises by the far the greater number of communists in Britain. There are a few other self-styled communist parties, but their slogans and tactics bear little or no relation to current conditions and some of these outfits devote an extraordinary amount of effort to attacking all other groups on the left, not least the CPB.

Elections and parliaments

Lenin insisted that a Communist Party in Britain should not boycott parliaments and elections. Fighting elections and utilising parliamentary representation were, in his view, an unavoidable front of the political class struggle. But Communist election campaigns should be conducted in a revolutionary way, with bold slogans and actions. Communist MPs should be held strictly accountable to the Party, using their position and status to inform, inspire and help mobilise the mass of the people.

This was a point of contention at the 1920 Unity Convention, although the resolution committing the CPGB to 'Parliamentary Action' was eventually passed with 186 delegates in favour and 19 against. Ever since the Caerffili by-election of 1921, the Party has contested elections at every level from local government to the Westminster Parliament and – in recent decades – the Scottish Parliament, the Welsh National Assembly and, until the 2016 EU referendum result, the EU Parliament.

Apart from MPs elected with Labour support in the 1920s such as Shapurji Saklatvala, the CP has only secured representation at Westminster through Willie Gallacher in West Fife (1935-40) and Phil Piratin in Mile End (1945-50). But between them, they demonstrated the immense value of Communist parliamentary representation, constantly exposing and attacking the anti-working class, capitalist and imperialist policies of Tory and Labour governments, working with left-wing Labour MPs while often facing ferocious hostility from right-wing MPs and ministers in both main parties. Throughout their period in the House of Commons, Gallacher and Piratin were subject to a strict regime of supervision, reporting and where necessary correction by the Party's parliamentary and local government department on behalf of the executive committee (EC).

Of course, the CP has faced formidable obstacles when it comes to securing MPs. The Labour Party, backed by its affiliated trade unions, was and still is the main electoral vehicle of the labour movement and working-class voters. The Westminster voting system has always been weighted heavily in favour of representation by the main parties, even before taking into account decades of Cold War, anti-Communist propaganda.

Given these realities, Communists have sought to influence Labour's election manifestos whenever possible, through affiliated trade unions and in alliance with parts of the Labour left. In the 1983 General Election, the Tories placed full-page adverts in the press listing the similarities between Labour and CP policies on the Common Market, nationalisation, nuclear weapons, trade union rights, immigration controls and the movement of capital under the headline: 'Like your manifesto, Comrade'.

Communist candidates have had more success at local level, where they are known as campaigners for working-class interests to a higher proportion of the electors. At various times, the Party has won substantial representation from East London and rural Norfolk to industrial South Wales, Manchester and Clydeside. Highpoints have included winning 215 councillors in the 1945-46 local elections and the elevation to mayoral posts of Joe Vaughan (Bethnal Green, 1920), Finlay Hart (Clydebank) and Annie Powell (Rhondda, 1979).

In recent decades, the CPB has re-entered the electoral arena, using the opportunity to distribute literature on a large scale, participate in public debates, secure party election broadcasts and challenge fascist candidates.

The Labour Party question

Lenin was aware that in the most recent General Election before the Unity Convention, the Labour Party had won more than two million votes (one-fifth of the total). Many more were soon to be added, taken mostly from the Liberal Party. Working-class electors would, Lenin argued, be more inclined to give a sympathetic hearing to Communists who shared the general objective of a Labour victory. A Labour government might benefit the people with some reforms; it would also benefit the Communist Party by exposing reformist limitations and the inability of social-democratic parties to bring about socialism.

Furthermore, Lenin insisted, the CP in Britain should seek affiliation to the Labour Party 'on condition of free and independent Communist activity'. Of course, he understood that Labour leaders would be likely to oppose the affiliation to their party of a body of Communist revolutionaries.

So be it ... Labour's leaders would be demonstrating their refusal to embrace working-class unity and the goal of socialism.

At the first Unity Convention, JF Hodgson proposed the British Socialist Party's position in favour of affiliation. The working class had to go through the experience of a Labour government in office in order to learn from its inevitable failures, with Communists opposing the election of Lloyd George or Winston Churchill and giving Labour leaders 'such support as the rope gives to the executed person' (Hodgson had been reading Lenin's *The Infantile Sickness of 'Leftism' in Communism* as it was first called in English). The CPGB could best influence these Labour-supporting workers from inside the Labour Party. William Paul opposed affiliation, pointing to the reactionary role that treacherous Labour MPs play, especially in times of crisis. Now that the left-wing revolutionary movement was growing in Britain, the CPGB should not tie itself to the Labour Party and parliament and thereby be discredited.

After its longest debate by far, the Unity Convention decided by 100 votes to 85 that the CPGB should apply for affiliation to the Labour Party. On August 6, the Second Congress of the Comintern endorsed affiliation – as a tactic but not a principle – after speeches from Sylvia Pankhurst and Willie Gallacher against and Lenin in favour.

All such applications were rejected by large majorities at the annual Labour Party conferences between 1920-24. A fifth application was rejected more narrowly in 1936, after an intensive campaign by the CPGB and its many Labour and trade union supporters, and again in 1943. A ferocious anti-Communist offensive widened the margin at the 1946 Labour Party conference and effectively put an end to the CPGB's affiliation attempts.

Subsequently, the CPGB mobilised against the Labour government's turn to the right after 1947 as it introduced NHS charges to help pay for a massive rearmament programme, developed nuclear weapons, embraced NATO and went to war in Malaya and Korea. But the aim remained to support – although not uncritically – the left against the right in the labour movement in line with the perspectives of the *BRS*. The defeat of the Communist and Labour Independent Group of MPs at the 1950 General Election represented a major setback, especially when many of the 'Bevanites' tended to take a pro-imperialist if less hawkish position on Cold War issues. Nonetheless, the Party's work in the trade union, peace, anti-racist and anti-colonial movements expanded and strengthened links with sections of the Labour left in the 1960s and 1970s, reflected particularly in the development of union 'Broad Lefts' and wider support for *Labour Monthly* and the renamed *Morning Star*.

Cooperation reached new levels during Jeremy Corbyn's leadership of the Labour Party between 2015 and 2019, although these were exaggerated and sensationalised by the anti-socialist press. Nonetheless, the British ruling class genuinely feared the prospect of Jeremy Corbyn winning office in Ten Downing Street, given his record as a committed socialist and anti-imperialist MP. Indeed, Britain's monopoly capitalists saw a Boris Johnson victory and Brexit as a price worth paying if it meant keeping Labour out of government and in opposition.

Despite defeat in the December 2019 General Election, the Labour Party still won ten million votes, one-third of the poll, and has hundreds of thousands of individual members and the affiliation of trades unions representing more than four million workers. Communists cannot ignore this elephant in the room, or imagine that denouncing it for being an elephant will somehow make it drop dead or go away.

Because the working class – as broadly defined in *Britain's Road to Socialism* – is the only class with the capacity to paralyse and overthrow capitalism, there can be no alternative to winning a deep and permanent shift to the left in the labour movement. That will, dialectically, be reflected and reinforced by a left turn in the Labour Party for as long as that party retains its working-class affiliations, organisationally and electorally. Thus, the perspective proposed in *BRS* is that of mass struggle creating the conditions for the election of a left government based on a Labour, socialist and communist majority; a government dependent on a popular democratic anti-monopoly alliance led by the organised working class and determined to implement a Left-Wing Programme. Reflected also in Scotland and Wales, this would mark a new stage in the revolutionary struggle for socialism.

However, the wider question remains: after six periods of Labour governments in office, spanning 33 years, is it still essential for the working class to go through the experience yet again in order to learn or re-learn the lessons of history? While working-class disillusionment with Labour governments has repeated itself over the decades, both as tragedy and as farce, political consciousness is not sufficiently hereditary. Thus, it may be necessary – albeit decreasingly so – for each generation to experienceLabour governments and learn lessons anew about the betrayals and limitations of social democracy. Standing aside from the left-right battle of ideas and policies within the Labour Party is sectarian posturing of the kind condemned by Lenin.

Affiliation of the CPB to the Labour Party is not a realistic prospect at present, despite increasing support for the *Morning Star* and its political perspectives – with an editorial line based on *BRS* – in the labour movement. Yet history demonstrates that conditions can change, making enhanced forms of cooperation between Communists and the Labour Party, or at least sections of it, possible in the future.

The trade union movement

Lenin urged Britain's Communists to forge the closest links with militant trade union organisations, including shop stewards committees. He wanted these workers to overcome their hostility to political parties and the electoral struggle, and to help build the Communist Party as a party of a new type, in constant contact with the masses and able to provide leadership.

Certainly, next to international solidarity, the most prominent and best-known area of the CP's work over the past 100 years has been that in the trade union movement. From the outset, Communists concentrated much of their efforts on organising and strengthening union organisation in workplaces and local communities through, for example, shop stewards committees and trades councils.

Initially, the CPGB pursued the Comintern line of a 'united front from below' of Communists, socialists and trade union militants. This produced advances for the CP-led National Minority Movement and some of its industrial sections such as that within the Miners Federation of Great Britain (MFGB). The National Left-Wing Movement (NLWM) also brought Communists and socialists together in the labour movement, as did the League Against Imperialism on the international front.

But after left-wing members of the TUC General Council capitulated to the Tory government and the mineowners in the General Strike, and the TUC and Labour Party leaderships intensified their purge of Communists in the labour movement,the CPGB broadened and sharpened its attacks on non-Communist trade union officials. The Comintern's 'Third Period' line strengthened this CPGB offensive, rather than creating or imposing it. The alliances with non-Communists in CP-led movements did not survive the divisions which opened up. The struggle between Party militants and reactionary, anti-democratic union leaderships led to the formation – backed ambiguously by the Comintern and the RILU – of 'Red' unions in 1929 such as the United Mineworkers of Scotland and the United Clothing Workers Union. In 1931, having opposed the unofficial continuation of a disintegrating coalfield strike, former chair of the central strike committee Arthur Horner was removed as secretary of the Miners Minority Movement, accused of 'Hornerism' and summoned to Moscow.

While the 'Third Period' analysis accurately foresaw the international capitalist slump which followed the 1929 Wall Street Crash, it overestimated the immediate revolutionary possibilities, causing the CP to turn too far to the left and alienate many of its left-wing allies. Unrelenting attacks on labour movement leaders, even those on the left and in the centre, are not necessarily conducive to forging unity with rank-and-file activists who do not see them as 'the main enemy', if an enemy at all. Yet the CPGB's fighting spirit in that period built the National Unemployed Workers Movement as an effective mass movement through its local campaigning, advice work, resistance to home evictions and the great hunger marches of 1927-36. Under the 'Class Against Class' leadership of general secretary Pollitt and editor Bill Rust, the Party also founded and sustained the *Daily Worker* from 1930, in the teeth of state persecution and a universal boycott by the big wholesalers.

As the CPGB began to break out of its isolation from much of the labour movement, the Comintern executive changed its line to the 'United Front' and 'People's Front'. The Party reached out to the Labour left and the ILP, while also building alliances – despite the TUC's fresh anti-CP offensive – at every level of the trade union movement in pursuit of achievable political and industrial objectives. In the industries recovering from the Great Depression, and those flourishing for the first time, Communists quickly came to the fore in rank-and-file and unofficial bodies. However, unlike some episodes during the 'Third Period', this was not done in order to attack union officials and build a base for 'Red' unionism; now the intention was to win the fight for policies and positions within the official union structures, bringing shop stewards committees and combines into them wherever possible.

Nobody embodied this approach better than Arthur Horner. He organised the rank-and-file with his paper, the *South Wales Miner*, before winning the presidency of the South Wales Miners Federation in 1936, followed by that of the National Union of Mineworkers in 1946. He used these positions not only to vastly improve the pay and conditions of his members, but also to strengthen and politicise miners and the working class generally – against vicious opposition from within the NUM, the TUC and in the capitalist press.

Not that the CP thereafter confined its activities to the labour movement's official channels. In the major dock strikes of 1949, for instance, the unofficial Port Workers Committees directed operations under the Communist leadership of Jack Dash, Ted Dickens and others (and under relentless attack from the police, courts, intelligence services and their agents in the labour movement and mass media). The TUC general council hit back with the expulsion of dozens of CP-led trades councils. In 1962-63, Charlie Doyle led an unofficial National Committee of Shop Stewards to organise power-station strikes which earned him the title of 'the most hated man in Britain' in the *Daily Mirror*.

Much of the Party's strength in industry derived from its organisation in the factories, mines, mills, ports and depots. At their peak, during the Second World War, there were Party branches or groups in more than 1,000 workplaces. But the branches were replaced by committees in 1944 and their members transferred to residential branches, partly to strengthen the CP's electoral work. Attempts to reverse this policy from 1948 were not wholly successful, although factory 'fortresses' were built or rebuilt in several hundred workplaces such as Shardlow's (Sheffield), Austin Aero (near Longbridge), Napier's (Acton), Metro-Vickers (Manchester), Rolls Royce (Derby), Ford's (Dagenham) and Fairey Aviation (Stockport), some with members in the hundreds.

During the 1950s, Communists rose to leading positions in a host of unions, including those for construction, furniture, foundry, tobacco, bakery and scientific workers, and in the National Union of Teachers and the Fire Brigades Union. CP leadership of the Electrical Trades Union (ETU) brought enormous benefits to all grades of members but also caused great alarm in ruling class circles in Britain and the US. Unfortunately, in the fierce inner-union struggle, some Communist ETU officials used the same underhand tactics as the anti-Communists to manipulate voting figures; they were found guilty of ballot-rigging in a highly-publicised court case in 1961. Communists were removed from high positions and all Party members were banned from office in the union for decades to come. The extraordinary coincidences underlying some of the 1961 court case 'evidence' against the union's Communist leadership have never been explained, although they point to involvement of the intelligence services in the whole affair.

The danger of more witch-hunts in the wake of the ETU case – Communists had previously been banned from office for political reasons in the Transport & General Workers and General & Municipal Workers unions – encouraged the Party to strengthen its links with allies on the left during the following decades. Unofficial 'Broad Left' networks of activists were built to win left policies and leadership elections. The CP-led Liaison Committee for the Defence of Trade Unions, based on a wide range of workplace shop stewards and union reps' committees, called national days of action against Labour's White Paper 'In Place of Strife' (1969) and the Tory government's Industrial Relations Act (1971), both of which were aimed at unofficial strikes and effective workplace organisation. Both measures were also abandoned, the latter after Communists and their allies organised mass action and forced the TUC to threaten a one-day general strike to free five dockers' leaders from Pentonville prison. The Communist-led occupation and 'work-in' to protect 6,000 jobs at Upper Clyde Shipbuilders in 1971-72 grabbed news headlines around the world, sparking solidarity strikes and a wave of copycat actions across Britain.

By this time, Communists had overcome decades of fierce anti-communism to occupy leading positions in the Scottish TUC. Following the 1972 miners strike, they organised with Labour allies to establish a Welsh TUC in defiance of many union leaders and the TUC general council.

Before and since, Communists have played a significant role in many of the biggest industrial battles of the 20th century, including the strikes by steelworkers (1934), apprentices (1937, 1941, 1951, 1964), dockers (1949, 1970, 1972), shipyard workers (1957, 1971-72), engineers (1957, 1970-71), car workers (1957, 1970s), power workers (1962-63), seafarers (1966), coal miners (1972, 1974, 1984-85), building workers (1972) and printworkers (1986-87), to name but a few.

Naturally, the Party's proud record has earned the active hostility of employers and a nest of anti-trade union, anti-Communist bodies such as the Economic League, Aims of Industry, Common Cause and the now defunct Information Research Department which operated from inside the government Foreign Office. These worked openly and secretly to smear Communists in the trade union movement and to exclude them from employment wherever possible.

From the foundation of the Party, Britain's intelligence services devoted substantial resources to combating what they considered 'Communist subversion' in industry. From the 1950s into the 1970s, the Security Service (MI5) had at least 60 desk officers in its London headquarters – liaising with many more officers, agents and informers in the field – wholly engaged in surveillance and disruption of the CPGB. A Security Service assessment in 1976 concluded that the Party's influence represented a 'major subversive threat' in the trade union movement and to the government's economic policy. Around the same time, MI5 estimated that almost half of the members of the CND national council were CP members, although a phone-tap on vice-president John Cox revealed that they were not engaged in any secretive or improper manipulation of the peace movement. Among the many Communist trade unionists subject to state surveillance and even burglary were Mick McGahey (NUM), civil service leader Margaret Witham, CP industrial organiser Bert Ramelson and technicians' leader Ken Gill (later the first-ever Communist president of the TUC). In 1979, MI5 also instigated the sacking of Derek Robinson ('Red Robbo'), chief convenor at British Leyland in Longbridge and the epitome of shopfloor trade union power, and ensured that the strike action which followed was undermined. This operation directly involved the new BL management, Prime Minister Margaret Thatcher's Cabinet Office, engineering union leader Terry Duffy and the bugging of the CPGB headquarters.

Yet there have been other important dimensions to Communist activity in the trade union movement, as well as the work of representing and supporting millions of fellow workers over the past 100 years. Robin Page Arnot and other Party members established and sustained the invaluable Labour Research Department. Communists have produced strategic plans for a wide range of different industries and services such as rail, coal, motors, the docks, healthcare and education. More widely, policies initiated by the Party have been adopted by many trade union bodies, not only on immediate workplace and occupational issues, but on national economic strategy, international solidarity, arms conversion and peace.

Nor did the CP forget unemployed workers when the long post-war expansion of the British economy came to an end. As unemployment soared towards three million, the Communist Party drew on its traditional strengths and alliances to initiate two People's Marches for Jobs in 1981 and 1983. From Liverpool and Glasgow to London, swelled by feeder marches and supported by rallies along the way, they won wide support at every level of the labour movement. In 1995, when unemployment had again risen above two million, the National Combine of Unemployed Workers Centres worked closely with the CPB to hold a ten-day 'March for Full Employment' from Liverpool to Sheffield.

Certainly, the CP has fulfilled its mandate from Lenin to forge the closest links with militant trade unionism. The alternative – isolation from the labour movement – can produce the grotesque parody of 'Marxism-Leninism' paraded by some ultra-left groups today.

The Communist Party today

The CP in Britain has been engaged in many more areas of activity than those prioritised by Lenin and the Party's founders in 1920. Vital issues of sex and race discrimination, gender, disabilities, health, national rights in Scotland and Wales, international relations and the environment have come to the fore to an extent not envisaged in 1920. Correspondingly, the Party's areas of organisation and campaigning have changed and expanded, reflecting changes in society at home and internationally.

Back in 1935, *For Soviet Britain* set out the policies that would emancipate women in a socialist society: equal opportunities in the labour market and at work; equal pay; time off with full pay and free medical care during pregnancy; nurseries, clinics and school meals for the children of working mothers; and labour-saving appliances in all new houses. While films and books encouraged young women to marry their boss for the ideal happy ending, Britain's Communists urged them to fight for equality and join the Women's Cooperative Guild instead. During World War Two, Communist women shop stewards initiated campaigns for equal pay and nursery facilities, taken forward by the Women's Parliament first proposed by the People's Convention. After the war, these and other demands were championed by the CP women's department and the National Assembly of Women (founded in 1952 and still active today) before eventually entering the mainstream of the trade union movement. The CPB publication *Women and Class* has been a vital weapon in explaining how women, like black people, are not only discriminated against but oppressed, and that this oppression is vital for the maintenance of capitalist society.

Among the proudest moments in the Party's history are Benny Rothman's Kinder Scout mass trespass in 1932 which helped win the right to roam in the countryside and the CP-led mass mobilisation against the British Union of Fascists and their police protectors at Cable Street in 1936.

On the ideological front, the CP has often assumed a central role not only in the education of its own members in Marxist-Leninist theory, but in the promotion of Marxist, socialist and progressive ideas in the wider labour and progressive movements. A host of schools, pamphlets, journals – from the *Communist Review* of the 1920s, *Labour Monthly* and the *Modern Quarterly* to the *Communist Review* of today – Communists have carried forward this battle against backward and reactionary thinking. The Marx Memorial Library & Workers School, founded in 1934 when the Nazis were burning books before burning people, is still going strong, now as a registered charity.

The 'Culture Matters' cooperative continues a long record of Communist and left-wing involvement in literary and other cultural ventures, and with solid trade union support. Together with socialist allies and the trade union movement, the CP has rescued the *Morning Star* as the daily paper of the left.

Since 1988, the CPB and the Young Communist League have worked hard to re-establish communist influence in the labour and progressive movements. But the challenges presented by capitalism in its imperialist stage are as large and perilous as ever. Communists face them inspired by the ideals, efforts and sacrifices of the many thousands who have gone before.

18

'Our history'

Preview of A Centenary for Socialism: Britain's Communist Party 1920-2020 (2020) Morning Star, 7 November 2020

It's been a long time coming.

Studies of Communist Party history in Britain have been published on a substantial scale over recent decades. Four volumes of 'official history' by party members James Klugmann and Nora Branson took the story from before the foundation of the Party in 1920 up to 1951. These were informative if somewhat orthodox accounts, written by historians in a position to reveal more but who chose to present the facts and defend them against the Party's right-wing and far left detractors.

Books by John Callaghan and Geoff Andrews were presented by their publishers as a continuation of the series. Unfortunately, however, the former tried too hard amidst a welter of useful information to portray a tired party in inexorable decline, either wrong or thwarted sooner or later at almost every turn. The less said about Andrews' one-sided apologia for the destructive impact of Eurocommunist revisionism, the better. He has composed a semi-fictional odyssey which ends with Odysseus slaying Penelope in a mercy killing.

Much else has been published, of course, usually from a hostile standpoint.

Henry Pelling wrote an early history which depicted Britain's Communists as a sinister, ruthless conspiracy contaminating the trade union movement and directed from Moscow. Very little else has been produced by right-wing historians of any substantial reputation.

Perhaps Britain's ruling class intellectuals have been happy to leave the hatchet jobs to far-left writers. Their efforts appear to have been mostly driven by the sectarian requirements of their own past or present political affiliations. Thus James Eaden and David Renton in *The Communist Party of Great Britain since 1920* (2002) are desperate to show how almost every major policy and action of the 'Stalinists' over 70 years was either misconceived, a failure, or a betrayal of the working class and the cause of world revolution. What little the Party fleetingly got right appears to have been mostly accidental. The authors' many errors of omission are even more telling than those of commission.

In recent years, a largely non-Communist academic school of CPGB historiography has flourished, enriched by access to party, British state, Soviet and Red International of Labour Unions archives in London, Moscow, Amsterdam and online. They reveal much about the internal workings and machinations of the CP and its interaction with foreign Communists and the British state.

While some prolific historians like Kevin Morgan have mined these usefully while placing undue emphasis on personal feuds and rivalries, the researches of Andrew Thorpe and Matthew Worley have undermined some well-worn anti-Communist myths about the Party's past.

Eminently readable accounts by the likes of Francis Beckett, Keith Laybourn and Dylan Murphy have tended to rely on previous stereotypes and – for the later period – on interviewees wielding a well-ground axe.

Many other books, pamphlets and articles deal with particular periods, episodes and personalities in the history of the Communist Party in Britain. Tom Sibley's biography of Bert Ramelson stands out in this last field, whereas Nina Fishman's semi-fictional Arthur Horner is forever in despair and on the verge of the quitting the Party (as he never did).

Now, at last, 21 party members and allies have written a comprehensive one-volume history to mark the Party's centenary this year. Ranged across 300 pages, the authors include distinguished labour movement historians such as editor Mary Davis, John Foster and Roger Seifert as well as party leaders and prominent trade unionists Liz Payne, Anita Halpin, Ann Field and Alex Gordon.

Their work has been arranged in a pattern which combines a thematic with a chronological approach, reflecting the class struggle on its political, economic and ideological fronts.

The first section highlights the role of the Party in the anti-racist, anti-fascist, anti-colonial and peace movements. Chapters also cover the Second World War, the Party's electoral strategies and – warts and all – the major internal crises in the Party and its relations with the international communist movement. These contents frequently give the lie to misrepresentations of the CP in Britain as undemocratic and economistic, as Comintern catspaws lacking commitment to the international struggle for socialism.

The second section gives due weight to the significant part played by Communists in the General Strike, the National Unemployed Workers Movement and the epic battles against post-war class collaboration, from 'Butskellism' and the Social Contract to anti-union laws and New Labour. Jonathan White outlines the emergence and rationale of the Party's

Alternative Economic and Political Strategy.

In the third section, on the battle of ideas, *Morning Star* readers will be familiar with the names of contributors Ben Chacko, Nick Wright, Christine Lindey and Andy Croft. They tell the story of the paper, its guiding political programme, the extraordinary work of the Party in the cultural sphere. Other chapters deal in depth with anti-Communism and the Party's policies and activities, past and present, in the women's movement and on the national question and the European Common Market.

Nobody interested in the history and present condition of the labour movement should be without this comprehensive, well-written and expertly informed book. It challenges preconceptions, explodes myths and provides a worthy testimony to 100 years of struggle, dedication and sacrifice on the part of one hundred thousand Communists across Britain.

Recommended reading

Max Adereth, *Line of March: An Historical and Critical Analysis of British Communism and its Revolutionary Strategy* (1994, 2020)
Keith Aitken, *The Bairns o' Adam: The Story of the STUC* (1997)
Geoff Andrews, Nina Fishman & Kevin Morgan eds, *Opening the Books: Essays on the Social and Cultural History of the British Communist Party* (1995)
Jim Arnison, *Decades* (1991)
John Attfield & Stephen Williams eds., *1939: The Communist Party of Great Britain and the War* (1984)
Bill Alexander, *British Volunteers for Liberty: Spain, 1936-39* (1982)
Keith Barlow, *The Labour Movement in Britain from Thatcher to Blair* (2008)
Francis Beckett, *Enemy Within: The Rise and Fall of the British Communist Party* (1998)
Noreen Branson, *History of the Communist Party of Great Britain 1927-1941* (1985); *History of the Communist Party of Great Britain 1941-1951* (1997)
John Callaghan, *Cold War, Crisis and Conflict: The CPGB 1951-68* (2003)
Trevor Carter, *Shattering Illusions: West Indians in British politics* (1986)
Maurice Cornforth ed., *Rebels and Their Causes: Essays in honour of A.L. Morton* (1978)
Andy Croft ed., *A Weapon in the Struggle: The Cultural History of the Communist Party in Britain* (1998)
Richard Croucher, *We Refuse to Starve in Silence: A History of the National Unemployed Workers' Movement 1920-46* (1987)
Jack Dash, *Good Morning, Brothers!* (1969)
Mary Davis ed., *A Centenary for Socialism: Britain's Communist Party 1920-2020* (1920)
Mary Davis, *Comrade or Brother? A History of the British Labour Movement* (2009 edn.)
Joe England, *The Wales TUC 1974-2004: Devolution and Industrial Politics* (2004)
John Foster, *Whose Nation? Democracy and the National Question in Britain* (2007)

John Foster & Charles Wolfson, *The Politics of the UCS Work-In* (1986)
Hywel Francis & David Smith, *The Fed: A History of the South Wales Miners in the Twentieth Century* (1980)
Eddie & Ruth Frow, *The Liquidation of the Communist Party of Great Britain: A Contribution to the Discussion* (1996)
Jim Fyrth ed., *Britain, Fascism and the Popular Front* (1985)
William Gallacher, *Revolt on the Clyde* (1936); *The Rolling of the Thunder* (1941); *Last Memoirs* (1966)
Wal Hannington, *Unemployed Struggles 1919-1936: My Life and Struggles among the Unemployed* (1936; 1977)
Kevin Halpin, *Memoirs of a Militant: Sharply and to the Point* (2012)
Arthur Horner, *Incorrigible Rebel* (1960)
Mark Howe ed., *Is That Damned Paper Still Coming Out?: The Very Best of the Daily Worker/Morning Star 1930-2000* (2001)
Allen Hutt, *British Trade Unionism: A Short History* (1975 edn.)
Martin Jacques & Frances Mulhearn eds., *The Forward March of Labour Halted?* (1981)
Douglas Jones, *The Communist Party of Great Britain and the National Question in Wales, 1920-1991* (2017)
Phil Katz, *Freedom from Tyranny: The Fight Against Fascism and the Falsification of History* (2010); *Yours for the Revolution: The Evolution of Tom Mann's Political Thought* (2023)
Ken Keable ed., *London Recruits: The Secret War Against Apartheid* (2012)
Harvey J. Kaye, *The British Marxist Historians: An Introductory Analysis* (1984)
Michael Keating & David Bleiman, *Labour and Scottish Nationalism* (1979)
Francis King & George Matthews, eds, *About Turn: the Communist Party and the Outbreak of the Second World War* (1990)
James Klugmann, *History of the Communist Party of Great Britain Volume 1: Formation and early years 1919-1924* (1969); *History of the Communist Party of Great Britain Volume 2: The General Strike 1925-1926* (1969)
Keith Laybourn and Dylan Murphy, *Under the Red Flag: A History of Communism in Britain* (1999)
Hugh MacDiarmid, *The Company I've Kept* (1966)
Stuart MacIntyre, *Little Moscows: Communism and Working-Class Militancy in Inter-War Britain* (1980)
John Mahon, *Harry Pollitt: A Biography* (1976)
Kevin Marsh & Robert Griffiths, *Granite and Honey: The Story of Phil Piratin, Communist MP* (2012)
Simon Meddick, Liz Payne & Phil Katz eds., *Red Lives – Communists and the Struggle for Socialism* (2020)
Andrew Murray, *The Communist Party of Great Britain: an historical analysis to 1941* (1995)
Will Paynter, *My Generation* (1972)
Phil Piratin, *Our Flag Stays Red* (1948; 2006)

Harry Pollitt, *Serving My Time* (1941)
Marjorie Pollitt, *A Rebel Life* (1989)
William Rust, *The Story of the Daily Worker* (1949; 2010)
Roger Seifert & Tom Sibley, *Revolutionary Communist at Work: A Political Biography of Bert Ramelson* (2011)
Brian Simon, *A Life in Education* (1998)
Jeffrey Skelley ed., *The General Strike, 1926* (1976)
Mike Squires, *Saklatvala: A Political Biography* (1990)
Henry Srebrnik, *London Jews and British Communism 1935-1945* (1995)
Brenda Swann & Francis Aprahamian eds., *JD Bernal: A Life in Science and Politics* (1999)
Andrew Thorpe, *The British Communist Party and Moscow 1920-1943* (2000)
Marc Wadsworth, *Comrade Sak: Shapurji Saklatvala MP, A Political Biography* (2020)
Matthew Worley, *Class against Class: the Communist Party in Britain between the Wars* (2017 edn)

Name Index

A

Aaronovitch, Dave 101
Aaronovitch, Sam 34, 101
Abbott, Diane 54
Ablett, Noah 174
Abraham, William ('Mabon') 211
Abse, Leo 154, 194
Ackland, Mary Valentine 19
Adenauer, Konrad 90
Adereth 114, 242
Airlie, Jimmy 42
Alexander, Bill 19, 110-14, 187, 242
Allende, Salvador 43, 72
Ambatielos, Betty 154
Andrews, Geoff 130–32, 239, 242
Aragon, Louis 205
Arnot, Robin Page 76, 78, 110, 182, 236
Arnison, Jim 242
Ashton, Jack 106
Askins, Betty 35
Attlee, Clement 27-8, 71, 204

B

Bain, Andy 56
Baldwin, Stanley 8
Barke, Jimmy 177
Barr, Sammy 42
Beauchamp, Kay 12
Beavis, Ivan 109-10, 121, 139-40
Beckett, Francis 240, 242
Bell, Julian 8, 68, 79
Bellamy, Ron 113-14, 121

Benfield, Bill 125, 141
Benn, Tony 49, 54, 104, 109, 113-14, 142, 160, 162, 193
Benton, Sarah 100, 102-3
Bernal, JD 17, 31, 244
Berry, Joe 121
Bevan, Aneurin 17, 20, 23, 28, 34, 71, 87, 92, 171
Bickerstaffe, Rodney 73, 113
Birch, Reg 94-5, 99, 228
Blackburn, Nancy 68
Blair, Tony 53, 56, 242
Bloomfield, Jon 99
Blunkett, David 109, 113
Bolton, George 107
Bowden, Maggie 105
Bowman, Dave 94
Braddock, Bessie 138
Bradley, Ben 13
Bradshaw, Laurence 32, 88
Bramley, Ted 22, 25, 86, 178
Branson, Noreen 2, 31, 143, 239, 242
Brockway, Fenner 17
Broggi, Moises 68, 73
Brooks, Gladys 43
Brown, Felicia 18
Brown, Gordon 56, 61
Brown, Isabel 17, 94
Bukharin, Nikolai 20, 78
Burns, Emile 186
Burns, Rabbie 136, 178, 210
Bush, Alan 18, 35-6, 94
Bush, George W 56, 94

C

Caballero, Francisco 18
Callaghan, James 46
Callaghan, John 46, 143–9, 239, 242
Callow, John 60
Cameron, David 58
Cameron. Ken 111, 158
Campbell, Beatrix 123, 124-5
Campbell, JR (Johnnie) 6, 21, 27,
    76–80, 82, 84, 87, 90, 95, 183, 224
Campbell, Kath 121
Campbell, RJ 198
Carter, Pete 98, 106, 108, 110-11, 113-
    14, 116-17
Carter, Trevor 242
Cartwright, Sian 141
Caudwell, Christopher 19
Chacko, Ben 64, 142, 241
Chalmers, Doug 115
Chalmers, Frank 107, 110
Chamberlain, Neville 19, 21, 84,
    208, 224
Chater, Tony 49, 50, 54, 98, 104–11,
    115, 118, 120-21, 135, 139-40,
    160-1
Chernyaev, Anatoly 135
Churchill, Winston 22–4, 26, 86, 137,
    153, 231
Chuter Ede, James 28
Clinton, Bill 141
Clinton, Chelsea 141
Cochrane, Archie 68
Cockburn, Claude 19
Cohen, Gerry 106, 110
Cohen, Nat 18
Cohen, Rose 20
Colvin, Ray 112
Connolly, James 163, 198
Cook, Dave 98, 101-2, 105
Cook, Don 36
Corbyn, Jeremy 61–3, 122, 141,
    231-2
Cornford, John 19

Cornforth, Maurice 94, 242
Costello, Mick 45, 100, 105-7,110
Cox, Dora 151-4, 212-13
Cox, Idris 12, 30, 79, 81, 92, 143-4,
    151–3, 179, 182–5, 186-7, 190-1
Cox, John 152, 158-9, 236
Coyle, Kenny 52-3, 119
Craig, Nares 70, 72-3
Cripps, Stafford 17, 20
Crome, Len 19
Cronin, Jeremy 140
Crow, Bob 61, 142
Crowther, Lord 193

D

Daggar, George 152
Dalyell, Tam 191
Darke, Marian 123
Dash, Jack 38, 149, 234, 242
Davies, D Ivor 43, 193
Davies, G Elfed 214
Davies, Harold 29
Davies, Ithel 201
Davies, Jack 212
Davies, Sephora 204-5
Davies, SO 29, 174, 198, 203-4
Davis, Mary 52, 64, 74, 114, 121,
    140, 173, 240, 243
Derfel, RJ (Robert Jones) 198-9
Dickens, Ted 234
Dickenson, Bessie 12, 81
Dickenson, Harold 81
Dimitrov, Georgi 15, 85, 177-8, 223-4
Dobb, Maurice 34, 94
Donovan, Ella 16
Doyle, Charlie 36, 37, 99, 234
Doyle, Mikki 94
Doyt, Sarah 67
Drakeford, Mark 142
Dubcek, Alexander 39, 93, 216
Durkin, Tom 105, 109, 110, 121, 140
Dutt, R (Rajani) Palme 19–21, 29,
    30, 32, 38, 76, 78, 81, 84, 86–88,
    91-2, 95, 134, 143–46, 153, 179,

186, 190, 224

E

Eden, Jesse 16
Engels, Frederick 26, 31, 175, 178, 218
Etheridge, Dick 94
Evans, Dai Dan 31, 167-72 185, 187, 208, 216
Evans, Gwynfor 187, 188-91, 207
Evans, Jack 121
Evans, Moss 111
Ewing, Keith 54
Ewing, Winnie 189-90

F

Falber, Reuben 124, 134
Faulkner, Hugh 16
Ferguson, Aitken 178, 181-2
Field, Ann 114, 240
Fine, Ben 109-10, 113
Fishman, Nina 163–66, 240, 242
Foley, Pete 128
Foot, Michael 117, 159, 162
Forman, Stanley 31
Foster, John 61, 64, 105, 110, 114, 121, 131, 240, 243
Francis, Dai 43, 171, 187, 193, 195
Franco, General Francisco 15, 17–19, 68, 73, 152, 180, 202, 223
Freeman, Bill 114-15
French, Sid 99, 228
Fryer, Peter 90

G

Gable, Gerry 35
Gagarin, Yuri 37
Gallacher, Willie 5, 8, 13, 15, 19–21, 24, 27, 76, 79, 81-2, 84, 136, 153, 174, 176, 178-9, 184, 206, 215, 229-30, 231, 243
Galloway, George 56, 136
Gandhi, Mahatma 202
Gaster, Jack 114

Gaughan, Dick 46
Geddes, Alec 82
Giles, GCT 26, 94
Gill, Ken 45, 50, 96, 100, 105, 107, 110, 114, 120, 131, 135, 162, 236
Gill, Tess 106
Glyndwr, Owain 211
Goebbels, Joseph 26
Gold, Harry 45
Goldman, Monty 119
Gollan, John 13, 32, 34, 38, 88, 90–92, 94, 98, 133-4, 184, 190, 215
Gomulka, Wladislaw 89
Gorbachev, Mikhail 52, 160
Gordon, Alex 62, 64, 240
Grahl, John 115
Gramsci, Antonio 46, 97, 130–32
Gray, John 114
Greaves, Desmond 188
Green, Royston 194
Greenshields, Bill 64
Griffiths, Gwyn 196
Griffiths, Jim 183
Griffiths, Robert 54, 62, 244
Guevara, Aleida 63

H

Haldane, JBS 17, 31, 152
Halifax, Lord 86, 141
Hall, Gus 114
Hall, Stuart 103, 110
Halpin, Anita 55, 240
Halpin, Kevin 51, 100, 105-6, 121, 131, 243
Halverson, Ron 106
Hannington, Wal 6, 13, 76, 80, 82-3, 152, 220, 243
Harris, Laurence 113
Harris, Oliver 169
Harrison, Doug 121
Hart, Finlay 211, 230
Hastings, Somerville 67
Hattersley, Roy 109, 117
Haxell, Frank 36

Hay, WF 174
Haylett, John 53, 54, 64, 114, 125, 137–42
Haylett family 137-8
Haywood, 'Big' Bill 198
Heath, Edward ('Ted') 41–44
Heathfield, Betty 108
Heinemenn, Margot
Henderson, Hamish 31
Hendy, John 54
Heseltine, Michael 49, 159, 226
Hill, Christopher 31, 67, 93, 182
Hilton, Rodney 31
Hitler, Adolf 14, 19, 21, 84, 87, 179, 202, 206, 207, 224
Hobsbawm, Eric 31, 46, 94, 101, 103, 110, 117, 118
Hodgson, JF 231
Hoffman, John 114
Home, Alec Douglas 208-9
Horner, Arthur 8, 10, 12, 13, 20, 67, 76, 79–82, 87, 154, 163–66, 169, 171, 179, 183, 187, 212, 225, 233, 234, 240, 243
Horner, John 93
Horthy, Nicholas 92
Hosey, Sean 40
Hoskins, Bob 31
Hudson, Kate 56
Hughes, Emrys 29, 203-4
Hunt, Alan 110
Hunt, Judith 98
Hussein, Saddam 48, 51, 157

I

Inkpin, Albert 8, 76-79
Innes, Bill 123

J

Jacks, Digby 40, 96
Jacques, Martin 53, 94, 98, 100, 102, 105-6, 117, 123–5, 157, 162, 243
Jagan, Cheddi 35
Jaruzelski, Wojciech 48, 159

Jeffery, Nora 30
Jennings, Humphrey 167
Johnson, Boris 63, 232
Johnson, Hewlett 26, 205
Johnson, Len 35
Johnson, Lyndon B 208
Johnston, Tom 183
Johnstone, Monty 113, 115, 117, 123
Jones, Bill (London) 93
Jones, Bill (Merseyside) 105, 138
Jones, Carolyn 51
Jones, Claudia 35
Jones, Glyn 179
Jones, Jack 41, 45, 138
Jones, Lewis 152
Jones, Richard 214
Jones, Tom ('Twm Sbaen') 43, 193
Jordan, Colin 35

K

Kadar, Janos 90–2
Kamenev, Lev 20
Kasrils, Ronnie 138
Katz, Phil 64, 151, 167, 211, 243, 244
Kelly, John 131
Kent, Bruce 48, 148, 159, 226
Kenton, Lou 19
Kerrigan, Peter 18, 30, 89, 92, 95, 177, 178
Kettle, Arnold 89, 92
Kettle, Martin 117
Keyworth, Florence 43
Khomeini, Ayatollah 48, 157
Khrushchev, Nikita 32, 33, 87, 88, 90-1, 93, 146, 215, 228
Kinnock, Neil 48, 53, 104, 109, 113, 117, 194-5
Kiszelly, Johnny 73
Klugmann, James 2, 40, 143, 239, 243
Knapp, Jimmy 113

L

Lane, Tony 104-5, 115

Larkin, Jim 198
Lawther, Will 165
Laybourn, Keith 240, 243
Leadbeater, Charlie 123
Lenin, Vladimir 3, 5, 53, 74, 173,
    175, 177, 178, 185, 201, 202, 209-
    10, 217–20, 223, 227, 229–32, 237
Lewis, Saunders 207
Lindey, Christine 241
Lindsay, Jack 182
Livesay, Michael 68
Livingstone, Ken 52, 104
Lloyd George, David 6, 231
Lom, Herbert 31
Loutit, Kenneth Sinclair 68, 71
Loveless, George 26
Ludmer, Maurice 35

M

MacCormick, John 178, 181-2, 184
MacDiarmid, Hugh 31, 177, 178,
    209-10, 243
MacDonald, Ramsay 6, 11, 12, 79,
    82, 202, 204
Mackenzie, Jacqui 139
Mackinnon, Alan 121
Maclean, John 173, 174, 178, 198,
    210, 227-8
Maclennan, Robert 176
Mahon, Alice 54, 141
Mainwaring, Bill 184, 213
Major, John 54
Mann, Tom 4, 18, 198, 243
Manuilsky, Dmitry 11
Mao Zedong 95, 209
Marshall, David 19
Marsland, Terry 120, 135
Marx, Karl 14, 26, 32, 55, 60, 63, 87,
    100, 128, 168, 171, 175, 178, 217-
    8, 220
Matthews, George 44, 89, 95-6, 98,
    105, 106, 124, 186, 243
Maxton, James 17
Mayo, Marj 109, 131

Mbeki, Thabo 140
McCarthy, Margaret 12
McCartney, Paul 137
McColl, Ewan 31
McCreery, Michael 95
McDonnell, John 63
McFadden, Alec 121
McGahey, Mick 43-4, 49, 94, 108,
    125, 192, 215, 236
McKay, Ian 105, 109
McLennan, Gordon 49, 50, 98, 105,
    108–10, 117, 123, 125, 133–36,
    139, 156, 157, 189, 191, 215
McLoughlin, Mike 121
McMichael, Joan 25
Miles, Gareth 196
Miliband, Ed 61
Milligan, Martin 31
Millington, Alan 121
Milne, Jimmy 43, 192
Milosevic, Slobodan 54
Mindszenty, Jozsef 91
Mitchell, Warren 31
Moffat, Abe 32, 94, 215
Moffat, Alex 93, 215
Molotov, Vyacheslav 79, 202
Mond, Alfred 76
Morgan, Kevin 240, 242
Morris, Max 89, 92, 95
Morrison, Herbert 22-3, 86, 224
Morton, AL 17, 182, 242
Mosley, Oswald 15, 16, 25, 35, 212
Moumbaris, Alex 40
Murdoch, Rupert 50, 114
Murphy, Dylan 240, 243
Murphy, JT 77, 79
Murray, Andrew 56, 122, 244
Myant 98, 107, 113, 117

N

Nagy, Imre 90-1, 93
Nasser, Gamal Abdel 33, 92
Negrin, Juan 19
Neruda, Pablo 31, 205

Newbold, J Walton 6
Nicholas, Islwyn 182
Nicholas, Nun 168
Nicholas, TE 31, 174, 177, 180, 185, 192, 197–210, 216
Nightingale, Florence 69
Norris, Stephen 137

O
Oestreicher, Paul 40
Ogilvie, Wendy 70
Osborne, George 58
Owen, Bill 31
Owen, Robert 198

P
Pallister, Minnie 174
Palmer, Aileen 68
Pankhurst, Sylvia 5, 198, 218, 227, 231
Papworth, Bert 94
Parry, Cyril 186
Paul, William 5, 231
Payne, Liz 64, 151, 167, 211, 240, 244
Paynter, Will 13, 31, 94, 169, 171, 187, 212, 244
Pearce, Bert 106, 171, 190, 194
Pelling, Henry 239
Penruth, Heather 196
Perlo, Victor 111
Pettifor, David 64
Phillips, WF 199
Picasso, Pablo 28, 72, 205
Pilger, John 54, 142
Pinochet, Augusto 161
Pinter, Harold 54
Piratin, Phil 16, 22, 24, 27, 86, 89, 91-2, 184, 229-30, 244
Pitt, Malcolm 105
Platts-Mills, John 27, 154
Pocock, Gerry 105
Polevoi, Boris 154
Pollitt, Harry 4, 8, 11, 15, 17-18, 20–22, 24, 27, 32, 76–81, 83–88,

153, 163-4, 184, 186-7, 206, 212-13, 222, 224, 233, 243-4
Ponomarev, Boris 135
Powell, Annie 153, 187, 208, 211–16, 230
Powell, Enoch 41, 130, 215
Powell, Margaret 19
Powell, Trevor 212-13, 216
Priestley, Frank 12
Priscott, Dave 106, 115
Pritt, DN 27, 72, 86-7

R
Rakosi, Matyas 91
Ramelson, Bert 19, 38, 45-6, 94, 98, 110, 114, 120, 123-4, 130, 134, 189, 236, 240, 244
Reagan, Ronald 48, 104
Redgrave, Michael 31
Rees, WJ (Will) 185, 190, 208, 216
Reid, Jimmy 42, 44, 190
Rhee, Syngman 28
Ritman, Pete 121
Rix, Mick 142
Roberts, Bryn 70, 99, 107, 151, 208, 211
Roberts, Ernie 107
Roberts, Evan 211
Roberts, Geoff 99
Roberts, Goronwy 208
Robeson, Paul 31, 72, 205
Robinson, Derek ('Red Robbo') 47, 51, 105, 111, 119, 121, 125, 127–29, 131, 135, 140, 236
Rosen, Harold 136
Rosen, Maurice 'Tubby' 16, 25
Ross, Willie 190
Rosser, Mary 111, 114, 118, 121, 135, 140-41
Rothermere, Lord 15
Rothman, Benny 14, 237
Rothstein, Andrew 76–9, 95, 110, 121, 154
Rowbotham, Sheila 43

Rust, Tamara 153-4
Rust, William (Bill) 8, 11, 21, 24, 26, 78, 81, 84–86, 224, 233, 244
Rutherford, Paul 45

S

Saklatvala, Shapurji 6, 76, 78, 220, 229, 244
Saville, John 32, 89, 92
Sawyer, Tom 113
Scanlon, Hugh 41, 45
Scargill, Ann 108
Scargill, Arthur 49, 50, 54, 108, 111, 160
Schaffer, Gordon 69
Seifert, Mike 105
Seifert, Roger 240, 244
Sibley, Tom 240, 244
Silverman, Sydney 29
Silverthorne, Thora 19, 67–73
Slipman, Sue 98, 101
Slovo, Joe 40
Smith, John 53
Smith, Joyce 72
Smith, Rose 12, 81, 153
Snowden, Philip 82
Solley, Lesley 27
Spratt, Philip 13
Springhall, Dave 84, 224
Starmer, Keir 63
Stephens, Wally 28
Stevenson, Graham 62, 122
Stewart, Bob 94
Suharto, General 38

T

Tanner, Jack 23
Temple, Nina 106, 111, 115-17, 124
Thaelmann, Ernst 68
Thatcher, Margaret 47–49, 54, 72, 103–5, 108, 110, 114, 117-18, 120, 123, 128, 157–60, 162, 195, 216, 236, 242
Thomas, Alun 187
Thomas, David 174
Thomas, Dylan 31

Thomas, George 192
Thomas, JH (Jimmy) 82
Thompson, Dorothy 31
Thompson, EP 31-2, 89, 92
Thompson, Harry 13
Thomson, George 190
Thorpe, Andrew 240, 244
Tito, Josef 27
Todd, Ron 162
Togliatti, Palmiro 79
Tomlinson, Eric (Ricky) 42
Torr, Dona 31
Tovey, Nidge 119
Trask, Roger 109, 114, 157
Tudor Hart, Alex 68
Turner, Ben 76
Turner, Beth 8
Tyler, Wat 36

U

Ulbricht, Walter 79

V

Vaughan, Joe 211, 230

W

Wadsworth, Marc 140, 244
Wallace, William 178
Warhust, Jan 121
Warner, Sylvia Townsend 14, 19
Warren, Bill 115
Warren, Des 42
Webb, Lily 12
Whitehead, Will 171
Whitfield, David 50, 104, 106-7, 109, 140
Williams, Hywel Davy 186-7
Williams, Jenny 141
Williams, John Roose 179-80, 208, 216
Wilson, Elizabeth 109
Wilson, Harold 37, 38, 41, 44, 96, 188
Wincott, Len 13
Windsor, Charles 192
Windsor, Elizabeth 45

Winnington, Alan 29
Wintringham, Tom 177
Wise, Audrey 43
Witham, Margaret 236
Woddis, Jack 94
Wolfson, Charlie 131, 243
Worley, Matthew 240, 244
Wright, Anita 122
Wright, George 193
Wright, Nick 122, 241
Wyatt, Robert 46
Wynn, Bert 93
Wyper, Hugh 192

Y

Yeltsin, Boris 125

Subject Index

7 Days 113, 115, 117, 124

A

Abyssinia (Ethiopia) 17, 202, 205
Afghanistan 47, 56, 59, 104, 141, 157
African National Congress (ANC), 35, 40, 122, 138, 161
Alternative Economic Strategy (AES) 96, 103, 109, 111, 113-15, 117-8, 122
Alternative Vote 59
Amalgamated Engineering Union (AEU/ AUEW) 20, 23, 30, 41-2, 95, 128
Angola 155
Anti-Apartheid Movement 35, 130, 138
anti-Communist bans and proscriptions 8, 10, 11, 14, 22-3, 26, 30, 33, 36, 72, 76, 78, 86, 149, 169, 178, 222, 224, 226, 233, 235
anti-fascism 10, 12, 15-20, 22, 25, 35, 52, 60, 68, 69, 77, 83-86, 111, 121, 136, 153, 177, 179-81, 202-3, 212, 223-4, 230; battle of DeWinton Field 15, 212; '43 Group' 25; see also Cable Street, 'Popular Front', 'United 'Front'
anti-racism 34-5, 41, 52-3, 59, 64, 99, 100-1, 113, 140, 214-15, 230
Anti-Racist Alliance 52-3, 140
anti-semitism 16, 32, 43, 88, 152; see also anti-fascism

Association of Nurses 68-70
ASLEF (Associated Society of Locomotive Engineers and Firemen) 37, 41, 56, 62, 141
Association of Indian Communists (Britain) 59

B

BNP (British National Party) 53
'Broad Lefts' in trade unions 38, 41-2, 45, 63, 113, 231, 235; in student movement 40-1, 96, 101, 228
British Empire 7, 13, 19, 21, 29, 34, 85, 144-46, 174, 176-7, 180-1, 186, 199, 223
British imperialism 7, 29, 34-5, 39, 48, 55, 98, 146, 159, 167, 186, 190, 192, 197, 202-3, 226
British Peace Assembly 209, 226
British Peace Committee 26, 72, 205
British/ Britain's Road to Socialism (BRS) 28-9, 39, 46, 50, 60, 64, 92, 95, 96, 98-9, 107, 109, 111, 117-19, 121-4, 125, 155-6, 161-2, 186, 188, 190-92, 194, 196, 215, 219-21, 228-29, 231-2
British Socialist Party 3-5, 217, 230
British-Soviet Friendship Society 37, 121, 154
British Union of Fascists (BUF) 15-16, 60, 69, 212
British Workers Sports Federation 14, 39, 198, 201

building workers union 30
Burston school strike 60

C

Cable Street, battle of 16, 60, 136, 237
Cambodia 39, 155
Campaign Against Racist Laws 41
Campaign for Trade Union Freedom 60
CARDRI (Campaign against Repression and for Democratic Rights in Iraq) 157
Caribbean Labour Solidarity 162
Central Labour College 198, 213
Chainmakers Festival 60
Chile 43, 57, 72, 96, 130, 161, 205, 227; Chile Solidarity Campaign 43; 130 Manuel Rodriguez Patriotic Front 43, 161
China 17, 19, 27-8, 57, 95, 140, 171, 202-3, 205, 209, 213, 222, 227; Communist Party of China 61, 209, 227
Christian-Marxist dialogue 39
civil service 26, 29, 42, 72, 185, 193, 236
'Class against Class' 11, 14, 75, 77-81, 110, 175, 222, 233, 244
CND (Campaign for Nuclear Disarmament) 34, 49, 56, 121, 130, 148, 154, 158-9, 209, 226, 236
CODIR (Committee for the Defence of the Iranian People's Rights) 157
Columbia, Justice for 55
'Comintern' 5, 7, 10-13, 15, 20-1, 27, 75-86, 124, 175, 177-79, 222-26, 231, 233, 240; see also 'Third Period'
Comment 94, 98, 100-2, 161
Communist Campaign Group (CCG) 50, 112-21, 127-8, 131, 140, 157, 228; Communist News

51, 125; Communist Campaign Review 50, 114, 117
Communist International see 'Comintern'
Communist Liaison 122, 229
Communist Party in Britain (CPGB / CPB): Unity conventions (1920, 1921) 4, 5, 217-8, 220, 227, 229-31; Labour Party affiliation 5, 6, 8, 10, 11, 17, 23, 51, 75-78, 218, 231; democratic-centralism 32, 54, 101, 119; 'Bolshevisation' 222; Draft Programme to the Comintern (1924) 175; Draft Programme (1939) 218; broad democratic alliance 46, 97, 99, 101, 110-1; anti-monopoly alliance 50, 59, 122, 189, 196, 232; workplace organisation 7, 12, 15, 23-4, 30, 49, 79, 81, 128, 153, 191, 222, 234; Left-Wing Programme 56, 60, 196, 221, 232; international solidarity: 7, 30, 63, 96, 120-1, 140, 227; 'Moscow Gold' 80, 143, 226; parliamentary politics 5, 75-6, 98, 193, 218, 220, 229, 232; electoral participation 5, 6, 11-14, 24, 30, 37, 43-4, 48, 54-59, 61-63, 75, 78, 82, 95, 117-8, 122, 133, 147, 212-14, 218, 227, 229-31, 234, 240; local councillors 8, 16, 22, 24-5, 36, 44, 86, 152, 214, 216, 230; Unity for Peace and Socialism 57, 59; occupations of hotels, tube stations (1940) 22, 86, 224 and barracks, mansions (1946) 25; national question in Britain 19-20, 29, 43, 63, 149, 173-96, 223, 237; 'progressive patriotism' 45, 173, 177-79, 182, 184, 186, 198, 199, 223; historians and History Group 2, 17, 10, 31, 143, 239-40, 243;

history pageants 18, 178; Party
membership 7, 9, 13, 20, 23, 25,
29, 32-3, 35-7, 39, 46, 76, 80-83,
87-8, 93, 96, 101, 104, 106, 112,
115, 118, 120, 123-4, 133, 146, 151;
revisionist purge (1980s) 50-1,
76, 110, 112-13, 131, 135, 228, 233;
re-establishment (1988) 111, 113,
116-17, 119-21; see also *British/
Britain's Road to Socialism*, 'Broad
Lefts', 'Class against Class',
Communist Campaign Group,
Eurocommunism, *For Soviet
Britain*, liquidationism, *Marxism
Today*, *Morning Star*, PPPS,
Straight Left faction
Communist Party of Britain
 (Marxist-Leninist) 95
Communist Party of the Soviet
 Union (CPSU) 32-34, 88, 94-5,
 99, 114, 124, 135, 143, 146, 157,
 160, 222, 224, 226
Communist Review (1929-53) 8, 176,
 186, 237; (post-1998) 51, 60, 125,
 155, 217, 237
Communist Unity Group 4, 217
Connolly Association 30, 43
Coordinating Committee of CPs in
 Britain 61, 227
Cornwall 178, 194, 196; *Communist
 Manifesto* in Cornish 196
Cotton Strike Leader 12
Country Standard 14, 58
Covid-19 64
Cuba 37, 40, 63, 206; Cuba
 Solidarity Campaign 55
culture and the arts 17-8, 31, 37, 64,
 83, 98, 101, 103, 148, 155, 171,
 177, 183, 188, 190, 192, 194, 196,
 214, 226, 228, 237, 241-2
'Culture Matters' 64, 237
Cyffro 192
Cyprus 57, 227
Czechoslovakia 19, 21, 26-7, 84, 99,

134, 144, 157, 167, 203, 207-8;
'Prague Spring' 39, 93-5, 97, 208,
216, 225

D
Daily Herald 2, 5, 7, 11
Daily Worker 11-12, 15, 19-24, 26,
 30, 33-4, 38, 67, 80-1, 83-90, 93,
 124, 152, 164-5, 179, 183, 222,
 224, 226, 233, 243, 244; Malaya
 atrocities 29
Democratic Left 51, 124-5, 135, 229
devolution for Scotland and Wales
 53, 135, 173-75, 178, 181-88, 190-
 1, 194-5, 214, 243
'dictatorship of the proletariat' 4,
 217-19
Durham Miners Gala 35, 60

E
Economic League 30, 36, 235,
Edinburgh People's Festival 31-2,
 148
electricians union (ETU / EEPTU)
 28, 30, 36, 50, 114, 149, 235
engineering workers (AUEW /
 AEU) 4, 6, 15, 17, 20, 22-3, 30, 36,
 41-2, 94, 96, 128, 133, 192, 228,
 235-6
England: national question and
 devolution 17, 175, 181-2, 186,
 191, 193-96, 223
environment 57, 64, 97, 122-3, 124,
 155, 237
equal pay for women 14, 22-3, 31,
 41-2, 44, 81, 121, 237
Eurocommunism 46, 81, 100, 116,
 156-8; in Britain 46, 50, 96-118,
 120-6, 131-2, 134-35, 139, 156-8,
 161-2, 228-9, 239
European Union / Common
 Market 34, 44, 53-4, 57-8, 61-64,
 96, 101, 107, 108, 114, 116-18,
 125, 149, 160, 162, 196, 204,

208, 209, 241; EEC referendum (1975); 44, 96; Single European Act (1987) 118, 162; 'No to EU' election campaigns 58, 61; EU referendum (2016) 61-2, 229, 231-2

F

Falklands War 48, 159, 226
fascism, see anti-fascism, Nazi Germany, Italy, Spain, Franco, Hitler, Mussolini
federalism in Britain 64, 173, 175, 177, 180, 183, 184-5, 188, 191-2, 196
feminism 97, 108-9, 116, 124, 131, 228
Finland: anti-Soviet war 21, 85, 203; Communist Party 122
Fire Brigades Union (FBU) 26, 30, 45, 93, 111, 158, 235
For Soviet Britain 14, 83, 177, 218, 237
France, Communist Party in 17-8, 46, 85, 100, 102, 134, 156, 203, 225
French imperialism 34, 36, 203;

G

gay rights and gender politics 44, 46, 49, 52, 97, 101, 108, 123, 237, 244
General and Municipal Workers Union 37, 235
General Strike and lock-out (1926) 9-11, 17, 67, 75-6, 81, 143, 175-6, 178-9, 211, 220, 233, 240, 243-4
Germany: GDR (German Democratic Republic) 36, 225; West Germany post-war rearmament 29, 216 and Communist Party 227; imperialism 34, 36; see also Nazi Germany

Greece, Communist Party in 57, 154, 227
Green Party 117, 123
Green Socialist Alliance 62
Greenham Common 48, 158
Grenada and New Jewel Movement 139, 162
Guardian newspaper 109, 117
Guinea-Bissau 155
Gulf War (1991) 51-2, 141
Guyana (British) 35

H

Highgate Cemetery 32, 55, 88
housework 14, 154, 237
housing 14, 25, 31, 35, 64, 118, 182, 215
Hungary 27, 39, 144, 148, 217; Soviet intervention (1956) 32, 33, 88-95, 146, 169, 170, 214, 225, 228
Hunger Marches 13, 67, 82, 152, 175, 220, 233

I

imperialism 3-5, 7, 13, 15, 20, 21, 23-4, 26-29, 34, 37-39, 48, 53, 55-59, 64-5, 84-5, 87, 95, 98, 119-20, 137, 144-46, 148, 155-6, 159-60, 162-3, 167, 177, 186, 190, 192, 223-27, 229, 233, 238 see also British, US, French and German imperialism
incomes policies 37-8, 45, 97, 106, 149
Independent Labour Party (ILP) 3, 11, 17, 68, 80, 83, 168, 173-76, 182, 197-8, 201, 223, 227-8, 234
India 7, 13, 57, 63, 122, 140, 202, 223, 227; Meerut Conspiracy Trial 13, 223; Communist Party (Marxist) 227
Indian Workers Association (GB) 35, 62
Indonesia 38, 227
industrial action 10, 12, 26, 30, 37,

41, 45, 47, 57, 75, 76, 80-1, 101, 124, 170, 235; apprentices 20, 22, 30-1, 36, 133, 235; docks strikes 4, 6, 26, 28, 38, 41, 149 and Pentonville Five 42, 96, 130, 235; equal pay 41; Grunwick's 45, 130; miners 49, 130 165, 199, 224; public sector 59; printworkers 50, 105, 113-5, 120, 121, 235; railways 41, 59, 199; Saltley Gates 42; seafarers 38, 51; Shrewsbury case 42; Upper Clyde Shipbuilders 42
Industrial Relations Act (1971) 41-2, 96, 130, 235
Institute of Employment Rights 51
International Brigades 13, 15, 18-19, 41, 43, 66, 68, 72, 73, 110, 138, 152, 193, 202, 223
international Communist movement 32, 33, 61, 87, 89, 95, 125, 146, 201, 222, 226, 240; Red International of Labour Unions 80, 83, 226, 233, 240; Cominform 148, 225; Moscow conferences of Communist and workers parties 227; annual International Meeting of Communist and Workers Parties 96, 227; see also 'Comintern', 'Third Period'
International Women's Day 29, 57, 61, 153, 227
Invergordon Mutiny 13
Ireland 7, 29, 120, 163, 174, 177, 185, 198, 207, 223; Communist Party 43, 61, 140, 161; conflict in the North 42-3, 51, 160-1; Irish Democrat 30; IRA 160-1
Israel 33, 61, 92; Six-Day War 39
Italy 10, 17, 19, 46, 68, 77, 84, 116, 156, 203, 223, 225; Communist Party in 46, 97, 100, 130, 134, 156, 158, 203, 225

J
Japan 4, 17, 84, 162
Jersey Communist Party 193
Jewish Ex-Servicemen's Association 16
Jewish Clarion 32, 88

K
Kinder Scout trespass 14, 237
Korea: South 28; War 29, 204-5, 226, 231; Workers Party of Korea (North) 122, 140
Kosovo 54
Kuwait 51

L
Labour Monthly 38, 76, 86-88, 182-3, 190, 194, 231, 237
Labour Party: and imperialism 28-9, 48, 98, 120; anti-Communist Party measures 5, 6, 8, 10, 11, 17, 23, 26, 51, 75-78, 218, 222, 226-7, 231, 234; left wing 11, 23, 33, 38, 40, 45-6, 48, 49, 52, 77-8, 87, 92, 96, 104, 121, 138, 160, 222-3, 229-31, 233; Labour Coordinating Committee 113-4; Labour Independent Group of MPs 27, 231; Bevanites 29, 231; Socialist Campaign Group of Labour MPs 52, 113; see also 'New Labour', Scotland (Labour Party), Welsh (Regional) Council of Labour
Labour Research Department (LRD) 7, 18
land 14, 176, 185, 200, 203, 225
Laos 39, 155
League Against Imperialism 13, 223, 226, 233
Leninist, The 107, 111, 119
Lexit: the Left Leave Campaign 62
Liaison Committee for the Defence of Trade Unions (LCDTU) 38,

41-2, 51, 60, 100, 115, 128, 221, 235
Liberal Party / Liberal Democrats 3, 6, 12, 40, 53, 59, 61, 75, 82, 86, 101, 110, 117, 118, 123, 174, 175, 186, 189, 201, 206, 222, 230,
Libya 61
Link 43
liquidationism: and the CPGB 54, 64, 91, 112, 117, 120, 131, 136, 147, 228, 243; *Marxism Today* 229; Young Communist League 120; *Morning Star* 64, 120, 135, 139; Communist Party of Britain 54

M
Malaya, war in 27, 29, 203, 226, 231
Manifesto for New Times 123-4
Manifesto Press 58
March for Full Employment (1995) 53, 236-7
Marx Memorial Library 14, 46, 60, 63-5, 121, 160, 237
Marxism Today 46, 47, 49, 51, 100-6, 108-10, 113, 115-7, 123-5, 131, 134-5, 147, 149, 157, 159, 161, 162, 190, 194, 215, 228-9
MI5 (Security Service) 26, 38, 42, 44, 47, 70, 96, 128, 141, 151-4 159, 164, 205, 213, 236; see also Special Branch
MI6 (Secret Intelligence Service) 205
Miners Federation of Great Britain 8, 20, 176, 233
Modern Quarterly 237
Molotov-Ribbentrop Non-Aggression Pact 21, 84, 202, 224
Morning Star 38-9, 44, 47-9, 52-8, 60-1, 63-65, 93-95, 98, 99, 103-15, 117-22, 124, 125, 127-31, 133-37, 139-43, 147, 148, 157, 159-63, 190-1, 222, 228, 231-2, 238, 239, 241, 243; Wapping plot 50; depleted uranium revelation 54;

journalists strike 54, 141
Movement for Colonial Freedom 35
Mozambique 155
Munich Agreement 21, 83-85, 202, 208, 220
Muslim Association of Britain 56

N
NALGO (National and Local Government Officers' Association) 51, 53, 109, 121, 162, 192
Namibia 122, 155
National Assembly of Women 30, 63, 154, 237
National Council for Civil Liberties 13
National Council of Labour Colleges (NCLC) 7, 168, 171
National Health Service 24-5, 28, 71, 215, 231
National Left-Wing Movement 76-8, 233
National Minority Movement 7, 8, 10, 76, 79, 80, 82, 151-2, 233
National Unemployed Workers Movement 6, 13-14, 76, 82, 152, 178-9, 233, 240, 242
National Union of Seamen 40, 51
nationalisation 10, 22, 25, 28, 86, 92, 113, 117, 165, 171, 182, 184, 215, 230
NATO 27, 29, 37, 54-5, 61, 109, 156, 158-9, 162, 192, 203, 206-7, 209, 215, 231
Nazi Germany 14, 19, 21-3, 26, 68, 84-6, 153, 167, 180, 202-3, 223-4, 237
New Communist Party 111, 122, 228-9
'New Labour' 3, 51, 53-8, 61, 125, 136, 195, 228, 240
New Politics Network 51, 125, 135
New Propeller 15

Nicaragua 120, 122
North Wales Quarrymen's Union 173
Notting Hill race riots 34-5
nuclear disarmament 29, 34, 48-9, 56, 61, 93, 120, 156, 158-60, 203, 215, 221, 226-7, 230-1
nuclear energy 114, 206
NUM (National Union of Mineworkers) 30, 43, 115, 163, 165, 170-71, 186-7, 225, 234; 1972 strike 43, 49; 1974 strike 49; 1984-85 strike 49, 108, 110, 228; Scottish Area NUM 176, 192; see also South Wales miners
NUPE (National Union of Public Employees) 70, 113, 154, 193
NUR (National Union of Railwaymen) 8, 37, 82, 113
NUS (National Union of Students) 24, 40-1, 96, 101, 161, 228; Broad Left 40, 96, 101, 228
NUT (National Union of Teachers) 26, 58, 64, 89, 212, 121, 214, 235

O
Old Oak Star 12

P
Palestine solidarity 39, 61, 120, 156, 158
PCS (Public and Commercial Services) union 72; see also civil service
peace and anti-war movement: Stockholm Peace Petition 29; British Peace Committee 26, 72, 205; World Peace Congress (Sheffield) 72, 226; British Peace Assembly 209, 226; Aldermaston March 34, 93, 226; Greenham Common 48, 158; European Nuclear Disarmament (END) 158-9; World Disarmament Campaign 158-9; Committee for Peace in the Balkans 54-5; Committee Against War in the Gulf 51-2, 141; see also CND, Stop the War Coalition, World Peace Council
People's Assembly and Charter 57-8, 60, 63, 221
People's Convention 22, 23, 86, 153, 221, 224, 237
'People's Front', see 'Popular Front'
People's Jubilee 45
People's March for Jobs (1981, 1983) 47-8, 104, 139, 236
PPPS (People's Press Printing Society) 49, 50, 54, 64, 106-8, 110-11, 113-4, 117-8, 120, 125, 135, 140-1
Plaid Cymru 142, 184, 186-9, 194, 215; see also Welsh National Party
Plebs League 198
Poland 4, 21, 32, 84-5, 89-91, 104, 171, 203, 220; Solidarnosc ('Solidarity') 48, 104, 107, 159-60
Poll Tax 51, 121, 195
'Popular Front' 16-21, 83, 85, 146, 177, 180-1, 212, 218, 222, 223, 233-4, 243
Portugal 180, 223
PR (proportional representation) 59, 136, 183, 189-91
Praxis Press 52

R
racism 34-5, 40-1, 46, 48, 52-3, 64, 95, 97, 109, 114, 119, 123, 130, 138, 140, 144, 185, 186, 237; see also anti-racism
railway industry 24, 41, 53, 59, 170, 188, 215, 236, 244; Beeching Plan 37; see also ASLEF, NUR, RMT, TSSA
Reasoner, The 89

Red Rag 43
Respect coalition 56, 136
RMT (Rail, Maritime & Transport) union 58, 61-2, 142
Romania 171
Russia 4, 5, 6, 20, 63, 74, 151, 152, 153, 177, 180, 201-2, 208, 213, 217, 220, 222; Russian language 137, 138, 139, 210; Communist Party of the Russian Federation 140; see also Soviet Union

S
Salford Docker 12
Scotland 13, 18-20, 29-32, 47, 55, 57, 59-61, 104, 107-8, 110, 112, 148-9, 169, 176, 192, 209, 215, 228-9, 232, 243; national question 20, 29, 43, 53, 63, 135, 149, 173-78, 181-96, 223, 227, 237; Labour Party 173-6, 178, 182-5, 188-91, 193-5; Communist Party 13, 32, 42-3, 63, 79, 83, 110, 121, 133, 149, 173-78, 181-96, 223, 237; Communist Labour Party 5; Communist Party of Scotland 124-5; Scottish Socialist Party 125; Scottish Workers Republican Party 114, 228; see also Scots Gaelic, Scottish Trades Union Congress, SNP, United Mineworkers of Scotland, Upper Clyde Shipbuilders
Scots Gaelic 31, 177-8, 188, 190, 192
Scottish Constitutional Convention 182
Scottish Council of Labour 190
Scottish Covenant Association 184, 187
Scottish Home Rule Association 175
Scottish Marxist 192
Scottish Trades Union Congress 32, 43, 48, 60, 104, 121, 176, 184, 187, 189, 192-4, 195, 235

Searchlight 35
SNP (Scottish National Party) 176-78, 180-1, 183-4, 187-8, 193-4, 195, 243
'Social Contract' 45, 96, 101, 240
Social Democratic Federation 3
Socialist Action 52, 141
Socialist Alliance 57, 62
Social Democratic Party 109, 110, 117
Socialist International 4, 217
Socialist Labour Party (1920) 4, 174, 217, 228
Socialist Labour Party (1996) 54
Socialist League (1930s) 17
Socialist Medical Association 67, 71-2
Socialist Party 62; Militant Tendency 157, 159
Socialist Workers Party 56, 62
South Africa 35, 40, 96, 114, 120-2, 138, 140, 155, 161, 227; South African Communist Party 40,140, 161
South Wales miners 13, 148, 168,171-2, 185, 208, 216, 243; South Wales Miners Federation (SWMF, the 'Fed') 12, 18, 67, 80-1, 87, 163-4, 167-9, 173-4, 179, 182, 197, 211-12, 234, 243; South Wales Miner 15, 234; South Wales Area NUM 43, 169, 170, 185-87, 193, 215; South Wales Miners Eisteddfod 148, 171, 185 and Gala 148, 171
Soviet Union 4-6, 13, 63, 74, 99, 106, 144, 151-3, 180, 209, 213, 220; achievements 20, 32, 85, 87, 144, 225; anti-Sovietism 20, 23, 26, 46, 84, 94, 116, 123, 131, 134, 135, 158, 159, 165; Nazi war danger 19, 20, 21, 84, 85, 202; 1930s internal repression 20, 32, 78, 88, 225; Non-Aggression Pact

21, 84, 202, 224; Finnish-Soviet War 21, 85, 203; World War Two 22-3, 86-7, 153, 203, 207; post-war reconstruction 203; Cold War 26-7, 47, 137; peace and arms control 34, 95, 120, 158, 160; international friendship and solidarity 22, 40, 70, 85-6, 99, 122, 151, 154, 157, 171, 185, 201; 'Moscow Gold' 80, 143; Hungary intervention 91, 93; Czechoslovakia intervention 93-5, 157; Afghanistan intervention 104; glasnost and perestroika 52, 120, 122, 160; collapse and counter-revolution 2, 52, 124,135, 140, 207; see also Communist Party of the Soviet Union (CPSU), Russia

Spain 17-19, 21, 46, 85, 100, 116, 134,156,158, 180, 205, 242; see also International Brigades

Special Branch 72, 128, 154, 159, 206; see also MI5

state power 28, 39, 40, 64, 95, 98, 111-2, 134, 179, 201, 218-9, 221, 225

Stalin, Khrushchev report on (1956) 32-3, 87-8, 90-1, 146

Straight Left faction 102, 107, 109, 111-13, 118-9, 122, 229

Stop the War Coalition 56, 209, 221

strikes, see industrial action

students 24, 37, 40, 56, 59, 89, 93-4, 96, 98, 100-1, 106, 131, 134, 161, 209, 228; see also NUS

Suez invasion 33, 92-3, 148

T

TASS (Technical & Supervisory Staffs, AUEW-TASS) 45, 96, 100, 120-21

tenants rights 16, 31, 36, 44, 92, 149, 179, 215, 221

Third International, see 'Comintern'

'Third Period' 10, 12, 77, 79, 81, 222-3, 233-4

Transport & General Workers Union (TGWU) 8, 33, 41-43, 47, 56, 149

Tolpuddle Martyrs 26, 58, 60

Trades Union Congress 8-9, 11, 13-14, 20, 23, 26-28, 36, 38, 41-2, 45-6, 48, 50, 53, 55-6, 58, 60, 62-3, 68, 70, 75-77, 80, 82, 96, 105, 110, 120, 128, 160, 162, 165, 171, 176, 185, 221-2, 233-36

Trotskyism, see ultra-leftism

TSSA (Transport & Salaries Staffs Association) 56

U

UKIP (United Kingdom Independence Party) 61-2

Ukraine 220; ban on Communist Party 227

ultra-leftism 17, 20, 27, 37, 41, 56-7, 95, 98, 101-2, 104, 116, 156, 160, 224, 226, 237

Unemployed Workers Centres, National Combine of 53, 236-7

Unison 67, 73

United Campaign to Repeal the Anti-Union Laws 54, 60

United Clothing Workers Union 79, 152, 233

'United Front' 76, 79, 83, 177, 218, 222, 234

United Mineworkers of Scotland 79, 176-7, 233

United Nations 51, 56-7, 156, 159, 170, 203, 205

Unite the union 62

Unity! 55, 60

Unity Theatre 17, 31

Upper Clyde Shipbuilders 42, 44, 96, 130, 235, 243

USA 4, 23, 34, 92, 122, 140, 144, 168, 198, 203, 208, 225; Communist Party of the USA (CPUSA) 111, 114
US imperialism 26, 29, 38-9, 55, 137, 144, 186, 197, 203

V
Vietnam 38, 96, 122, 227

W
Wales 61, 67, 152-3, 167-74, 197-202, 205-7, 209, 215-16, 220, 232, 243; national question 19, 29, 53, 173-75, 179-81, 183-90, 192, 194-5, 198, 209, 214, 223, 237; Labour Party 173-75, 183-90, 194-5, 209; South Wales Labour Federation 173; South Wales Socialist Society 174, 217; South Wales Communist Council 4, 174, 217; Communist Party 13, 29, 43, 59, 63, 83, 112, 115, 128, 149, 153, 179, 180-1, 183-87, 189-90, 192, 223, 230, 237; National Eisteddfod 179, 181, 183, 187, 197, 205; see also Plaid Cymru, South Wales miners, Wales Trade Union Congress, Welsh language, Welsh National Party,
Wales Trades Union Congress 43, 48, 60, 104, 141-2, 173, 183, 189, 190, 192-95, 235, 243
Wapping dispute 50, 113-5, 121
Warsaw Pact (Treaty) 27, 33, 39, 90, 93-4, 156, 225
Welsh language 142, 174, 177-83, 185, 187, 189-90, 192, 194, 196-99, 207-9, 211, 216; *Communist Manifesto* translation 185, 196
Welsh Language Society 189, 192, 196
Welsh National Party 61, 178-81, 183-4, 189-90, 206-7; see also

Plaid Cymru
Welsh (Regional) Council of Labour 183, 186, 187, 190
West Indian Gazette 35
Women Against Pit Closures 49, 108, 221
women's rights and liberation 8, 14, 22-3, 25, 29-31, 41-44, 52, 57, 61, 81, 97, 100, 101, 121, 153, 158, 227, 237; Working Women's Charter 44, 81; Women's Charter (1931) 81; Women's Liberation Conference 15, 43, 67, 141; Charter for Women (2002) 55; Women's TUC 60; see also National Assembly of Women
Workers Music Association 17
Workers Socialist Federation 5, 227
World Federation of Democratic Youth 24, 52
World Peace Council 28, 31, 72, 205, 209, 226

Y
Y Cymro 180, 201, 202
Young Communist League (YCL) 7, 9, 17, 20, 24, 52, 65, 67, 93, 96-7, 116-7, 121, 131, 133, 137, 151, 228, 238
Yugoslavia 27, 54-5

Z
Zimbabwe 155

Readers' Notes

About the author

Robert Griffiths was born in Cardiff and studied Economics at Bath University before becoming a parliamentary research officer, Wales president of the trade union TASS, a TUC tutor and senior lecturer in Political Economy and Labour History at the University of Wales College, Newport. His previous books include *Streic! Streic! Streic!* (1986), *Driven by ideals – a history of ASLEF* (2005), *Killing No Murder – South Wales and the Great Railway Srike of 1911* (2009), *Granite and honey: the story of Phil Piratin, Communist MP* (2012) with Kevin Marsh, *Marx's Das Kapital and capitalism today* (2018) and *Reddest of the Reds: SO Davies, MP and miners' leader* (2019). He was first elected general secretary of the Communist Party of Britain in 1998.

ESSENTIAL READING ON CHINA

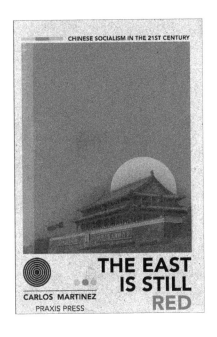

China, after its revolution, has achieved the greatest improvement in life of the largest proportion of humanity of any country in history. In *China's Great Road*, John Ross explains how China achieved this step forward. His unequivocal conclusion is that socialism is responsible for this advance. *China's Great Road* analyses Chinese reality and argues socialists worldwide can learn from China.

Carlos Martinez argues in *The East is Still Red* that the decisive role of the Communist Party of China and its commitment to building 'socialism with Chinese characteristics' needs to be more widely understood especially in the West.

https://redletterspp.com/collections/china

OTHER PRAXIS PRESS TITLES

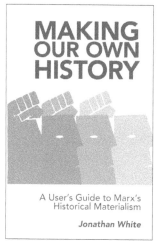

MAKING OUR OWN HISTORY by Jonathan White
A brilliant introduction to the Marxist approach to understanding and participating in social change.

MARX200
Leading scholars and activists from different countries – including Cuba, India and the UK – show that Marx's ideas continue to provide us with the analysis we need to understand our world today.

A PROMETHEAN VISION by Eric Rahim
"This small book is a very useful account of how Marx came to develop his materialist conception of history." Michael Löwy, *New Politics*

LINE OF MARCH by Max Adereth
A new edition of Max Adereth's historical analysis of British communism, focusing on the development of the party's various programmes. First published 1994.

1000 DAYS OF REVOLUTION
A fascinating account of the Allende Presidency, the dilemmas of peaceful and armed struggles for socialism, the role of US imperialism and domestic right-wing forces, and a self critical evaluation of the role of Chilean communists.

HARDBOILED ACTIVIST by Ken Fuller
A critical review of the work and politics of writer Dashiell Hammett, crime fiction legend, communist and staunch opponent of McCarthyism.

For more details, contact praxispress@me.com

ORDER online at www.redletterspp.com

COMMUNISTS/REBELS/ FEMINISTS/AGITATORS/ THINKERS/WRITERS/ TROUBLEMAKERS

www.manifestopress.coop

A CENTENARY FOR SOCIALISM

BRITAIN'S COMMUNIST PARTY 1920-2020

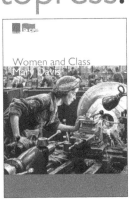

The political life and times of Claudia Jones

David Horsley

Women and Class
Mary Davis

RED LIVES
COMMUNISTS AND THE STRUGGLE FOR SOCIALISM

Empire and Ukraine 2022
Andrew Murray

Marx's Das Kapital and capitalism today
Robert Griffiths

2nd edition

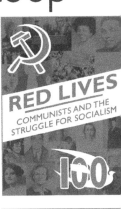

The Impact of the Russian Revolution on Britain
Robin Page Arnot

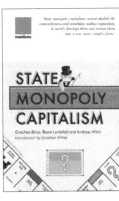

Granite and honey
the story of Phil Piratin, Communist MP
by Kevin Marsh and Robert Griffiths

Foreword by John Callow

Reddest of the Reds
S O Davies, MP and miners' leader
Robert Griffiths

STRUGGLE OR STARVE

The Life and Times of James Connolly
C Desmond Greaves

THE CAUSE OF LABOUR IS THE CAUSE OF IRELAND

THE CAUSE OF IRELAND IS THE CAUSE OF LABOUR

The Woman Worker

STATE MONOPOLY CAPITALISM

Gretchen Binus, Beate Landefeld and Andreas Wehr
Introduction by Jonathan White